ADOBE PHOTOSHOP ELEMENTS

ADVANCED EDITING
TECHNIQUES AND TRICKS

TED PADOVA

**New
Riders** | VOICES THAT MATTER™

Adobe Photoshop Elements: Advanced Editing Techniques and Tricks
Ted Padova

New Riders
www.peachpit.com
Copyright © 2022 by Pearson Education, Inc. or its affiliates. All Rights Reserved.

Peachpit Press is an imprint of Pearson Education, Inc.
To report errors, please send a note to errata@peachpit.com.

Executive Editor: Laura Norman
Production Editor: Charlotte Kughen
Compositor: Bronkella Publishing LLC
Indexer: Cheryl Lenser
Technical Editor: Doug Sahlin
Graphics: tj graham art
Cover Design: Chuti Prasertsith
Interior Design: Bumpy Design

ISBN-13: 978-0-13-784402-9
ISBN-10:   0-13-784402-6

1 2022

This book is dedicated to Brandon Creasey.

The memories are so wonderful, but the pain is still with us.

About the Author

I've been a professional photographer on and off for almost 60 years. I first started working in photography in 1963 at the Army Aviation Test Office at Edwards Air Force Base in Edwards, California. I shot on glass plates using the Fairchild Flight Analyzer, developed the plates, and made contact prints. It was crude but an interesting first introduction to photography.

A few years later, I joined the Peace Corps and spent several years in a Venezuelan fishing village and the Amazon jungle in Ecuador. It was early in my Peace Corps service that I acquired my first SLR and became thoroughly engrossed in photography.

After my tour in the Peace Corps, I went to the New York Institute of Photography in New York City when it was a resident school. After a short time in Manhattan, where I shot all over the city, I acquired a diploma in Commercial Photography and headed off to my home in California.

Throughout the time I was working on my baccalaureate degree and going to graduate school, I shot weddings that paid for my education. When I had time off from school, I worked in a small trailer I converted into a dark room, where I processed B&W film and made enlargements.

I began teaching secondary school after finishing my university degree and was given a class to teach in photography. For more than 30 years, I've been involved in teaching photography and digital image editing. I owned a digital imaging and photo finishing company for more than 16 years. That's where much of my work was spent on the back end of photography.

Photography has never been a regular job for me, but it's been a delight and a great love. I wouldn't want to spend all my time in a full-time job in photography, and I'm quite certain that is the reason it's still a first love for me.

In years past, my heroes in the photography world were the great photographers of all time, such as Ansel Adams, Richard Avedon, Bert Stern, Irving Penn, Annie Leibovitz, and several others. But today, my heroes are the many young people I come across in teaching and some young modern-day professionals.

I've been working with computers for more than 40 years. I had the luxury of learning applications slowly over time. When Photoshop 1.0 was introduced, I taught all the tools and menu commands and just about all that could be done in Photoshop in my one-day university classes at UC Santa Barbara and UCLA. The same went for Adobe Illustrator all the way through version 3.2. Today, however, one could spend a week covering just color in Photoshop or Illustrator without getting into various tools and commands to handle other edits.

The young people today who can jump into Photoshop 2022 or Elements 2022 and become knowledgeable and skilled in a short time are truly my heroes. I'm simply amazed at how fast young people learn such a complicated set of applications so quickly. It took me more than 40 years to know a little about the applications I work with today. If I had to start learning now, I just might retire and go fishing.

The following are some of the other books I've authored:

- *Photoshop Elements For Dummies* (coauthored with Barbara Obermeier), versions 4 through 2022
- *Photoshop Elements All-in-One For Dummies* (coauthored with Barbara Obermier) versions 6 through 13
- *Photoshop 3* (coauthored with Bill Harrel)
- *Photoshop Color Correction* (coauthored with Don Mason)
- *Photoshop Color Correction For Dummies* (coauthored with Don Mason)
- *Photoshop 4 Instant Expert*
- *Photoshop Tech Support* (coauthored with Ken Oyer)
- *Adobe Creative Suite* (coauthored with Kelly Murdock) versions CS – CS5
- *Adobe Master Class Illustrator Illuminated* (coauthored with Barbara Obermeier)
- *Adobe InDesign Interactive Digital Publishing*
- *Acrobat PDF Bible* (versions 3 through 10)
- *Creating Acrobat PDF Forms*
- *Acrobat PDF Forms Bible* (coauthored with Angie Okamoto)
- *Acrobat Complete Course*
- *Adobe Reader 7 Revealed*

Acknowledgments

Far too much credit is given to the person whose name appears on the cover of a book. A book like this is not the result of one individual's hard work. It's a team effort, and the success of the project largely depends on the team working well together toward a common goal. That's exactly what has happened with the result of what you're holding. I cannot express enough gratitude to a marvelous group of individuals who indeed worked together as a cohesive team to finish this book.

I am particularly grateful for two individuals without whom this book would never have seen the light of day. I first contacted Nancy Davis, executive editor in the IT Professional Group at Pearson. I pitched the idea for this book to Nancy, and she put me in contact with my executive editor at Peachpit, Laura Norman. I soon found Laura a great partner and true advocate who championed the proposal though the Peachpit network and ultimately gained approval to move forward. Without Nancy and Laura, this book would never have been published, and I'm very grateful to have had them on my team.

A true unsung hero for this project was my tech editor, Doug Sahlin. Doug is not only a technical editor but also an author. Having a background in authoring as well as tech editing gives him additional perspective, which no doubt contributes to his analysis down to the minutia. I'm grateful to Doug for his careful review to make sure this book is technically correct.

What starts out as a book idea turns into a manuscript. For many authors, the manuscript is a coordinated flow of gibberish that needs fine-tuning and a smooth flow. The people who take the raw data and help assemble it into something you can read is handled by the project editor and their team. My gratitude is extended to Charlotte Kughen, my project editor, and her team that includes Compositor Tricia Bronkella and Proofreader Sarah Kearns. Additional thanks are extended to Tammy Graham, who handled the graphics, and Cheryl Lenser, who wrote the index.

I want to thank many models for working with me in photoshoots: Camille Sedar, Bernadette Baro, Cindy De Vera, Chanel Pepino, Kat Smokedlin, Liezel Escodero, Dina Lopez, and Jakielyn Lopez. Family members Bonnie Butterbredt-Creasey, Bruce Butterbredt, Courtany Jensen, John Jensen, Brian Kaus, Brittany Kaus, Hudson Jensen, Harleigh Jensen, Stella Kaus, and Sayla Kaus.

Also, thank you to my friends for posing for some photos: Fernando Grecia, Jr., Henk Loonstra, Henri Galen, Andre van den Dungen, and LC Caro. And a special thank you to Zoe Andrei Lim for posing on her fourth birthday.

Pearson's Commitment to Diversity, Equity, and Inclusion

Pearson is dedicated to creating bias-free content that reflects the diversity of all readers. We embrace the many dimensions of diversity, including but not limited to race, ethnicity, gender, socioeconomic status, ability, age, sexual orientation, and religious or political beliefs. Books are a powerful force for equity and change in our world. They have the potential to deliver opportunities that improve lives and enable economic mobility. As we work with authors to create content for every product and service, we acknowledge our responsibility to demonstrate inclusivity and incorporate diverse scholarship so that everyone can achieve their potential through learning. As the world's leading learning company, we have a duty to help drive change and live up to our purpose to help more people create a better life for themselves and to create a better world.

Our ambition is to purposefully contribute to a world where:

- Everyone has an equitable and lifelong opportunity to succeed through learning.

- Our products and services are inclusive and represent the rich diversity of readers.

- Our content accurately reflects the histories and experiences of the readers we serve.

- Our content prompts deeper discussions with readers and motivates them to expand their own learning (and worldview).

While we work hard to present unbiased content, we want to hear from you about any concerns or needs with this Pearson product so that we can investigate and address them. Please contact us with concerns about any potential bias at https://www.pearson.com/report-bias.html.

CONTENTS

INTRODUCTION

Many new photographers typically ask, "What is the best application for editing photos?" In online forums, people always respond with Lightroom and Photoshop. Those applications are fine for the photographers who want to spend as much time in front of a computer as they do behind the camera. However, if you're the kind of photographer who wants to spend more time behind the camera and less time editing photos, then you don't need the expensive subscription applications. If you're a scrapbooker; an amateur who likes to take family photos; a person who takes many travel, wildlife, or photos of your kid's sports activities; or even a professional wedding or portrait photographer, then Photoshop Elements provides you with all the tools you need to perfect images that express your vision for how you want the final photos to appear.

Photoshop Elements comprises three separate applications: the Organizer, the Photo Editor, and Adobe Camera Raw. Throughout this book, you find content only on the Photo Editor and Adobe Camera Raw; there is no mention of the Organizer. If you want an introduction to Photoshop Elements that covers the Organizer, then I suggest you check out *Photoshop Elements For Dummies*, which I coauthored with Barbara Obermeier.

> **NOTE:** When you open the Photo Editor, you see an option to choose one of three separate workspaces: Quick, Guided, and Expert. All photo editing addressed in this book is handled in the Expert mode with an occasional reference to using Guided Edits in the Guided mode. Therefore, when you see an instruction to open a photo, open the photo in Expert mode to be able to follow along with the book.

For several years, Adobe has invested much research and development into features using Adobe Sensei technology. (Adobe Sensei is Adobe's term for artificial intelligence.) As you work with tools and menu commands, Photoshop Elements uses Sensei technology to learn from the edits you make so that it can help you refine adjustments you make to your photo.

When you open the Enhance menu in the Photo Editor Expert mode, you see a huge number of commands that perform automated editing tasks. Many of these commands use Sensei technology, and Adobe is continuing to improve the features to help make editing photos in Elements a one-click operation to enable you not to have to think too much about the way to edit your photos.

All the automated features are fine for the novice user. However, to harness the real power of Photoshop Elements, you need to use manual editing and move away from the automated features. That's what this book is all about. In the chapters ahead, you find material covering many ways to apply edits to your photos using the powerful tools in Elements without using automated commands.

As you delve deeply into Photoshop Elements, you'll find it much easier to use than other high-end professional photo-editing applications. In this book, I show you how to use Elements to edit photos so you achieve professional results.

Online content

NOTE: You can find video trainings by Ted on www.YouTube/TedPadova.

Accessing the bonus chapters

Your purchase of this book includes two bonus chapters that are accessed from your Account page on peachpit.com.

You must register your purchase on peachpit.com to access the bonus content:

1. Go to peachpit.com/advancedpse.

2. Sign in or create a new account.

3. Click Submit.

4. Answer the question as proof of purchase.

5. Access the Bonus Content from the Registered Products tab on your Account page.

If you purchased a digital product directly from peachpit.com, your product will already be registered. However, you still need to follow the registration steps and answer the proof of purchase question before the Access Bonus Content link will appear under the product on your Registered Products tab.

If you encounter problems registering your product or accessing the online chapters, go to peachpit.com/support for assistance.

Figure Credits

Screenshots: Microsoft; Adobe

Figure 2.15: vitalez/Shutterstock

Figure 8.1 (a): njene/Shutterstock

Figure 8.1 (b): Coleman Yuen/Pearson Education Asia Ltd

Figure 8.9: frenta/123RF

Figure 8.20: Shutterstock

Figure 8.21: Shutterstock

Figure 10.9: Masson/Shutterstock

Figure 10.38: Filipe Frazao/Shutterstock

Figure 11.36: gyn9037/Shutterstock

Figure 12.10: candy18/Shutterstock

Figure 12.16: frenta/123RF

Figure 12.24: Lorraine Swanson/Shutterstock

Figure 13.1: Everett Collection/Shutterstock

Figure 13.24: Przemek Tokar/Shutterstock

Figure 15.4: iofoto/123RF

Figure 15.6: Alex Zabusik/Shutterstock

PART I

USING PLUG-INS AND PRESETS

In short, this part covers apps outside the Photoshop Elements Photo Editor: plug-ins and the Camera Raw Editor. Throughout this book, I talk about using Elements+ (a plug-in that costs $12 USD). Although it's not essential for many topics in the book, it is necessary for some advanced techniques I discuss. I talk about the Camera Raw Editor in this first part because your first step in performing any series of editing tasks should be in the Camera Raw Editor.

CHAPTER 1
USING PLUG-INS AND PRESETS

Chapter Goals

Photoshop Elements is a professional photo editing program. Although it's not as powerful as Adobe Lightroom or Adobe Photoshop, if you're not a dedicated photo editor and you want to polish up and perform some essential edits on photos, the program offers you more than enough in terms of functionality and feature-rich tools and menu options. However, there are a few things you might want to use that the program doesn't support. For example, you may like working with features that are found in Photoshop but not in Photoshop Elements, such as Curves, Color Balance, Channel Mixer, or Layer Styles. Fortunately, you have all these features and many more available in a plug-in, and the good news is the plug-ins are very low cost.

If you want to get the most out of Photoshop Elements, I recommend acquiring some affordable, low-cost plug-ins so that you have access to some advanced tools for editing and an array of features you find in Photoshop. In this chapter, I explain how to add plug-ins and suggest some plug-ins you can use with the Photoshop Elements Photo Editor. You find out how to

- Install third-party plug-ins
- Search online for plug-ins and install them
- Install the NIK Collection plug-in from Google
- Take advantage of using Elements+ for advanced editing tools

This chapter appears first in this book because it's critical that you understand plug-ins, how to install them, and which particular plug-in I cover throughout this book. As I take you on a journey through discovering methods for improving photos, correcting color, adjusting brightness and contrast, and adding your own personal touches to artistic images, I explain features in Photoshop Elements where you can make various edits, and I cover editing tasks that can only be accomplished by use of a plug-in.

I've made every effort to show what you can do in Elements without the aid of a plug-in, but there are a few instances where I talk about some tasks you can perform only with a plug-in. Just be aware upfront that if you want to take full advantage of all the editing discussed throughout this book, you need to purchase one plug-in for $12, which is a very reasonable price for all the power the plug-in offers you. The plug-in I use the most is covered later in this chapter in the section, "Using Commercial Plug-ins."

Adding Plug-Ins

A plug-in is simply a mini app installed in your Elements workspace. The plug-in often has tools and menus that enable you to perform edits that are traditionally not offered by Photoshop Elements. Plug-ins are provided by Adobe Systems and by third-party developers. Some plug-ins require purchase, whereas others are free.

Finding Plug-Ins

The easiest way to find plug-ins for Photoshop Elements is to simply do an Internet search for "Photoshop Elements Plug-ins." You'll get many results of sites that host both free and commercial plug-ins.

A huge number of sites host plug-ins for Photoshop, but unfortunately, there are fewer plug-ins available for Photoshop Elements. Among the free plug-ins available for Photoshop Elements, there are a few that are quite impressive, and there are also a few powerful commercial plug-ins that can add to your image editing.

One site that hosts many free and commercial plug-ins for Photoshop Elements is The Plugin Site (https://www.theplug-insite.com/products/). This site lists plug-ins in three groups: Commercial, Freeware, and Discontinued. Plug-ins are listed by name, along with a short description for what the plug-in will do for you, as shown in Figure 1.1.

FIGURE 1.1 Commercial plug-ins available from The Plugin Site.

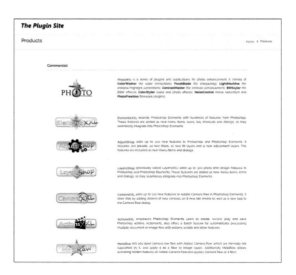

Click a plug-in name in the list to visit that plug-in's details page. If you decide you want to try it, click the Download or Try link or button to start the download.

Installing Plug-Ins

After downloading a plug-in, look in your Downloads folder (or any other location where you save downloads) and examine the file extension. If a file ends in .exe, the file is executable on Windows. If the extension is .dmg, the file is executable on a Macintosh computer. If the extension is .zip (Mac and Windows) or .rar (Windows), then the file is compressed and needs to be expanded.

To expand a compressed file, you can often double-click on the file. On Windows, you can right-click a compressed file and choose Expand from the pop-up window. On the Mac, you can right-click with a two-button mouse or Control + click to open a context menu and choose Open.

If you need to manually move a plug-in to a folder where Elements can find it, you have different paths on Windows and the Macintosh:

- On Windows, open the Program Files folder and then open the Adobe folder. Look for the Photoshop Elements folder and open it. Scroll down to the Plug-ins folder and open it, as shown in Figure 1.2. Copy the new plug-ins to this folder.

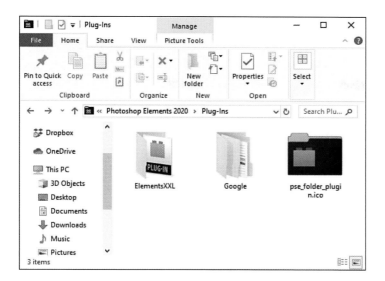

FIGURE 1.2 Open the Photoshop Elements Plug-Ins folder and copy newly installed plug-ins to this folder.

- On the Macintosh, open the Applications folder and the Photoshop Elements subfolder to see the Support Files folder. Open it, and you can see the Plug-ins folder, which looks like Figure 1.3 after you open it. Copy all newly installed plug-ins to this folder.

TIP: If you're not certain whether a plug-in is installed properly in the Photoshop Elements folder after running an installer, just open the folder and look for the new plug-in. If it's not there, check your download location and copy the plug-in to the Elements Plug-ins folder.

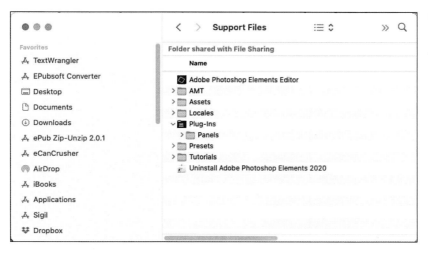

FIGURE 1.3 Open the Support Files folder on the Mac and copy plug-ins to the Plug-ins folder.

Working with Free Plug-Ins

There are a huge number of free plug-ins you can use with Photoshop Elements. Some Photoshop plug-ins also work with Elements, and you can use some Photoshop Presets with Elements. The number of plug-in options you have available are far beyond the scope of this book to discuss all of them.

To illustrate using some free plug-ins, I selected a few to look at for installing and using with Elements. Which versions of Elements are supported depends on the plug-in. Many developers tell you what versions of Elements the plug-in supports on their download website. If you don't know whether your version of Elements is supported by a plug-in, you can try it to see if it works.

Using Harry's Filters

TIP: Harry's Filters is available on The Plugin Site in the Freeware area at https://www.theplug-insite.com/products/harrysfilters/index.htm.

Harry's Filters is a free plug-in that's available only for Windows for Photoshop and Photoshop Elements. This plug-in offers you limitless ways to add different moods and special effects to your images. You can download Harry's Filters from a number of different sites. Just do a Google search to find a site supporting the installer download.

Harry's Filters provides you with a whopping 69 special effects that you can apply to images to change colors and moods, warp images, add special noise effects, and use adjustment sliders to control intensities.

When you run the installer, you can choose to install in Photoshop Elements and Photoshop if you have both installed. When installing with Elements, the installer deposits the plug-in in the Elements plug-ins folder. Launch Elements, open an image in the Photo Editor, and choose Filter > The Plug-in Site > Harrys Filters (version number) to open the Harrys Filters dialog box shown in Figure 1.4.

FIGURE 1.4 Open the Harry's Filters dialog box from the Filters menu.

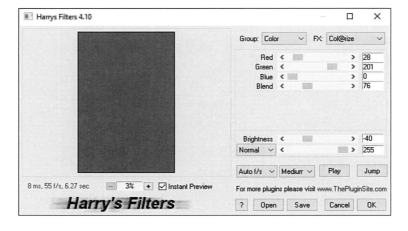

In Figure 1.5, I used Harry's Filters to colorize a photo. I added a new Solid Color Adjustment Layer and chose a warm color. I opened Harry's Filters and chose Color from the Group drop-down list and Colorize from the FX drop-down list. I also reduced Opacity on the Adjustment layer.

FIGURE 1.5 Colorizing an image with Harry's Filters.

Using the NIK Collection

The NIK Collection has been around for a long time. It was initially developed by Nik Software in 1995 and later acquired by Google. Google had the software for a few years before announcing there would be no more upgrades to the product. A company by the name of DxO acquired the NIK collection and upgraded the product to version 2.

The original NIK collection is still available as a free plug-in; the NIK Collection 2 requires purchase. To download the free version, do an Internet search for NIK Collection 1.2.15 downloads. Run the installer and install in Photoshop Elements. As of this writing, the NIK Collection is compatible in Elements versions through Elements 2022.

NIK Collection is an impressive set of various filters with a huge number of presets. The different sets include the following:

- **Analog Efex Pro:** This set of filters can add a vintage look to your photos.

- **Color Efex Pro:** These filters enable you to enhance color and create different moods.

- **Dfine:** These presets offer many different methods for reducing noise.

- **HDR Efex Pro:** These filters offer various methods for adding HDR (High Dynamic Range) effects to your image.

TIP: The NIK Collection plug-in is one of the best plug-ins you can find for both Adobe Photoshop and Photoshop Elements. Do an Internet search for "Nik Collection free download" to find links for free downloads.

- **Sharpener Pro:** This set provides various sharpening effects.

- **Silver Efex Pro:** This set includes diverse effects that you apply to black and white photos.

- **Viveza:** These filters enable you to apply various adjustments to areas of an image, such as apply structure, color, exposure changes, and shadow recovery to selected areas of a photo.

In Figure 1.6, I used the Color Efex Pro filter to create an infrared look on a photo. On the left side of the window, there are many different presets for creating different effects. On the right side of the window, you find several panels with sliders where you can fine-tune the settings. This interface is common for most of the different sets in the NIK Collection.

FIGURE 1.6 Efex Pro used to create an infrared image.

Using Commercial Plug-ins

There are two plug-ins for purchase that greatly extend Photoshop Elements image editing: Elements+ and Elements XXL. These two plug-ins bridge the gap between some essential Photoshop features and Photoshop Elements.

Both plug-ins offer a variety of different editing opportunities you don't have with Photoshop Elements. In my opinion, the most beneficial features both plug-ins offer you are the following:

- **Curves:** Photoshop Elements offers a Color Curves dialog box where you can make a few brightness adjustments similar to some Levels adjustments. However, Color Curves, shown in Figure 1.7, is very limited. Notice the curve is limited to the sliders in the Color Curves dialog box. You can't plot points on the curve, and you can't eliminate any points. Elements limits you to the slider adjustments and a few presets. Furthermore, you cannot make curve adjustments to individual channels. You're limited to making adjustments in the RGB channel only. To compare a more flexible Curves dialog box to the Elements Curves dialog box, see the section "Working with Curves" later in this chapter.

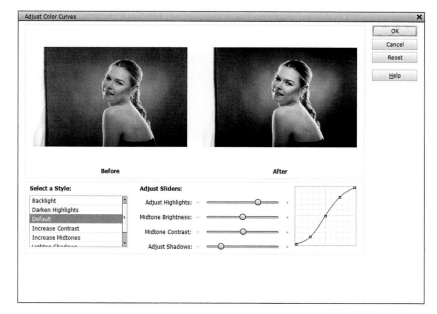

FIGURE 1.7 Limited curves adjustments in the Photoshop Elements Color Curves dialog box.

- **Layer Styles:** Elements has its own form of Layer Styles in the Styles panel. The styles you can use are limited to presets where you can apply a variety of effects. In Photoshop, the Layer Styles dialog box offers you blending opportunities, including Blend If sliders, that enable you to make adjustments to underlying layers. As discussed in later chapters, having access to blending layers and using the Blend If feature in both the commercial plug-ins discussed here offer you a huge range of options for correcting skin colors, matching colors when compositing images, and changing moods with your photos.

- **Smart Objects:** In Photoshop, you can convert any layer to a Smart Object. Once a layer is converted to a Smart Object, all the editing you perform is said to be nondestructive. Nondestructive editing simply means you can return to the original layer and dismiss all edits, or you can later return to an edit to refine it. The plug-ins don't create a Smart Object like you find in Photoshop; instead, they create a link to the original file, and it behaves much like a Photoshop Smart Object.

- **Paths:** Photoshop offers a Paths panel where you can create vector paths, but Elements doesn't have a Paths panel. Both plug-ins offer you a Paths panel where you can create paths, fill, and stroke them. In Premiere Elements 2022, a Pen tool was introduced where you could create paths in Premiere Elements. It's safe to assume that a later version of Photoshop Elements will include both a Pen tool and Paths panel. However, as of Elements 2022, no Pen tool or Paths panel is available.

The two most critical features for taking Photoshop Elements to a new level for image editing are the Curves dialog box and the Layer Styles blending features. In addition, you have the Channel Mixer where you can mix channel data using Color Lookups (see Chapter 4), additional editing opportunities using the Camera Raw Editor (see Chapter 2), and another selection method using Color Range (see Chapter 3).

Both Elements+ and Elements XXL are great additions to Photoshop Elements and offer you much more professional editing tools than you have with just Photoshop Elements. The most distinguishing difference between them is the price. Both plug-ins are available on Windows and Macintosh. Elements+ is available for $12 USD plus applicable taxes. Elements XXL costs $49 USD plus applicable taxes.

Using Elements+

I've chosen to include Elements+ in this book simply for the reason that I want to help keep your investment at a minimum. For only $12 USD, you can add a lot of functionality to Photoshop Elements. Throughout this book, where an exercise requires using the plug-in, I provide an alert to inform you that you need Elements+ to perform the steps in editing a photo.

> **TIP:** You can download a trial version of Elements+ and follow the steps in the chapters ahead. If you plan to pursue some professional editing opportunities, you might want to purchase the plug-in.

You can download Elements+ from http://elementsplus.net. You can also download the plug-in from The Elements Plus site at https://elementsplus.net. You can download a trial version that offers only Color and Tone adjustments. When you purchase and install Elements+, a new panel is installed in the fx Effects panel, as shown in Figure 1.8.

Working with Curves

There are fifteen different categories in the Effects > Elements+ tab. The first button in the top-left corner in the Elements+ panel is the Color and Tone Adjustments, which is where you access the Curve settings. Click Curves, and the Curves dialog box opens, as shown in Figure 1.9.

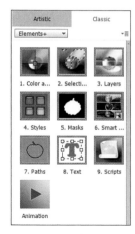

FIGURE 1.8 The Elements+ tab in the Effects panel.

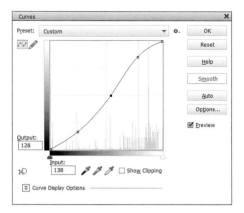

FIGURE 1.9 The Elements+ Curves dialog box.

NOTE: One disadvantage when using the Elements+ Curves dialog box is you cannot click and drag a point on the path. You must select a point and then use the arrow keys to move points up down, left, and right.

Notice how many more features you have in this dialog box compared to Elements Color Curves. A disadvantage in this dialog box compared to the Photoshop Curves dialog box is that you need to predetermine the channel you want to adjust. For example, if you want to change brightness settings in the Red channel, you need to choose Red before opening the Curves dialog box. In Figure 1.10, you can see the Color and Tone dialog box.

FIGURE 1.10 Select the channel with the Color and Tone dialog box before opening the Curves dialog box.

You make your adjustments and then reopen Curves and choose another channel before making another adjustment. It's a bit of a hassle, but overall, Curves in Elements+ offers you much more than Elements Color Curves.

Throughout this book, I describe making curves adjustments as we look at editing photos.

Examining Blending Styles

The first button in the second row is for the Styles dialog box, in which the options simulate the Photoshop Layer Styles. When you click the button, you see the dialog box shown in Figure 1.11.

FIGURE 1.11 The Elements+ Styles dialog box.

In the General Blending section, the Blend Mode pop-up menu displays a list of blend modes, as shown in Figure 1.11, including two advanced blending options not available in Elements: Subtract and Divide. The Styles dialog box also includes Blend If, where you can control blending on the currently selected layer and layers below the selected layer. Blend If also permits you to create smooth transitions by splitting the slider handles.

> **NOTE:** The Styles options are much better in the Elements XXL plug-in, but the cost for that plug-in is more: $49 USD.

The one disadvantage in using Elements+ rather than Elements XXL is that the Blend If adjustment is much inferior to the XXL plug-in. Therefore, if Blend If is an important feature to you, you might want to spend $49 for the Elements XXL plug-in.

Elements+ has a wealth of features and tools. At the top of the Effects panel, the drop-down menu contains 19 different categories with multiple choices for each category. Rather than describe all the different options available to you now, the following chapters detail some of the more beneficial tools and commands you will find useful in your image editing.

Using Elements XXL

Elements XXL is another plug-in that provides you with similar features as Elements+. Elements XXL offers you a few more Photoshop-like tools, and it integrates much better in the Elements interface than Elements+ does. The critical tools such as Curves, Blending Styles, Smart Objects, and Paths are all available with Elements XXL. The major difference between the plug-ins is price. Whereas Elements+ costs $12, Elements XXL costs $49.

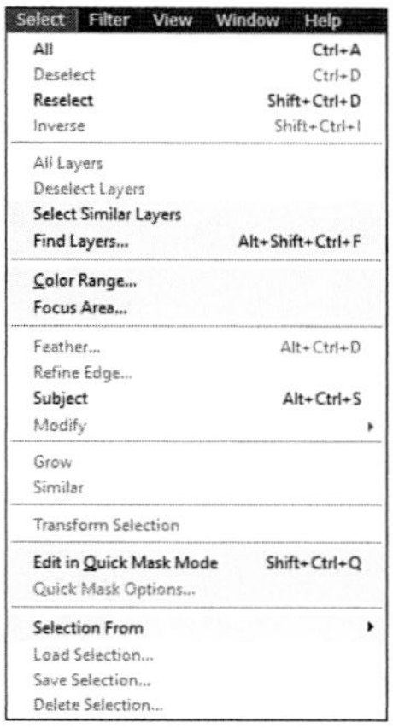

When you install Elements XXL, all menu items introduced by the plug-in appear highlighted with blue, as shown in Figure 1.12. You can disable the blue highlight for menus and tools by opening File > Automation Tools > Elements XXL; then disable Colorize Icons Menu Items.

One critical difference between Elements+ and Elements XXL is Elements+ doesn't offer the same blending opportunities in Layer Styles. The Blend If sliders are very crude in Elements+, and no advanced blending options are available. If you use Elements XXL, you can purchase the additional plug-in Layers XXL to get much better blending than available in Elements+. However, buying the additional plug-in drives the cost to as much as you spent purchasing Photoshop Elements.

FIGURE 1.12 Elements XXL menu items highlighted in blue.

The Curves dialog box in Elements XXL is much more impressive than Elements+ because you can individually edit each channel in the same dialog box (see Figure 1.13).

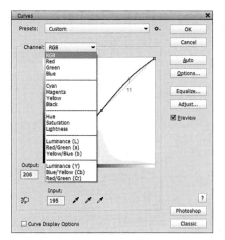

FIGURE 1.13 The more impressive Curves dialog box in Elements XXL.

Another advantage you have with Elements XXL is that you can try all the features during a trial period. With Elements+, you can only try the single Color and Tone set. All other tools and options are disabled in the trial version.

Before purchasing either plug-in, download both and use the trial versions. With Elements XXL, you can easily disable the plug-in by dragging it out of

TIP: Before you make a purchase for any software, download a trial version if one is available so you can try it out before making the purchase.

the Elements plug-in folder. Disabling Elements+ is more complicated. Several files are installed in the Photoshop Elements folder when you run the Elements+ installer. The only way to disable the plug-in is to uninstall it. If you have to uninstall and then reinstall later, the next time you launch Elements, you need to wait some time. Upon installation, the Elements Cache file needs to be rebuilt. This can take several minutes.

Working with Custom Color LUTs (Lookup Tables)

LUTs are color lookup tables used for making color corrections on images. LUTs are commonly used in video editing to balance color between cameras. With Photoshop and Photoshop Elements, you use LUTs for color grading, changing moods, balancing color, and adding special effects. LUTs are a series of Adjustment Layers set up as presets you can apply as layers to an image and make opacity adjustments to control intensity.

Elements+

NOTE: It's not necessary to copy the Photoshop 3DLUTs folder and paste into your Photoshop Elements folder. If you store the LUTs outside the Elements 3DLUTs folder, you need to search for a LUT when using it with Elements+. Keeping LUTs you use with Elements in your Photoshop Elements folder just makes it easier to keep them organized

Using LUTs is not something you can do with Elements without the help of a plug-in. If you install Elements+, you can take advantage of free LUTs available for download on the Internet. In addition, you can use LUTs installed with Lightroom and Adobe Photoshop. If you use Photoshop, open the Program Files > Adobe > Adobe Photoshop > Presets folder. Look for the 3DLUTs folder. Copy it and paste in your Photoshop Elements Presets folder.

Installing LUTs for Use with the Photo Editor

As I said earlier, you can find a number of LUTs available for free download as well as commercial packages you can purchase. To locate free downloads, do an Internet search. One helpful set of LUTs is a set for changing skin tones. You can download the set from https://godownloads.net/skin-tone-luts-for-light-skin-photoshop-free-download/.

After downloading LUTs or copying Photoshop LUTs, create a folder in your Elements folder and name it LUTs. Be sure to remember the directory path to access the settings when you want to apply a LUT to an image.

Elements+

NOTE: To see some of the benefits for working with Color LUTs, take a look at Chapter 12.

Using LUTs with Elements+

LUT stands for Color Lookup Table. You'll find many uses for using color LUTs to change the mood and drama or feeling of a photo and apply color grading to your images. In Chapter 12, I provide you with techniques and methods for color grading your photos. For now, just understand that using color LUTs can be a great benefit to you when editing your images.

Remember, Photoshop Elements has no support for using LUTs. You need the help of a plug-in to use the LUTs you installed. With Elements+ installed, open the Photo Editor and open an image. Click *fx* at the bottom of the Photo Editor panel to open the Elements+ tools. If you don't see the Elements+ tools, open the panel menu and choose Elements+.

As I mentioned earlier in the section "Using Elements+," the top-left button in the first row is the Color and Tone settings. Drag the button on top of your Image; alternatively, you can click the button. The Color and Tone dialog box opens. Scroll down to Color Lookup, select it, and click the green check mark for Apply in the top-right corner. A New Layer dialog box opens. Accept the defaults and click OK

At this point, the Color Lookup dialog box opens, as shown in Figure 1.14.

FIGURE 1.14 The Elements+ plug-in Color Lookup dialog box.

In the Color Lookup dialog box, you locate LUT files by selecting from the 3DLUT File drop-down list. In the example shown, I used the Red.CUBE LUT I downloaded as part of a free set of LUTs from the Internet.

Also, in the dialog box, you have two choices for Dither Order. The default is Data Order – RGB and Table Order – BGR. These settings refer to the byte order. BGR (Blue, Green, Red) is a legacy Microsoft standard. In terms of practice, you will find that changing the orders can greatly influence the colors you apply to an image. As a matter of rule, leave the defaults alone. If you want to test the opposite byte orders, reverse the settings and explore the results.

As you scroll through the various LUTs in the Color Lookup 3DLUT File menu, you see a dynamic preview for the changes respective to the item you choose in the menu. Move the dialog box aside the Elements Image Window and carefully look at the results before you commit to a choice. If you decide to change your mind, you have to delete the adjustment layer and start over. You cannot edit the Adjustment layer like you can in Photoshop. Once you choose the LUT you want to use, click OK.

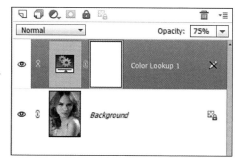

After clicking OK in the Color Lookup dialog box, you are returned to the Photo Editor window. In the Layers panel, you can see the adjustment layer that was applied to your image, as shown in Figure 1.15.

FIGURE 1.15 A new adjustment layer with the effect chosen from the 3DLUT File menu.

Look over your image. In many cases, the full opacity amount of 100% may be too much, and you might want to lower it. You can also use different blend modes, as I discuss later in Chapter 4, "Working with Layers." You can also use Blend If sliders to tweak adjustments.

I took an edited image and decided to turn the warm tones to much cooler tones. I applied the Padora.cube 3D Color LUT in Elements+. The result was a much cooler image as shown on the right in Figure 1.16.

TIP: For more information on using Color Lookup Adjustment Layers, see Chapter 4.

FIGURE 1.16 A warm image (left) and the same image after applying a cooler tone (right).

Adding Actions

Actions are installed in the Photoshop Elements Photo Editor when you install the program. An *action* is a set of instructions that performs one or more edits on an image. Almost all menu commands and tool adjustments are said to be "actionable" (in Photoshop), meaning you can include almost any edit function or operation as an instruction in an action. However, in Photoshop Elements, you cannot create your own actions. You can load precreated actions, and you can play actions. Some Photoshop actions can work in Elements if all the menu commands and tool adjustments are the same. If you install a Photoshop action that calls an instruction not available in Elements (such as opening the Channel Mixer), the action won't work in Elements.

FIGURE 1.17 The Actions panel showing Adobe actions and actions installed with the Elements+ plug-in.

In addition to preinstalled actions by Adobe, you can download free action sets, or, if you have Photoshop, you can create actions and install them in Photoshop Elements. If you install the Elements+ plug-in, a series of actions are also installed with your Elements+ installation. In Figure 1.17, you can see a list of actions installed with Elements+. To open the Actions panel, choose Window > Actions or click the More tab at the bottom of the Panel Bin and click the Actions tab. To separate the Actions panel from the other panels in the group, drag the tab away from the group.

Installing Actions

Actions are loaded in the Actions panel and don't need to reside in any specific location on your hard drive. When you open the Actions panel from the top-right corner (see Figure 1.17), you navigate your computer's hard drive to locate actions you have installed. For convenience, you might think of adding actions to an Actions folder inside the Photoshop Elements folder.

Running an Action

In Figure 1.17, you see a Play button. You select an action in the Actions panel and click the Play button to run the action. Some actions run seamlessly to completion of all steps. Other actions may have stops for user input. For example, an action may create a Hue/Saturation Adjustment Layer and then stop. After the Adjustment Layer is created, you need to move sliders to make adjustments. Since every photo is unique, no single adjustment can be used for all images. Once you make an adjustment and click OK, the action proceeds to run through other steps.

In Photoshop, stops in actions are denoted by a small icon adjacent to a step in the sequence. Unfortunately, Elements does not show any indicator for a stop in the action. Stops do work, however. When a stop occurs, you typically see a dialog box open and waiting for you to make an adjustment. After you click OK, the action continues to run.

This section offers you a basic understanding for actions, how they are created, and where to install them. In forthcoming chapters, I talk about creating actions in Photoshop and how to install and run them in Photoshop Elements.

Understanding Advantages of Actions

To demonstrate how an action might be useful for you, let's assume you take a number of photos and in the Camera Raw format. You make edits and save the files and want to keep them in Camera Raw in case you want to change the edits. If you want to share the photos with another user, you might want to deliver the photos as JPEG. Therefore, all the Raw files need to be saved as JPEG. Opening each file and saving as JPEG can take quite a bit of time.

Instead, you can have an action that opens a file, saves as JPEG, closes the file, and then proceeds to the next file. In this example, you could conceivably convert hundreds of files from the Camera Raw format to JPEG in a matter of seconds.

This is but one example where using an action can save you much time.

> **NOTE:** Actions cannot be created in Photoshop Elements. You can, however, copy actions from many different sites that offer downloads. You can use Photoshop to create different action sets as long as all action steps are executable in Elements.

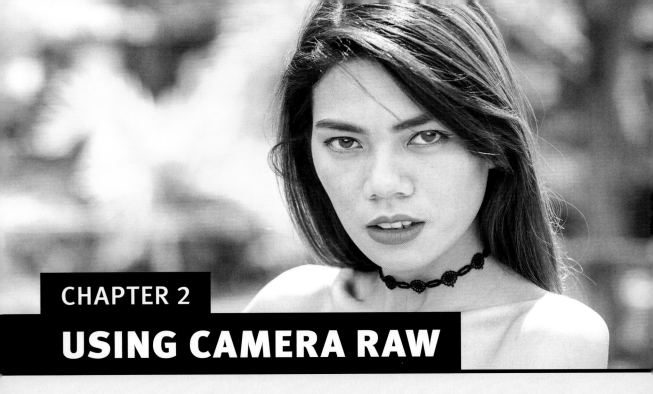

CHAPTER 2
USING CAMERA RAW

Chapter Goals

This chapter is all about using Adobe Camera Raw (ACR). If you use a version of Photoshop Elements prior to version 2021, I explain how to use the earlier version of ACR. For users of version 2021 and later, you'll find that version addressed in this chapter.

The topics covered in this chapter include the following:

- Working in the user interface for ACR prior to version 2021
- Working in the user interface for ACR for version 2021 and later
- Using the Camera Raw Panels
- Opening JPG, TIFF, and other file formats in Camera Raw
- Working with 8-bit and 16-bit images
- Synchronizing edits among multiple images
- Applying different edits to a single image
- Working with the Elements+ Camera Raw Editor

When you download images off your camera's memory card and you begin editing, your first stop should be the Camera Raw Editor. Of course, this means you must have shot and saved your files in the RAW format. Most DSLR cameras, mirrorless cameras, and even some smartphones provide options for saving in the Raw format. Some cameras provide options for saving in both Raw and JPEG file formats.

The Camera RAW format contains all the information captured by the camera's sensor. In the Adobe Camera Raw (ACR) editor, you can choose what data ultimately appears in your image. For example, suppose you have highlights blown out. You might be able to recover data using the Adobe Camera Raw Editor; however, in such a case, you may have to sacrifice some detail in the shadows. The point is that Adobe Camera Raw enables you to choose what data ultimately appears in the photo.

Image editing can be viewed from two points of view. The first includes edits you make to improve an image quality. These are generally edits most photographers would agree that are necessary: underexposure, overexposure, poor color balance, lack of sharpness, and so on. These are the issues that most often need to be corrected.

The essential editing needs to be performed first before you go about the second type of editing, which includes edits you make that aren't right or wrong. They're edits you make to create your personal view for presenting the image. You may want the image to appear warmer or cooler, you may want to apply special effects, or you may even want to intentionally break some traditional photographic rules. The result is your personal touch for how you want your final image to be presented.

You should address the first type of edits in the Camera Raw Editor before you open a photo in the Photo Editor. (The Camera Raw Editor is a separate application that opens on top of the Photo Editor.) You can handle the second type of edits using the Photo Editor along with tools and menu commands in the Elements Photo Editor.

There was a significant user interface (UI) change when Elements 2021 was introduced. Most of what you could do in the earlier versions is still available in the new ACR (Adobe Camera Raw) Editor and vice versa. Because some people may still be using an ACR prior to version 2021, I'll start with presenting the old version. Then, in the second half of this chapter, I'll talk about the new version available in Elements 2021 and later versions.

Working in ACR Before Elements 2021

NOTE: If you are using Elements 2021 or later, jump down to the section "Working on 16-Bit Images." You can skip the first part of this chapter and move on to using ACR version 2021 and above.

The old ACR editor was in use for Photoshop Elements 2020 and previous versions. Almost all of what you can do in the 2021 release is available in the 2020 release. The major difference between the two is the UI. Let's take a look at what was available in the 2020 and earlier releases of ACR.

Opening Files in the Raw Editor

The Raw Editor is a separate application from Photoshop Elements. The Raw Editor window opens on top of the Photo Editor window and provides you with a number of tools and panels used for adjusting brightness, contrast, and color.

TIP: Any file you can open in the Photo Editor can also be opened in Camera Raw. If you have a file saved in Raw format, choose File > Open in Camera Raw. You can select one or more files, click Open, and all the selected files open in Adobe Camera Raw,

If you have a camera or cell phone that saves files in Camera Raw format, from the Desktop you can double-click a raw file to open it in the Raw Editor. If you're in the Photo Editor, choose File > Open and select a raw file to be opened in the Raw Editor.

You're not limited to raw files, however. You can also open any .psd, .tif, or .jpeg file in the Raw Editor. If you have one of these file types, choose File > Open in Camera Raw. When you open the file, it opens in the Raw Editor.

Figure 2.1 shows you what you see the Raw Editor window.

NOTE: Figure 2.1 shows the Raw Editor in Photoshop Elements version 2020 and earlier.

FIGURE 2.1 The Camera Raw Editor.

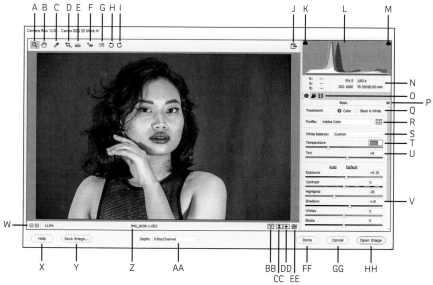

In the old UI, you find the following tools and panels:

A. **Zoom tool (Z):** Click with this tool to zoom in. To zoom out, press Alt/ Option and click with the tool.

B. **Hand tool (H):** Use the Hand tool to move around the document window. If you're using another, you can press the space bar to access the Hand tool temporarily.

C. **Eyedropper tool (I):** Use the Eyedropper tool to sample color in the photo. This tool is tied to White Balance. When you click in a photo, the sample adjusts the Temperature slider. When you press Shift and click, the Tint slider is adjusted. Use the eyedropper tool to adjust white balance by clicking on a neutral gray area in the photo. If you use a gray card and shoot one photo with a subject holding the gray card, you can easily adjust white balance by clicking on the card.

D. **Crop tool (C):** Use this tool to crop images in the Raw Editor. However, most often, you'll want to crop images in Expert mode in the Photo Editor.

E. **Straighten tool (A):** As with the Crop tool, you are best off straightening images in the Photo Editor, but if you need to do it in the Raw Editor, use this tool.

F. **Red Eye Removal tool (E):** Use this tool for removing red eye that occurs with indoor flash. You click and drag a marquee around the subject's eyes, and the Raw Editor removes red eye.

G. **Camera Raw Preferences (Ctrl/@@cmd + K):** Click this icon to open the Preferences dialog box. I talk about preferences later in this chapter in the section "Changing Program Defaults."

H. **Rotate Left (L):** Click this icon to rotate to the left by 90°. Press Alt/ Option, and the icon changes to Flip Horizontal.

I. **Rotate Right (R).** Click to rotate the photo to the right by 90°. Press Alt/ Option, and the icon changes to Flip Vertical.

J. **Full Screen (F):** Click to zoom to full screen. Click again to zoom back to the default view.

K. **Shadow Warning:** Click this button and you see clipping in an image for shadows represented by blue overlays. Clipping means that no detail is shown in that area of the image.

L. **Histogram:** See "Histogram" in the section "Using the Basic Panel." As you make adjustments in the Basic panel, look at the Histogram as you move the sliders. You look for a bell-shaped curve as you move the sliders. This helps you get a more precise adjustment.

M.   Highlight Warning: Click this icon, and you see a red overlay in areas where highlights are blown out.

N.   ITPC data: You see a readout for the f-stop, shutter speed, ISO, and lens used for the shot.

O.   Panel icons: Click an icon, and the respective panel opens in the Panel Bin. The first icon is for the Basic panel, which opens by default. The second icon is for the Detail panel. The third icon is for the Calibration panel.

P.   Defaults drop-down list: Click the icon, and a drop-down list opens, as shown in Figure 2.2. You have choices for choosing Camera Raw defaults that take you back to the original unedited image. You can also choose a previous settings adjustment or custom settings, and you can clear imported settings if you import any camera raw settings.

FIGURE 2.2 A drop-down list showing camera raw defaults.

Image Settings
Camera Raw Defaults
Previous Conversion
Custom Settings
Clear Imported Settings

Q.   Treatment: Choose either Color or Black and White.

See the "Using the Basic Panel" section later in this chapter for more information.

R.   Profiles: You can chose from a number of different color profiles to help you get the adjustment close to a particular scene.

S.   White Balance: White balance balances the color temperature of your images. A cooler temperature results in a bluish tint, and a warmer color temperature is displayed as a yellow-orangish tint. You can use the slider to make your photo appear cooler or warmer.

T.   Temperature: Temperature is measured in degrees Kelvin. The higher the number, the cooler the temperature. Conversely, the lower the number, the warmer the temperature.

U.   Tint: Tints are created by adding white to any hue found on the color wheel, which desaturates and lightens the hue.

V.   Panel Bin: By default, the Basic panel opens in the Panel Bin.

W.   Zoom settings: Press the Z key to access the Zoom tool. You can zoom in or out of an image in a number of ways. Click the Zoom tool on an image to zoom in. Press Alt/Option and click to zoom out. Right-click the Zoom tool on an image, and a context menu opens where you can choose from a number of different fixed zoom levels.

In this area, press the down-pointing arrow in the lower-left corner of the editor window to access the same fixed zoom levels in a pop-up menu. Also, you can use Control/⌘ + and Control/⌘—or press the +/– buttons in the lower-left corner to zoom in and out.

X. Help: Click this button to open the Help section of Adobe's website where information related to the Raw Editor is provided.

Y. Save Image: Click this button to open a dialog box where you can choose options for saving your image with Adobe's Digital Negative (.DNG) format. For information related to choices in this dialog box, take a look at the section "Using Sidecar Files" later in this chapter.

Z. File name: This is merely information and not a button. You see the name of the file you're currently working on reported here.

AA. Depth: For 16-bit images, choose 16 Bits/Channel. The alternate choice is 8 Bits/Channel.

For more on bit depth, see the "Working on 16-Bit Images" section later in this chapter.

BB. Before/After (Q): Click this button to cycle through before/after views displayed adjacent to each other vertically, horizontally, and split screen.

CC. Swap Before/After Settings (P): You can make a series of edits in one or more panels and click this button to return to a state before you started making edits. Click again and all the edits return.

DD. Copy Current Settings to Before (Alt/Option): You make edits in a panel and then you can copy the edits and apply them to the Before image preview.

EE. Toggle Between Current Settings and Defaults: Click this button to see your image at the default settings. Click again and you see the image with the edits you made.

Defaults are not necessarily the original image captured by your camera. You can, for example, choose to open images with some automatic corrections applied. When you toggle this button, you see the defaults after automatic corrections were applied.

To learn more about changing defaults, see the "Changing Program Defaults" section later in this chapter.

FF. **Done:** Click Done and all your edits are applied and the image is closed. When you open the image, it is shown in the Raw Editor with the last edits you made.

GG. **Cancel:** Click Cancel and the image closes with no edits applied.

   Alt/Option + Cancel: The Cancel button changes to Reset. When you press Alt/Option and click Reset, all edits from the time you opened the image are returned to Camera Raw defaults.

HH. **Open Image:** Click this and the image opens in the Elements Photo Editor with the edits you applied.

   Alt/Option + Open Image: When you press Alt/Option, the button changes to Open Copy and a copy of the edited Raw image opens in the Elements Photo Editor. The original raw image remains unaffected and is closed as the copy is opened.

Using the Basic Panel

The Basic panel is the center of your Camera Raw Editor world. Settings you make in the Basic panel in the legacy version of ACR and the new version of ACR are virtually the same. There are just a few differences in the UI.

The lion's share of the edits you make are handled in the Basic panel. Adobe logically positions tools and panels across an application interface. In normal workflows, you begin on the left and work toward the right or at the top and work down through tools and settings.

You start your edits at the top of the Basic panel and then work down. As you work your way through the tools, you may find that many settings need to be finessed by toggling between different adjustments. For example, you can adjust Contrast; later, when you get to Clarity, you'll see that Clarity also adds some contrast. Therefore, you may need to return to the Contrast slider to tweak the contrast a bit. This back-and-forth editing is common for many adjustments. You typically make minor adjustments to your photos. Be certain to not overdo it when moving the adjustment sliders.

TIP: If you want to return a slider to the default position after moving it, double-click the slider.

Figure 2.3 shows the Basic panel with all the sliders set to default values.

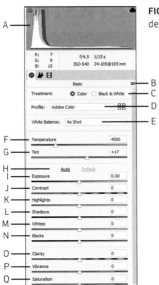

FIGURE 2.3 The Basic panel with the sliders at the defaults.

Each of the different settings for the Basic panel are identified as follows:

A. Histogram: When you open an image in the Raw Editor, first take a look at the Histogram. You want to see whether the image is skewed to the left where the data shows more shadow information or to the right where you find more highlight data. The ideal image has no clipping (cutting off data) on either side of the Histogram, and more data appears in the center (something like a bell curve). As a start, click the clipping warning buttons (items K and M in Figure 2.3) to show clipping in highlights and shadows. Notice in Figure 2.4 that the clipping indicators are shown, and the Histogram shows that the file has a lot of shadow data (skewed to the left).

FIGURE 2.4 The Histogram showing the clipping indicators and data skewed to the left.

B. Default Options: When you click the small icon to the far right of the panel title, a menu opens where you can make some choices for default settings. I'm waiting to look at the menu options until the section "Changing Program Defaults."

C. Treatment: Choose between Color or Black and White.

D. Profile: The drop-down menu displays choices for a number of profiles from which you can choose to begin your editing tasks. To the right of the menu is a grid icon that displays thumbnail views of each preset. The default preset is Adobe Color. Leave the default for the moment. You'll read more about working with profiles later in this chapter.

E. **White Balance:** The default white balance is As Shot, meaning the white balance you have in your camera settings are used as the default in the editor. You can change the white balance in several ways. Select the Eyedropper tool in the toolbar and then click on a white, medium gray, or black area in the photo. Clicking with the Eyedropper tool sets a custom white balance. If you click several times, you can scroll back through your edits and press Ctrl/⌘ + Z to Undo. Each successive Undo takes you back one step. Hence, you can, for example, click with the Eyedropper tool 10 times and undo 10 times to return to the original setting.

The other means for changing white balance is to adjust the Temperature and Tint sliders, as mentioned next.

F. **Temperature:** As you move the Temperature slider to the left, your image appears with more blue, which results in a cooler image. Conversely, moving the slider to the right adds more yellow; the result is a warmer image.

G. **Tint:** Move this slider to the left to add more green. Move it to the right to add more magenta. Together these sliders let you add/subtract more blue, yellow, green, and magenta.

To return to the default settings, you can choose As Shot from the White Balance menu, or you can double-click a slider. For example, if you move the Temperature slider from its default value of 5500 to 7000 and then double-click the slider, you return to the default 5500 value.

H. **Auto/Default:** If you want the Raw Editor to make its best guess for all the adjustments, click the Auto button. To return to the default setting, click the Default button.

Generally speaking, it's a good idea to begin your edits by clicking Auto and then working down the panel to fine-tune the settings.

I. **Exposure:** Move the slider left to darken the image. Move the slider right to lighten the image. Press Alt/Option and drag a slider to see any clipping as you make the adjustments. In Figure 2.5, you can see the clipping appear as red when you depress the Alt/Option key and move the slider. For highlight clipping, the clipping is shown in either R, G, or B. Shadow clipping is shown as black.

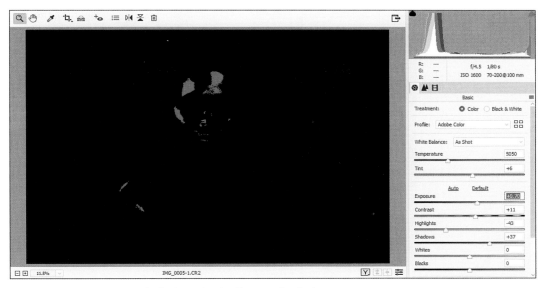

FIGURE 2.5 Clipping shown in black when adjusting Exposure for shadows.

J. Contrast: Move the slider left to decrease contrast. Move the slider right to increase contrast.

K. Highlights: In some cases where highlights are blown out (no data appears in the white areas of the image), you may be able to bring in some detail. Press the Alt/Option key and move the slider left to see any clipping warnings as you add more highlight data or right to decrease highlights. When you see clipping, move the slider to the point where the clipping first begins to appear. Be sure to press the Alt/Option key as you drag a slider to see clipping.

> **TIP:** When taking photos with your camera, strive to get proper exposure correct in-camera as much as possible. With regard to capturing detail in highlights and shadows, if you shoot an image with a lot of highlights, set your exposure for the highlights. Additionally, you might use one f-stop less of exposure compensation to capture detail in the highlights. When in the Camera Raw Editor, you can recover detail much easier for the shadows than for the highlights.

L. Shadows: This adjustment works the opposite of the Highlight slider. To increase detail in shadows, move the slider right. To decrease detail, move the slider left. Holding the Alt/Option key displays clipping if it occurs in the image. In Figure 2.6, you can see the tiny bit of clipping when adjusting shadows.

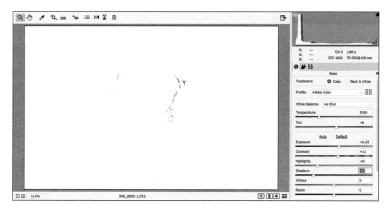

M. **Whites:** This slider brightens whites in the image. Press Alt/Option to detect clipping. When you see clipping occur, move the slider back to where you just begin to see the clipping.

N. **Blacks:** This slider helps add richer blacks in an image. Press Alt/Option to detect clipping. When you see clipping occur, make the final adjustment just before you see the clipping.

O. **Clarity:** Move this slider to the right to adjust midtones and add more contrast. Move to the left to reduce contrast in midtones.

P. **Vibrance:** Adjusting Vibrance can add some snap to your photos by brightening colors, but be careful about adding too much vibrance. Doing so makes your photos appear unrealistic.

Q. **Saturation:** When you move the slider left, you desaturate the image. Moving the slider right increases saturation. You can convert the image to grayscale by moving the Saturation slider all the way to the left, thus eliminating all color.

Working on 16-Bit Images

When you make adjustments for brightness, contrast, and color in the Photo Editor, you need to access several different dialog boxes to perform all edits:

▪ You use the Enhance > Adjust Lighting > Levels dialog box for brightness and contrast adjustments.

▪ You use the Enhance > Adjust Lighting > Shadow/Highlights dialog box to make adjustments in the shadows and highlights.

▪ You use the Enhance > Adjust Color > Adjust Hue/Saturation dialog box for hue and saturation adjustments.

■ You use the Convert to Black and White dialog box for converting color
images to black and white.

You handle all of these edits in the Basic panel in the Camera Raw Editor.

Another advantage you have with the Raw Editor is that all the edits you
make are nondestructive. You can always return to the original image as shot
by your camera and edit the image using completely different settings.

The convenience for having adjustments in a single window and the ability to
edit images nondestructively are not the only benefits you have with Camera
Raw editing. Look at the bottom of the Raw Editor window where you see
Depth. When you click the Depth drop-down list, you see two choices,
as shown in Figure 2.7: 8 Bits/Channel and 16 Bits/Channel. This is one
of the most important settings you have in the Camera Raw Editor. When
you work on 16-bit images, you have more data to work with, which
results in less destruction of the image data.

FIGURE 2.7 The Depth menu in
the Raw Editor.

Understanding Bit Depth

When you work on an 8-bit photo, the image is said to have a total of 256
levels of gray. This breaks down to 8 bits per channel (RGB channels). Think
of the level of grays as data in the image.

Some cameras can take photos at 10, 12, 14, and 16 bits. The level of grays correspondingly is shown in Table 2.1.

TABLE 2.1 Levels of Gray According to Bit Depth	
BIT DEPTH	**LEVELS OF GRAY**
8 bits	256
12 bits	4,096
14 bits	16,384
16 bits	65,536

When you convert images to 16 bit, you theoretically have much more data to
work with. Ideally, it's best to have an image that was originally shot in 16 bit
from your camera. However, fudging it a little with the Raw Editor provides
you with images with more data.

Editing 8-Bit Versus 16-Bit Images

Understanding the differences between 8- and 16-bit images is much easier
when using an example. Figure 2.8 shows an image I took in a hotel conference
hall with no flash and very low light. (The original image is an 8-bit image saved
as a JPEG file.) You may have some photos that were shot with similar exposures.

FIGURE 2.8 An under-exposed photo shot in a room with low lighting.

If you choose Enhance > Adjust Lighting > Levels or press Ctrl/⌘ + L, the Levels dialog box opens. If you move the Highlight Input Level slider (right slider) toward the left to around 55, as shown in Figure 2.9, the image brightens.

FIGURE 2.9 The Levels adjustment on an 8-bit image.

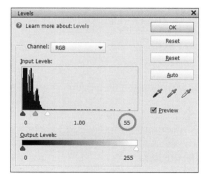

If you first open this image in the Raw Editor, convert it to 16-bit from the Depth menu, and then open it in the Photo Editor to apply the same Levels adjustment, the result is less gaps in the tone curve.

If you return to the Levels dialog box after making the same levels adjustment on both the 8-bit and 16-bit images, you see results as shown in Figure 2.10. On the left is the 8-bit image after the Levels adjustment. On the right is the 16-bit image after the same Levels adjustment. The gaps between the data points in the left dialog box show areas where no data exist. Elements needs to reconstruct the data through interpolation. In the right screen shot, which shows the Levels dialog box for the 16-bit image, you see much more data.

When you work on 16-bit images in Elements, most of the adjustments you can make from menu commands in the Enhance menu are available to you, as well as all the adjustments in the Raw Editor. Before printing or sharing the file on social media, you need to change the bit depth to 8 bit by selecting Image > Mode > 8 Bits/Channel.

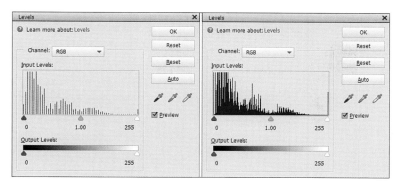

FIGURE 2.10 After levels adjustment on an 8-bit image (left) and a 16-bit image (right).

Obviously, the image used in this example is one you wouldn't print. It's low resolution and doesn't have sufficient data to produce a nice-looking photo. However, it might be something you could post on social media. When it's absolutely necessary to rescue images for Facebook, Instagram, Twitter, or other social media outlets, you can use the Raw Editor and convert images to 16 bit to resurrect some photos you desperately need to tell a story. In Figure 2.11, you can see the original image used in this example on the left and the edited version on the right.

FIGURE 2.11 The Original image opened in the Photo Editor (left) and the final edited image (right).

Editing Multiple Images in the Raw Editor

To edit multiple images with the same edits applied to all images, you need to first open the images you want to edit in the Raw Editor. The best way to open multiple raw images is to load them in the Organizer. In the Organizer, select the files you want to open and right-click to view the context menu. Select Edit with Photoshop Elements Editor, as shown in Figure 2.12.

NOTE: This book covers only the Photo Editor and the Advanced editing mode for intermediate and advanced users. If you're not familiar with the Elements Organizer, take a look at my introductory book on Elements for the version you have: *Photoshop Elements For Dummies* (Obermeier/Padova, John Wiley & Sons).

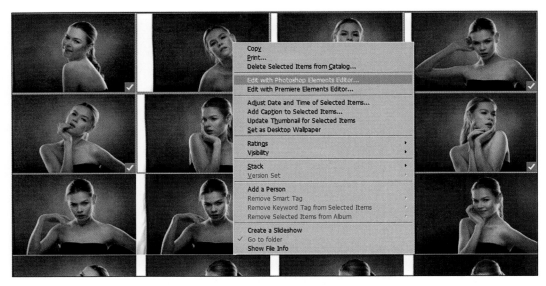

FIGURE 2.12 Multiple Camera Raw files selected in the Organizer and targeted to open in the Photo Editor.

If you have JPEG, PSD, or TIF files and want to open them in the Raw Editor, you need to open the Photo Editor and choose Open in Camera Raw. In the Open dialog box, select the files you want to open. Press Shift and click for a contiguous selection or press Ctrl/⌘ while you click each photo in a noncontiguous selection.

The photos you open are displayed as thumbnails in the panel on the left. To apply the same edits to all the images, click the first image, press Shift, and click the last image to select all the images. You can double-check the selection by examining the thumbnails. All selected images appear with a gray highlight, as shown in Figure 2.13.

TIP: Before performing individual edits, save and close the files except the one you want to start with additional edits. The Photo Editor behaves sluggishly when many high-resolution images open at the same time.

With the images selected, you can make adjustments in the Basic panel and the Sharpen and Noise Reduction panel, and you can crop and straighten images. When finished with your editing, click Open.

Back in the Photo Editor, the images are opened. As you can see in Figure 2.14, each open photo has a tab at the top of the editor window.

There are not that many edits you can perform on 16-bit images in the Photo Editor. However, there are a few tools and menus you can use. For example, you can adjust lighting using the Enhance > Adjust Lighting submenu commands, you can sharpen using Enhance > Unsharp Mask, and you can use a variety of filters. If you plan on making any of these adjustments, keep the files at 16 bit when you save them. If you don't intend to use tools and commands available to 16-bit images, choose Image > Mode > 8 Bits/Channel. Reducing the bit depth saves memory and space on your hard drive.

FIGURE 2.13 Multiple edits applied to multiple images in the Raw Editor.

FIGURE 2.14 Multiple files opened in the Photo Editor indicated by the tabs above the selected file.

One thing you cannot do with 16-bit images is duplicate backgrounds. So, if you want to edit a duplicate background, you need to first reduce the file to 8-bit mode by choosing Image > Mode > 8 Bits/Channel.

Applying Multiple Raw Edits to a Single Image

Quite often, you may find photos that requite different adjustments in different areas of a photo. When you move sliders in the Basic panel and sharpen photos, the edits are applied to the file open in the Raw Editor. The Elements Camera Raw Editor makes no provision for selecting a specific area in a photo. All adjustments are globally applied to the entire image.

In Figure 2.15, you can see a photo where a single set of edits won't work as well as if I dissect the image and edit parts separately. In this photo, I could make some edits for the foreground mountain area, but the same edits won't work for the sky, the bay, and the mountain in the distance. In essence, I need to break this photo into four different parts.

FIGURE 2.15 A photo that can benefit from editing separate parts.

In Photoshop, you have a filter where you can open a photo from the Photoshop window into the Raw Editor. Unfortunately, in Photoshop Elements, you can only access the Raw Editor when you open a file. If a file sits in the Photo Editor window, you have to close the file and select File > Open in Camera Raw. This inconvenience necessitates creating separate layers and saving each layer as a separate file. The saved files are then opened in the Raw Editor, where each file is edited and saved. Then you have to merge the files into a composite.

To perform the steps, you need to have some understanding of working with layers and creating Layer Masks. If you don't know how to create a Layer Mask, flip ahead to Chapter 5, "Masking Photos," to read more about selections and Layer Masks.

Creating Multiple Layer Masks

To begin the editing, you need to create copies of the background into separate layers:

1. Open a file you want to edit in Camera Raw. Choose a file you think may need separate adjustments. For this example, I'm using the photo shown in Figure 2.15.

2. Create a new layer from the background by pressing Ctrl/⌘ + J. In this case, I pressed the keys four times to create four copies of the background as separate layers.

3. Create Layer Masks for each separate area of the photo that requires a separate adjustment. Use the quick Selection tool to create a selection. Then click the Add a Mask tool.

4. Name each layer as you create the masks. In my example, I named the layers as shown in Figure 2.16.

> **NOTE:** Remember that when using any selection tool where you have black and white defining selections, black conceals and white reveals.

Notice the white areas in the Layer Masks. When you edit the respective layer, only the area within the white is affected.

Add Layer Mask

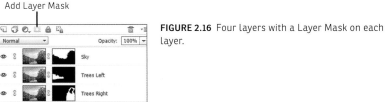

FIGURE 2.16 Four layers with a Layer Mask on each layer.

Creating Separate Files from Individual Layers

After you've created the Layer Masks, you need to create separate files for the individual layers. Because you can't open the file in the camera Raw Editor from the Photo Editor workspace, you need save each layer separately to a file by following these steps:

1. Save the file with the layers and Layer Masks. Give it a name like *composite.psd* or some such name.

2. Duplicate the file by choosing File > Duplicate.

3. Delete all layers (including the Background) except the first layer with the mask and save it with a new filename. In my example, I saved the files as SkyEdit, TreesLeftEdit, TreesRightEdit, and RiverEdit.

4. Save the first layer as a new file.

5. Continue returning to the composite. Duplicate the file and delete all layers except the one you want to keep. Save each one with a new filename.

In my example, I now have four separate files made up of the four individual layers with the Layer Masks. At this point, I'm ready to edit each file in the Camera Raw Editor.

Editing Separate Files in Camera Raw

After you have separate files, you need to edit them in Adobe Camera Raw. This example continues with the file shown earlier in Figure 2.15:

1. In the Elements Photo Editor, select File > Open in Camera Raw. Make necessary adjustments in the first image. Click Open Image after completing the edits. Save the figure as a new composite.

2. When you open the image in Camera Raw, you lose the Layer Mask. Therefore, you have to create a new mask. Unless you have a lot of white in your photo, this should be easy to do. You can use the Magic Wand tool and select the white. Inverse the selection by pressing Ctrl/⌘ + Shift + I. Then click the Add a Mask icon in the Layers panel.

3. After completing all the masks on the new files, you need to merge them. Open the original photo you started with. Drag each layer from the new files to the original photo. You use the original photo in the event that some data may have been missed when you created the masks. The background will fill in any gaps. In Figure 2.17, you can see the new layers I added to the original background. Note that the layers carry the new names from the files that I edited in the Camera Raw Editor.

FIGURE 2.17 Drag the edited files to the original background image.

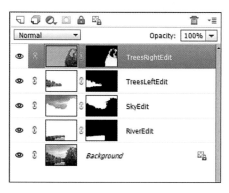

4. Follow the same steps for all layers to bring each layer into the new composite. In Figure 2.18, you can see the original file I used on the left and the final edited image on the right. Not all images require this level of complexity, but now you know what to do with an image that requires editing certain areas in the photo separately.

FIGURE 2.18 Original unedited image (left) and after multiple Camera Raw edits (right).

Working in ACR in Elements 2021 and After

The old ACR editor was in use for Photoshop Elements 2020 and earlier. All of what you can do in earlier versions of ACR is available in the 2021 release. The major difference between the earlier versions of ACR and the 2021 and later version is the UI. Let's take a look at using the 2021 version of ACR.

Launching the Camera Raw Editor

The first time you launch the Camera Raw Editor in the ACR 2021 and later, a welcome screen opens and prompts you to make a choice for the UI you want to use. In Figure 2.19, you can see the initial screen after launching the Camera Raw Editor.

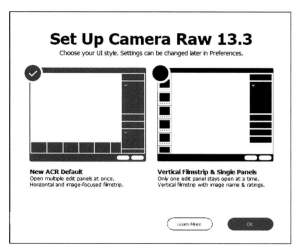

FIGURE 2.19 The Camera Raw Editor welcome screen.

Notice that you can decide if you want the filmstrip to appear on the bottom of the image window (left in Figure 2.19) or along the left side of the image window as it was in the legacy version of ACR (right in Figure 2.19). The choice on the left also permits you to open multiple edit panels rather than a single panel.

Click the UI style you want and then click OK. The raw file you selected opens in the Raw Editor. As you can see in Figure 2.20, much has changed in the user interface. Everything you may have used in previous versions of the Camera Raw Editor are available in this upgrade, but the settings have been moved around a bit.

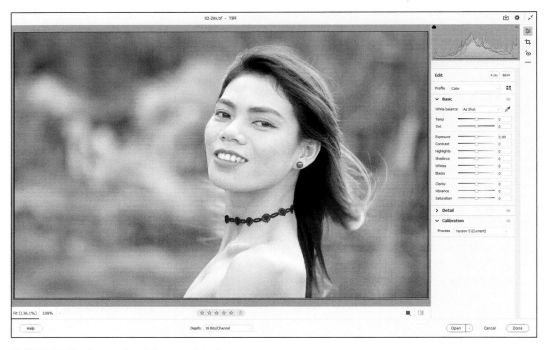

FIGURE 2.20 The Camera Raw Editor user interface.

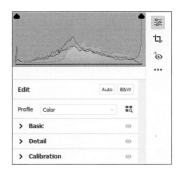

FIGURE 2.21 The Panel Bin showing a list of panels.

Becoming Familiar with Tools and Buttons

On the right side of the Raw Editor below the Histogram, you see, by default, the Basic panel. If you don't see the Basic panel, you may see a list of the available panels, as shown in Figure 2.21.

In this case, below the Profile drop-down list, you see three items with right-pointing arrows: the Basic panel, the Detail panel, and the Calibration panel. Rather than icons corresponding to panels as in the earlier version of ACR, this new version shows text labels. Click one of the arrows to open the respective panel in the Panel Bin.

In Figure 2.22, you can see the toolbar at the top right and various buttons around the interface.

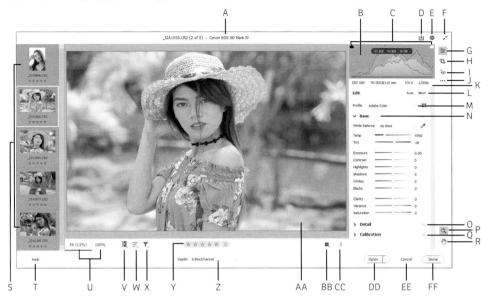

FIGURE 2.22 The Camera Raw Editor tools.

The buttons and settings in the Camera Raw Editor in Elements 2022 include the following:

A. **Camera Data:** A display at the top of the ACR window shows the camera model used for the active shot in the image window.

B. **Histogram:** The Histogram displays data in your image. In the three RGB channels, you can see how the data falls across a measure of grays from 0 to 255. You can also see if clipping (cutting off data) occurs if there is a spike (high column) on either side of the Histogram.

C. **Shadow/Highlight clipping warning (U/O):** Click the button on the left to see clipping in an image for shadows represented by blue overlays. Clipping means that no detail is shown in that area of the image. Click the button on the right or press O to see clipping of highlights represented as red overlays and click U to show shadows as blue highlights.

D. **Convert and Save Image:** Click this icon to open the Save Options dialog box. For more on Save Options, see the section "Using Save Options" later in this chapter.

E. **Open Preferences (Ctrl/⌘ + K):** Click this to adjust the Raw Editor Preferences, which I talk about more later in the section "Changing Program Defaults."

F.   **Toggle Full Screen Mode:** Press the F key or click this button to expand the Raw Editor workspace to full screen. Press F again, and you return to the default view.

G.   **Edit:** If you click the Crop tool (the next tool in the list) or the Red Eye Removal tool (item I) and you want to return to the default edit mode, click this tool.

H.   **Crop tool (C):** You can crop images in the editor much the same as you crop in the Elements Photo Editor. If you click on the Crop tool, another panel opens in the Panel Bin (item K), as shown in Figure 2.23. Settings you have available in the Crop panel include the following:

FIGURE 2.23 The Crop panel.

- **Aspect Ratio:** Click the default size, and a drop-down list opens where you can choose from a number of different aspect ratios.

- **Angle:** Move the slider to change the angle for the crop.

For more on straightening images, see Chapter 8.
- **Straighten tool (A):** The Straighten tool functions the same in the Raw Editor as you find in the Elements Photo Editor.

- **Rotate Left (L):** Click the tool button or press the L key to rotate the image 90° left. Keep pressing L to rotate the image in 90° increments.

- **Rotate Right (R):** Click the tool button or press the R key to rotate the image 90° right.

- **Flip Horizontal:** Click the button adjacent to the Rotate Right button and the image flips horizontally.

- **Flip Vertical:** Click the last button in the Rotate & Flip category to flip the image vertically.

- **Crop Adjustments:** Notice the marks at the corners of the photo in Figure 2.23. They're also along the horizontal and vertical centers at the edges of the photo. Click and drag a corner or center item to shape the crop. If you move the cursor outside the marks, you see a semicircle with two arrowheads. Click and drag to rotate the image. If you place the cursor at the corners, you see a diagonal line with two arrowheads. Click and drag to crop down or up.

  To return to the default editing mode, click the Edit button (item F).

I. **Red Eye Removal tool (E):** Removes red eye from a subject's eyes. Use the tool to draw a marquee around an eye to remove red eye.

J. **More Image Settings:** The fly-out menu offers options for changing default settings for the open image.

K. **Panel Bin:** By default, the Basic panel is open.

L. **Edit:** Two options are available here. The Auto setting makes an adjustment for autocorrecting image color and brightness. To see what adjustments are affected, open the Basic panel. The other option is the Black and White adjustment. Click this button, and all color is eliminated so the image appears as a black-and-white photo.

M. **Profile:** From the drop-down menu, you have several choices for using different profiles. For more on using profiles, see "Working with Profiles" later in this chapter.

N. **Panel Bin:** In Figure 2.22, you see the Basic panel open in the Panel Bin.

O. **Detail:** Click the right-pointing arrow to open the Detail panel. For information related to settings in the Detail panel, see "Sharpening and Reducing Noise" later in this chapter.

> **TIP:** Choose 100% views or greater when you make adjustments to sharpness and noise reduction.

P. **Zoom tool (Z):** If you move the cursor into the document window, the cursor changes to a Zoom tool. Click to zoom in or press Alt/Option and click to zoom out.

Q. **Calibration panel:** You have few choices here. From a drop-down menu, choose a default or a legacy version of Camera Raw.

R. **Hand tool (H):** Press the H key on your keyboard or click the Hand icon in the toolbar to access the Hand tool. Alternatively, you can press the spacebar. Click and drag around an image to move it within the editor workspace.

S.   Filmstrip: The filmstrip is only visible when two or more photos are open in the Raw Editor. You can view the image thumbnails vertically along the left side of the window or horizontally along the bottom of the image window. To change from vertical to horizontal and vice versa, right-click an image thumbnail and choose the orientation you want.

T.   Help: Click this button to open the Help section of Adobe's website where information related to the Raw Editor is provided.

NOTE: Items V through X only appear when more than one file is open in the Raw Editor.

U.   Zoom settings: You also have fixed zoom option choices in the pop-up menu. Click to open the menu and make choices for the zoom level you want. Click in the text box and change the value to jump to a zoom level. You can also zoom in and out of an image by pressing Ctrl/⌘ + − (the minus sign) to zoom out and Ctrl/⌘ + + (the plus sign) to zoom in.

V.   Show/Hide Filmstrip: Click the button to hide the filmstrip. Click again to show the filmstrip.

W.   Sort menu: Click to open the menu and choose from different sort options. You can sort by Capture Date, File Name, Star Rating, or Color Label. You can sort by ascending or descending order. When making a menu choice, the thumbnails in the filmstrip are sorted accordingly.

X.   Filter menu: You can filter images by Star Rating, Color Label, Marked or Not Marked for Deletion, and Rejected or Not Rejected. For marking for deletion and rejection, open a context menu on a thumbnail and choose one of the options.

Y.   Star Ratings: Stars: Click a star to rate the photo. When you open the file in the Organizer, you can sort photos by star ratings. Adding stars to photos helps you organize images in the Organizer and provides a means for rating photos.

Z.   Depth: For 16-bit images, choose 16 Bits/Channel. The alternate choice is editing in 8 Bits/Channel mode.

AA.   Image window: The active image is displayed here.

BB.   Before/After (Q): Click this button to cycle through before/after views adjacent to each other vertically, horizontally, and split screen.

CC.   Toggle Between Current Settings and Defaults: Click this button to see your image with the defaults. Click again to see the image with the edits you made.

Defaults are not necessarily the original image captured by your camera. You can, for example, choose to open images with some automatic corrections applied. When you toggle this button, you see the defaults after automatic corrections were applied.

To learn more about changing defaults, see the "Changing Program Defaults" section later in this chapter.

DD. Open: Click to open the image in the Elements Photo Editor with the edits you applied.

> **Alt/Option + Open:** When you press Alt/Option, the button changes to Open Copy and the edited raw image opens in the Elements Photo Editor. The original raw image remains unaffected and is closed as the copy is opened in the Photo Editor.

> **Alt/Option + Cancel:** The Cancel button changes to Reset. When you press Alt/Option and click Reset, all edits from the time you opened the image are returned to defaults.

EE. Cancel: Click Cancel, and the image closes and no edits are applied.

FF. Done: Click Done to apply all your edits and close the image. When you open the image, it is shown in the Raw Editor with the last edits you made.

Sharpening and Reducing Noise

The second panel in the Panel Bin is the Detail panel. The same adjustments are found in the legacy version of ACR.

The Detail panel has three sections, as you can see in Figure 2.24. At the top, you find adjustments for Sharpening. Below Sharpening is Noise Reduction, and the final group is Color Noise Reduction.

Sharpening Images

By default, some sharpening is applied to images when you open them. Figure 2.24 shows you default slider adjustments when an image is opened in the Raw Editor. If you want to eliminate the default amount of sharpening, move the sliders to zero.

FIGURE 2.24 Click the Detail icon in the Panel Bin to open the Detail panel.

Before making any adjustments in this panel, you should view your image at a 1:1 ratio. Open the Zoom menu from the lower-left corner of the editor window and choose 100%. This adjustment zooms the image to an actual size, where you can see more clearly any artifacts that might appear if you sharpen too much. Use the Hand tool to move the image around and locate an area such as a subject's eye or contrasting colors in images. Sharpening actually increases contrast along the differences of tonal edges of subjects and the background or along edges of contrasting colors.

TIP: Be very careful when sharpening images. If you apply too much sharpening, you will see strong contrast lines between differing tonal values. Your images may look fine on your monitor but when printed, you may see obvious artifacts or halos. Back off the sharpening after printing some test prints to reduce contrast.

The sliders provide you adjustments for the following:

- **Sharpening:** The Sharpening slider increases contrast between colors and at the edges of color transitions. As a general rule, keep the Sharpening slider between 70 and 90. If you're sharpening portraits or shots with people, keep the Amount to 50 or less.

- **Radius:** Radius is the number of pixels the editor looks at on either side of the line of contrast between two contrasting colors or the edges of subjects. Increasing radius will show strong contrast along lines of contrasting pixels. It's best to keep this adjustment low, such as between .8 to 1.2.

- **Detail:** This adjustment increases sharpness in detail. Although it increases sharpness, it may also result in adding more noise to images shot at higher ISOs. In many cases, keep this setting off, or at least keep it to 20 or lower.

- **Masking:** Masking looks at the solid colors in the image where no contrasting values exist. To use this slider, press Alt/Option. The image area turns white. As you move the Masking slider to the right while keeping Alt/Option depressed, you begin to see solid colors appear as black (see Figure 2.25). Black areas are where no sharpening is applied. The white areas are where sharpening occurs. Move this slider to the right as far as needed to eliminate sharpening in solid colors.

FIGURE 2.25 Press Alt/ Option when adjusting masking.

Adjusting Noise

By default, adjustments are made to reduce color noise. You see noise in color areas represented by varying colors of different pixels. As you reduce the noise, the colors disappear in solid color areas. Before adjusting noise, press Ctrl/⌘ + 1 to zoom to an actual size. You can see adjustments more clearly when viewing the photo at actual size.

Noise adjustments involve the following:

- **Noise Reduction:** Move this slider to reduce overall noise.

- **Detail:** This item represents how much detail remains in the color noise area. As you increase the adjustment, you regain some detail. Keep this adjustment low to avoid emphasizing the color noise.

- **Contrast:** Zoom in to 800% to 1600% to see results while moving this slider. You make some adjustments for the contrast in the noise areas. Move the slider to around 50 to bring back some detail in the highlights.

Noise often shows up in images shot at high ISOs and when you expand the dynamic range to capture more detail in highlights and shadows. For example, when you move the Highlight and Shadow sliders in the Basic panel to the far edges, you will usually see some noise.

When you make adjustments on images with a lot of noise, first set all the sharpening sliders to zero and start your editing in this section. You don't want to sharpen the noise because it will introduce more noise in your image. First, make all noise adjustments and then go to the sharpening sliders and make those adjustments,

Slider adjustments you may make to reduce color noise include the following:

- **Color Noise Reduction:** Move the slider to adjust overall color noise.

- **Detail:** Move this slider up to regain some detail lost after reducing color noise. Whereas the Color Noise Reduction adjustment blurs the image, this adjustment results in sharpening the softness introduced with the Color Noise Reduction adjustment.

- **Smoothness:** This adjustment blurs the color noise, so it appears like the color noise disappears. Add a little bit of color smoothness to further reduce the color noise.

Using the Calibration Panel

There's not much to do in the Calibration panel. Your only adjustment is to choose a version of the Raw Editor. Most of the time, you leave this menu command at the default, which is the current version of the Raw Editor. If you have legacy files edited in earlier versions of the Raw Editor, you might choose a menu option equivalent to the version from which the file was edited.

Working with Filmstrips

When you select multiple raw files in the Organizer or you select multiple raw files in the Open dialog box and click Open, the files open in the Raw Editor and are visible in the Raw Editor filmstrip.

TIP: If you select files in the Photo Editor that are not in a Raw format, you need to choose File > Open in Camera Raw. If you open files from the Organizer, the files must be in the Raw format to open in the Raw Editor. You cannot open other file formats in the Raw Editor from the Organizer. If you choose Raw files from the Organizer, you can open them from the Organizer and the files open in the Raw Editor.

You can select photos in a contiguous or noncontiguous order in the film-strip. To select photos in noncontiguous order, click a photo in the filmstrip and press Ctrl/⌘ + click the desired photos. In Figure 2.26, you can see photos selected in noncontiguous order.

FIGURE 2.26 To make a noncontiguous selection, press Ctrl/⌘ and click each image to add to the selection.

By default, the filmstrip is across the bottom of the ACR window. If you want to view the files vertically on the left side of the ACR window (as in Figure 2.26), you can open a context menu on an image thumbnail and choose Film-strip Orientation > Vertical, as shown in Figure 2.27.

FIGURE 2.27 Right-click on a thumbnail to open a context menu.

As you can see in Figure 2.27, you have a number of options in the context menu. Among those are the following:

- **Select All:** Click the menu command or press Ctrl/⌘ + A to select all photos in the filmstrip. To deselect all selected images, press Ctrl/⌘ + D. All images but the first image are deselected.

■ **Set Rating:** From the submenu, you can choose a star rating. Star ratings are the same as star ratings you can use in the Organizer.

For more on star ratings, see Chapter 5.

■ **Mark for Deletion:** If you have a photo in the group you don't want to use, click this command and the photo is moved to the Recycle Bin/Trash Can. Be careful. If you click Mark for Deletion, the photo is moved out of its folder and to the trash. If you empty the Recycle Bin (Windows) or Trash Can (Mac), the file is deleted.

■ **Filmstrip Orientation:** Choose the orientation in the submenu.

■ **Show Filename:** Click this command, and the filenames of the photos are displayed below each thumbnail.

■ **Show Ratings & Color Labels:** Displays start ratings and color labels.

Synchronizing Edits

The great advantage for opening multiple files in the Raw Editor is that you can apply the same adjustments to multiple images. If you have several photos taken under similar lighting conditions and you want to make brightness and contrast adjustments, you can select multiple files and adjust sliders in the Basic panel. Likewise, you can sharpen multiple images, crop multiple images to the same size, and employ all the other editing options you have in the Raw Editor.

Synchronizing Defaults

Suppose you make some different edits to several different files. Let's further assume you have one unedited image to which you want to apply the same edits you made for your second edited image. To apply previous edits to another image, first select the image with the edits you want to copy. Press Ctrl/⌘ and click the image you want to edit.

Next, open the defaults menu. Click the More Image Settings icon (the icon of three bullets below the Red Eye Removal tool on the right side of the ACR window) to open the Defaults fly-out panel shown in Figure 2.28. Select Apply Previous Settings. The edits made to the previously edited file are now applied to the selected file.

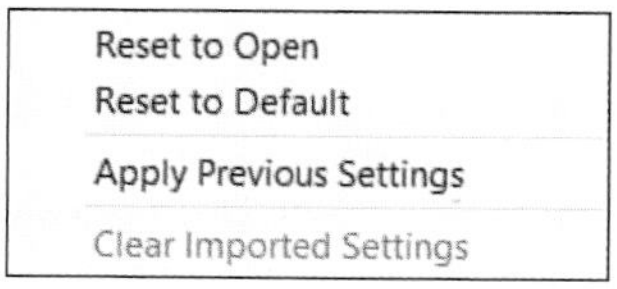

Reset to Open
Reset to Default
Apply Previous Settings
Clear Imported Settings

FIGURE 2.28 Click the three dots below the Red Eye tool to open the More Image Settings menu.

Working with Profiles

Earlier in this chapter when I discussed working in the Basic panel in the section "Using the Basic Panel," I talked about making settings changes using the default Adobe Color profile. When you open a raw image, this profile is selected by default. However, there are many other profiles you can use. You can install custom profiles created by third parties, you can set up a number of favorites to access the profiles you use most frequently, and you can create custom profiles.

There's quite a bit to understand when talking about Camera Raw profiles. Let's start by looking at the panels Adobe provides for you when you first install Elements.

FIGURE 2.29 Profile thumbnails displayed after clicking the Browse icon.

Looking at the Adobe Camera Raw Profiles

When you install Photoshop Elements, Adobe installs many different profiles, including the default Adobe Color profile. If you click the down-pointing arrow adjacent to Adobe Color, the drop-down menu opens and reveals five additional profiles. You can also click the Browse Profiles icon adjacent to the drop-down list, or you can choose Browse from the drop-down list to see thumbnail images for the profiles. If you mouse over a thumbnail, you see a dynamic preview of what your photo will look like if you use that profile. In Figure 2.29, you can see some of the thumbnails for the Adobe Color group along with several other collapsed groups.

Aside from the default Adobe Color profile, which is for general use, other included profiles are the following:

- **Adobe Monochrome:** This profile renders an image as black and white with optimized sensitivity for how colors render as different tones and increased contrast.

- **Adobe Landscape:** This profile adds enhancements to sky hues (blues) and foliage hues (greens).

- **Adobe Portrait:** This profile provides optimum protection and enhancements for skin tones.

- **Adobe Standard:** Adobe Standard adds subtle tonal and color adjustments to the image. The result is an expected look and feeling of a photograph. Like Adobe Color, this is generally a good starting point for many images.

- **Adobe Vivid:** Adobe Vivid adds an increased level of contrast and saturation.

Additionally, you'll notice items such as Camera Matching, Artistic, B&W, Modern, and Vintage. To get familiar with these other choices, open some images and try applying different profile settings to different images.

Managing Profiles

If you right-click a profile (or Control + click on a Mac with a one-button mouse), a context menu opens. The menu shown in Figure 2.30 offers the following options for managing profiles:

- **Profile Info:** Click this item in the menu and a dialog box opens to provide a very brief description of the profile.

- **Add to Favorites:** This option lets you add the profile to a Favorites list.

- **Remove from Favorites** (available when you right-click on a Favorite): This command enables you to delete the item from the Favorites. You can also delete Favorites Adobe installed when you installed Elements. To learn more about Favorites, see "Creating a Favorites List" later in this chapter.

Profile Info...
Add to Favorites

Manage Profiles...
Reset Favorite Profiles
Reset Hidden Profiles

Import Profiles & Presets...

FIGURE 2.30 Open a context menu on a profile thumbnail.

- **Manage Profiles:** This command opens the Manage Profiles dialog box, which contains a listing of all profile groups. If you want to display a group, click the check box next to the profile. To hide a profile, click the box to remove the check mark. Enabled profiles are visible in the Basic panel.

- **Reset Favorite Profiles:** If you have added a number of profiles and you want to return to the defaults, select this command.

- **Reset Hidden Profiles:** If you have hidden any profiles, selecting this command brings them back and unhides them.

- **Import Profiles and Presets:** Choose this command to open the Import Profile and Presets dialog box. You can load custom profiles by selecting a profile and clicking the Open button. If you want to return to the list option, click the Back button at the top of the Basic panel. The Back button appears after you click Browse in the Profile area of the Basic panel.

Creating a Favorites List

Adding profiles to a Favorites list enables you to quickly access those profiles you use most often. As shown in Figure 2.31, I added a number of different profiles to my Favorites list, including a custom profile I created.

By default, the installed profiles appear in a Favorites list. You can open the list by clicking the down-pointing arrow adjacent to Favorites at the top of the Profile Browser panel. As you view different profiles, notice the star icon in the top-right corner of each profile thumbnail. Click the star, and that profile is added to your Favorites list. To eliminate a profile from your Favorites list, click the star icon again in the Favorites panel.

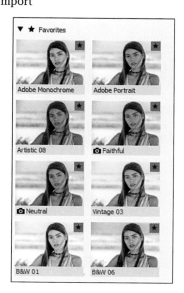

FIGURE 2.31 A number of profiles added to the Favorites list.

Working with XML Files and Preferences

There are a few things you should understand when it comes to sharing edited raw images and changing default settings. Our first stop in learning how to deal with file sharing and changing defaults is examining the Preferences dialog box.

Changing Program Defaults

Some default settings can be applied in the Camera Raw Editor Preferences dialog box. To open the Preferences dialog box, you must open an image in the Raw Editor, but note that any settings you make in the Preferences dialog box won't have an effect on the open image. The Preference settings only take effect when you quit and reopen the Raw Editor.

With the Raw Editor open, click the Open Preferences tool in the toolbar or press Ctrl/⌘ + K. The Preferences dialog box opens, as shown in Figure 2.32.

FIGURE 2.32 Press Ctrl/⌘ + K to open the Preferences dialog box.

There are six areas in the Preferences dialog box with different settings. These include the following:

- **General:** In the General area, you make choices for raw default settings. Choose from Adobe Default or Camera Settings. If you prefer your Camera Raw settings, open the drop-down list and choose Camera Settings.

- **DNG File Handling:** This section covers working with Adobe Digital Negative (DNG) files. Adobe created its own raw format and named it Adobe Digital Negative. New profiles are added as new versions of Photoshop and

Photoshop Elements are updated. If you update your version of Photoshop Elements and your camera profile has not yet been updated to the newest version of Photoshop Elements ACR, you can convert your camera's raw image to a DNG file. DNG file support is always available during new application upgrades. You can download the free DNG converter file from https://helpx.adobe.com/camera-raw/using/adobe-dng-converter.html.

Embed XMP in DNG in the Sidecars drop-down menu means when you make edits in the Raw Editor, by default a text file called an XMP file known as a sidecar file is created that holds all your edit information. The Raw file itself is not edited. The XMP file holds the edit information apart from the photo itself. Choose this item if you want to embed the XMP file inside the DNG file.

If **Update embedded JPEG Previews** is checked, embedded previews are updated as files are edited.

- **Panels:** If **Use Compact Layout** is enabled, you can see all the sliders in panels like the Basic panel. If you uncheck the box, the panels appear larger, and you need to scroll the panel to see adjustments at the bottom.

- **Filmstrip:** From the Orientation drop-down menu, you can choose horizontal or vertical to change the default.

  When **Show Filenames** is enabled, filenames display at the bottom of each thumbnail.

  Enable **Show Ratings and Color Labels** to have all star ratings and color labels appear at the bottom of each thumbnail. See Figure 2.33, where filenames, star ratings, and color labels appear on thumbnails.

- **Zoom and Pan:** Type a value in the text box to set the default zoom level.

  When you click on the image window, the image zooms to the default zoom level, and the cursor changes to a zoom tool with a minus symbol indicating that you can click to zoom out. When the **Use Lightroom Style Zoom and Pan** check box is enabled, after zooming in, the cursor changes to the hand tool where you can pan the image inside the ACR window.

- **Keyboard shortcuts:** Enabling Use Legacy Shortcuts literally has no effect. You can use Ctrl/⌘ + Z or Ctrl/⌘ + Alt/Option + Z to step back through edits in the panels. Legacy files are treated identically where the shortcuts work the same.

FIGURE 2.33 Thumbnails in the filmstrip appearing with filenames, star ratings, and color labels.

Using Save Options

The icon at the top-right corner of the ACR window is the Convert and Save Image icon (refer to Figure 2.34). Additionally, you see a tool tip when the cursor is placed over the icon.

FIGURE 2.34 The Convert and Save Image icon.

Click this item, and the Save Options dialog box opens, as shown in Figure 2.35. In this dialog box, you have choices for specifying the location where you want to save photos, the filenaming convention, the file extension choice, and some specifics related to the Adobe Digital Negative format. Most of these options are self-explanatory.

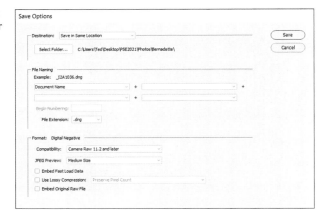

Using Sidecar Files

In the Preferences dialog box, you have some choices for handling sidecar files. Sidecar files (which have a .xmp extension) are text files written in XML that contain all the data related to editing a raw file. You can examine an .xmp file by opening it in a text editor.

.xmp files are like tape recordings. All the edits are recorded and documented for each edit you make. When you click Done or you click Open Image in the Raw Editor, the sidecar file is written. In a desktop view, you can see the sidecar file adjacent to the raw image. In Figure 2.36, notice the desktop view of a number of Camera Raw files along with .dng and .xmp files. The .xmp files indicate that the raw files have been open and adjustments have been made to the images. Where no .xmp file appears adjacent to the raw file, the raw image has not yet been edited.

FIGURE 2.36 Desktop view of raw and xmp files.

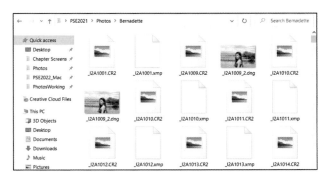

If you delete the sidecar file, all edits are deleted, and the original raw image remains in its unedited version. It's the same file you copied from your memory card to your computer.

It's important to understand that the sidecar file needs to accompany your original raw image when you copy the image to another computer or share the image with another user. That is, it's important if you want to retain all the edits you made in the raw file.

NOTE: When you copy photos that have been edited in Camera Raw to a network server or another computer, or you send it to another user, be certain to also copy/send the sidecar file.

Using Elements+ Camera Raw

If you have a raw photo you want to edit using the Elements+ Raw Editor, you need to first open the file in the Elements Photo Editor in expert mode. Furthermore, you need to convert any 16-bit files to 8-bit before you can edit a file using Elements+ Camera Raw.

Elements+

If you have the Elements+ plug-in installed, you gain more editing options in the Elements+ Camera Raw Editor. To access the Elements+ Camera Raw Editor, open the Effects panel and choose Elements+ from the drop-down list at the top of the panel.

In the lower-left corner of the Effects panel, click or drag the camera icon to a photo open in the Photo Editor.

The best way to handle editing using the Elements+ Raw Editor is to first use the Elements Raw Editor. Adjust brightness and contrast in the Basic panel and open the file in the Photo Editor. Click the Photo icon in the Elements+ panel or drag it to the photo to open the Elements+ Camera Raw Editor, as shown in Figure 2.37. If your photo is 16-bit, Elements+ prompts you to convert the bit depth before opening the file.

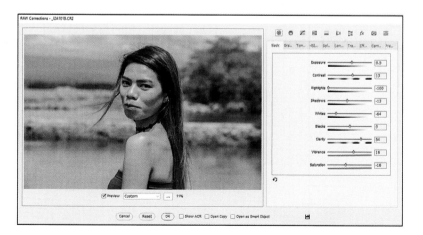

FIGURE 2.37 The Elements+ Camera Raw Editor.

As you can see in Figure 2.38, there are some additional tools and panels available in the Elements+ Camera Raw Editor.

A
B
C
D
E
F
G
H
I
J
fx
Basic
Gra..
Ton..
HSL..
Spl..
Len..
Tra..
Eff..
Cam..
Pre..

FIGURE 2.38 The Elements+ tools.

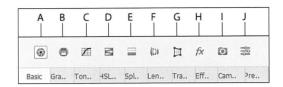

The tools shown in Figure 2.38 include the following:

A. **Basic:** The Basic panel is identical to the Basic panel in the Elements Raw Editor from the Exposure setting all the way down to the adjustment for Saturation. Choosing Profiles and adjusting Temperature is not available in the Elements+ Camera Raw Editor.

B. **Gradient Filter:** The Gradient Filter lets you adjust similar settings you have in the Basic panel to a gradient. For example, if your photo has more blown-out highlights at the top of the photo, but the foreground appears with good brightness and contrast, you can create a gradient so you can adjust the top portion of the photo and make more gradual adjustments as the gradient moves down. You have two tabs. One tab is for Adjustments (sliders for adjusting brightness and contrast) and the other tab is for masks, where you decide how the gradient is applied in the photo.

C. **Tone Curve:** Tone Curve offers several preset curve adjustments in a drop-down list from which to choose. If you click the Edit button, the Curves dialog box opens where you can make custom Curves adjustments. When you click Edit and apply a Curves adjustment, the Elements+ plug-in creates a new Adjustment Layer where the Curves adjustments are applied. When you click OK, you return to the Photo Editor view and don't return to the Elements+ Raw Editor.

D. **HSL/Grayscale:** HSL/Grayscale panel offers you options for adjusting the Hue, Saturation, and Luminance separately, as shown in Figure 2.39. These adjustment options are not something you have available in the Photo Editor.

Hue
Saturation
Luminance
Reds
0
Oranges
0
Yellows
0
Greens
0
Aquas
0
Blues
0
Purples
0
Magentas
0

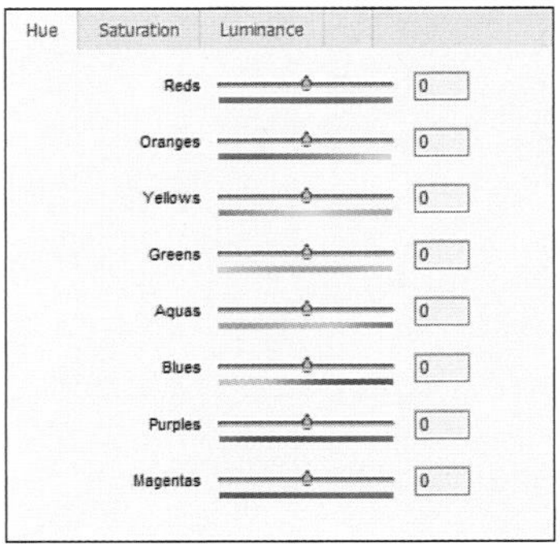

FIGURE 2.39 The HSL tab in the Elements+ Raw Editor.

E.   Split Toning: Split toning offers you sliders to set the highlight and shadow hues and adjust the saturation for highlight and shadow to create a split tone photo like the one in Figure 2.40.

FIGURE 2.40 Split toning lets you set hues and saturation values for highlights and shadows.

F.   Lens Correction: Lens correction offers you settings to remove chromatic aberration (fringe colors due to lens distortion).

G.   Transform: The Transform tab provides settings for correcting barrel distortion you might get from some lenses.

H.   Effects: The Effects panel provides settings for Dehazing, adding Grain, and adding Vignettes.

I.   Camera Calibration: Camera Calibration lets you set adjustments to correct for color shifts.

J.   Presets: If you make adjustments and want to apply the same settings to other photos, click the Save button in the Presets tab.

At the bottom of the Elements+ Camera Raw Editor, you see an option for opening the photo as a Smart Object. Inasmuch as you don't have many editing opportunities with Smart Objects in the Photo Editor, there are many different edits you can apply to Smart Objects using Elements+. If you want to continue editing with Elements+, check the box for Open as Smart Object.

After you finish edits in the Elements+ Camera Raw Editor and open a photo in the Photo Editor, you see all edits as you made them in the Raw Editor, including such edits as Tone Curve adjustments, Split Toning, and adding Vignettes.

PART II

SELECTIONS AND LAYERS

This part begins with coverage of all the selection tools and the ways you can make selections. Then I move on to important concepts relative to using layers and creating Layer Masks. Throughout this book, almost all editing sequences use layers and the Layers panel, so if you're not already skilled at working with layers and creating Layer Masks, make sure to study Chapters 4 and 5. The last chapter in this part covers sharpening images.

CHAPTER 3
MAKING SELECTIONS

Chapter Goals

Seasoned users of Photoshop Elements probably already know the importance of selections and how to create them. If that's the case for you, skim through this chapter to see if there is anything new to you. Less-experienced users should know that making selections is one of the most frequently used and important tasks in Elements. Study this chapter and become familiar with all the selection methods described herein. This chapter helps you

- Become familiar with all the selection tools
- Understand all the tool options for each selection tool available in Elements+
- Find out how to refine a selection
- Become familiar with the Select menu commands
- Become familiar with additional tools available for creating selections

When you perform tasks like compositing images; making color corrections; editing portraits; changing backgrounds; and adjusting brightness, contrast, and color, selections are essential. When you create a selection, the selected area in the image is the target for all the editing you perform. For example, if you select a sky and want to add some saturation and vibrance, then the saturation and vibrance edits you make are applied only to the sky. When you haven't made a selection in the photo, all edits are applied globally to the entire image.

To give you an indication of how important selections are, look over the Tools panel and the menus. Elements has ten different selection tools in three different groups (found in the Select group in the Tools panel) and an entire menu devoted to working with selections. This chapter shows you many ways to create and use selections.

Using Selection Tools

The selection tools are grouped in the Tools panel along with the Move tool (see Figure 3.1). The selection tools are contained in three groups:

- The geometric tools

- The lasso tools

- A miscellaneous category with several other types of selection tools

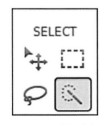

FIGURE 3.1 The Selection tools in the Tools panel

Creating Geometric Selections

The geometric selection tools include the Marquee Rectangle tool and the Elliptical Marquee tool. The Marquee Rectangle tool is the default in the Tools panel. To select the Elliptical Marquee tool, you can press M on your keyboard or open the Tool Options panel. Each tool has additional settings that you can make in the Tool Options panel. Figure 3.2 shows the tool options for the geometric selection tools.

FIGURE 3.2 Tool options for the geometric selection tools.

With both the Marquee Rectangle tool and the Elliptical Marquee tool, you can create a selection from center by pressing the Alt/Option key as you drag with the tool. To create a constrained square or circle, press the Shift key. To create a square from center or circle from center, press both Alt/Option and Shift as you drag.

Using the Geometric Selection Tools

In the Tool Options panel, notice the two tools on the left (refer to Figure 3.2). Click either icon to select the respective tool and then drag in the image window to create a selection.

TIP: If you find yourself accidently pressing the M key so the tool switches when you didn't intend for it to, you can adjust the setting to prevent this from happening. Open the Preferences (Ctrl/⌘ + K), and in the General panel, check the box for Use Shift Key for a Tool Switch. Click OK. Now you need to press Shift + M to change between tools.

Next to the tool icons are four option icons, which are (from left to right):

TIP: With all selections, to add to a selection, you press the Shift key, click and drag to add to the selection. To remove from a selection, you press the Alt/Option key, and click and drag to remove from a selection.

- **New Selection:** This icon is selected by default when you click a selection tool. This tool enables you to create a new selection on the image. If you have a selection currently active when you click the New Selection icon, the first selection is deselected, and you can draw a new selection.

- **Add to Selection (Shift):** If you've created a selection and release the mouse button, and then decide you want to add to the selection, click this icon and draw around the area you want to add to the selection. Alternatively, you can add to the selection by simply pressing the Shift key, and then clicking and dragging around the area you want to add to the selection.

- **Subtract from Selection (Alt/Option):** To subtract from a selection, click the third icon and drag around the area you want to remove from the selection. Alternatively, simply press the Alt/Option key when you drag a selection tool.

- **Intersect with Selection (Alt/Option + Shift):** Draw one selection, and then click this tool or press the Alt/Option + Shift keys as you make a second selection. The area where the two selections intersect becomes the new selection.

Notice the Refine Edge button in the Tool Options in Figure 3.2. You find this button in the geometric selection tools and most of those tools in the miscellaneous group. I talk about Refine Edge in more detail later in this chapter in the "Refining Selections" section.

You can use a slider to add some feathering with selections made from these tools. As you drag the slider to the right, you add more feathering to your selection. When feathering selections, you must first make an adjustment for the feather amount and then create the selection. You cannot create a selection and apply feathering after the fact.

Additionally, below the Feather slider is a menu (adjacent to Aspect). You can choose to create a fixed ratio selection by choosing Fixed Ratio in the dropdown menu and type values in the text boxes below the list. Additionally, you can restrict the selections to fixed sizes. As one example, you might want to create a 3-inch by 3-inch selection, so you would choose Image, Crop to crop an image to exactly 3 × 3 inches.

Creating Single-Row and Single-Column Selections

In Photoshop, you have two additional geometric selection tools: the Single Row Marquee tool and the Single Column Marquee tool. These tools create a selection that's 1-pixel wide either horizontally (row) or vertically (column).

They can be handy when you want to remove a horizontal or vertical line in a photo.

In Elements, you don't have a separate tool to create a 1-pixel selection. However, you can still create a selection that's 1 pixel wide or tall. To do so, follow these steps.

1. Choose File > Open and select an image to open. To make this more useful, try to find an image that has a seam you want to remove—for example, a white line across the photo either horizontally or vertically.

2. Open the Aspect drop-down list and choose Fixed size.

3. Add dimensions for the size by typing in the text boxes. For a horizontal line, type a large value, such as 25 inches, in the W text box. (You need to specify the unit of measure when you type a value.) Type 1 px in the H text box for the height.

4. Click in the document window. You should have a selection horizontally across the photo.

5. Move the selection to just below the line you want to remove. You can nudge the selection by using the arrow keys. Just be certain you have a selection tool active in the Tools panel.

6. Press the V key to select the Move tool. When you have a selection tool active, you move a selection when you press the arrow keys. When you have the Move tool selected, you move content within a selection.

7. Duplicate the area below the line you want to remove. Press Alt/Option and press the up (or down) arrow key to duplicate 1-pixel of content across the photo. When you press Alt/Option, you create a duplicate as you drag a selection. If you need to move the content, release the Alt/Option key and press the arrow keys to place the duplicate content precisely.

This is a particularly handy technique when you create composite images, and you find seams that aren't exact so there are white lines showing in the composite photo.

Using Lasso Tools

Lasso tools are used for creating free-form selections. Click the Lasso tool in the Tools panel (or press L (or Shift + L) on your keyboard) to find three different Lasso tools in the Tool Options panel. The Lasso and Polygonal Lasso tools, which are shown on the left of the tools in Figure 3.3, have the same options. The Magnetic Lasso tool, shown on the right side of the tools in

Figure 3.3, has options for changing width, contrast, frequency, and feathering. The Width and Contrast sliders for the Magnetic Lasso tool provide a tighter selection as you move the sliders to the left when there's sufficient contrast on the edges in the area you select. The Frequency slider adds more points on the selection path as you move the slider to the right. To feather a selection for creating smoother transitions, you need to move the Feather slider the desired amount before you make a selection.

Feathering Geometric Selections

You can create rounded corners on selections by using the Marquee Rectangle tool and setting a Feather amount before you create the selection. The amount you feather the selection depends on the resolution of your photo. For low-resolution photos, you use less feathering. For higher-resolution images, you use more feathering. Select the Marquee Rectangle tool, set a Feather amount, and then draw a rectangle. If the rounding of the corners is too little or too much, undo the edit, change the amount, and draw another selection.

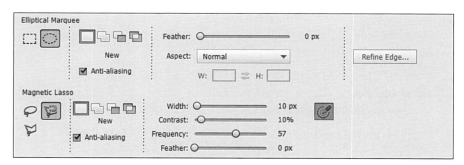

FIGURE 3.3 Lasso tools in the Tool Options panel.

NOTE: Remember that pressing Shift and moving the mouse adds to a selection, and pressing Alt/Option and moving the mouse deletes from the selection.

If you want to use the Lasso tool to create a geometric selection rather than a free-form selection, you can make straight-line selections. For example, to select a triangle, press the Alt/Option key and click. Keep the mouse button down as you release the Alt/Option key. Move the cursor and press the Alt/Option Key again and click in a second location. Keep the Alt/Option key depressed and move the mouse to a third location. This technique may seem complicated if you haven't used it before, but with a little practice, it becomes second nature. Alternatively, you can click the Add to Selection icon in the Tool Options panel.

The Polygon Lasso tool enables you to draw straight-line selections without having to use modifier keys. The Magnetic Lasso tool traces the edge of a subject you want to select. Don't worry if the first selection you make isn't precise. You can return to a selection with the Lasso tool and add to or remove from a selection. To close a selection with the Magnetic Lasso tool, drag to return to the point of origin. When the cursor moves close to that point, you will see an "o" icon indicating that you can close the selection when you click the mouse button.

NOTE: When making selections, look at the photo and determine what area in the image will be the easiest to select. For example, if it's easier to select a background than a foreground, select the background. If you want to make edits on the foreground, you simply inverse the selection. To inverse a selection, choose Select, Inverse or press Ctrl/⌘ + Shift + I.

TIP: When the Magnetic Lasso tool is selected, you see an icon on the far right of the Tool Options panel. If you use a tablet, you can tap this icon to use pressure sensitivity to change the Magnetic Lasso selection width.

Using Miscellaneous Selection Tools

The third category contains five tools that have distinct differences, but they're all somewhat automatic selection tools. These tools use some intelligence as you're making selections. The tools in this group include the following.

Quick Selection Tool

Perhaps the most frequent selection tool you will use is the Quick Selection tool. Click in an area you want to select and drag around. Elements includes like tones within the selection. When you find some area that's not part of your desired selection, press the Alt/Option key to remove it from the selection. Then, as you drag around, Elements disregards common colors and tones from the selection. In essence, the Quick Selection tool learns what you're trying to select as you drag through an image. In Figure 3.4, you can see the tool options for the Quick Selection tool.

FIGURE 3.4 Options for the Quick Selection tool.

A marvelous addition to this tool is the Select Subject button (on the far right in Figure 3.4). When you have an image open that clearly shows a subject and you click this button, Adobe Sensei technology is used to create the selection. (Adobe Sensei technology is a form of artificial intelligence that's used throughout the Elements Photo Editor with many tools and menu commands.) Alternatively, you can access the command by choosing Select, Subject. You can use the menu command regardless of what tool you have selected.

In Figure 3.5, I opened an image and clicked the Select Image button. You can see the selection the Photo Editor automatically created. It needs a little fine-tuning, but as you can see, the Select Subject option does a good job selecting subjects in photos.

FIGURE 3.5 Click the Select Subject button to automatically select a subject in a photo.

For more on using brushes, see Chapter 7.

The Quick Selection tool behaves like a brush, so another option for the tool is Brush Settings (refer to Figure 3.4). Click Brush Settings, and the Brush Settings dialog box opens, as shown in Figure 3.6. The settings are similar to settings you apply to brushes. You can change the Hardness, the Spacing, and the Roundness of the brush tip. If you have a tablet, you also can alter the Pen Pressure setting. You can also change the Angle by dragging in the Angle box.

FIGURE 3.6 Change the brush tip attributes for the Quick Selection tool.

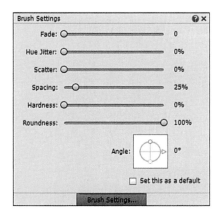

Selection Brush Tool

The Selection brush behaves similar to a paint brush. You paint in the area where you want a selection. In the Tool Options, you can choose Mask or Selection from the drop-down list, as shown in Figure 3.7. If you choose Mask, the tool options change, as shown at the bottom of Figure 3.7.

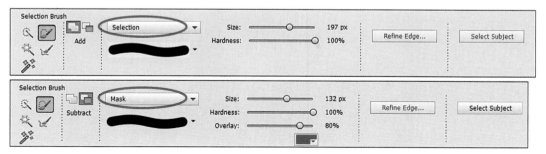

FIGURE 3.7 Choose Mask or Selection for the Selection Brush tool. When you choose Mask, the tool options change.

When you choose Mask, the area where you paint turns into a Quick Mask, represented by default as a red overlay. Once you have a mask, you can choose Selection from the drop-down list, and the mask converts to a selection. As you paint, having the mask active gives you a guide to show you where the selection is created when you choose Selection from the drop-down list. In Figure 3.8, you can see a mask in the photo where I painted the face of the subject. Note at the bottom of the Tool Options, you can change the color of the mask. Click the default red color swatch, and the Elements Color Picker dialog box opens so you can choose a different color.

FIGURE 3.8 Use the Selection Brush to paint a mask and then convert the mask to a selection.

The Size, Hardness, and Overlay sliders in the Tool Options for the Selection Brush should be self-explanatory. Notice that this tool also includes a button for Select Subject, as do all the selection tools in this group.

Magic Wand Tool

The Magic Wand tool is used to sample where you click within a tolerance range you set with a slider. If the tolerance is 32, the range is 16 pixels lighter and 16 pixels darker than the sampled area. You can adjust the tolerance value when you're making selections. If you click and make a selection, and you don't see all the area you want contained within the selection, add more to the tolerance. If you select too much, lower the tolerance and click again. If you have a selection and want to delete some area, press Alt/Option and click in the area you want to remove from the selection.

> **NOTE:** When you use the Magic Wand tool, quite often you may have some tiny areas within a selection that are not selected. To add these unselected areas to the selection, choose Select, Modify, Expand. Adjust Expand by a value of 5 to 10 pixels. Click OK and then choose Select, Modify, Contract. Set the Contract value to the same value you entered for the Expand value. All stray pixels are added to the selection.

- In Figure 3.9, you see check boxes for Sample All Layers, Contiguous, and Anti-Aliasing. If you have multiple layers and the Sample All Layers check box is enabled, the sampled area includes all layers. If you disable Contiguous, the selection moves throughout the image sampling values in a noncontiguous area where you click and within the Tolerance range. When Contiguous is enabled, the selection moves outward from the area where you click and includes only those pixels in a contiguous area.

FIGURE 3.9 Options for the Magic Wand tool.

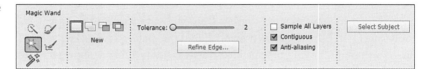

Refine Selection Brush Tool

This tool is used in conjunction with other tools. If you make a selection using the Quick Selection tool, you can use the Refine Selection tool to paint over the edges of the selection to refine it. A good example is when you select hair on a subject. The Quick Selection tool won't grab individual strands of hair. After you make a selection, use the Refine Selection Brush to paint along the edges of the hair to add individual stands of hair to the selection. Adobe Sensei technology (a form of artificial intelligence) is used to assess neighboring pixels and include those similar to the pixels selected and disregard pixels not similar to the selection.

In Figure 3.10, you can see the Tool Options for the Refine Selection Brush.

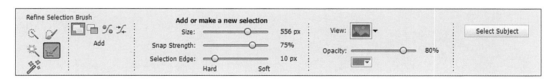

FIGURE 3.10 Options for the Refine Selection Brush.

Notice in Figure 3.10 the two new tools for the Refine Selection Brush. The curve with the −/+ symbols and the two arrows are used for pushing a selection and smoothing a selection. After using the Refine Selection Brush, you can further refine the selection by selecting these tools and use the sliders to make adjustments. When you move the cursor outside a selection, the inside of the cursor shape turns to a minus to indicate you can push the selection inward to refine an edge. When the cursor is inside a selection, you can push the selection outward to grab more of the area you want to select. When you move to the edge of a selection, you can smooth it out. The center of the cursor appears with a square. Move around the edge of a selection with the square close to the edge, and you can pick up small areas like strands of hair.

Auto Selection Tool

This tool provides you with a little bit of magic. The Tool Options for this tool include four icons in the Rectangle section, as shown in Figure 3.11. You select one of the icons and then drag around the area you want to select. Elements intelligently selects an item within the boundaries of the shape you created.

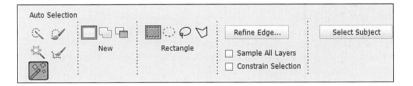

FIGURE 3.11 Options for the Auto Selection tool.

As an example of how this tool works, in Figure 3.12, I drew a rectangle around the face and hair of the subject. Elements assumed I want to select the subject's head, and after some minor subtractions from the selection, you can see the result in Figure 3.12.

FIGURE 3.12 Selection created after using the Auto Selection tool.

Don't feel you need to master every tool. If some tools are new to you, play around with them to see which tools you prefer to use when making selections. No one tool can do the job, so be prepared to frequently change tools to refine selections.

Using the Select Menu

The Photo Editor has a separate menu for working with selections. Many commands help you shape and refine your selections. Figure 3.13 shows the Select menu.

Working with Selections

The Select menu is divided into separate categories. I call the first four items *handling selections*. The All command selects the entire canvas. The Deselect command deselects an active selection. I don't find the Reselect command necessary because you can only reselect a selection (backward) once. In other words, if you have multiple selections and deselect all of them, you can only reselect the last selection. You can achieve the same thing using Undo or moving backward in the History panel.

FIGURE 3.13 The Select menu.

> **NOTE:** The History panel (choose Window, History or press F10) shows you edits you make in a photo editing session. The number of edits is determined in the Photo Editor Preferences in the Performance pane. The default is 50, meaning the last 50 edits you make in a document are recorded in the History panel. You can step back to any edit listed in the panel and continue editing from that point forward. You can change the number of History states by editing the number in the Preferences dialog box. The number of different History states can be any number between 2 and 1,000. However, be aware that the higher the number, the more memory is required by Elements. You may find your computer slowing down if you push the number too high. If you find Elements operating sluggishly, lower the number of History states.

> **TIP:** Memorize the keyboard shortcut (Ctrl/⌘ + Shift + I) to inverse a selection.

Inverse is a term commonly misused by people authoring books and videos on using Photoshop and Photoshop Elements. Many people refer to the action as invert, but that is incorrect. The Invert command, found in the Adjustment Layers menu or by pressing Ctrl/⌘ + I, inverts the content of a selection; dark pixels turn light and light pixels turn dark, or colors change to opposite colors. The Inverse command inverses a selection, so all content not currently selected becomes selected and all selected areas are deselected when you inverse a selection. This is a handy command you will frequently use.

Refining Selections

The next category contains four items beginning with Feather. You can draw a selection and feather it after the fact. Feathering creates a soft edge. In Figure 3.14, you can see the results after I feathered a selection. I first drew a rectangle selection, and then I feathered it, which resulted in the corners becoming rounded. I inversed the selection to create a border, and then I darkened the border to create a vignette. For more on creating vignettes, see Chapter 15.

FIGURE 3.14 A selection feathered and inversed.

The next command in this category is Refine Edge. When you create a selection and then choose Refine Edge, the Refine Edge dialog box opens. You can move the cursor on the image to trace the edge of your subject. Elements grabs additional information as you go. Compare Figure 3.15 where Refine Edge was used to Figure 3.16, where a raw selection was created. You can see individual strands of hair selected in Figure 3.15.

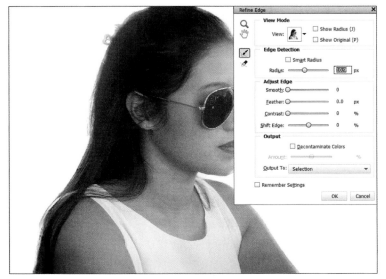

FIGURE 3.15 Refine selections with the Refine Edge dialog box.

The next item is Subject. You don't need to create a selection to use this command. When you open an image and choose Subject, Elements looks at your photo, sees the subject(s) in the photo, and makes its best guess for selecting the subject(s).

In Figure 3.16, I opened a file and chose Select, Subject. Notice the selection doesn't include some extra hair that the Refine Edge settings were able to capture.

The last item in this category, Modify, offers several submenu items. You can choose to create a border for a selection, and the size of the border is determined in a dialog box that opens after you select Border. Smooth refines a selection. If you use the Lasso tool and have a few jagged edges, using the Smooth command takes away some jaggies.

FIGURE 3.16 Elements makes its best guess at creating a selection around the subject in the photo.

Expand and Contract follow the Smooth command. When you choose these menu commands, the selection expands/contracts the number of pixels you specify in a dialog text box. One way you can use the commands is after creating a selection with something like the Magic Wand tool and small gaps exist within the selection. You can expand, then go back and contract, and you pick up some unselected areas.

The Grow and Similar commands occupy the next category. When you choose Grow, the selection grows outward to select pixels within the tolerance range specified in the Magic Wand tolerance setting. When you use the Magic Wand tool and choose Contiguous in the Tool Options panel, the selection travels out and selects pixels contiguous to the area where you click the cursor. When you choose Similar, Elements examines the entire image and selects like pixels within the tolerance range.

Transforming Selections

The next category has a single item used for transforming selections. When you create a selection and choose Select, Transform Selection, you see a bounding box with handles much like when you use the Transform tools when you select Image, Transform and choose a submenu item.

This is a very handy command when you're editing portraits. For example, if I want to select a subject's eyes, I might first create a circle using the Elliptical Marquee tool while pressing Alt/Option + Shift to draw from center. The subject's eyes are not perfectly circular. If I choose Select, Transform Selection, I can then fudge the edges to create the selection I need. As you can see in Figure 3.17, the selection contains a bounding box and handles.

FIGURE 3.17 Use Transform Selection to size and distort a selection.

Saving, Loading, and Deleting Selections

If you spend a lot of time creating a selection, you might want to save the selection and reload it at a later time to continue editing the selected area. To save a selection, choose Select, Save Selection. In the Save Selection dialog box, choose New for the selection, and type a name for the selection in the Name text box. In Figure 3.18, I created a selection that took quite some time to refine. I named my selection Hair. As you can see, the hair in this photo looks great on the model but presents a challenge for the person trying to select the image.

NOTE: You can also create a Layer Mask that also saves a selection, in a way. You might want to choose Save Selection instead of creating a Layer Mask when you spend a lot of time creating a selection on a Background, but then decide you want to duplicate the entire layer. If you duplicate a layer with a selection, only the selected area is duplicated. If you save the selection and then deselect and duplicate the layer, you can load the selection on the new layer. For more on Layer Masks, see Chapter 5.

FIGURE 3.18 A complex selection.

After saving a selection, you can save the file to update it and close it. When you reopen and choose Select > Load Selection, the Load Selection dialog box opens. From the Selection drop-down list, choose the name you provided when you saved the selection. In my example, I used the name Hair. Therefore, I choose Hair from the list. Choose New Selection from the Operation list, and the selection is loaded. You can then go about editing your photo. In my example, I added a texture from the Graphics panel and produced the image shown in Figure 3.19.

FIGURE 3.19 A texture added as a new background to the subject.

Creating Selections with Elements+

If you purchase the Elements+ plugin, you have a few more options when you want to create selections. The two additional options include Color Range and Channels.

Elements+

Using Color Range

Photoshop includes the Color Range dialog box. In Elements, it doesn't exist. However, if you install the Elements+ plugin, you have a Color Range dialog box similar to the one in Adobe Photoshop.

In the Effects (*fx*) panel, click number 2. Selections to open the Selections settings in Elements+. When the Selections dialog box opens, click the Show All Commands check box. The Select Color Range command is at the top of the dialog box. Click the Select Color Range command and click the green check mark at the top-right corner. The Color Range dialog box opens as shown in Figure 3.20.

Notice you have three eyedropper tools in the Color Range dialog box. The center window shows a preview of the image. Click around the preview area or click in the photo to create a selection. When you sample an area, the range of the sample turns white in the preview in the Color Range dialog box. You can use the plus Eyedropper and minus Eyedropper tools to add to or delete from the selection. Move the Fuzziness slider to refine the selection by adding more or taking away some of the selection. After you click OK, all the white area becomes part of a new selection.

Loading Selections from Channels

Another item you don't have available in Elements is a Channels panel. Quite often, you may find it easier to create a selection from one of the three RGB channels. In Figure 3.21, I created a black-and-white adjustment layer using the Elements+ plugin. I edited the brightness and contrast a little with Levels and then opened the number 2. Selections style from the Elements+ panel and loaded the selection from the Red channel. The final selection grabbed most of the subject along with strands of hair, as shown in Figure 3.21.

Creating Selections from Paths

Paths can be vector shapes, text, or illustrations created in programs like Adobe Illustrator or Adobe Photoshop with the Pen tool. You can have vector shape layers in Elements in the form of shapes you can add as new layers. If you draw a shape on a background or raster layer, Elements automatically creates a new layer and places the shape you draw on the layer. Since shapes are vector objects, they cannot reside on the same layer as a raster image. Text, likewise, is a vector object; when you add text to a photo, a new layer is created where the text resides.

Let's take a look at creating vector objects and converting them to selections.

Working with Shapes

The star icon (adjacent to the Eye Dropper tool in the Tools panel) is the Custom Shape tool. When you click the Custom Shape tool, the Tool Options panel displays a number of choices for creating shapes. There are quite a few preset shapes along with the Custom Shape tool. When the Custom Shape tool is selected, you have access to a menu and pop-up panel where additional shapes are organized in Groups. If you choose All Elements Shapes from the Shapes drop-down list, all the shapes installed with Elements appear in a scrollable list, as shown in Figure 3.22.

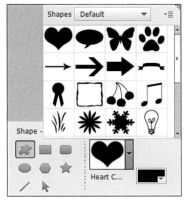

FIGURE 3.22 Shapes available in a scrollable panel.

Raster Layers Versus Vector Layers

Vector shapes and drawings are comprised of mathematical formulas that tell the printing device to move from one x,y coordinate to another. Vector shapes contain no resolution. They print at the resolution of the printing device. Raster images, on the other hand, are individual pixels that form shapes. Pixel-based images contain resolution within the image. Therefore, if you print a 72 ppi (pixels per inch), it prints at that resolution. If you want higher resolutions, you need to have the file set to a higher resolution. Additionally, when you size a vector object, you won't lose any image quality. When you size raster images up, the larger you size the image, the more resolution it loses.

Raster data and vector data cannot reside on the same layer. A layer is either a raster layer or a vector layer. When you choose File, Place, the placed file is a vector image. When you use any one of the Type tools, all the type you create resides on vector layers. When you use the Shape objects from the Tools panel, all the shapes are vector objects and reside on vector layers.

There are limitations for editing vector objects. You cannot apply filters to vector objects, you cannot use selection tools, and you cannot use any of the Enhance menu commands. To take full advantage of all Elements tools and menu commands, you must convert vector layers to raster layers by choosing Simplify Layer from the Layers panel menu.

Suppose you want to use a shape as a selection and place a photo inside the shape. That's easy enough to do in Photoshop Elements. Open an image and duplicate the Background by dragging the Background in the Layers panel to the New Layer icon in the Layers panel, or you can press Ctrl/⌘ + J. It's usually a good idea to duplicate a background when you begin a new edit on a photo. If you don't like the results, you can easily return to the original.

Click the Custom Shape tool, and in the Tool Options panel, select a shape. When you select a shape, the cursor changes to a plus symbol. Click and drag on the photo to draw the shape. If you accidently release the mouse button too soon, press Ctrl/⌘ + T to create a free transformation. Move the handles on the bounding box to extend the shape where you want to cover the photo. When you release the mouse button, the shape is added to a new layer. At this point, you should see the background, background copy, and the shape in the Layers panel, as shown in Figure 3.23.

FIGURE 3.23 The Layers showing a shape on a new layer.

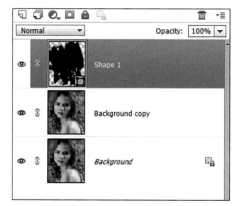

Creating a selection from the shape is easy enough in the Layers panel. To create a selection from a shape, first select the shape layer and then press Ctrl/⌘ as you click on the shape to select the shape. You want to create the mask on the background copy, so select the background copy layer before proceeding. The next step is to create a layer mask. With the selection active on the target layer, click the Add a Mask button in the layers panel. This adds the mask on the selected layer—in this case, the Background copy.

At this point, you can select the shape layer and press Backspace/Delete to delete the area around the shape. Click the eye icon to hide the Background. The image and layers panel should look something like Figure 3.24.

FIGURE 3.24 Final image shown inside a shape selection

Pasting into Selections

You can use Layer masks to confine photo contents within a selection, and you also can use the Paste Into command from the Edit menu. For this example, I used text and created a selection from the text; then I pasted different images inside the text characters to create the image shown in Figure 3.25.

1. Choose File, New Blank File. Set the Background Contents to transparent and decide how large you want the document to be. Set Resolution to 150 ppi.

2. Choose a bold font. For this exercise, I used Azo Sans Uber Regular. Set the font size to 90 points.

3. Press Ctrl/⌘ and click on the layer in the Layers panel to select the text.

4. With the text selected, click the Add a Mask icon at the top of the Layers panel.

5. Press Ctrl/⌘ and click the mask to create a selection for the text. Select the Marquee Rectangle tool in the Tools panel. Press Alt/Option and drag through the selection except the first character. The Alt/Option key deletes from the selection as you keep the key depressed and drag through the selection.

6. Keep the new document open and open a document and select a subject using one of the selection tools.

7. Press Ctrl/⌘ + C to copy the selection.

For more on Layer Masks, see Chapter 5.

8. Bring the document with the character selection to the front and choose Edit, Paste into Selection.

9. Repeat steps 5 through 8 for the remaining characters. In Figure 3.25, you can see the final result for creating a type mask with photo images contained within the mask. Figure 3.26 shows the layer panel for this exercise.

FIGURE 3.25 Different photos pasted into text selections.

In my example, I copied several different images and pasted them into separate selections. If you want a border on the type, create a new layer and select the text in the Layer Mask. Choose Select, Modify, Expand. In my example, I expanded the selection 2 pixels. Fill with black or any other color you desire. When you examine the Layers panel, it should look like Figure 3.26.

FIGURE 3.26 Layers panel showing the layers created for pasting images into text selections.

CHAPTER 4
WORKING WITH LAYERS

Chapter Goals

When Layers were introduced in Photoshop 3.0, it was revolutionary. Today it's hard to believe a program like Photoshop Elements or most of the Adobe Creative Cloud applications could exist without support for Layers. Layers are vital to all your photo editing needs. In this chapter, you learn to do the following:

- Create layers
- Use commands in the Layers panel and the Layers menu
- Create Adjustment Layers
- Work with Smart Objects
- Work with all the blend modes
- Move layers around the layer stack
- Copy, delete, and modify layers

Photoshop was introduced in early 1990. The first version of Photoshop was amazing to people who worked with the program. We could adjust images with the same adjustment tools we use today (Curves, Levels, and Hue/Saturation). But compared to today's release of Photoshop, there was still much left to be desired.

Photoshop 2 offered a few more features, but it was still limited compared to the recent releases. For example, to create a drop shadow in Photoshop 2, we had to use the Calculate commands and Channel Operations. There were no methods for blending and no layers to set up with Layer Masks.

When Photoshop 3 was introduced, Adobe revolutionized software and began a path toward phenomenal opportunities for graphic designers and photographers. More than any other single feature introduced in Photoshop, Layers and a Layers panel were by far the most important contribution to the program we've seen in 30 years of development. Fortunately, when Photoshop Elements was introduced, Adobe implemented layers in the program, and we could do much in Elements that we can do in Photoshop with regard to layers.

If you don't have a strong background for using layers, then this chapter provides you with a foundation for using and working with layer commands and settings.

Understanding Layers

If you're an advanced user, you can skim through this chapter and focus on any areas where you find some new information. For the novice users, this chapter is vital to all the editing you do in Photoshop Elements.

The Layers panel is where you find Layers. In Figure 4.1, you see a photo open in Elements where I added several different layers, which you can see in the Layers panel. Layers are like pieces of clear acetate. You can have the layer appear without any data, in which case the layer(s) below the target layer are visible. The top layer can be partially opaque, in which case the layer(s) below the target layer show a portion of the contents of a layer. Lastly, a layer can be completely opaque, in which case all data below the target layer is hidden.

FIGURE 4.1 A photo with multiple layers.

There are a number of different types of layers. You can make a copy of one layer and create a second identical layer to add to the first layer. You can create Adjustment Layers that affect luminosity, brightness and contrast, color, gradients, and patterns. You can blend the contents of one layer with another. You can mask a layer and show only a portion of the layer. You can group layers, name layers, rename layers, merge layers, add innumerable layers, delete layers, and flatten layers. In short, you have a huge number of editing opportunities respective to working with layers.

In the Layers panel in Figure 4.1, you see multiple layers ordered from top to bottom. This group of layers is commonly referred to as the *layer stack*. Throughout this chapter, I make references to the layer stack.

Examining the Layers Panel

The Layers panel has several tools, drop-down lists, and menu commands. The layer stack has an order from top to bottom. Depending on what you assign to a layer, layers from top to bottom control various levels of visibility on the layers lower in the stack.

In Figure 4.2, you can see a description of the various tools and menu items in the Layers panel. If working with layers is new to you, spend some time looking over the toolbar to become familiar with the following editing options:

- **Blending Mode menu:** This menu contains 25 choices for blending one layer with another. For a detailed description of blending modes, see the "Blending Layers" section later in this chapter.

- **New Layer:** When you click the New Layer icon, a new layer is added to the layer stack. If you press Alt/Option and click the New Layer icon in the Layers panel, press Ctrl/⌘ + Alt/Option + J, or use the Layer panel menu and choose New Layer, a New Layer dialog box opens where you can name the layer, label it with a color, set the blending modes, and create a Clipping Mask (for more on Clipping Masks, see Chapter 5).

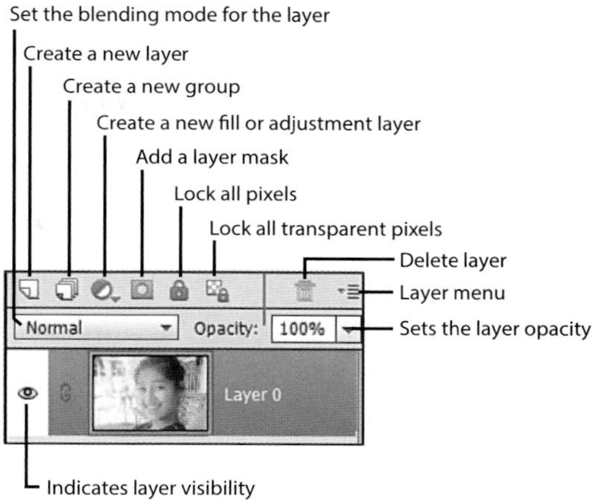

- **New Group:** You can select multiple layers and then click this button to nest them in a group.

- **New Fill or Adjustment Layer:** This icon has a drop-down list of various choices you have for making Adjustment Layers and creating different fills for layers. For more information on Adjustment Layers, see the "Working with Adjustment Layers" section later in this chapter.

Set the blending mode for the layer
Create a new layer
Create a new group
Create a new fill or adjustment layer
Add a layer mask
Lock all pixels
Lock all transparent pixels
Delete layer
Layer menu
Sets the layer opacity
Indicates layer visibility

FIGURE 4.2 The tools and menu items in the Layers panel.

- **Add a Layer Mask:** Layer Masks are a powerful tool. They enable you to mask out (or hide) part of a layer. There's a lot to creating masks, and you can find more information on Layer Masks in Chapter 5.

- **Lock All Pixels:** Click this button to lock the layer in the stack. No editing can take place on a locked layer. Click the lock icon again to unlock a locked layer.

- **Lock All Transparent Pixels:** Click this button to lock a layer's transparency. A transparent area on a layer contains no data, and it's represented by a checkerboard design. Click the icon again to unlock transparency.

- **Layer Opacity:** The Opacity adjustment slider controls how transparent the layer appears. At 100% opacity, the full strength of the layer is displayed. As you move the slider left and lower the opacity, you add more transparency to the layer. In a layer stack, reducing opacity reveals more data on layers below the target layer.

- **Delete Layer:** Select a layer and click the trash can icon, and the layer is deleted. When you click Delete Layer, a confirmation dialog box asks you to confirm the deletion. To bypass the dialog box, press Alt/Option and click the icon.

- **Layer menu:** Click the icon on the far-right side of the Layers panel (to the right of the Delete Layer icon), and a drop-down list opens where you can use menu commands for managing layers.

- **Layer Visibility:** Click the eye icon to hide a layer. Click it again to show the layer. Press Alt/Option and click the eye icon, and all layers but the one you click are hidden. Press Alt/Option and click again, and all layers are made visible.

Creating New Layers

There are several ways you can create new layers using tools and techniques. You can create a new layer as a blank empty layer, a duplicate of another layer, an adjustment that is applied to layers lower on the layer stack, a layer containing a fill, a layer copied from another document, or a vector layer. The methods available to you include the following:

- **New Layer icon:** You can click the New Layer icon in the Layers panel to create a new layer. You can drag an existing layer or the Background from the layer stack and drop it on the New Layer icon to duplicate a layer. You can also use any of the options noted earlier in the section "Examining the Layers Panel."

- **Ctrl/⌘ + Shift + N or Ctrl/⌘ + Alt/Option + J:** Use the keyboard shortcut to create a new layer. Using either of these commands opens the New Layer dialog box.

- **Ctrl/⌘ + Click New Layer icon in the Layers pane:** Creates a new layer below the selected layer.

- **Ctrl/⌘ + J:** Duplicates the selected layer.

- **Drag a layer to the New Layer icon in the Layers panel:** Duplicates the layer.

- **Layers panel menu:** Open the Layers panel menu and choose New Layer. This option opens the New Layer dialog box.

- **Layer menu:** Select New and choose from Layer, Layer from Background, Layer via Copy, and Layer via Cut.

FIGURE 4.3 The New Fill or Adjustment Layer menu.

- **Adding Adjustment or Fill Layers:** The New Fill or Adjustment Layer menu contains several commands to create fill layers and Adjustment Layers. The menu choices are shown in Figure 4.3. Additionally, you can create the same Fill and Adjustment Layers from the Layer menu. For more on Fill Layers, see the "Creating Fill Layers" section later in this chapter. For more on Adjustment Layers, see the "Working with Adjustment Layers" section later in this chapter.

- **New layers from text:** Click the Horizontal Type Tool (T), which is the default Type tool in the Tools panel. Click in a document window, and Elements automatically creates a new layer for the text. This layer and the following layers created when you add a shape are considered Vector Layers containing vector objects. Vector objects are like drawings you create in Adobe Illustrator or similar programs. You cannot use some editing features on vector layers, such as most of the commands in the Enhance menu. To apply many edits on a vector object, you need to first select the layer, open the Layer menu or the Layer Panel menu, and choose Simplify Layer. This action converts a vector object to a raster object. Vector objects are math-based plotting paths from one x, y coordinate to another. Raster objects are pixel based, and you can edit the pixels.

- **New layers from shapes:** Click a shape in the Tools panel or Tool Options panel and draw a shape on a layer. Elements automatically creates a new layer for the shape. The resultant shape is a vector object.

- **Place a photo:** Choose File > Place and open a TIFF, PSD, or JPEG file. Elements automatically creates a new layer for the placed object. In actuality, the layer contains a Smart Object. To learn more about Smart Objects, see "Working with Smart Objects" later in this chapter.

- **Pasting data:** Paste data you copy from one file into another document, and Elements automatically creates a new layer for the pasted data. If you choose Edit > Paste into Selection or press Shift + Ctrl/⌘ + V, the data are pasted into a selection, and a new layer is not created.

- **Adding graphics:** When you add graphics from the Graphics panel, Elements creates a new layer. In Figure 4.4, you see the Graphics panel displaying Backgrounds. When you select a Background from the panel, Elements automatically creates a new layer and adds the background image as a new layer.

FIGURE 4.4 The Graphics panel showing the Background choices.

- **Adding effects:** From the Effects panel, click an effect, and Elements automatically creates a new layer to apply the effect.

- **Guided edits:** Elements creates layers when using some Guided Edits.

For more on Guided Edits, see Chapter 7.

- **Dragging layers from documents:** You can drag one layer from a document to another document window. Essentially, this is like copying and pasting data. When you drag and drop a layer, Elements copies the layer to a new document. Take a look at Figure 4.5. The document on the right contains a layer mask (as shown in the Layers panel). The document on the left was originally a texture. When you drag the layer and Layer Mask from the document on the right to the file containing the texture, both the subject and mask are copied to the new document as a new layer.

TIP: You can also duplicate a layer in one document to another open document in the Document Window. When you choose Duplicate Layer, the dialog box shows you a Document drop-down list showing all open documents. Choose the target document you want the duplicate to reside in and click OK.

FIGURE 4.5 Dragging a layer from one document to another creates a new layer in the target document.

Creating Fill Layers

There are three types of fill layers you can create in Elements: solid color fills, gradient fills, and pattern fills. You can use menu commands in the Layers menu for creating New Fill Layers. You also can use Fill Layers in the Adjustment Layers drop-down list in the Layers panel. When you create a Fill Layer using the Layer > New Fill Layer command, you are creating Adjustment Layers just like using the Adjustment Layers drop-down list and choosing a fill layer.

Filling Layers Options

When filling a layer with color, you have several options. You can use the Layer menu and choose New Fill Layer; then you choose Solid Color, Gradient, or Pattern. You can also use the Adjustment Layer menu in the Layers panel and choose Solid Color, Gradient, or Pattern. Either method creates a new Adjustment Layer, and it's nondestructive—meaning you can return to the layer and edit it. You also can create a new layer and press Shift + Backspace/Delete to open the Fill Layer dialog box. In this dialog box, you can choose to use the current Foreground color, Background color, and another option labeled Color. When you choose this option, the Elements Color Picker opens. Choose a color (or Pattern) and click OK. The color is added to the current selected layer. If you want to change the color using this method, you need to add a new color fill.

Adjustment Layers are nondestructive, meaning you can return to edits, change the edits, or delete the Adjustment Layers, and no permanent changes are made to your document. One thing to keep in mind is that the

Adjustment Layers drop-down list is not accessible when you have a 16-bit image open in the document window. Likewise, the Layer Menu commands for creating fill and Adjustment Layers are grayed out and not accessible. You must convert an image to 8-bit by choosing Image > Mode > 8 Bits/Channel before applying fill and Adjustment Layer edits.

Creating Solid Color Fills

You can fill layers with a color, reduce the opacity so the color appears transparent, and use blending modes to describe different ways a color interacts with layer data. To create a solid fill, follow these steps:

1. Open a photo in the Photo Editor. This example uses the color fill to apply color to a photo.

2. Convert the photo to black and white if you open a color image by selecting Enhance > Convert to Black and White.

3. Create a Solid Color Fill layer by selecting Layer > New Fill Layer > Solid Color in a document. Alternatively, you can choose Solid Color from the Layers panel Adjustment Layers drop-down list. The New Layer dialog box opens.

4. Type a name for the layer and click OK. The Elements Color Picker opens. (See Figure 4.6.)

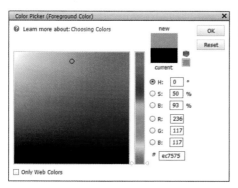

FIGURE 4.6 Select a color in the Color picker for the color fill.

5. Choose a color for the fill and click OK. A new layer with the fill and a Layer Mask is created.

6. Use the Opacity slider in the Layers panel to bring the opacity down. Lower the amount so you can clearly see the layer below the color fill.

7. If you change your mind, you can double-click the Color Swatch icon on the new fill layer in the Layers panel to reopen the Color Picker. Choose another color and click OK.

TIP: When using two colors for a color fill, just be certain the top color layer has a lower opacity than the bottom color layer, so it blends the layers.

For more on Layer Masks, see Chapter 5. For more on Adjustment Layers, see "Working with Adjustment Layers" later in this chapter.

When you create a Color Fill layer, a Layer Mask is automatically created for you. There is no hidden area in the mask by default. All the color is applied to the layer below the color fill. Additionally, you can create multiple color fill layers to blend colors. Color fills are very handy when you want to create a color tint for a photo. In Figure 4.7, you can see a black-and-white photo I colorized using two fill layers. I created a composite layer above the fill layers and applied a Levels Adjustment Layer.

FIGURE 4.7 A black and white photo with two color fill layers.

Creating Gradient Fills

For a detailed explanation for color grading and color grading photos, see Chapter 10, "Color Toning and Color Grading."

The second type of fill layer you can create from both the Layer menu and the Adjustment Layers drop-down list in the Layers panel is a Gradient Fill. Gradient Fills offer you many opportunities to color grade your photos and create different moods to help tell a story. To add a Gradient Fill, follow these steps:

1. Open a photo in the Photo Editor.

2. Choose Layers > New Fill Layer > Gradient or choose Gradient from the Adjustment Layers drop-down list in the Layers panel. The Gradient Fill dialog box opens, as shown in Figure 4.8.

   At the top of the Gradient Fill dialog box, you see the Gradient drop-down list. From the list, you can choose from a number of presets that Elements provides you for gradient choices. The default is the Black, White gradient.

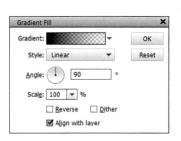

FIGURE 4.8 The Gradient Fill dialog box.

3. **Open the Gradient Editor.** The default gradient is the Black, White gradient shown in Figure 4.8, You can edit the gradient and add your own color scheme in the Gradient Editor shown in Figure 4.9. Choose the Black, White gradient in the Gradient drop-down list in the Gradient Fill dialog box, and the Gradient Editor opens.

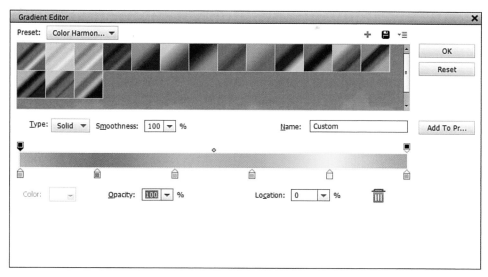

FIGURE 4.9 The Gradient Editor.

> **NOTE:** The Style drop-down list provides choices for different gradient styles such as linear, radial angle, reflected, and diamond. The default is the linear style. You can rotate the angle to any angle within 360°. The Scale slider adjusts the size of the gradient. Dithering adds some noise. Reverse reverses the gradient. If the default is black to white and you check reverse, the gradient is drawn from white to black. Align with Layer aligns the gradient in the document.

4. On either side of the gradient in the Gradient Editor, you see two icons known as the Stops. Double-click one of the Stops to open the Elements Color Picker dialog box. Choose a color in the Color Picker and click OK. Then double-click the Stop on the other side and choose another color for the other side of the gradient. These edits let you decide the colors you want to use on either side of the gradient. You also can add intermediary colors by clicking below the gradient to add a Stop and then clicking the Stop to open the Color Picker to choose a color.

5. Click OK to return to the document window.

6. In the Layers panel, click Normal to open the Blend Modes list. In this example, I chose Soft Light.

To learn more about blend- ing layers, see "Blend- ing Layers" later in this chapter.

For more information on sampling color, see Chapter 9.

7. Gradients are best used with blending modes in the Layers panel. In Figure 4.10, you can see a Gradient Adjustment Layer applied to an image. I sampled colors in the original image to create the gradient from blue to red and chose Soft Light for the blending mode. These settings added some contrast to the image. Gradient maps are also useful when Color Grading photos and videos.

FIGURE 4.10 A photo with a Gradient Fill layer added in the Layers panel.

Using the Gradient Editor

From the Preset drop-down list, you have several categories for additional gradient presets. On the right side of the dialog box is a plus symbol. Click it, and you can load gradient presets from downloads and others who share gradients. The Type drop-down list offers two choices. The default is solid. The second option is Noise. If you click Noise, three sliders appear for RGB color values. A Randomize button randomizes the values to create various linear configurations using the colors you choose in the sliders.

If you choose Solid from the Type drop-down list, you can adjust Smoothness, and you can name the

gradient in the Name text box. After creating a new gradient, you can add it to your presets by clicking the Add to Preset button.

The two icons on top of the gradient are opacity Stops. Select the Stop on the left or right and change the opacity amount in the Opacity text box. To add additional opacity Stops, click above the gradient to add a Stop. All the Stops above and below the gradient can be moved left or right. The diamond-shaped icons adjust the balance between Stops.

FIGURE 4.11 The Pattern Fill dialog box.

Creating Pattern Fills

The last fill option you have in the Layer menu and Adjustment Layers menu is the Pattern Fill. When you choose Pattern Fill from either menu, the Pattern Fill dialog box opens. The options you have in the Pattern Fill dialog box are shown in Figure 4.11.

You can scale the size of the pattern by adjusting the Scale slider. If you click the down-pointing arrow, you open the Patterns dialog box shown in Figure 4.12. Click the icon in the top-right corner to open the Patterns menu, and you find several menu choices. Among those choices is Load Patterns. If you load a pattern, back in the Pattern Fill dialog box, you can add the new pattern to your pattern presets by clicking the page icon.

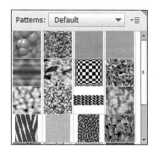

FIGURE 4.12 The Patterns dialog box.

Choose a pattern in the Patterns dialog box and click OK. A layer or selection is filled with the pattern you chose. The patterns are repeating images and quite often are displayed as artificial, so they and may not fit your vision for the photo you ultimately want. Use filters, blurs, or blending modes to shape the pattern to your liking if the pattern looks too symmetrical. In Figure 4.13, I used the Leaves pattern from the Nature Pattern Group in an Adjustment Layer, added a Soft Light blend mode, and reduced opacity to 18%.

FIGURE 4.13 A Pattern Fill as an Adjustment Layer with a Soft Light blend mode and a reduced opacity.

Using the Layers Panel Menu

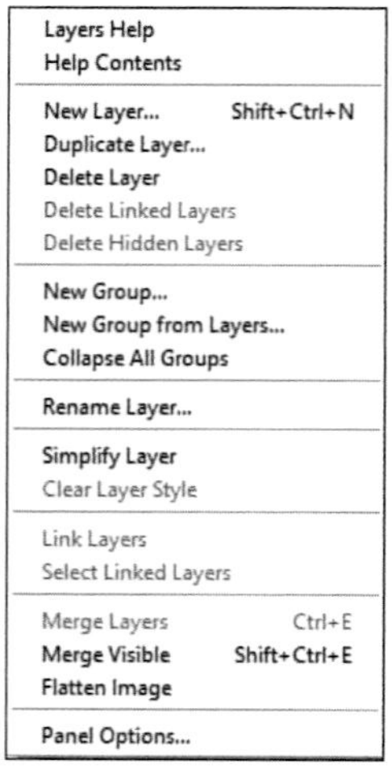

When you click the icon to the right of the Layers panel, the Layers panel menu opens, as shown in Figure 4.14. The menu items offer commands to help you manage layers. The commands include the following:

Layers Help	
Help Contents	
New Layer...	Shift+Ctrl+N
Duplicate Layer...	
Delete Layer	
Delete Linked Layers	
Delete Hidden Layers	
New Group...	
New Group from Layers...	
Collapse All Groups	
Rename Layer...	
Simplify Layer	
Clear Layer Style	
Link Layers	
Select Linked Layers	
Merge Layers	Ctrl+E
Merge Visible	Shift+Ctrl+E
Flatten Image	
Panel Options...	

FIGURE 4.14 The Layers panel menu.

- **Layers Help:** Opens the Adobe Help web page for help with using layers.

- **Help Contents:** Opens a web page displaying help contents for using Photoshop Elements.

- **New Layer:** Select this command, and Elements creates a blank new layer.

- **Duplicate Layer:** A selected layer is duplicated.

- **Delete Layer:** Select a layer and choose this command to delete it. You can also select multiple layers to delete. A warning dialog box opens to confirm your choice. You can dismiss future displays of the warning dialog box by checking the Don't Show Again check box. You can also drag a layer to the Delete icon (the trash can) to delete it. To prevent the warning dialog box from opening, press Alt/Option and drag a layer to the Delete icon, or simply select the layer you want to delete, press Alt/Option, and click the Delete icon in the Layers panel.

- **Delete Linked Layer:** If you have some layers linked (read more about linking layers later in this list), select one of the linked layers and then choose this item to delete all layers in the linked group.

- **Delete Hidden Layers**: If you click the eye icon on one or more layers, you can hide the target layers. Choose this menu item, and all hidden layers are deleted.

- **New Group:** Choose this item to create a new group. The group is empty when you create it. To add layers to the group, click and drag one or more layers to the group.

- **New Group from Layers:** Select multiple layers in the Layers panel and choose this item. A new group is created containing all the selected layers you added to the group.

- **Collapse All Groups:** You can see all layers in a group by clicking the right-pointing chevron to expand the group. You can click it again to collapse the group. If you have multiple groups, you can collapse them all by choosing this item.

- **Rename Layer:** If you want to rename a layer, choose this item. Additionally, you can double-click a layer name in the Layers panel to type a new name.

- **Simplify Layer:** If you have a vector object or a Smart Object, you can use this item to convert vector objects to raster images. You cannot change pixels in vector objects or Smart Objects in Elements while they remain vector layers or Smart Objects. For example, you cannot use any filters, Enhance menu commands, or many tools with vector objects and Smart Objects. To use these editing features, you first need to choose Simplify Layer from the Layers menu or Layers Panel menu.

- **Clear Layer Style:** In the Styles panel, you have a number of different styles you can add to a layer. Click this to delete a style from a layer.

- **Link Layers:** Select two or more layers and click this item. When layers are linked, you can move them together in the layer stack. You can link layers in a contiguous order in the layer stack or a noncontiguous order. In Figure 4.15, you can see three layers I linked from a noncontiguous order in the layer stack. When I moved the layers above the Background copy layer, they moved together as shown on the right side of Figure 4.15 and are grouped in a contiguous order.

TIP: You create a contiguous selection by clicking one item in a series, pressing the Shift key, and clicking another item in the same series. All items contained within the first and last selections are contained within the whole selection. A noncontiguous selection is made by depressing Ctrl/⌘ and clicking individual items in a nonlinear fashion.

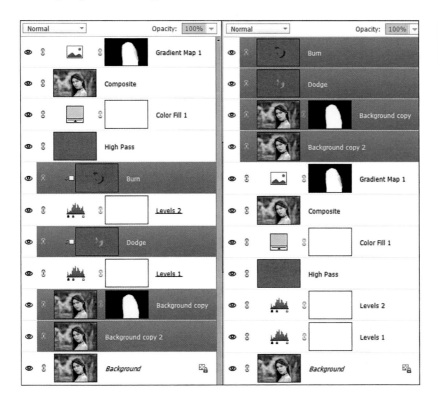

FIGURE 4.15 Linked layers in a noncontiguous order (left). After moving in the Layer stack (right).

- **Select Linked Layers:** To select linked layers, you need to select one layer in the linked group and then choose this menu item. All layers linked in the same group are selected.

- **Merge Layers:** When two or more layers are selected, this menu item is active. If only one layer is selected, the menu item changes to Merge Down. Merge Layers merges all layers in the document. Merge down merges the selected layer with the one below it in the layer stack. To use keyboard shortcuts to merge layers or merge down, press Ctrl/⌘ + E.

- **Merge Visible:** Choose this item to merge all visible layers. Any layers that are hidden are not merged together.

- **Flatten Image:** Choose this item to merge all visible layers. If any layers are hidden, a dialog box opens and prompts you to decide whether you want to discard hidden layers.

- **Panel Options:** Click this item to open a dialog box where you can choose different thumbnail sizes for the thumbnail images in the Layers panel.

Creating Composite Layers

At times, you may have several layers that contribute to the image you're editing and some layers that can be dismissed. You may not want to delete the unused layers because you may later decide to use them. Layers are handy when you want to create *what-if* scenarios.

Suppose you want to keep all layers, but you want to apply a filter or some other edit to some of the layers in the stack. To do so, you might create a composite layer from the layers you want to experiment with.

In Figure 4.16, you see three layers visible in the Layers panel. If you want to eliminate layers from the composite layer, you need to hide the layers you don't want to add to the composite. You cannot select layers for the composite and expect only those layers will be added to the composite. Creating a composite image uses all visible layers in the Layers panel.

To create a composite layer from these three layers, use a keyboard shortcut to merge the layers. Press Alt/Option + Ctrl/⌘ + Shift + E. This action creates a new composite layer from the selected layers. On the right side of Figure 4.16, you see the composite layer that I created from the visible layers on the left side of the figure. Notice layers 2 and 3 are hidden.

This action is different than using any of the Merge commands. A completely new layer is created and merged from the visible layers.

TIP: Remember to use Ctrl/⌘ + Alt/Option + Shift + E to create a composite layer, and also remember to make all layers you want in the composite visible in the layer stack.

It's important to remember the keyboard shortcut. You don't have a menu command for this action, and it is something you will continually use when working with layers.

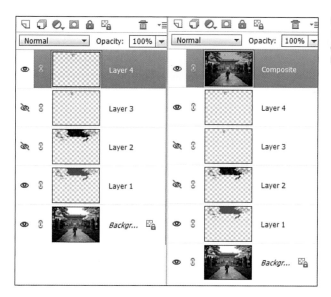

FIGURE 4.16 A composite layer (top right) is created from the visible layers (left).

Working with Adjustment Layers

Earlier in the section "Creating Fill Layers," I talked about the Create Fill or Adjustment Layer drop-down list. The first three menu items on this list are used to create fills. The remaining menu commands are used for Adjustment Layers.

The great advantage for using an Adjustment Layer is that Adjustment Layer edits are nondestructive. You can delete the layer at any time, and there's no effect on your image other than deleting the edits from the Adjustment Layer. If you want to refine edits made in an Adjustment Layer, you can double-click the layer and bring up the dialog box used for the edits. For example, if you apply a Levels adjustment and move the midtone slider too far right to darken midtones, you can double-click the Levels Adjustment Layer and move the slider a little left to lighten midtones.

If you use the Enhance > Adjust Lighting > Levels, make a levels adjustment in the dialog box, and then save your image, the edit is permanent. You can't go back and refine the levels setting. However, if you use a Levels Adjustment Layer and save the file, you can still go back and refine the levels adjustment as long as you save the file with the layers intact.

Another additional advantage you have with Adjustment Layers is the layer opacity adjustment. You can create an adjustment with an Adjustment Layer and reduce opacity to lessen the effect. All in all, Adjustment Layers offer you much power when editing your photos.

NOTE: You must convert all 16-bit images to 8-bit before attempting to create an Adjustment Layer.

Creating Brightness Adjustment Layers

The first two items below the Fill Adjustment Layers are Levels and Brightness/Contrast. As a matter of rule, forget about using the Brightness/Contrast Adjustment Layers. Likewise, avoid using the Enhance > Adjust Lighting > Brightness/Contrast command. You have much more precise editing available in the Levels dialog box and Color Curves dialog box; if you have Elements+ installed, the Curves dialog box is used for adjusting brightness and contrast as well as editing in the Adobe Camera Raw editor.

To create a Levels Adjustment Layer, open the Create Fill or Adjustment Layer drop-down list and choose Levels. Likewise, you can use the Layer > New Adjustment Layer > Levels menu command. The Levels dialog box opens, as shown in Figure 4.17. You can move the sliders to adjust brightness and contrast.

Unfortunately, you can't use Adjustment Layers with 16-bit images. If you open a 16-bit image in the Photo Editor, you can choose Enhance > Adjust Lighting > Levels or press Ctrl/⌘ + L. The Levels dialog box opens and offers the same adjustments as the Adjustment Layer Levels dialog box. However, if you try to add a Levels Adjustment Layer to a 16-bit image, all the tools in the Layers panel are grayed out and cannot be used until you reduce the bit depth to 8 bit.

FIGURE 4.17 The Levels dialog box (left) from a Levels Adjustment Layer (right).

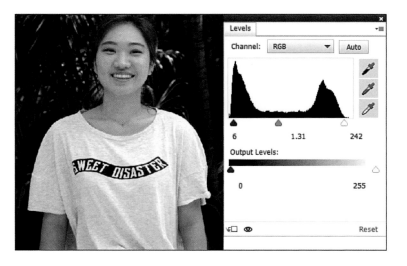

You have a trade-off and need to make a decision. If you want to keep the document in a nondestructive editing mode, then you must change the bit depth to 8-bit. If you want to keep nondestructive editing, then you must make adjustments on Adjustment Layers or new layers. When in 16-bit mode, you cannot duplicate the background, so all the editing you make in 16-bit mode is destructive.

When working with 16-bit images, your workflow should be to edit the photos in Camera Raw first. After you open the file in the Elements Photo Editor, if you need to refine some brightness/contrast, color, and other 16-bit mode edits, make your edits on the background. Then convert the photo to 8 Bits/ Channel to continue with additional editing.

Creating Hue/Saturation Adjustment Layers

Open the Create Fill or Adjustment Layer drop-down list and choose Hue/ Saturation. The Hue/Saturation dialog box opens, as shown in Figure 4.18. In this dialog box, you can make adjustments for Hue (color), Saturation (amount), and Lightness (brightness). From the Channel drop-down list, you can choose from different colors.

If you want to colorize a black-and-white photo, check the Colorize check box. Note also that while the Hue/Saturation dialog box is open, you can dynamically adjust opacity from the Opacity slider in the Layers panel.

In Figure 4.18, I colorized a black-and-white photo to create a cooler image.

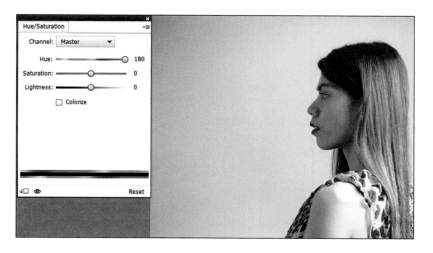

FIGURE 4.18 The Hue/ Saturation dialog box from the Hue/Saturation Adjustment Layer.

Creating Gradient Maps

Gradient maps are quite different from Gradient Fills. You use gradient maps with different blending modes to tone images. Here is just a quick explanation of gradient maps.

When you choose Gradient Map from the Create Fill or Adjustment Layer drop-down list, the Gradient Map dialog box opens. There are fewer choices in the Gradient Map dialog box than you have with the Gradient Fill dialog

For a more thorough discussion on using gradient maps for toning images, see Chapter 10.

box. However, you can access the Gradient Editor much the same as you can with the Gradient Fill dialog box by clicking on the gradient in the Gradient Maps dialog box.

In Figure 4.19, I added a gradient map to warm up the photo. While in the Gradient Map dialog box, I could also access the Opacity sliders and the blending modes drop-down list. In Figure 4.19, I set the opacity to 24% and chose Screen for the blending mode. For more on blending modes, see "Blending Layers" later in this chapter.

FIGURE 4.19 The Gradient Map dialog box from a Gradient Map Adjustment Layer.

Using Photo Filters

Photo Filter Adjustment Layers are similar to the Solid Color Fill layers. The main difference between the two is that you apply color to the luminosity in a photo. Solid Color fills can cover an image 100% opaque color at 100% opacity. Photo Filters apply color to the brightness areas of a photo and retain detail in the image even at 100% opacity. The Photo Filter Adjustment Layers dialog box has a list of 20 preset color choices, as well as an opportunity to choose colors in the Elements Color Picker. In addition, the Photo Filter provides you with an option for affecting all layers below the Photo Filter Adjustment Layers by clicking the icon in the lower-left corner of the Photo Filter dialog box.

In Figure 4.20, I clicked the Filter radio button. This choice enables me to select one of the preset colors. If you click Color and then the color swatch in the dialog box, the Elements Color Picker dialog box opens.

For the effect I wanted for this photo, I chose a cooling filter and reduced the opacity to 56%.

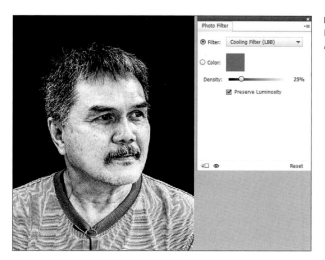

FIGURE 4.20 The Photo Filter dialog box from an Adjustment Layer.

Inverting Images

You can use an Adjustment Layer to invert an image. Inverting an image renders an appearance like a negative. This is the same effect as when you choose Filter > Adjustments > Invert or press Ctrl/⌘ + I.

Using Threshold

The Threshold dialog box displays all pixels as black or white. Any pixel values less than 50% turn to white. Any pixel values greater than 50% turn to black. The Threshold Adjustment Layers command is handy for using with text scans. It eliminates some grays around the text and renders the text more crisply. You can also use Threshold Adjustments for special effects when blending layers.

Posterizing Photos

When you choose Posterize from the Create Fill or Adjustment Layer drop-down menu, the result is a posterized image much the same as when you choose Filter > Adjustments > Posterize. You can use this adjustment to create special effects. In Figure 4.21, I posterized an image, set the blend mode to Difference, and added a few Levels Adjustment Layers.

TIP: If you scan documents with text, use the highest resolution your scanner can handle. Most consumer-grade scanners offer resolutions from 1200 to 2400 dpi. When you scan text, you want the highest resolutions for crisp text.

FIGURE 4.21 The result of using the Posterize Adjustment Layer.

Using Elements+ Adjustment Layers

Elements+

If you have Elements+ installed, you have access to additional Adjustment Layers. Unfortunately, you can't use any of the Elements+ Adjustment Layers in 16-bit mode, but you do have access to additional settings that can be helpful when working on your photos.

Using Elements+ Curves

Open the Color and Tone settings by clicking on the Color and Tone button in the Styles panel with Elements+ selected from the drop-down list in the Effects panel. At the top of the Color and Tone dialog box, click Curves. The Curves dialog box opens, as shown in Figure 4.22.

NOTE: When you click the diagonal line to plot a point on the line, you must use the arrow keys to move the point. You cannot click and drag points in the Curves dialog box. To move a point a distance of 1 pixel, press an arrow key on your keypad. To move a point 10 pixels, press Shift and press an arrow key.

NOTE: The Curves adjustment with Elements+ opens the Curves dialog box. After you make an adjustment and click OK, the adjustment is added as a new layer. However, the layer is not exactly like an Adjustment layer. All the Adjustment Layers enable you to revisit the last settings and tweak the adjustment. When a Curves layer is created with Elements+, you can't revisit that last settings. If you need to make a different edit with Curves, you need to delete the layer and create a new Curves adjustment.

In the Curves dialog box, you can adjust the brightness and contrast by clicking on the diagonal line to plot points and move them. There are six primary adjustment presets available in the Preset drop-down list you can make using curves, as well as an almost infinite number of combinations you can make by moving points on a path. Generally, adjustments fall into the following categories:

- **Lighten image:** Click a point in the center of the diagonal line in the Curves dialog box and move it up and to the left to light the photo.

FIGURE 4.22 The Elements + Curves dialog box.

- **Darken image:** Click a point in the center of the diagonal line in the Curves dialog box and move it down and to the right to darken the photo.

- **Lighten with less contrast:** Move the black point (lower-left corner) up to lighten the photo with less contrast.

- **Darken with less contrast:** Move the white point (top-right corner) down to darken with less contrast.

- **Darken with more contrast:** Move the black point (lower-left corner) to the right to darken with more contrast.

- **Lighten with more contrast:** Move the white point top-right corner) left to lighten with more contrast.

Try to understand the direction you move the points to brighten or darken with more or less contrast and remember you must use the arrow keys on your keyboard to move the points. In Figure 4.22, you can see an S-shaped curve for editing brightness and contrast.

You find a few limitations in the Elements+ Curves dialog box compared to the Curves adjustments in Adobe Photoshop. You cannot adjust the individual RGB Channels and you cannot drag points on the diagonal line.

NOTE: Points on a curve in Elements+ can only be moved by selecting a point and then striking an arrow key. You cannot click and drag points on the path using Elements+.

As noted earlier, you have one limitation when using the Curves adjustment in that you can't click and drag points on a path. Another limitation is that you can't select individual color channels in the Curves dialog box. When using the Levels adjustment or a Levels Adjustment Layer, Elements provides a menu to choose color channels. When using Elements+ and adjusting curves on color channels, you must first select the color channel when you first open the Color and Tone dialog box. Select the channel and then click Curves. If you want to make adjustments on all channels, you must select each channel individually and make the adjustments. You are further limited when using curves with Elements+ in that each adjustment you make on individual channels does not produce a layer. Therefore, if you don't like the result, you have to start over and make adjustments to all three color channels (in RGB documents).

Editing Elements+ Adjustment Layers

After you create an Adjustment Layer with Elements+, you can't double-click the layer to return to the adjustment. You need to open the Color and Tone dialog box again, and from the menu choices, choose Edit Adjustment Layers. If you have multiple Adjustment Layers in the Layers panel, select the layer you want to adjust, and Elements+ opens the respective Adjustment Layer.

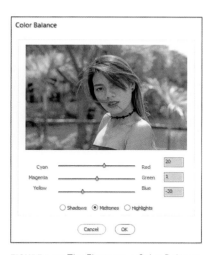

FIGURE 4.23 The Elements + Color Balance dialog box.

Adjusting Color Balance

Elements+ includes a Color Balance adjustment. Open the Color and Tone Settings and choose Color Balance. The Color Balance dialog box opens, as shown in Figure 4.23. In this dialog box, you can adjust the CMY and RGB values to balance color. If you have a magenta shift in your image (or some other color shift), you can use this dialog box to make corrections to color. Because you're working with an Adjustment Layer, you can apply blending modes, opacity settings, and return to the dialog box using the Elements+ Edit Adjustment Layers option in the Color and Tone dialog box.

Using the Channel Mixer

The Color Balance adjustments work with highlights, shadows, and midtones. The Channel mixer, on the other hand, works with the three channels (Red, Green, and Blue). You can adjust intensity of one channel to produce brighter colors and amplified color values. When you choose Channel Mixer in the Elements+ Color and Tone dialog box, you arrive at a dialog box where you make choices for colors and blending modes. The defaults are None for the color choice and Normal for the Blending Mode. In Figure 4.24, you can see some color adjustments I made in the Channel mixer to slightly change the colors.

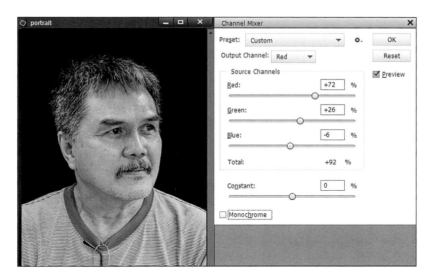

FIGURE 4.24 The Elements
+ Channel Mixer.

Using Selective Color

You can use the Selective Color Adjustment Layer to change colors of items in a photo. A good use for Selective Color is when you want to change the color of clothing. In Figure 4.25, I selected the model's dress and opened the Selective Color adjustment from the Color and Tone settings in Elements+. The model's dress is red in the original photo. In the Selective Color dialog box, I changed the red to blue.

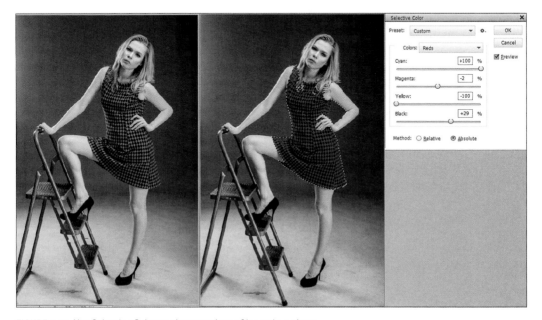

FIGURE 4.25 Use Selective Color to change colors of items in a photo.

TIP: Chapter 1 discusses Color Lookup as it is used with Elements+. What I didn't show you is that after choosing a Color Lookup, you create an Adjustment Layer. As an Adjustment Layer, you have access to layer blend modes and opacity adjustments.

Working with Color Lookup

When you choose Color Lookup in the Color and Tone dialog box in Elements+, the New Layer dialog box opens. Click OK, and the Color Lookup dialog box opens, as shown in Figure 4.26.

Elements+ has a number of preinstalled lookup tables (LUTs) you can choose to apply to a new Adjustment Layer. In addition, you can load LUTs by selecting Load 3D LUT; locate LUTs on your computer, select one, and click the Load button.

FIGURE 4.26 The Elements+ Color Lookup dialog box.

For more on adding LUTs to Elements and working with them, see Chapter 10.

Working with Smart Objects

Smart Objects are layers converted to a special kind of layer that's non-destructive. In Photoshop, you can create Smart Objects and perform many different kinds of edits and always return to the original layer undamaged by any edits.

In Photoshop Elements, you can have Smart Objects, but the editing you can perform is very limited. For example, you cannot apply any filters; most of the Enhance menu commands are not accessible, and you cannot create Layer Masks. You can create selections, although you cannot perform any edits that change pixels like using the Clone Stamp tool, Dodge/Burn tools, Healing Brushes, and so on.

You can create a Smart Object and create a new blank layer above it. You can then use the various tools to place the edits on the new blank layer. You can also use Selection tools on Smart Objects to create selections.

Placing Photos

If you choose File > Place and place a photo on an open document, the placed photo is converted to a Smart Object on a new layer. Perhaps the only real value to Smart Objects in Photoshop Elements is if you need to scale an image. You can scale down and back up, and you won't lose any resolution. The scaled document remains intact.

Using Elements+ with Smart Objects

Elements+ offers you more options when editing Smart Objects. You can create a Smart Object by placing an image on a document in the Photo Editor, or you can open the Elements+ panel and click the Layers button. Check the box for Show All Commands and select Convert to Embedded Object. Click the Green Apply check mark. This creates a Smart Object.

You're limited as much with Elements+ as with the Photo Editor tools and menus when working with Smart Objects. However, among the Elements+ options, you have Smart Filters in the second row in the Effects panel.

Select the Smart Object in the Layers panel and click Smart Filters. In the Smart Filters dialog box, choose a filter to apply to the Smart Object layer. In Figure 4.27, I created a Smart Object and applied the Plastic Wrap Smart Filter.

FIGURE 4.27 The Plastic Wrap filter from the Smart Filter gallery.

If you want to edit the Smart Object, you can return to Elements+ and choose Split Smart Object. You are returned to the original layer before applying the Smart Filter.

Blending Layers

One of the great benefits you have for working with layers is the blending options. You can blend one layer with another or blend through the entire layer stack. You can use blending options to darken, lighten, and add contrast (among other things) to layers below the blend.

Understanding Blend Modes

When you open the Blend Modes drop-down list in the Layers panel, you see 24 different choices in addition to the Normal blend mode. In Photoshop, there are 26 choices—not counting the Normal blend mode. The Subtract and Divide blend modes are available in Photoshop but not in Photoshop Elements. For Elements users, this is not any major disadvantage because you probably wouldn't use these two blend modes. As a matter of fact, you'll find around six of the options are ones you'll use most frequently.

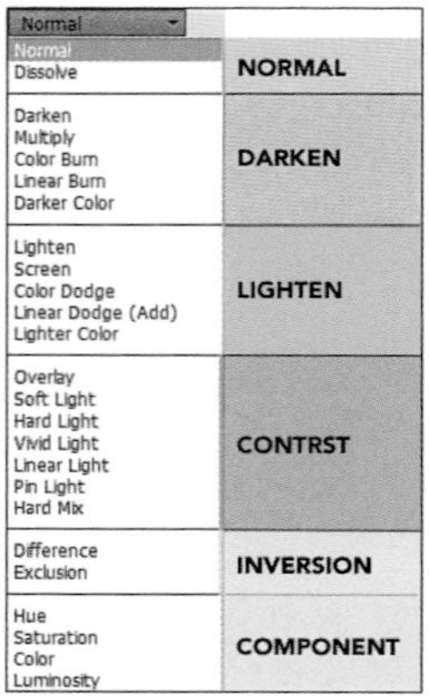

FIGURE 4.28 Blend modes listed according to category.

As you can see in Figure 4.28, blending options are divided into six groups. Beginning at the top of each group, you find the strongest application of an effect at the top with lesser degrees of the effect as you move down the list. For example, Darken is the strongest darken effect. As you move to Multiply, darkening is less. Move down to Color Burn, and the darkening is less than Multiply, and so on.

The first thing to familiarize yourself with in the blend modes is the three primary groups. The group beginning with Darken darkens the layer(s) below it. The group beginning with Lighten lightens the layer(s) below it. The group beginning with Overlay adds contrast to the layer(s) below.

Also, realize that after you apply a blend in a layer, you can also use the Opacity slider in the Layers panel. You can reduce the amount of the effect by moving the opacity slider. You can use all the Adjustment Layers options and apply blend modes to them. You can also mask out areas of a layer and blend only a portion of one layer to the layer(s) below.

Working with the Normal Modes

Beginning at the top of the Blend Modes drop-down list, you find Normal and Dissolve. Normal does nothing. It's the default choice in the Layers panel and produces no effect on other layers.

Dissolve is something you will rarely use, or you may never have a use for it. If you choose the Dissolve blend mode, it creates a spatter of pixels. If you use Dissolve at 100% Opacity, it has little effect. The more transparency you add by adjusting the Opacity slider, the more obvious the effect.

In Figure 4.29, I created a 25% gray layer atop a radial Black to White gradient in a layer below the gray layer. In the Layers panel, you can see the Difference blend mode applied with an Opacity of 32%. The result shows a spattering of pixels. The more transparency you add by lowering the Opacity, the farther the dots distance themselves from other pixels.

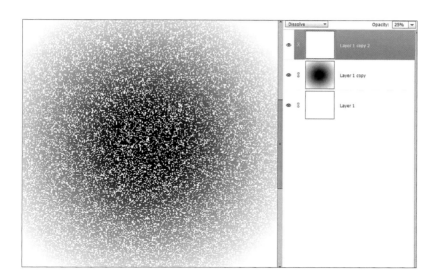

FIGURE 4.29 The Dissolve blend mode applied to a layer.

Working with the Darken Modes

The Darken blend modes includes five choices. When you choose the topmost option, the darkening of the layer(s) below is strongest. All of the choices in this group result in some form of darkening of the layer(s) below.

Using Darken

When you choose Darken from the Blend Modes list, Elements darkens all pixels greater than 50% gray. All pixels below 50% gray are not changed.

In Figure 4.30, you can see a black-and-white gradient in the gradient layer. Below the layer is the Solid Color layer. If we choose Darken from the Blend Modes list and apply it to the top layer, notice the color layer darkens up to the midpoint of the Solid Color layer. The bottom half of the Solid Color layer is unaffected.

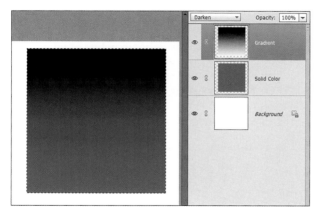

FIGURE 4.30 The Darken blend mode darkens all pixels greater than 50% gray.

The Darken blend mode darkens up to 50% grays and then leaves the rest of the blend unaffected.

Using Multiply

Multiply takes all the black in one layer and adds it to all the black in the layer(s) below. All the 100% white pixels are ignored. Any gray pixels with a slight amount of black are affected.

Take a look at Figure 4.30 and compare it to Figure 4.31. In Figure 4.31, you see darker pixels toward the bottom of the image and the darker areas are much richer than what you see in Figure 4.30. The difference is slight, but you can see a much richer black in the Multiply mode since all levels of black are made darker.

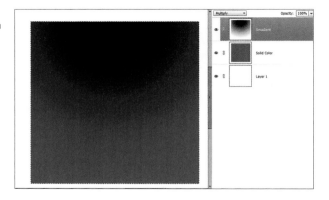

FIGURE 4.31 The Multiply blend mode provides much richer blacks than the Darken blend mode.

Using Color Burn, Linear Burn, and Darker Color

Dissect the name of the Color Burn mode. You have color, and you have burn. Color implies that color is affected. Burn is a darken technique in Elements. Therefore, you can expect that the result of using this blend mode is that the target layer gets darker and the colors are affected.

As the name implies, when you use Color Burn, the target layer gets darker and colors are added. (You can target more than one layer.) Blacks and whites are unaffected; only all the levels of gray other than black and white are affected.

In Figure 4.32, you can see the darkening effect in the top half of the image and that the colors are more intense in the top half. As you move down the gradient to the lighter areas, no darkening or color changes are visible.

Color Burn has no effect on white pixels in the document.

NOTE: One thing to note is that Color Burn is one of eight blend modes that react differently with opacity adjustments. They don't introduce transparency at all levels of the Opacity adjustment. Once you move the slider below 50%, the effect is not proportionately reduced in transparency. The eight maverick blend modes that behave in this manner include Color Burn, Linear Burn, Color Dodge, Linear Dodge, Vivid Light, Linear Light, Hard Mix, and Difference.

FIGURE 4.32 Darkening the target layer and adding color with Color Burn.

Linear Burn does the same thing as Color Burn, but the white pixels are affected. They become darker.

Darker Color is almost identical to Darken. In some cases, the difference is indistinguishable. In other cases, the effect of Darker Color is a little more extreme than the Darken blend mode. For all intents and purposes, you will rarely use Darker Color, Color Burn, or Linear Burn.

Working with the Lighten Modes

The lighten modes are opposite the darken modes. Lighten is the opposite of Darken, Screen is the opposite of Multiply, and so on. The end result with all modes is a lighter image:

- Lighten is the exact opposite of Darken. It lightens all pixels less than 50%. In Figure 4.33, you can see the result of using the Lighten Blend Mode applied to a gradient.

- Screen is the exact opposite of Multiply. The target image is lightened a little less than the Lighten Blend Mode. It shows everything that's 100% white and hides everything that's 100% black.

FIGURE 4.33 The Lighten
blend mode.

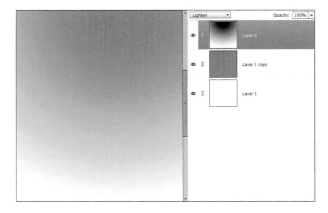

- Color Dodge is the opposite of Color Burn. Whereas Color Burn keeps 100% white as white, Color Dodge keeps 100% black as black. This Blend Mode lightens the target image and adds color. In Figure 4.34, you can see the effects of Color Dodge.

FIGURE 4.34 The Color
Dodge blend mode.

- The Linear Dodge blend lightens the image much brighter than Color Dodge. Keep in mind that you would rarely use the various blends at 100% Opacity. You would often reduce opacity and/or use the Blend If sliders you can only find with the Elements+ plugin.

- The Lighter Color blend mode is an extreme version of Lighten. 100% black is unaffected while all grays to white are lightened.

Working with Contrast Blend Modes

This group has various blend modes that primarily increase contrast by brightening the bright areas of the target layer and darkening the dark areas of the target layer. All 50% gray values are unaffected. Grays above 50% are darkened, and grays below 50% are lightened.

Using the Overlay Blend Mode

The Overlay blend mode, like other blend modes in this group, adds some contrast to the target image by brightening the brighter pixels and darkening the darker pixels. This blend mode is like using the Multiply blend mode and the Screen Blend mode together. Everything 50% gray remains the same. Everything brighter than 50% gray gets brighter. Everything lighter than 50% gray gets lighter.

In Figure 4.35, you can see the darkening at the top of the image and the brightening at the bottom of the image. Compare the document with the Layer thumbnail image, and you can see more contrast appears in the document.

FIGURE 4.35 The Overlay blend mode.

> **NOTE:** When I speak of grays related to blending modes, I'm not talking about color. Rather, it is brightness values that are affected. For example, 50% gray means a brightness value of 50%. Therefore, any color can be used for blending. It's the brightness of the color that produces the effect on the target layer.

The Overlay mode with a gradient blending to the image below is a little harsher in the transitions of blacks to grays. Granted, you can adjust opacity, but you still end up with some sharper transitions. A better way to use the blend mode when you want to add more contrast to a photo is to create a Levels Adjustment Layer. Don't make any brightness/contrast adjustments. Just add a Levels Adjustment Layer and choose Overlay on the Levels layer for the blend mode. In Figure 4.36, you can see the result of using this technique on the same photo used in Figure 4.35.

FIGURE 4.36 The Overlay
blend mode using a Levels
Adjustment Layers.

Using Soft Light Blend Mode

Soft Light is a milder version of Overlay. Depending on the target image and the layer you blend with it, using Soft Light may not show much more difference than the Overlay blend mode. If you are in an editing session where you use Overlay, switch back and forth between Overlay and Soft Light. Choose the one that appeals to you. Sometimes Soft Light can offer you a little less contrast.

Using Hard Light Blend Mode

When you use Hard Light, the result in the target layer is a more diluted color. As an exercise, take a photo and duplicate the background. Add a Gaussian Blur to the top layer. Push the blur slider far to the right to create a massive blur.

After blurring the top layer, select it and choose Hard Light. You'll notice the colors in the photo are slightly faded back and the contrast is lowered. In Figure 4.37, you can see the result of these steps on the same image shown in Figures 4.35 and 4.36.

FIGURE 4.37 The Hard
Light blend mode.

Using Vivid Light Blend Mode

Vivid Light leaves 100% black as black and 100% white as white on the target layer. All values in between are brightened, as you can see in Figure 4.38. Fully saturated colors appear differently. If the color is not fully saturated, like a very bright color, then the blacks stay black, whites stay white, and all grays in between get brighter.

FIGURE 4.38 The Vivid Light blend mode.

Using Linear Light Blend Mode

Linear Light has a similar effect except 100% black does not stay at 100% black and 100% white does not stay at 100% white. All colors, including black and white, are brightened.

Using Pin Light Blend Mode

Pin light is simply a combination of Lighten and Darken. All values above 50% gray are darkened, and all values below 50% gray are lightened.

Using Hard Mix Blend Mode

Hard mix reduces colors to eight values (RGB, CMY, blacK and White). The result on the target layer is all colors are reduced to only those eight values. If you reduce opacity, you begin to introduce more colors.

In Figure 4.39, you see the Hard Mix applied to a Levels layer, and the opacity was reduced to 38%. The color in the photo has been reduced to eight colors, much like reducing colors in a GIF image with the end result creating some posterization.

FIGURE 4.39 The Hard Mix blend mode.

Working with the Inversion Group

The blend modes in this group are modes you probably won't use too often. You might find some use for artistically creating certain looks to your images, but as a general edit for improving images, they aren't as useful as blend modes in the darken, lighten, and overlay groups:

■ Difference blend mode produces the difference between two colors. If you draw a circle and color it red (255, 0, 0 in the RGB values), duplicate it on another layer, and then overlay the circles slightly, the overlapping area displays the difference when you use the Difference blend mode. The overlapping area is black (0,0,0 RGB values). Mathematically, red is 255,0,0. When you choose Difference, it's 255,0,0 minus 255,0,0, which results in black or 0,0,0.

■ One of the most beneficial aspects of Difference is when you want to align two layers of the same image. In Figure 4.40, you can see the layers misaligned after using the Difference blend mode. When you use Difference to check layer alignment, you should see 100% black on the blend layer. If you see any edges of the underlying layer, the layers are out of alignment. Notice in Figure 4.40 that the layers are out of alignment.

■ Exclusion blend mode produces the exact same result as Difference with the exception that it doesn't invert the midtones.

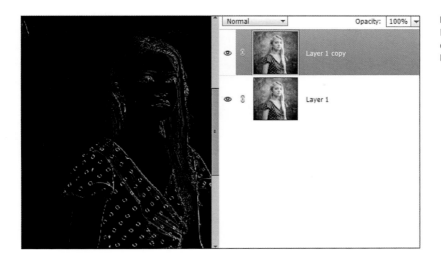

FIGURE 4.40 Using the Difference blend mode to detect misalignment of layers.

Working with the Component Group

The Component group blends color in your photos:

- Hue blend mode changes color. The color affected is the primary or dominant color in the image. If there is no dominant color in an image, the blend mode produces no effect.

- If you create a solid color Adjustment Layer, the Saturation blend mode increases that color in the target image. This blend mode only controls the amount of color. It has no effect on the hue.

- The Color blend mode applies a color throughout the target image. Again, if you create a solid color Adjustment Layer and choose the Color blend mode, the chosen color is applied throughout the photo on the target layer.

- This blend mode has no effect on color. It increases brightness.

Knowing the Most Important Blend Modes

When you try to remember each blend mode and know precisely what they do, it can be very overwhelming. The best way to get a handle on using blend modes is to choose the ones that are most useful. Fortunately, I can suggest which you should focus on.

The blend modes you are likely to use often include Multiply, Screen, Overlay, and Soft Light.

Using the Multiply Blend Mode

There are many uses for the Multiply blend mode. As I mentioned earlier, Multiply adds all levels of black from one image to the target image. One particular use for Multiply is in working on vintage photos or photos that are overexposed with low contrast, as shown in Figure 4.41.

FIGURE 4.41 Overexposed photo with low contrast.

For more on adding data to photos, see Chapter 13, "Editing Vintage Photos."

To resurrect this photo, I need more data. I can add data using the Multiply blend mode. In Figure 4.42, you can see the Background layer was duplicated twice. I used the Multiply blend mode on the duplicate layers. By using the Multiply blend mode, I can move on to adjusting brightness and contrast, sharpening, and removing stains and scratches. At this point, I have an image ready to add the additional edits after using the Multiply blend mode.

FIGURE 4.42 The Multiply blend mode adds more data to the photo and begins to bring the image to life.

Using the Screen Blend Mode

The Screen blend mode is another blending option you will frequently use. One particular edit that's handy is when you want to accent some highlights in a photo, such as highlights on hair. Take Figure 4.43 as an example. You can see some hair highlights on the left side of the model's hair. In this photo, I want to bring out the hair highlights just a little more.

FIGURE 4.43 Very slight highlights in the hair.

In Figure 4.44, I created a Layer Mask to protect the face and some of the clothing.

For more on Layer Masks, see Chapter 5.

Again, I can use an Adjustment Layer on the isolated hair without making an adjustment; I just use it as a placeholder for a blending mode choice. I added a Levels Adjustment Layer and chose Screen for the blending mode on the Levels layer. I reduced opacity to bring the brightness down.

FIGURE 4.44 Using the Screen blend mode to bring out some hair highlights.

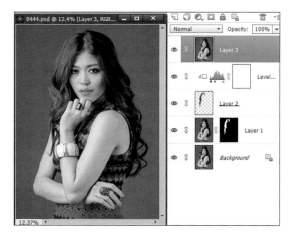

Using the Overlay Blend Mode

The Overlay mode is one you might use the most of all the blend modes. You can do so much more than adding contrast when working with this mode. As an example, look at Figure 4.45. I have two images—one with a brick wall (left) and the other with a face (right). In this example, I want to blend the face into the wall.

FIGURE 4.45 Two images set up for blending layers.

In Figure 4.46, you can see the results of merging these two photos and using the Overlay blend mode with a few other blend modes. I took a copy of the face, converted to black and white, and added it as a layer to the brick wall photo. I masked the face and used the Overlay blend mode to create a realistic look for the face to blend in with the wall. I duplicated the Face layer and applied the Screen blend mode to make the face brighter.

I made a levels adjustment in the Levels layer, and I clipped the layer to the Face Copy layer to tweak the brightness levels.

To learn more about clipping layers, see Chapter 5.

To balance the color, I sampled a color from the brick wall and filled the Color Blend layer with the sampled color (Layer 1), then changed the blend mode from normal to Color.

FIGURE 4.46 The face photo blended with the brick wall to create a surrealistic look.

Using the Soft Light Blend Mode

Soft Light is another blend mode affecting contrast. It's a lesser application for adding more contrast than the Overlay mode. However, beyond adding contrast to a layer, Soft Light is a great mode for color grading in Elements.

In Figure 4.47, I created a Gradient Adjustment Layer, and I created a custom gradient in the Gradient Editor. I applied the Soft Light blend mode to this layer. I then added a Levels Adjustment Layers to make a Levels adjustment, and I reduced the opacity of the Soft Light layer to 40%.

For more on color grading, see Chapter 10.

FIGURE 4.47 Color grading using a gradient map and the Soft Light blend mode.

Often, you'll find that using more than one layer with more than one blend mode may be needed to create the effect you want, such as the example used in Figure 4.47. If you haven't worked with layer blend modes, practice using the four basic modes (Multiply, Screen, Overlay, and Soft Light) on your photos. You can quickly learn the outcomes for using each of these blend modes with a little practice. After you become familiar with them, branch out and experiment with the other blend modes.

Using Keyboard Shortcuts with Blend Modes

Sometimes, you just don't know what blend mode you want to use for an effect. It's helpful to scroll through all the blend modes and observe the results in the Document window.

If you know what blend mode you want, and you want to jump to that mode, there are a number of keyboard shortcuts you can use to scroll through to all blend modes. In Figure 4.48, you can see the keyboard shortcuts associated with blend modes. The shortcuts work with layers, and many tools have blend mode choices in the Tool Options panel. When a tool is selected that accommodates blend modes, pressing the keyboard shortcuts is applied to the Tool Options. For example, if you have the Marquee rectangle tool selected and press Shift + Alt/Option + M, the Multiply blend mode is applied to the selected layer. However, if you have the Brush tool selected, the Multiple blend mode is applied to brush strokes. The Marquee Rectangle doesn't have blending options available in the Tool Options panel, but the Brush also has a drop-down list for Mode where all the blending modes are available.

To quickly change from a tool so you can use the shortcuts with layer blend modes, press the V key to access the Move tool. Use the keyboard shortcuts, and then press a shortcut key to return to your tool. For example, if you're using the Brush tool and then you want to change a layer blend mode, press V and then press a shortcut to access a blend mode. Press the B key to return to the Brush tool.

Keyboard shortcuts to access specific blend modes in the layers panel and Tool Options panel are shown in Figure 4.48.

FIGURE 4.48 Keyboard shortcuts for accessing blend modes.

LAYER BLEND MODES KEYBOARD SHORTCUTS

NORMAL = Shift + Alt/Option + N
DISSOLVE = Shift + Alt/Option + I

DARKEN = Shift + Alt/Option + K
MULTIPLY = Shift + Alt/Option + M
COLOR BURN = Shift + Alt/Option + B
LINEAR BURN = Shift + Alt/Option + A

LIGHTEN = Shift + Alt/Option + G
SCREEN = Shift + Alt/Option + S
COLOR DODGE = Shift + Alt/Option + D
LINEAR DODGE = Shift + Alt/Option + W

OVERLAY = Shift + Alt/Option + O
SOFT LIGHT = Shift + Alt/Option + F
VIVID LIGHT = Shift + Alt/Option + V
LINEAR LIGHT = Shift + Alt/Option + J
PIN LIGHT = Shift + Alt/Option + Z
HARD MIX = Shift + Alt/Option + L

DIFFERENCE = Shift + Alt/Option + E
EXCLUSION = Shift + Alt/Option + X

HUE = Shift + Alt/Option + U
SATURATION = Shift + Alt/Option + T
COLOR = Shift + Alt/Option + C
LUMINOSITY = Shift + Alt/Option + Y

Managing Layers

There are a few things you need to know when working with layers. Among those are keyboard shortcuts for working with layers, ordering layers in the layer stack, grouping and ungrouping layers, and deleting layers.

Using Keyboard Shortcuts with Layers

There are some actions you will frequently use when working with layers. To speed up your editing sessions, you should learn some keyboard shortcuts. Some of the most frequently used shortcuts are the following:

- **Duplicating a layer, Ctrl/⌘ + J:** When you first begin a new editing session, it's generally a good idea to duplicate the background and work on a copy. If you don't like the edits and want to start over, it's easy to delete one or more layers and return to the original background image. Additionally, you may find it necessary to duplicate other layers frequently. Become familiar with this keyboard shortcut. You'll use it frequently.

- **Create new blank layer, Shift + Ctrl/⌘ + N or Ctrl/⌘ + Alt/Option + J:** When you want to create a new blank layer, use this keyboard shortcut. When you invoke the shortcut, the New Layer dialog box opens. Type a descriptive name for the layer and click OK. The new layer is added on top of the selected layer.

- **Group selected layers, Ctrl/⌘ + G:.** The advantage for creating a group of layers is that you can apply adjustments to the entire group. For example, you can change opacity equally for all layers in the group, and you can add different Adjustment Layers above a group and apply the same adjustment to the group.

- **Ungroup layers, Shift + Ctrl/⌘ + G:** You can use this shortcut to ungroup layers that were previously grouped.

- **Merging selected layers to a new layer, Shift + Ctrl/⌘ + Alt/Option + E:** Using these keys, you merge all visible layers into a composite image as a new layer.

Of course, there are additional keyboard shortcuts available to you. If you find yourself using other actions where a keyboard shortcut is available, then use it.

Reordering Layers

If you want to reorder layers, click to select a layer you want to move and drag it up or down in the layer stack to change the order. If you want to move a background up from the bottom position, you need to first convert it to a layer. Click the lock icon in the Background layer to convert it to a layer.

To move several layers in a contiguous order, select one layer, press Shift, and select the last layer among those you want to move. Click and drag one of the selected layers to move up or down the stack.

To move layers in a noncontiguous order, select a layer and press Ctrl/⌘ + click to select another layer. Continue clicking with the key modifier depressed to select additional layers in a noncontiguous order. Click and drag to a new position in the layer stack. When you move the group, the layers are moved and ordered together. To make this a little more clear, take a look at Figure 4.49.

On the left side of Figure 4.49, layers are selected in a noncontiguous order. When we move the layers to reorder in the layer stack, the selected layers are placed in a contiguous order, as shown on the right side of Figure 4.49.

FIGURE 4.49 Layers selected in a noncontiguous order (left), then moved together in the layer stack (right).

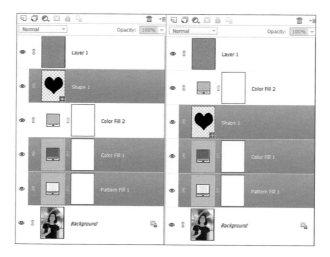

Deleting Layers

When you want to remove a layer in the layer stack, select the layer and choose Delete layer from the Layers panel menu. Likewise, you can choose Layer > Delete Layer in the Layer menu. You can also drag a layer to the trash can icon in the layers panel. When you invoke any of these actions, a warning dialog box opens and prompts you to confirm deleting the layer(s). If you want to delete a layer without the warning dialog box opening, press Alt/Option and drag the layer to the trash can icon in the Layers panel or select a layer you want to delete and press Alt/Option and click the Delete icon in the Layers panel.

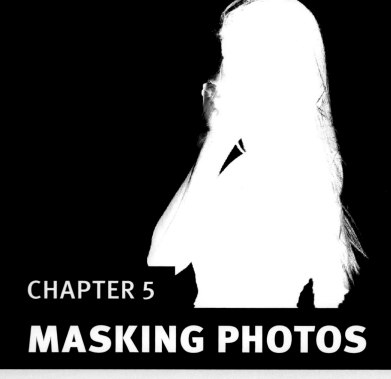

CHAPTER 5

MASKING PHOTOS

Chapter Goals

Masks are essential in much of your Photoshop Elements editing. You need masks so that you can return to selections for further editing. If you had to make a selection each time you wanted to edit the same selection, your editing sessions would be infinitely longer. The goals for this chapter include

- Becoming familiar with Layer Masks
- Creating blank (or empty) and negative masks
- Creating Layer Masks with Adjustment Layers
- Managing Layer Masks
- Creating and working with Luminosity Masks

Layer Masks are as essential to perfecting your Photoshop Elements editing as layers are. Creating and working with Layer Masks is quite simple, but as you begin working with them, it can be confusing.

A Layer Mask masks out portions of a layer so only the selected area is revealed while the unselected area is concealed. It's a selection that's saved on a layer, which means you can return to it as long as it remains intact. In essence, you create a selection and then create the Layer Mask. The selection is saved and the unselected area is hidden. It's analogous to using masking tape when painting walls. You use masking tape around molding to prevent paint from being applied to the wood molding. Likewise, a Layer Mask prevents edits from being applied to portions of a photo or underlying layer(s).

Understanding Layer Masks Basics

I used Layer Masks in several examples in Chapters 3 and 4, but I haven't explained how to create them, modify them, and manage them. The first step in learning about Layer Masks is to understand exactly what a Layer Mask is and what it can do for you.

Getting Familiar with Layer Masks Essentials

A Layer Mask is like a piece of clear acetate. If you paint a portion of the acetate black and then place it over an object, you can see through the clear area, but the black paint hides what's below it. In terms of using Layer Masks, black hides and white reveals layer data.

Black at 100% hides all data in a photo where the mask is created. Less than 100% produces a translucent effect. In Figure 5.1, you can see a Layer Mask with a gradient. On the far left of the mask, the value is 100% black. Black hides the data in the image. As you move right, the gradient slowly moves from black to grays and eventually to 100% white.

All gray areas are translucent, meaning you can see the image ghosted. The degree of ghosting depends on how little or how much gray is in the mask. As you move from dark grays to light grays, the image data become more visible. In other words, 80% gray hides more data than 20% gray.

On the far right, where the gradient is 100% white, image data shows at full strength.

100% Hidden   Translucent   100% Visible

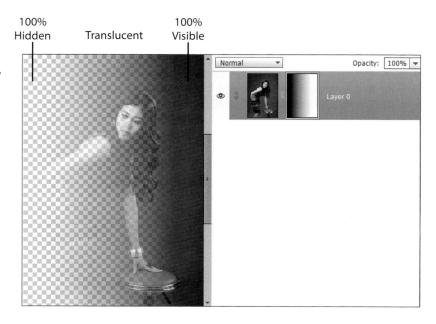

FIGURE 5.1 A gradient Layer Mask hides all black, shows grays as translucent, and white as 100% visible.

Creating Layer Masks

NOTE: You must convert 16-bit images to 8-bit images before you can convert a background to a layer. Note that almost all menu items in the Layers panel and the Layer menu are grayed out when your photo is in 16-bit mode.

As a matter of practice, it's a good idea to duplicate the background before you convert it to a layer. When you duplicate the background by dragging it to the New Layer icon in the Layers panel, choosing Duplicate Layer from the Layers panel menu, or pressing Ctrl/⌘ + J, you create a duplicate layer of the background. This enables you to work on a copy of the background while you keep the original background intact in case you need to return to the original. You must also convert 16-bit images to be 8-bit images to duplicate a layer.

To create a Layer Mask, you must be on a layer. A Layer Mask cannot be added to a locked background. If you want to apply a Layer Mask to a background, click the lock icon on the Background layer. Alternatively, you can right-click on the Background layer to open a context menu and choose Layer from Background or choose Layer > New > Layer from Background. You can also simply double-click a background to convert it to a layer. When you use any of these methods to convert a background to a layer, the New Layer dialog box opens. You can type a name for the new layer or leave the default name of the layer as Layer 0 and click OK. The background is now a layer to which you can add a Layer Mask.

Creating Empty Layer Masks

To create a Layer Mask, select the layer where you want the mask and click the Add a Mask button in the Layers panel. This creates a blank Layer Mask where the mask is completely white. With a white mask, all data on the layer is visible.

Creating Negative Masks

When you use the Add Layer Mask tool (the tool to the left of the Lock) in the Layers panel, a Layer Mask by default is filled white. This shows all data on the layer because white reveals and black conceals.

If you want to have the mask filled with black, perhaps to introduce just a small amount of white that shows a small portion of the layer data, press the Alt/Option key and click the Add Layer Mask button in the Layers panel. You create a new Layer Mask, and it is filled with black.

Creating Adjustment Layers

When you create an Adjustment Layer, the new Adjustment Layer automatically adds a Layer Mask. The Layer Mask by default is filled white; therefore, the entire adjustment is applied to the layer where you add the Adjustment Layer. In Figure 5.2, you can see a Hue/Saturation Adjustment Layer added to a photo. In this figure, I reduced Saturation slightly in the Hue/Saturation dialog box.

FIGURE 5.2 Creating a new Adjustment Layer auto-matically creates a Layer Mask.

NOTE: All editing on Adjustment Layers is nondestructive. You can edit, save, return to the edit, and change it.

The nice thing about using Adjustment Layers and Layer Masks is that all the editing is nondestructive. You can double-click the adjustment in the layer–in this case, the Hue/Saturation adjustment–and open up the last settings. You can refine the edit and click OK, and the edit is updated with no permanent damage on the layer data. Likewise, you can edit the Layer Mask and return to it later to refine the masked area, again without damaging the layer data. For more information on Adjustment Layers, see Chapter 4, "Working with Layers."

Creating Layer Masks from Selections

One of the most beneficial ways to use a Layer Mask is to create one from a selection. You create a selection and use the Add Layer Mask tool in the Layers panel, and the Layer Mask shows white for the selected area and black for all the area outside the selection.

In Figure 5.3, if I want to change subject's skin tones, I first make a selection of the area that I want to edit and click the Add Layer Mask tool in the Layers panel. The reason you create a Layer Mask is two-fold. You can easily return to the mask and apply or modify the adjustment to the masked area, and you can nondestructively make your edits. You can always delete the mask to return to the original.

FIGURE 5.3 A Layer Mask created from a selection.

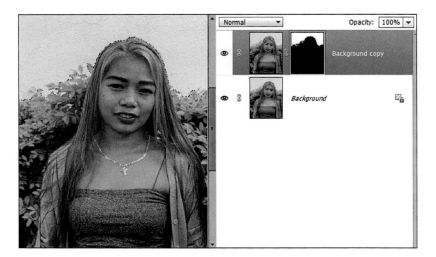

If you create a selection and choose to save the selection, as I explained in Chapter 4, you can easily apply new edits. However, you cannot modify a previous adjustment, and you cannot edit the layer nondestructively.

Showing and Hiding Layer Masks

Sometimes you may want to temporarily hide a Layer Mask to see data on the layer without the mask. To temporarily hide a Layer Mask, press the Shift key and click the Layer Mask. The Layer Mask hides, and it displays a red X over the mask to let you know the mask is not visible, as shown in Figure 5.4.

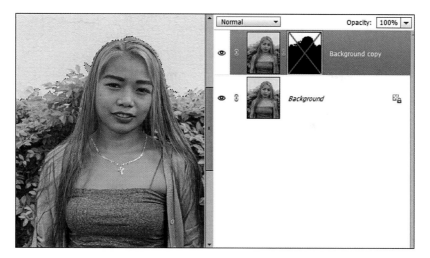

FIGURE 5.4 Hiding a Layer Mask.

Linking and Unlinking Layer Masks

When you create a Layer Mask, by default the Layer Mask is linked to the layer. A link icon appears between the layer and the mask. If you move the mask or transform it by rotating, scaling, distorting, and so on, both the mask and the layer are affected. If you click the Link icon, the icon disappears, and the layer and mask become unlinked. Anything you do to the layer or the mask is independent of the other. You can, for example, unlink the layer and mask and transform the mask by rotating it.

For more on unlinking layers and masks, see Chapter 4.

Inverting a Layer Mask

Suppose you create a new Layer Mask, and you want to convert the default color white to a negative mask (filled with black). You can fill the mask with black, and you also can invert the mask by first selecting the mask and then pressing Ctrl/⌘ + I. When you use the Invert command shortcut, a white mask turns black and a black mask turns white. If you know ahead of time that you want the selected area of the photo masked out, press Alt/Option and click the Add Layer Mask icon in the Layers panel. This action also inverses the mask.

Painting on Layer Masks

When you create a Layer Mask by clicking the Add Layer Mask tool and selecting the mask in the Layers panel, the default foreground color changes to white. Likewise, if you press Alt/Option and click the Add Layer Mask button in the Layers panel to create a negative mask and then select the mask, the foreground color likewise changes to white. In other words, whenever you create a Layer Mask and select the mask, the foreground color automatically changes to white.

If you want to mask an area and increase a selection in the mask by painting, you need to use a white foreground color to increase the mask visibility. You need to use black as the foreground color to reduce the selection.

In Figure 5.5, I created a selection by using the Select > Select Subject menu command. I then refined the selection by choosing Refine Edge in the Select menu to select the hair. When I created a Layer Mask, I pressed Alt/Option to inverse the selection so the background would be the active area. As you can see in Figure 5.5, there's a lot of black inside the selection. If I want to select the subject, I need to inverse the selection.

FIGURE 5.5 The Layer Mask shows the background is selected.

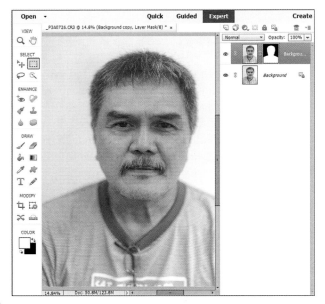

To show the mask in the document window, press the Alt/Option key and click the mask. The mask then appears much larger in the document window, which makes it much easier to paint, as shown in Figure 5.6.

FIGURE 5.6 The Layer Mask in full view in the document window.

If you need to edit the mask, you can paint with white to reveal more of the image data or paint with black to hide more data and shrink the selection. Be certain to double-check the Tool Options panel for the Brush tool. You want the opacity set to 100%, and you should choose a hard edge brush tip.

Changing Background Colors

In the example image in Figure 5.5, I created a mask that hid the subject and revealed the background. At this point, I could use a Solid Color Adjustment Layer and apply it to the background. I could also simply press Ctrl/⌘ + click on the mask to select the background. With the selection active, you can open the Color Picker, choose a color, and click OK.

Once the color you want is the foreground color in the Tools panel, press Alt/Option + Backspace/Delete, and you fill the selection with the foreground color.

In Figure 5.7, you can see the result of filling the background of the example image with a new color.

TIP: If you want to open the Fill Layer dialog box where you can choose from different fill options, blend modes, and opacity settings, press Shift + Backspace/Delete.

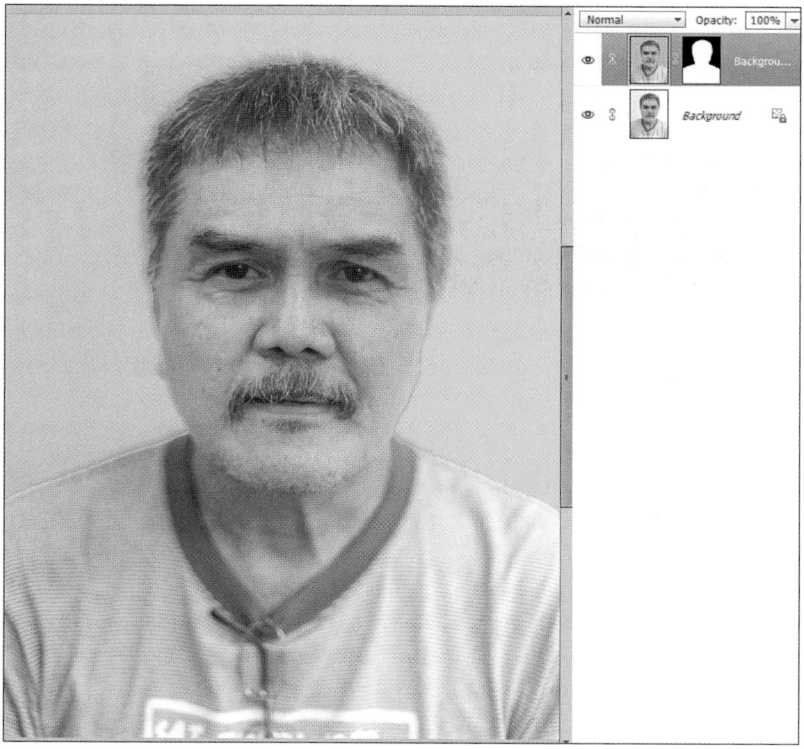

FIGURE 5.7 Fill the Background selection with a new color using the Fill Layer dialog box.

Copying Layer Masks

If you create a Layer Mask and you want to use the same mask on another layer, you can easily copy the mask and paste it to a layer.

In the Layers panel, press Alt/Option and click and drag a Layer Mask to another layer. If you have a mask on the target layer, Elements asks you to confirm whether you want to replace the mask with the copy. Click OK in the Replace Layer Mask dialog box to replace a mask.

Deleting Layer Masks

To delete a Layer Mask, you select the mask and drag it to the Delete icon or choose Layer > Layer Mask > Delete. If you choose the menu command, Elements deletes the selected mask without warning. If you click the Delete icon or drag the mask to the Delete icon, Elements prompts you in a warning dialog box to apply the mask or delete the mask. If you have a mask selected, and you press Alt/Option and click the Delete icon or drag the mask to the Delete icon, the mask is deleted without warning.

Be careful to select the mask and not the layer or the content on the layer when you want to delete only the mask. If you select the layer (to the left of the Layer Mask) or the content on the layer and drag it to the Delete icon, the entire layer (content and Layer Mask) is deleted.

Copying a Layer Mask to Another Document

If for some reason you want to copy a Layer Mask to another document, you must copy the layer containing the mask to the target document. You cannot copy just the mask to a secondary document using drag and drop.

To copy a layer and the mask, click the layer containing the mask and drag to another document. You must click on the image and not the mask in the layer to copy to another document.

Creating Clipping Masks

A clipping mask clips the data in the current layer to the underlying layer. You have two ways you can create a clipping mask. If you know ahead of time that you want to create a clipping mask, you can create the clipping mask at the time you create a new layer. When you create a new layer, the New Layer dialog box opens. Check the box for Use Previous Layer to Create Clipping Mask, as shown in Figure 5.8. Likewise, when you create Adjustment Layers, you see a tiny icon in the lower-left corner of the Adjustment Layer dialog box. Click the icon to creates a clipping mask.

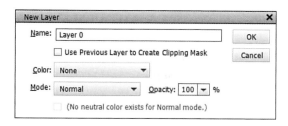

FIGURE 5.8 Check the box for Use Previous Layer to Create Clipping Mask to create a clipping mask.

NOTE: A clipping mask takes the selected area in one layer and clips the second layer to the selection.

The other way you create clipping masks is after you create a layer. Suppose you create a layer, add a Layer Mask to the layer, and then want to contain the data above the Layer Mask to the mask. To make this easier to understand, take a look at Figure 5.9.

I created a Layer Mask on the Background Copy layer. I want to clip Layer 0 to the heart shape in the Layer Mask. To create a clipping mask, press Alt/Option and move the cursor to the line separating the layers. You should see the cursor change to a square with a down-pointing arrow adjacent to the square. When you see the cursor change, click and the clipping mask is created. The result in this example is shown in the Document window in Figure 5.9.

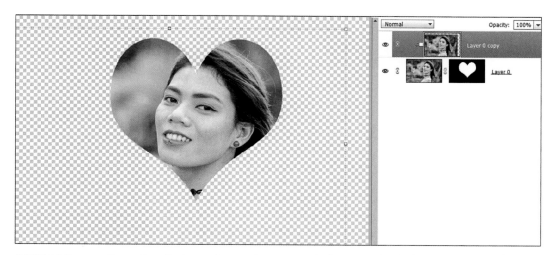

FIGURE 5.9 To manually create a clipping mask, move the cursor to the line separating the layers and press Alt/Option and click.

Creating Luminosity Masks

Luminosity is the brightness in a photo. Therefore, a luminosity mask is a Layer Mask that masks out areas of brightness. In Photoshop Elements, you can create separate luminosity masks for highlights, shadows, and midtones.

Having the ability to mask out different brightness areas of a photo means you can apply different brightness, contrast, and color adjustments separately to the different levels of brightness.

Adjusting Highlights and Shadows Using a Luminosity Mask

If you apply a Levels adjustment to a layer, you apply the brightness/contrast adjustment to all brightness areas. If you want to isolate the highlights or shadows, you need to create a luminosity mask. In Figure 5.10, you can see a photo that's a little underexposed. This photo needs some brightening adjustments, particularly in the midtones and shadows. If I use a Levels adjustment, the highlights, shadows, and midtones are all changed with the same adjustment. In this photo, I want to make only the shadows brighter and adjust the midtones to make them brighter.

FIGURE 5.10 An underexposed photo.

Luminosity masks are often much better methods for adjusting brightness in photos than using levels, curves, and brightness/contrast tools. To see how a luminosity mask is created and used for adjusting brightness, follow these steps:

1. Open a file that needs a brightness contrast adjustment in the Photo Editor. In this example, I'm using the photo shown in Figure 5.10.

2. Press Ctrl/⌘ + J twice to duplicate the background and create two additional layers.

3. Select the top layer and choose Enhance > Convert to Black and White. In the Convert to Black and White dialog box, choose an option for the conversion. Because my example image is a portrait, I choose the Portraits style, as shown in Figure 5.11. Click OK after choosing a style from the Style list.

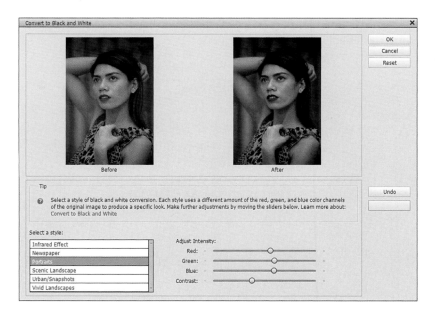

FIGURE 5.11 Choose Enhance > Convert to Black and White to convert the color to grayscale.

4. The top layer is now black and white. Select the first copy (above the Background) and choose Levels from the Adjustment Layer menu in the Layers panel.

   You can make a levels adjustment, but it's not necessary to do so now. You can return to the Adjustment Layer's Levels dialog box later.

5. Select the layer you converted to black and white. Press Ctrl/⌘ + A to select all the data on the layer.

6. When you create an Adjustment Layer, the adjustment creates a mask. In this case, the Levels adjustment has a mask on the layer.

7. Press Alt/Option and click the mask in the Levels 1 layer and press Ctrl/⌘ + V to paste the black-and-white layer's data into the mask.

8. Press Ctrl/⌘ and click to select the highlight data in the mask.

NOTE: When you load the selection for the layer containing the black-and-white photo and press Ctrl/⌘ + click, you load the highlights. If you want to adjust shadows, simply inverse the selection.

9. At this point, the highlights are selected. To select the shadows, you need to inverse the selection by choosing Select > Inverse or pressing Ctrl/⌘ + Shift + I.

10. To make a levels adjustment on the shadows, press Ctrl/⌘ and click the Layer Mask on the Levels layer. Pressing Ctrl/⌘ + clicking on the mask selects the white in the mask. Since I inversed the mask, the white area is now the shadows.

11. Apply a levels adjustment to the shadows.

12. Double-click the Levels icon in the Levels 1 Adjustment Layer to reopen the Levels dialog box. Adjust the levels sliders to create the final look you want. In Figure 5.12, you can see the layers used in this example and the final levels adjustment for the shadows.

FIGURE 5.12 The final image after adjusting the luminosity layer for the shadows.

Adjusting Midtones

At this point, you know how to create luminosity masks for highlights and shadows. Now let's move on to creating a luminosity mask for midtones. Using the same image after adjusting shadows in Figure 5.12, I can make further edits to the midtones:

1. If you followed along and you have adjustments like those shown in Figure 5.12, open the Layers panel menu, hide the top black-and-white layer by clicking the eye icon in the Layers panel, and choose Flatten Image. A dialog box asks you to confirm that you want to delete hidden layers. Click Yes to delete the top layer.

2. Select the Background and press Ctrl/⌘ + J twice to create two copies on two new layers.

3. Convert the Layer 1 copy (top layer) to a black-and-white image by selecting the top layer and choosing Enhance > Convert to Black and White. Again, choose the option that best represents your image in the Convert to Black and White dialog box. In my example, I choose Portrait.

4. Select the top layer and choose Filter > Adjustment > Invert or press Ctrl/⌘ + I.

5. Select both the top two layers and choose Merge Layers in the Layers panel menu to merge the two layers.

6. In the Layers panel, open the Blend Modes drop-down list and choose Darken.

7. Press Ctrl/⌘ + A to select all in the top layer and choose Edit > Copy or press Ctrl/⌘ + C.

8. Select the Background and create a new Levels Adjustment Layer by choosing Levels from the Create New Fill or Adjustment Layer drop-down list in the Layers panel.

9. Select the mask in the Adjustment Layer by pressing Alt/Option and click the mask. Press Ctrl/⌘ + V to paste the composite layer data.

10. Press Ctrl/⌘ + click to select the mask brightness levels.

11. Hide the top layer by clicking the eye icon in the Layers panel on the top layer.

12. Adjust midtones by double-clicking the Levels icon and making midtone adjustments in the Levels dialog box.

13. Select the layer and click the Delete icon to delete the layer. For the final image, flatten the layers.

In Figure 5.13, you can see the results of these edits. Compare the final results to the original photo in Figure 5.12.

FIGURE 5.13 The final image after adjusting the luminosity layer for the midtones.

PART III

SHARPENING AND EFFECTS

Regardless of how good your camera and lenses are, all digital files require some level of sharpening, and Chapter 6 provides an explanation of how to sharpen your images. Chapter 7 looks at using some effects you can apply to your images using the Effects panel.

SHARPENING PHOTOS

Chapter Goals

Just about every digital camera produces images a little bit soft. Some cameras are much sharper than the lower-end models, but even the best sensors aren't quite as crisp as you might like. In this chapter, you learn how to

- Sharpen photos using Adobe Camera Raw
- Sharpen images using the High Pass filter
- Use the Photo Editor Sharpen tools

When you use any one of a variety of sharpening effects in Elements, you find that sharpening typically is the result of increasing contrast between light and dark pixels adjacent to each other. You should always zoom in on a photo after applying sharpening to ensure the amount of sharpening isn't too much, and you don't see halos in the sharp contrast areas.

Using Camera Raw Sharpening

In Chapter 2, "Using Camera Raw," I explain how to make adjustments in the Camera Raw Editor and use the Detail panel shown in Figure 6.1. As a first stop in your image-editing process, it's generally a good idea to visit the Camera Raw Editor and apply adjustments in the Basic and Detail panels.

FIGURE 6.1 The Sharpen/Noise Reduction panel.

In Chapter 2, I also discuss applying different brightness adjustments to selected parts of a photo. You can use the same principle for sharpening photos when using the Camera Raw Editor. You may find a need to sharpen an entire image a little, sharpen the face and hair a little more, and sharpen the eyes, lips, teeth, and eyebrows a little more. It all depends on the image and the amount of sharpening that's needed and how much you can apply without degrading the photo.

When you use the Detail panel, think of making slight adjustments. Don't overdo it and let some of the other sharpening agents in Elements finalize your edits after leaving the Camera Raw Editor.

Working with the High Pass Filter

One of the best sharpening tools at your disposal in Photoshop Elements is the High Pass filter. You use the filter along with a blend mode to add contrast, and it results in sharpening.

Sharpening an Image with the High Pass Filter

Sharpening an image with the High Pass filter is one of the best sharpening techniques at your disposal. The technique is relatively easy, as you can see if you follow these steps:

1. Open an image in the Photo Editor.

2. Press Ctrl/⌘ + J to duplicate the Background layer.

8-Bit Versus 16-Bit

Make sure the image is reduced to an 8-bit image. You cannot duplicate photos at 16-bit. To check the bit depth, choose Image > Mode. You should see 8 Bits/Channel grayed out. When the command is grayed out, the photo is already an 8-bit image. If it's not grayed out, click 8 Bits/Channel in the menu and the file is reduced to 8 bits.

3. Select the top layer and choose Filter > Other > High Pass. The High Pass dialog box opens, as shown in Figure 6.2.

FIGURE 6.2 The High Pass filter dialog box.

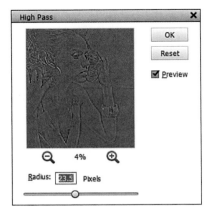

4. The Radius slider is used to apply more or less sharpening. Be careful to not overdo it by moving the slider to the right too far. As a general rule, you want to move the Radius slider to where you first begin to see an outline of the subject. Move the slider back slightly so the subject outline is not too obvious. Click the magnifying glass with a minus (–) symbol to zoom out. When you have the right adjustment, click OK.

5. After you create a High Pass layer, open the Blend Modes menu and choose Overlay. As I explained in Chapter 4, "Working with Layers," the Overlay group of blend modes adds more contrast to the layers below the target layer.

You have to be careful to not move the Radius slider too far in the High Pass filter dialog box. If you need a little more sharpening, duplicate the Background again and apply another High Pass filter, or you can simply duplicate one High Pass layer to add additional sharpening. In the Layers panel, reduce the Opacity if you see any halos in the sharp contrast areas. In Figure 6.3, you can see two High Pass filter layers. On the High Pass 2 layer, I reduced opacity to 32%.

In Figure 6.4, you can see the original raw image opened in the Photo Editor on the left. On the right side, you see the photo after using the High Pass settings shown in Figure 6.3.

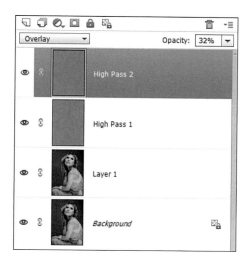

FIGURE 6.3 Layers panel showing two High Pass filter layers.

In this example, I explained sharpening the entire photo using the same settings. In some cases, you may want to apply different amounts of sharpening to different areas of a photo.

FIGURE 6.4 Before adding the High Pass filter (left) and after adding the High Pass filter (right).

Sharpening Different Areas of an Image

Sometimes a global sharpening adjustment isn't as good as sharpening different parts of an image. For example, with a portrait, maybe you want to apply a global sharpening adjustment to the entire image and add more sharpening separately to the hair, eyes, eyebrows, and lips. In this case, you need to create some multiple Layer Masks and mask out areas outside the hair, eyes, eyebrows, and lips.

In Figure 6.5, I start with applying a High Pass filter to the entire image. This sharpens the model's clothing and overall sharpening to the subject. After applying the High Pass filter, choose Overlay for the blend mode.

FIGURE 6.5 High Pass filter applied to the photo and set to Overlay blend mode.

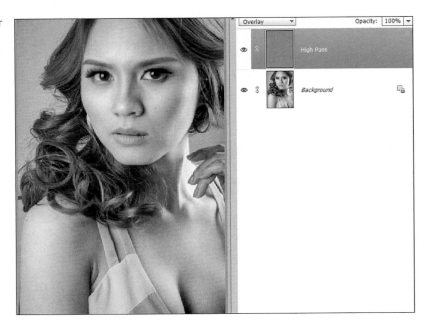

Notice in Figure 6.5, the sharpening is slight. The images need some more sharpening on the face and hair. If you intend to use multiple sharpening effects on an image, start by making your first sharpen edit very low and slowly build more sharpening as you move the other areas of the photo.

After applying the High Pass filter to the entire photo, duplicate the background by pressing Ctrl/⌘ + J. Move the Background copy layer above the High Pass filter layer. Duplicate two more times to create three copies of the Background. I named the three layers from top to bottom Hair Layer, Lips Layer, and Eyes Layer.

I then created selections for the eyes and brows, lips, and hair. When making selections for these components, you don't have to be precise. I used the Refine Edge dialog box to refine each selection but didn't worry about the final selections being too precise. I created Layer Masks for each layer. The original unedited image appears in Figure 6.6.

For more on creating Layer Masks, see Chapter 5, "Masking Photos."

After the Layer Masks are created, you can load selections on each layer and apply the High Pass filter to the selected area. You also set the blending mode to Overlay for each layer. The radius for each filter setting differs according to how much sharpening you can apply without creating any halos. In Figure 6.7, you can see the layers and the final edited image. Compare Figure 6.6 with Figure 6.7 to see the difference.

You can create before/after looks by selecting all layers except the background and creating a new composite layer by pressing Ctrl/⌘ + Alt/Option + E. Hide all layers by clicking the Indicate Layer Visibility icon (the eye icon) on each layer except the background to see the before image. Show the composite layer to show the after image. Toggle the Composite layer eye icon to toggle the before/after looks.

FIGURE 6.6 Original unedited image.

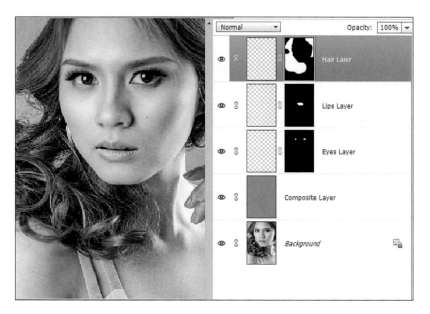

FIGURE 6.7 High Pass filter applied differently to selected regions of the photo.

Using Photoshop Elements Sharpening Tools

You have a few tools in the Photo Editor for sharpening images. You can use the Enhance > Adjust Sharpness menu command and open the Adjust Sharpness dialog box, and you can use the Sharpen tool in the Tools panel.

Using the Menu Options

Using the same image as shown in Figure 6.6, I can create multiple layers and create Layer Masks for eyes, brows, lips, and hair. I can apply a sharpening effect to the photo and then add sharpening to the contents of each layer mask.

To sharpen the photo, choose Enhance > Adjust Sharpness. The Adjust Sharpness dialog box opens, as shown in Figure 6.8. In the Adjust Sharpness dialog box, you can apply sharpening to the overall photo, and you can target highlights and shadows with different amounts of sharpening.

The slider for Amount sets the amount of sharpening. The Radius determines the number of pixels surrounding edge pixels affected by the sharpening. As you increase the Radius, the sharpening becomes more obvious. You can easily oversharpen an image by pushing the Radius slider too far right. From the drop-down list, you can choose from Gaussian Blur, Lens Blur, and Motion Blur. Try each option and choose the one that works best for your image.

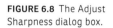

FIGURE 6.8 The Adjust Sharpness dialog box.

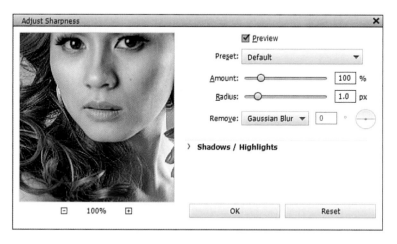

In Figure 6.9, you can see the layers and Layer Masks used to apply sharpening to the same areas as were applied in Figure 6.7. This time, I used the Adjust Sharpness menu command.

FIGURE 6.9 Layers and Layer Masks set up to apply sharpness to different areas of the image.

When we compare the results of sharpening with the High Pass filter and sharpening with the Adjust Sharpness options, the High Pass filter adjustments appear to be a little better, although the difference is slightly noticeable. The Adjust Sharpness controls do a good job sharpening an image.

In Figure 6.11, you can see the sharpness adjustments using the High Pass filter (left) and the Adjust Sharpness controls (middle).

Using Unsharp Mask

Unsharp Mask is another menu command in the Enhance menu. Unsharp Mask is a traditional technique used by printers in print shops. It looks for pixels that differ in surrounding areas (determined by the Threshold adjustment) and increases contrast according to the Amount adjustment. When you choose Enhance > Unsharp Mask, the Unsharp Mask dialog box opens, as shown in Figure 6.10.

The Amount slider adjusts the amount of sharpness applied to an image. The Radius determines the number of pixels surrounding edge pixels affected by the sharpening. The Threshold looks for differences in pixels surrounding the area. As you move the Threshold slider to the right, the area is increased, and it results in less sharpening.

In Figure 6.11, you can see the three methods used for sharpening an image. Using any one of the three creates some sharpening, and there's little difference in the results. Using the High Pass filter has a tiny bit of an edge over the other two methods.

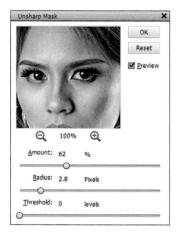

FIGURE 6.10 The Unsharp Mask filter.

FIGURE 6.11 Three sharpening methods applied to the same image: High Pass filter (left), Adjust Sharpness controls (middle), and Unsharp Mask filter (right).

Using Sharpening Tools

The Tools panel includes a Sharpen tool. You use this tool like a Brush tool. You click and drag around the area you want to sharpen. The tool is handy when you want to sharpen delicate areas like eyebrows and eye lashes. When using the tool, though, you should create a new layer and apply the edits to that new layer.

In the Tool options panel, select Sample All Layers. Select the new layer (the Sharpen Layer in Figure 6.12) and move the Sharpen tool to the document window. Drag through the area you want to sharpen. You can reduce opacity in the Layers panel by moving the Opacity slider or typing a value in the Opacity text box.

Be careful when using the Sharpen tool. It's easy to sharpen too much and can result in obvious halos in the image. If you can't reduce opacity enough to eliminate halos, select the top layer, press Ctrl/⌘ + A to Select All, and press Delete. The sharpening effects are deleted, and you can start over.

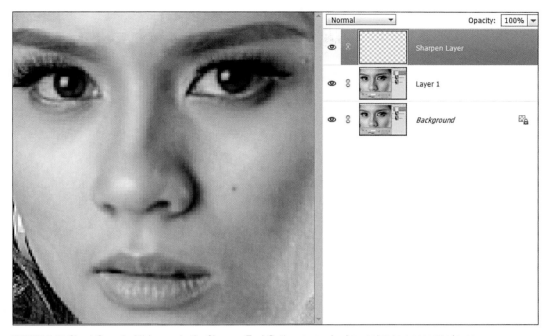

FIGURE 6.12 Check Sample All Layers in the Sharpen Tool Options to apply sharpening to a separate layer.

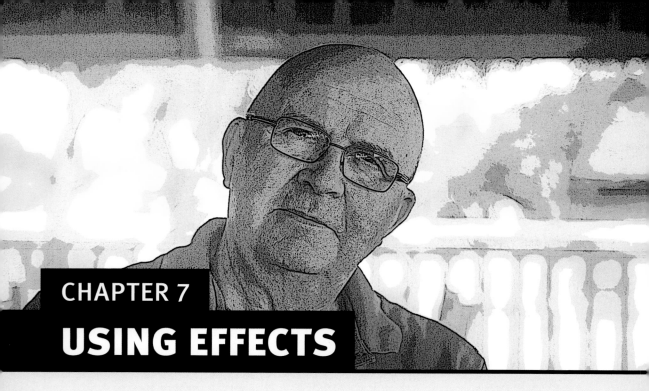

CHAPTER 7
USING EFFECTS

Chapter Goals

This chapter describes methods for having some fun and adding some artistic effects to your photos. This chapter explores using many different effects Elements offers. In this chapter, you find out how to do the following:

- Work with the Effects panel and explore many different effects that you can add to your photos
- Add picture frame effects
- Create vignettes
- Apply color effects
- Add special effects for artistic expression
- Add effects using Elements+

In Photoshop Elements, you have a variety of effects you can apply to images using the Styles panel. Some effects, like drop shadows, bevels, and flows, are available in the Styles panel.

In Photoshop, you can apply certain effects similar to those in Elements, and you also have some blending options in a Layer Styles panel. Unfortunately, Elements doesn't include any blending options in a Layer Styles panel. You can, however, use Elements+ and gain some limited use of blending options similar to what is available to Photoshop users.

You can create other effects by using a wide assortment of Guided Edits, and you can also apply different effects using tools and menus. The number of effects that you can create in Photoshop Elements are limitless. I can't cover every effect you can apply to your photos in this book, but I can offer an assortment of edits to get you started in looking at some useful ways to present your photos.

In this chapter, you'll see ways of using the Elements Styles and Effects, find out how to create a variety of different effects, and later examine some of the blending options you have available when using the Elements+ plugin.

Working with Effects

The Effects (*fx*) panel has a number of effects that you can apply to photos with some simple clicks and others that you can use in a series of more complicated adjustments. The effects panel has 41 effects adjustments in eight groups. If you install Elements+, another group is installed in the Effects panel with many additional effects and editing options. In this section, I just scratch the surface of the many ways you can use effects in Photoshop Elements.

Creating a Painterly Image

There are a number of Guided Edits in Elements that provide step-by-step instructions to apply different effects to a photo. A painterly effect is one of the Guided Edits you can use, but the results are not as impressive as when you add a painterly effect manually. In Figure 7.1, you can see the results of using the painterly Guided Edit.

When you use Guided Edits, you make some choices in the steps to customize some things in a painterly effect. However, in this example, I'm bypassing the Guided Edits and creating a painterly effect from scratch.

To give you an idea of where I'm headed with applying a painterly effect in this example, take a look at Figure 7.2. On the left is the original image, and on the right is the same image with a painterly effect applied to it. The effect is quite different from Figure 7.1.

FIGURE 7.1 A painterly effect created in the Guided Edits panel.

FIGURE 7.2 A painterly effect (right) applied to the original photo (left).

To create a painterly image similar to the image on the right in Figure 7.2, follow these steps:

1. Open a photo in the Photo Editor. Use a photo with good contrast that's been adjusted for proper exposure, brightness, and contrast. For this example, I used the photo shown in Figure 7.2 on the left.

2. Press Ctrl/⌘ + J to create a copy of the Background layer.

3. Name the Layer Smart Blur.

4. On the Smart Blur layer, choose Filter > Blur > Smart Blur. In the Smart Blur dialog box, first choose one of the quality options (Low, Medium, or High). The choice you make depends on the image you use. Look for outlines defined in white with the majority of the image in black.

   Choose Edge Only and then adjust the Radius and Threshold sliders. In Figure 7.3, you can see the adjustments I made in the Smart Blur filter dialog box.

5. Click OK in the Smart Blur filter dialog box.

6. Press Ctrl/⌘ + I to invert the image.

7. Duplicate the layer and keep the name as Smart Blur copy. In Figure 7.4, you can see the Layers panel displaying the edits thus far.

8. Select the Smart layer (above the Background) layer and change the blend mode to Dissolve.

9. Add a layer mask to the Smart layer. Create a layer mask by clicking the Add Layer Mask button in the Layers panel.

10. Select the Brush tool and open the Tool Options panel (see Figure 7.5). Select a soft-edge brush and move the size slider to somewhere between 200 and 400.

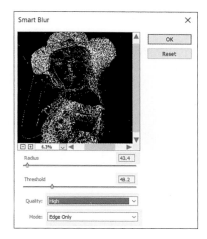

FIGURE 7.3 Adjustments in the Smart Blur filter dialog box.

FIGURE 7.4 The layers panel with the Smart Blur and Smart Blur copy layers.

FIGURE 7.5 Brush settings in the Tools panel.

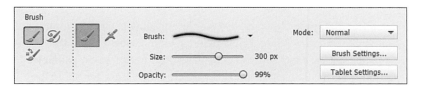

11. Set the default colors to black foreground/white background by pressing the D key on your keyboard.

12. Select the Smart Blur copy layer (at the top of the layer stack) and click the eye icon to hide the layer. We hide the top layer so we can see painting in the Layer Mask and where it will hide part of the image.

13. Click the Layer Mask to select it and then use the Brush tool to paint black on the Layer Mask. Paint random strokes and leave some white areas. In Figure 7.6, you can see the brush strokes I applied to the Layer Mask and the vibe area in the image in the Document window.

FIGURE 7.6 Paint the Layer Mask with random brush strokes.

14. Unhide the top layer by clicking the eye icon on the Smart Blur copy layer.

15. Add a Levels adjustment layer by selecting the Background and clicking Levels from the Create New Fill or Adjustment Layer drop-down list in the Layers panel. Make some levels adjustments for brightness values. Bring up the highlights and take down the shadows. The exact settings you use depends on your image. Make the adjustments that add a little more punch to the image.

16. Add a Hue/Saturation adjustment layer by choosing Hue/Saturation from the Create New Fill or Adjustment Layer drop-down list in the Layers panel. Again, exact settings depend on your image. In my example, I bumped up the Saturation a little by moving the Saturation slider to the left, and I increased the lightness slightly. At this point, your Layers panel should look like Figure 7.7. The Hue/Saturation dialog box is also shown in Figure 7.7.

17. Duplicate the background by selecting it and pressing Ctrl/⌘ + J.

18. Move the Background copy above the Hue/Saturation layer by clicking the new background copy and drag it up in the Layers panel so that it's above the Hue/Saturation layer.

19. Name the layer Gaussian Blur. This helps identify the adjustments made to the layers.

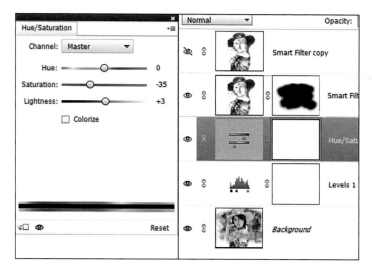

FIGURE 7.7 Add a Hue/Saturation adjustment layer.

20. Choose Filter > Blur > Gaussian Blur. Set the radius to a high value to add quite a bit of blur. In my example, I set the Radius adjustment to 36.0. The Gaussian Blur dialog box is shown in Figure 7.8.

21. Select the Gaussian Blur layer and select Soft Light in the Blend Mode drop-down list.

22. Select the Background and press Ctrl/⌘ + J to duplicate it.

23. Move the Background copy to the top of the layer stack.

24. Choose Linear Light from the Blend Modes drop-down list in the Layers panel. At this point, your layers pane should look like Figure 7.8.

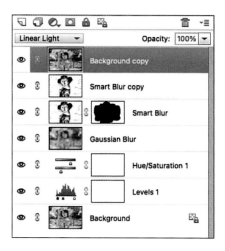

FIGURE 7.8 Layers panel showing all layers up to this point.

25. Select all layers and press Ctrl/⌘ + Alt/Option + Shift + E to create a composite layer. Leave the blending mode to Normal. The composite layer should be at the top of the layer stack.

26. As a final edit, add a little bit of texture to the image with a Texturizer filter. Click the composite layer and choose Filter > Texture > Texturizer. In the Texturizer dialog box, press Ctrl/⌘ + 1. This zooms the view to 100%. From the Texture drop-down list, you have several choices. You can use artistic freedom here and choose Brick, Burlap, Canvas, or Sandstone for the texture. In this example, I use Sandstone to add a subtle texture, as shown in Figure 7.9. Move the Scaling and Relief sliders to create the look you desire.

Turn back to Figure 7.2 and look at the original (on the left) and compare it to the final image (on the right) with the painterly effect added to it.

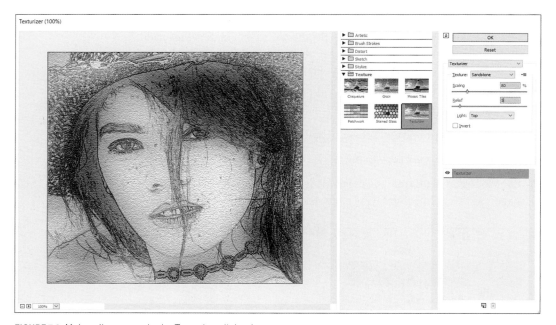

FIGURE 7.9 Make adjustments in the Texturizer dialog box.

Creating a Watercolor Effect

Like the painterly effect, the watercolor effect is another task you have with a Guided Edit. The Guided Edit walks you through steps to produce an effect similar to what you see in Figure 7.10.

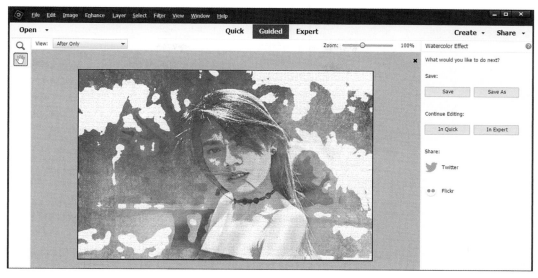

FIGURE 7.10 Watercolor effect made in the Guided Edits panel.

You can also create a watercolor effect using your own adjustments to create something a little different than what you see in Figure 7.10.

In Figure 7.11, you see an original image on the left and a watercolor effect created manually in the Photo Editor on the right.

FIGURE 7.11 Original photo (left) and after producing a watercolor effect (right).

To produce a similar watercolor effect on one of your photos, follow these steps:

1. Open a photo in the Photo Editor. Use a photo that is corrected for brightness and contrast.

2. Create two copies of the Background layer by pressing Ctrl/⌘ + J twice.

3. Change the name of the top layer to Smart Blur Edge.

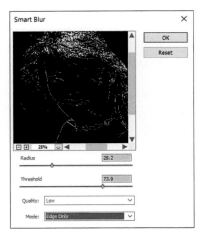

FIGURE 7.12 Settings in the Smart Blur dialog box.

FIGURE 7.13 Settings for the second Smart Blur filter.

4. Select the top layer and choose Filter > Blur > Smart Blur. In the Smart Blur dialog box, produce an effect similar to what you did earlier to achieve the effect shown in Figure 7.3. Set the Quality to Low and choose Edge Only for the mode. Depending on your image resolution, you might need to move the Radius and Threshold sliders to produce an outline in white. Be careful to not move the sliders to produce too much white. In my example, I used the values you can see in Figure 7.12.

5. Select the layer and press Ctrl/⌘ + I to invert it.

6. Set the blending mode to one of the Darken modes. In my example. I used Linear Burn. Try different modes to see which one works best for you.

7. Name the first layer (the one above the Background copy) **Smart Blur Normal**. At this point, you should have a Background, a layer named Smart Blur Normal, and the top layer named Smart Blur Edge.

8. Select the Smart Blur Normal layer and choose Filter > Blur > Smart Blur. Choose High for Quality and set the Mode to Normal. Leave the Radius and Threshold settings alone. These settings are the same as when you set up the first Smart Blur. See Figure 7.13.

9. Duplicate the Smart Blur Normal layer. At this point, you should have three layers above the background. Name this new layer Smart Blur Paint.

10. Invert the Smart Blur Normal layer by pressing Ctrl/⌘ + I.

11. Open the Blend Mode drop-down list in the Layers panel and choose Color Dodge.

12. Paint random strokes on the layer. Keep the layer selected and use the Brush tool to paint over the layer, making random strokes like you did when creating the painterly image. Use the default foreground color and any brush tip that you like.

13. You may want to add one Levels Adjustment layer above the Smart Blur Paint layer and another above the Smart Blur Normal layer and adjust the Brightness/Contrast to your liking. At this point, the Layers panel should look like Figure 7.14.

14. Select all layers above the background and press Ctrl/⌘ + Alt/Option + Shift + E to create a composite layer and name it Composite Texture.

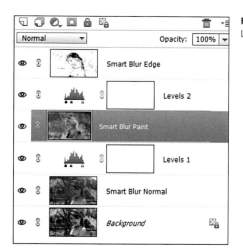

FIGURE 7.14 Layers panel showing the layer adjustments.

15. Select the Composite Texture layer and choose Filter > Texture > Texturizer. Press Ctrl/⌘ + 1 to zoom to 100%. Choose a texture from the Texture drop-down list. In my example, I chose Canvas. Make other adjustments as you see fit. In my example, I set the Scaling to 70% and the Relief to 6, as shown in Figure 7.15.

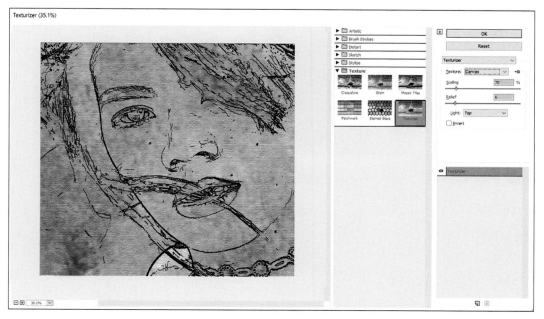

FIGURE 7.15 Make adjustments in the Texturizer dialog box.

16. Click OK, and the final image for my example looks like the right side of Figure 7.11.

Creating an Oil Painting Effect

In Photoshop, you can create an oil painting effect with the Filter > Stylize > Oil Paint filter, but Photoshop Elements doesn't have much available to you for this effect.

In Elements, open the Effects panel and choose Painting from the drop-down list. In the Painting pane, you have three choices: Fluorescent Chalk, Oil Painting, and Watercolor Painting.

When you apply the Oil Painting effect on a photo, you get a simulated oil painting effect; however, the effect doesn't include much in the way of brush strokes. In Figure 7.16, you can see an image where I applied the Oil Painting effect from the Effects panel.

FIGURE 7.16 Oil Painting effect applied from the Oil Paint option in the Effects panel.

An alternative to using the Oil Painting effect is to apply a texture in the Texturizer dialog box. Unfortunately, Elements doesn't provide any brush strokes textures. However, you can add custom textures to the Texturizer.

You can search the Internet and look for free texture downloads to load in the Texturizer filter. Most images you download are JPEG images. After you've downloaded a texture, convert it to black and white using Enhance > Convert to Black and White. Save the file as a .psd file. You can save the file anywhere on your hard drive. If you use many custom textures, you may want to keep a folder of textures inside your Photoshop Elements folder and a duplicate folder on your hard drive where you keep other assets.

Choose Filter > Texture > Texturizer to open the Texturizer dialog box. On the right side of the Texturizer adjacent to the drop-down list, you see two tiny icons: a down-pointing arrow and menu icon. Together they act as a button (see Figure 7.17). Click the button to open a drop-down list, and the only available menu command is Load Texture. Click it to launch an Open dialog box. Navigate to a folder where you downloaded textures and click Load to load one of your saved textures.

After you've loaded a texture, you can adjust the Scaling and Relief items by moving the sliders. You can see a dynamic preview of the texture changing as you move the slider back and forth. Choose the settings that work best for you and click OK.

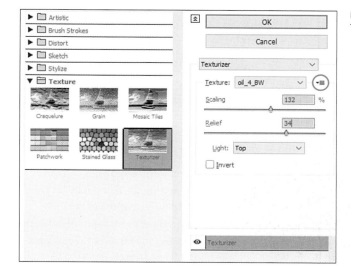

FIGURE 7.17 Open the menu and choose Load Texturizer.

The texture is applied to your photo. You can add Adjustment Layers for Levels and Hue/Saturation to fine tune the effect. Once again, the final result isn't like what you can accomplish in Photoshop, but you can create a slight oil painting effect a bit better than the Oil Painting effect offered in the Guided Edits panel. The result of my edits is shown in Figure 7.18.

FIGURE 7.18 Oil painting effect from a custom texture.

Adding Depth of Field to Photos

Depth of field is best created in a camera while you're taking pictures. You should think about the kind of image you want as you take photos.

Depth of field is merely a measure of what's in focus and what's out of focus. Using your camera, you control depth of field by setting the f-stop. The larger the number, the greater the depth of field, which results in more of the area being in focus. For example, an f-stop of f/2.8 is a very narrow depth of field and results in the subject you focus on being in focus and the foreground and background being out of focus. When you use higher f-stops—such as f/11, f/16, and f/22—the foreground, midground, and background are all in focus.

Having only your subject in focus results in the viewer's attention being devoted to the subject. As the background is increasingly out of focus, distracting elements are less obvious and won't take the viewer's attention away from what is important in the photo.

Sometimes you may have photos that were taken at higher f-stops where you don't want foregrounds/backgrounds in focus. If this is the case, you need to use Elements to help you remove some focus from the foreground and background.

In Figure 7.19, I have a photo that has some nice depth of field. The background is blurred, and the foreground is a little out of focus. It looks like I can improve a little on this image. The subject is soft and needs some sharpening. I could also add a little more blur to the foreground and a slight bit of blur to the background.

FIGURE 7.19 Original image that needs some sharpening and little more depth-of-field blurring.

In Figure 7.19, I need three separate layer masks: one layer mask for the background, one for the foreground, and another for the subject. I'll blur the background slightly, add more blur to the foreground, and sharpen the subject.

Use the following steps to create more depth of field in a photo:

1. Set the Feather amount to 10 to 20 pixels and then use the Quick Selection tool to create a selection of items near the subject to take them slightly out of focus. The amount depends on the resolution of your photo. For 150ppi, set the Feather adjustment to 10 pixels. For 300 ppi, set the adjustment to 20 pixels. You just want a little feathering on the selection. Name the layer Weak Blur.

2. Create another selection and Layer Mask for the background. This area will receive the strongest blur. Therefore, name this layer Strong Blur.

3. Create a selection for the subject and add a Layer Mask. Name this layer Subject. The Layers panel at this point should look like Figure 7.20.

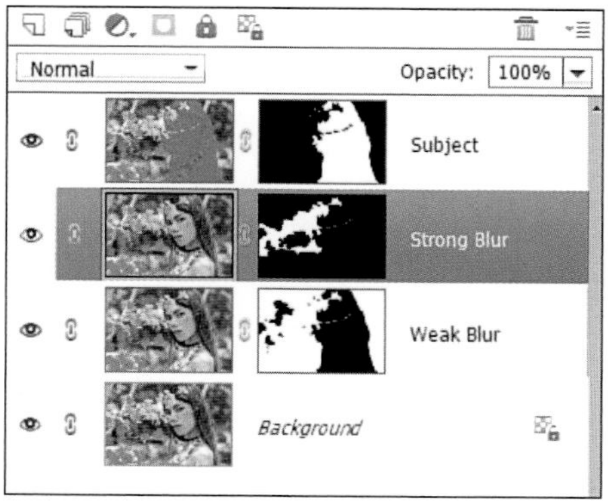

4. Select the Weak Blur layer, press Ctrl/⌘, and click to create a selection from the Layer Mask. This selection should be the area close to the subject.

FIGURE 7.20 Layers and Layer Masks set up to blur foreground/background.

5. Choose Filter > Blur >Gaussian Blur. In the Gaussian Blur dialog box, set the blur amount by moving the Radius slider. This setting should be a lower amount than the Strong Blur layer. In my example, I set the blur amount to 15 pixels. Click OK to return to the document window.

6. Select the Strong Blur layer and load the selection from the mask by pressing Ctrl/⌘ and clicking. Choose Filter > Blur > Gaussian Blur to open the Gaussian Blur dialog box. Set the Radius to a stronger blur than the setting used for the Weak Blur layer. In my example, I set 30 pixels for the blur amount and clicked OK.

7. Select the subject layer. This is the area you want to keep in focus. The photo needs some sharpening, so with the layer selected, choose Filter > Other > High Pass. Move the radius slider to where you can see a definitive outline in the image. Click the Minus Zoom tool to zoom out if needed. Move the cursor inside the preview area and click and drag to move the image around within the preview. Click OK when the adjustment looks right.

8. Change blend mode. Select the Subject layer and choose Overlay for the blend mode in the Layers panel. The final image in my example appears in Figure 7.21. Notice how the subject in the image stands out a little more than the raw image shown in Figure 7.20.

FIGURE 7.21 Final image after blurring foreground/background and sharpening the subject.

Creating Picture Edges Effects

There are a number of effects that you can use for creating picture frames, adding vignettes to photos, and creating some grunge on the edges of photos. Whether you display photos on social media or print pictures, adding some of these effects can provide some interesting alternatives to a standard photo with no special edges.

Working with Picture Frame Effects

You can download various borders and picture frames from the Internet. There are many that require purchase, but you can find some free options if you spend some time poking around. Many sites are filled with ads and require you to sign up by supplying contact information before downloading. However, there are some sites that let you download without having to wade through all the nonsense. It just takes a little time. Search for "grunge borders," which are a nice artistic alternative to picture frames.

To create a picture frame, follow these steps:

1. Open a photo in the Photo Editor.

2. Resize your photo by choosing Image > Resize > Image Size. In the Image size dialog box, set the resolution to **150**. If the Width amount at the top of the dialog box is higher than 2000 pixels, check the Resample check box at the bottom of the dialog box and type **2000** for the width or height. Start with these values to size down the image if your image size is very large. Click OK when finished with these adjustments.

3. Press D on your keyboard to set the default black foreground and white background colors.

4. Choose Image > Resize > Canvas Size. Choose Percent for the unit of measure for the Width and Height. Type **115** in both text boxes, as shown in Figure 7.22. This adds a border of 15% of the image size around the photo. If you want more or less border, increase or decrease the size of the border.

> **TIP:** You can also add more canvas area by using the Crop tool. Select the Crop tool in the Tools panel, and in the Tool Options panel, choose No Restriction from the drop-down menu. Drag open a crop rectangle. Move the sides outside the image area to extend the canvas. Shape the crop zone as desired, and click the green check mark.

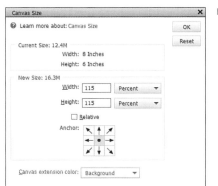

FIGURE 7.22 Size up the canvas size to 115%.

5. Search the Internet for free downloads for borders and frames. Download an image from one of the sites offering free downloads. You can find an assortment of free downloads at https://www.vecteezy.com/free-vector/free-download-vector-borders-and-frames.

6. Open your downloaded border file. Drag the border onto the open image file. The border image comes in as a layer.

7. If your border is already transparent, you don't need to create a layer mask. If the border doesn't have transparency, create a selection of the border and add a layer mask. This should be easy to do. The border is probably transparent or on a white background. If it's white, use the Magic Wand tool. Set the tolerance to **10** and uncheck Contiguous in the Tool Options panel. Click and press Ctrl/⌘ + Shift _ I to inverse the selection. Click the Add Layer Mask button in the Layers panel.

8. You can distort the border by disproportionally sizing. Press Ctrl/⌘ + T to transform the border. Drag any of the handles to resize and fit the border within the image.

9. Select the photo layer below the border layer. Choose the Eraser tool and select a dry or rough bristle brush. Click and drag around the edges of the photo to roughen up the edges. Figure 7.23 shows my example to this point.

FIGURE 7.23 Erase the edges to roughen up the sides and size the border to fit around the image.

10. To add contrast to the border, create a Levels adjustment layer. In the New Layer dialog box, check Use Previous Layer to Create Clipping Mask. This applies the Levels adjustments to only the border and not the photo.

11. Select the Marquee Rectangle tool and create a rectangular selection at the middle of the border. Sample a color in the photo that contrasts with the edges around the photo. With the selection active, open the Adjustment Layer menu and choose solid color. The sampled color is the fill inside the selection.

12. Click the Link icon between the layer and the mask for the border if you have a layer mask on that layer. Select the mask and press Ctrl/⌘ + T to Transform the mask. Rotate the mask about 10 to 15 degrees clockwise.

13. Click the icon between the Solid Fill and the mask to unlink them.

14. Select the mask and press Ctrl/⌘ + T. Rotate the mask in the opposite direction the same amount as the first rotation—or whatever looks good to you.

15. Select the layers and press Ctrl/⌘ + Alt/Option + E to create a composite layer. The Layers panel at this point should look like Figure 7.24.

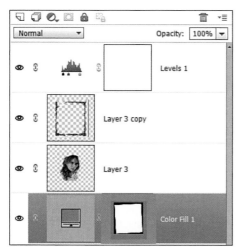

FIGURE 7.24 The Layers panel showing the steps thus far.

Figure 7.25 shows the final image.

FIGURE 7.25 Final image with a grunge border and solid fill layer.

Creating Vignettes

A vignette helps bring the viewer's attention toward the center of a photo by darkening the edges. A simple vignette is easy to create:

1. Open an image and duplicate the Background by pressing Ctrl/⌘ + J.

2. Add a new layer by clicking the Add a New Layer icon in the Layers panel. You should have the Background layer, a duplicate of the background, and an empty layer in the Layers panel.

3. Select the Rectangle Marquee tool. In the Marquee Tool Options panel, move the Feather slider right to somewhere between 50 and 75 pixels. The amount depends on your image resolution. You may need to raise the feather amount or lower it.

4. Press D on your keyboard to select the default black foreground and white background colors.

5. Draw a rectangle about ½ inch around the photo and inverse the selection by pressing Ctrl/⌘ + Shift + I.

6. Fill the outside selection with black by pressing Alt + Backspace/Delete. Your Layers panel should look something like Figure 7.26. Apply a Multiply blend mode. Duplicate the layer if you want a darker border.

7. Reduce the opacity if the border is too dark. I created a much darker image to show the result in this printed book.

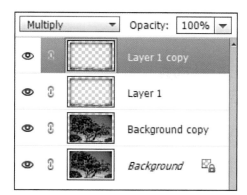

FIGURE 7.26 Layers panel showing the feathered border.

8. If the feathering is not enough or too much, delete the border layer and start again by changing the feather amount.

Figure 7.27 shows the before (left) and after (right) views. Notice that the vignette is strong in this example to show the effects clearly.

For more on creating grunge borders, see Chapter 12.

FIGURE 7.27 Before (left) and after (right) adding a vignette to the photo.

Creating Custom Borders

You can create custom borders using paper and poster paint and then scan the paintings. You typically need to brighten up the blacks if you use this method. Another way to create a custom border is to do it in the Photo Editor.

To create a custom border in the Photo Editor, follow these steps:

1. Create a new document by choosing File > New > Blank File. Use either the Elements defaults or set the size and resolution to your liking. The Elements default size is 6x4 inches at 300 ppi. Set the orientation to the width and height that matches your photo—either portrait or landscape.

2. Click the Brush tool and open the Brush tip choices drop-down menu. Choose a brush with a grunge edge, like the Spatter brush number 27 shown in Figure 7.28.

FIGURE 7.28 Choose a grunge edge brush tip.

3. Click Brush Settings and move the brush inside the Document Window. Notice the rotation on the brush tip. If it's not perpendicular to the canvas, you may want to rotate it. If you need to adjust the angle of the brush tip, drag the circle icon in the Brush Settings dialog box to the degree you want the tip. You can move the tip to the Document Window and check the rotation. If you need to adjust the angle more, rotate the angle in the Brush Settings. Work back and forth between viewing the brush tip in the Document Window and adjusting the angle. In my example, I rotated the brush tip −45°, as shown in Figure 7.29.

FIGURE 7.29 Changing the rotation of the brush tip in the Brush Settings.

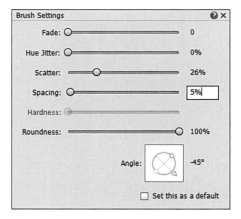

4. Leave about .5 to 1 inch white around the edges without painting. After you complete painting the canvas, drag the layer with the brush strokes to a photo. The document comes in as a layer at the top of the layer stack, as shown in Figure 7.30.

FIGURE 7.30 Drag the painted image to a photo.

5. Convert the background to a layer and drag it to the top of the layer stack. If you have a background on the photo, create a selection of the subject and add a Layer Mask. The final image with a custom border is shown in Figure 7.31.

FIGURE 7.31 Final image with a custom border.

If you want to change the color of the area outside the subject, press Ctrl/⌘ and click on the mask to create a selection. Select the subject layer and inverse the selection so all but the white border is selected. Fill the selection with a color of your choice. In Figure 7.32, I changed the color in the example image.

FIGURE 7.32 A different color painting.

Using Color Effects

There are many different ways to add color to black-and-white photos. In this section, I describe just a few that Elements offers.

Creating Sepia Effects

Sepia tints work well with vintage photos. You can apply a sepia tint in many different ways in the Photo Editor. First, be certain to convert all color images to grayscale using Enhance > Convert to Black and White or add a Hue/Saturation adjustment layer and move the saturation slider far left to −100. The mode should remain as an RGB Color mode.

Here are but a few ways you can add a sepia tint to a black-and-white photo:

- **Effects panel:** Open the Effects panel and choose Monotone Color from the drop-down menu. The Monotone Color panel offers six color tints you can apply to a photo. Among those is the Tint Sepia. Click Tint Sepia and a sepia tone is added to the photo.

- **Actions panel:** You have two actions in the Actions panel: Sepia Toning and Sepia Toning with Grain. The latter adds some grain to the photo along with the sepia effect.

- **Color Fill adjustment layer:** Actually, you can use an Adjustment Layer to tint a photo any color. From the Adjustment Layer menu in the Layers panel, choose Color Fill. Add a sepia toning effect from the Color Picker. For starters, try using R=160, G=140, and B=95 color values in the Color Picker. These values get you in the range of a sepia tone.

- **Levels adjustment layer:** Add a Levels adjustment layer. In the Levels dialog box, open the Channel drop-down list. Choose the Red channel. Click the midtone triangle and type **1.41**. Open the Channel list again and choose the Green channel. Add **1.12** to the midtone value. Select the Blue channel in the Channel list and set the midtone value to **.60**. You can vary the settings for stronger or weaker sepia effects. The higher the Red channel setting and the lower the Blue channel setting, the more sepia is added to the photo.

Each of these methods automatically creates a new layer in the Layers panel. You can further adjust the sepia effect by lowering the opacity.

In Figure 7.33, you can see a sample of all four methods for applying a sepia tone.

| Sepia Tint Monochrome Color Effects | Sepia Toning With Grain Action | Color Fill Adjustment Layer | Levels Adjustment Layer |

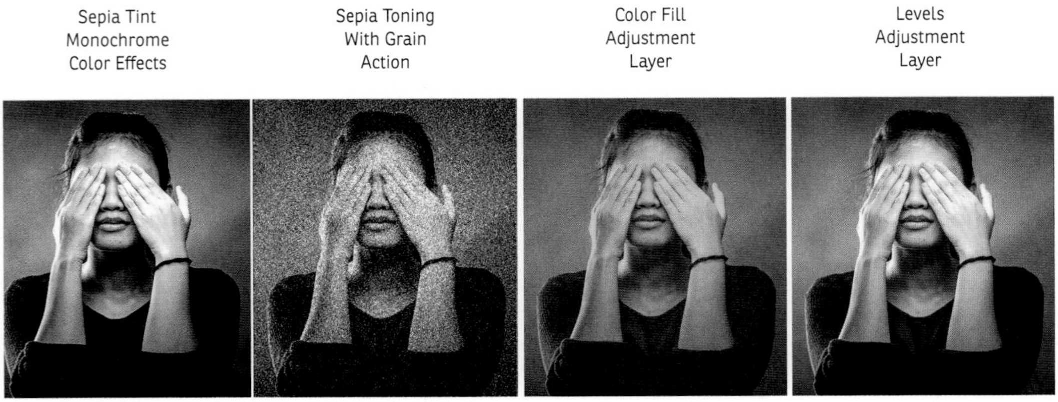

FIGURE 7.33 Four different methods for applying a sepia tone.

Colorizing Black-and-White Photos

If you want to colorize a black-and-white photo, you have several methods you can use. Additionally, if you have a color photo, you can retain some color in the photo while converting the rest of the photo to black and white. You can also create a selection in a black-and-white photo and convert the selection to color. Let's take a look at the methods available to you.

Using the Colorize Menu Command

Photoshop Elements 2020 introduced a new menu command that enables you to quickly convert a black-and-white photo to color. In Figure 7.34, you see a black-and-white photo. If I want to quickly colorize the photo, I might choose Enhance > Colorize Photo.

FIGURE 7.34 A black-and-white photo to be colorized.

When you choose Enhance > Colorize Photo, the Colorize Photo dialog box opens, as shown in Figure 7.35. You have four choices in the right panel for applying color to a photo. Click on one of the thumbnail images to change colors. The first two thumbnails use warmer tones, and the last two use cooler tones. At the bottom of the dialog box, you can toggle between before and after views. Click OK, and the color tones you choose from among the thumbnails are applied to the black-and-white photo.

FIGURE 7.35 Add color to a photo in the Colorize Photo dialog box.

Painting Colors

When you use the Colorize menu command, you have few choices for what colors appear in your photo. You're limited to four options from the thumbnail choices in the Colorize Photo dialog box.

If you choose to paint color on a photo, you have total freedom for what areas you want to paint in what colors. In Figure 7.36, I have a black-and-white photo I want to colorize. Here are the steps to colorize a photo by painting:

1. Create selections for the areas you want to color. In my photo, I want to add color to the hair, pants, plate, skin tones, and the background. Therefore, for this image, I needed to create five duplicate layers and add a layer mask for each layer. I name the layers Hair, Pants, Plate, Skin, and Background. For each layer, I chose the Soft Light blending mode.

2. Choose a color for the foreground color. Don't be concerned with what color you choose; you'll change the Hue later. You want to choose a color that shows contrast between the areas you paint and those areas outside each painted region. Double-click the Foreground color in the Tools panel and the color you want for the corresponding layer.

Photo courtesy of Courtney Jensen.

FIGURE 7.36 Black-and-white photo to paint with color.

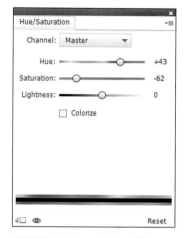

FIGURE 7.37 Move the Hue slider back and forth to view the color effects applied to the image.

3. Press Ctrl/⌘ and click on a layer mask to create a selection. Paint over the selected area.

4. With the layer set up for the Soft Light blend mode, create a Hue/Saturation adjustment layer. In the Hue/Saturation dialog box shown in Figure 7.37, move the Hue slider back and forth to tweak the color you want for the area you edit.

5. Move on to another layer; create a selection and paint again. Create a Hue/Saturation adjustment layer and choose a color value in the Hue slider. You can also increase or decrease saturation by moving the Saturation slider. If you don't get the color right using the Hue slider, try to check Colorize and see what kind of results you get. You can also reduce opacity in the Layers panel for a Hue/Saturation adjustment layer. In Figure 7.38, you can see the layers, Layer Masks, and Adjustment Layers I used in the example image.

6. Once again, be certain you set the blend mode to Soft Light for each layer. Set the adjustment layers blend mode to Normal. The results of my example are shown in Figure 7.39.

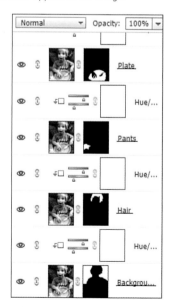

FIGURE 7.38 The Layers panel with Layer Masks and Hue/Saturation Adjustment Layers.

FIGURE 7.39 The final colorized photo.

Using Special Effects

This section offers information on some miscellaneous effects that you can create in Elements for some artistic expression.

Creating Pop Art Effects

Pop art began in the 1950s. It was used extensively on products such as soup cans, spray cans, and later on cartoons and portraits. Andy Warhol developed a style of pop art and made it very popular. Pop art generally has strong vibrant colors applied to black-and-white photos with little or no gray tones.

Photoshop Elements has a Guided Edit that walks you through steps to create pop art from your photos. The end result is four different applications of the effect with a single color applied to each copy of the photo. Figure 7.40 shows a photo where I applied the Pop Art Guided Edit.

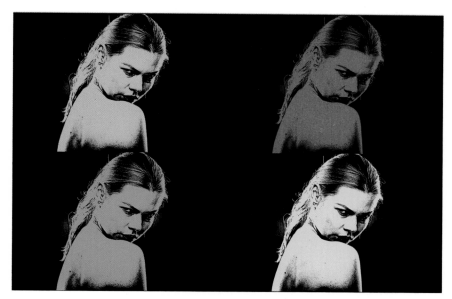

FIGURE 7.40 Pop Art effect applied with a Pop Art Guided Edit.

If you want to apply more than one color to an image to create a pop art effect, you can manually walk through some steps to create the effect:

1. To create a pop art effect, you can decide whether you want to use a complete black-and-white photo to begin with or one that simulates grayscale. By simulate, I mean you convert it to a bitmap. If you want to use a bitmap image, you may want to duplicate your document by opening a document and choosing File > Duplicate. Create selections you want in one document and add layer masks for each selection.

2. On the second document, choose Image > Mode > Bitmap. (If your file is RGB color, you need to first convert to grayscale and then convert the grayscale image to bitmap.) When you choose Image > Mode > Bitmap, the Bitmap dialog box opens, as shown in Figure 7.41. Choose 50% Threshold in the Method drop-down menu. Set the Output to the same resolution as your original image.

3. Convert back to RGB by choosing Image > Mode > Grayscale. Then return to the menu and select Image > Mode > RGB Color. Drag any layers with layer masks to the bitmap image.

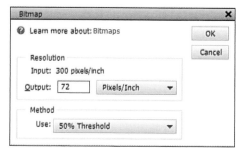

FIGURE 7.41 The Bitmap dialog box.

4. If working with a portrait image, you might want to color the skin tones first. If you want an average flesh tone color, open the Color Picker and choose R=235, G=206, and B=155. If you want more saturated skin color, choose R=168, G=86, and B=43.

5. Press Ctrl/⌘ and click on the layer mask. Create a new layer and fill the layer with the skin color. Choose Multiply for the blend mode. If the color interferes with other parts of the image, add a layer mask from the selection. At this point, my example image looks like Figure 7.42.

FIGURE 7.42 Fill the top layer with the skin tone color and choose Multiply for the blend mode.

In Figure 7.43, you can see an example of a bitmap image colored with a pop art effect. If you don't want to use a bitmap image, you can add an Adjustment Layer and choose Threshold. This option converts an image to 100% black and white. You can determine the amount of black or white by moving the Threshold slider left and right.

FIGURE 7.43 Pop art effect added to a bitmap conversion.

Posterizing Images

You can posterize a photo and then turn it into a pop art type image. To posterize a photo, open a photo in the Photo Editor and choose File > Save for Web. In the Save for Web dialog box shown in Figure 7.44, choose GIF for the mode and choose the number of colors you want to reduce in the photo from the Colors drop-down list on the right. In my example, I use four colors.

Choose Restrictive for the color table. The Restrictive setting uses a standard 256-color table used by Windows and Mac. Click Save after making your changes in the Save for Web dialog box.

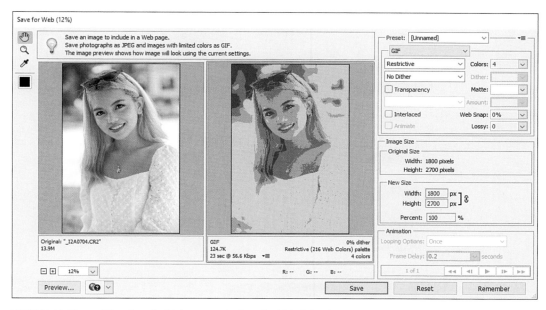

FIGURE 7.44 Choose File > Save for Web to open the Save for Web dialog box.

Open the GIF file you saved from the Save for Web dialog box. The image is posterized, and the colors were reduced to a total of four colors. The current color mode is Indexed color. You need to convert the photo to RGB Color if you want to print the file or apply other edits. Choose Image > Mode > RGB Color. In Figure 7.45, you can see the example used here after reducing colors to four.

If you want to create a pop art image, you can create multiple selections to isolate the four colors. You may need to work on selections using the lasso and Quick Mask tool. After working on the selections, apply colors to the different areas of the image. Figure 7.46 shows an example of colors applied to a posterized image.

FIGURE 7.45 GIF image with four colors.

FIGURE 7.46 Final image with a pop art effect.

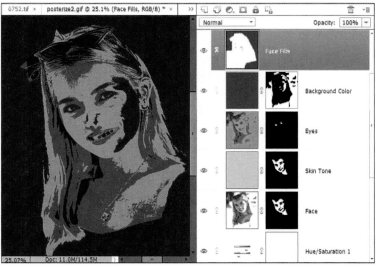

Adding Photo Effects with Elements+

There are many effects that you can create using Elements or Elements+. What I show you in this section are a few that you can use to create some artistic flair to your photos.

Elements+

Orange/teal color grading is a very popular effect for Photoshop users, and it's often used in video production and travel photos to help create depth and separate the subject from a background. You could create a Gradient Map and color grade the photo, but we have some other advantages when using the Elements+ plugin.

Open a file in the Photo Editor and click the Effects tab. Choose Elements+ from the Effects panel drop-down list. There are many different methods you can use to add an orange/teal color grading effect. Perhaps the easiest is to use the Camera Raw dialog box in Elements+.

Click the Camera icon in the Elements+ panel to open the Raw Corrections dialog box. The Elements+ Raw Editor has many more panels and settings than the Elements Camera Raw Editor. Click the Camera Calibration tab to open the Camera Calibration settings, as shown in Figure 7.47.

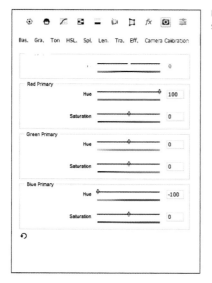

FIGURE 7.47 Elements+ Camera Calibration settings in the Camera Raw Editor.

Move the Red Primary Hue slider all the way to the right to 100. Move the Blue Primary Hue slider to the left to –100. That's it. Figure 7.48 shows the effect applied to a photo. When you use the Elements+ Camera Raw Editor, your edited file comes in as a new layer. To reduce the color a bit in the final image, I lowered the opacity on the orange/teal layer to 75%.

In the Elements+ Scripts panel is an item labeled Photo Effects. Open the drop-down list at the top of the Scripts panel and choose Photo Effects. The Photo Effects appear as shown in Figure 7.49. The Looks item has a number of submenu items. If you click Looks and then click the Play button (the right-pointing arrow), the Looks submenu items appear.

FIGURE 7.48 Photo with an orange/teal color grading effect.

FIGURE 7.49 The Elements+ Photo Effects panel.

A number of the effects of the Looks submenu items are shown in Figure 7.50. You can see the results by selecting the respective items in the Photo Effects panel. I used one example image to display results for applying the various submenu items. Obviously, other photos might serve some effects better. For example, the Looks>Clear Sky effect would be best used on a landscape photo.

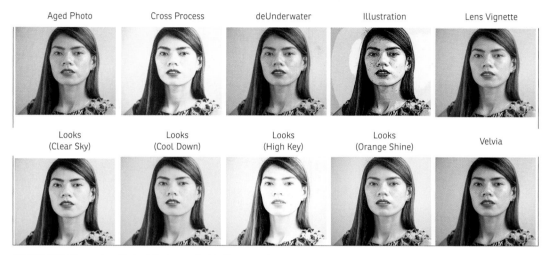

FIGURE 7.50 Elements+ Photo Effects applied to the same image.

PART IV

PHOTO COMPOSITING

There are some basic rules you need to follow when combining images from one photo with images from another. You must match horizon lines, address proper perspective, and match color and brightness between the photos. Chapter 8 covers everything you need to make your composited images appear realistic.

CHAPTER 8

COMPOSITING IMAGES

Chapter Goals

The ability to composite images is perhaps one of the techniques that best illustrates the power of a photo editor. Image compositing is taking two or more images, or taking different areas in a single image, and bringing them together in another photo for either realistic final results or artistic expression. For example, poor uncle Ezekiel couldn't make it last Christmas, but you want him in the family photo, so you take one photo of him and add it to your group photo.

There's much to consider when compositing images or applying edits to different parts of a single image: lighting, perspective, and the right composition to make it appear realistic. It's important to become familiar with certain rules to follow for compositing images so the final result looks realistic. You need to be certain subjects don't float on backgrounds, the luminosity and brightness closely resemble all components, that the colors match, and hue/saturation levels are similar.

This chapter covers the many considerations you need to make when compositing images. You find out how to do the following:

- Become familiar with essentials for compositing images
- Understand perspective
- Use Photomerge
- Match color
- Add shadows
- Add photos to high grass

Knowing Compositing Essentials

There are some important essentials you should know when compositing images. As you examine photos, you should carefully look at the images you want to bring together. In some cases, it may be next to impossible to bring images together. In other cases, you might want to choose one image over another because your steps to composite with one image might be easier than with another image.

Here are some of the most important essentials for compositing images:

- **Perspective:** Perhaps the single most important essential for image compositing is matching perspective between images. You need to become familiar with perspective rules and know something about horizon lines and vanishing points. When you have a mismatch in a composite image, the viewer immediately can see that the final image is a fake. People floating in air, proportion distortions, and unrealistic rotations are immediately viewed as fake by anyone seeing your final photos.

  Figure 8.1 shows an exaggerated example, but it gives you the idea of issues in perspective. The image on the left shows the subject floating in air and obviously not properly placed in this composite. The problem is the horizon line for the background is where the water meets the sky. In the subject image on the right of Figure 8.1, the horizon line is at the top of the subject's head, and the composite looks more realistic.

- **Resolution:** The resolutions of two or more images don't have to be exact, but they should not be extremely different, such as 72 ppi for one image and 300 ppi for the other. When compositing images, choose Image > Resize > Image Size. Set identical resolutions for both images. If you need some scaling, you can scale images on the composite layers. Be careful to not upsize a photo. Increasing resolution can severely degrade your images.

- **Brightness and contrast:** Adjust brightness and contrast after bringing one image into another. You can use a Levels Adjustment Layer and clip the Adjustment Layer to the layer where you adjust brightness and contrast. You should try to get a close match for brightness and contrast between images in the composite.

FIGURE 8.1 Horizon lines don't match in the left image; the right image is a closer match of horizon lines.

> **NOTE:** The amount of noise introduced in photos at higher ISO numbers varies greatly between different cameras. Older DSLR (Digital Single Reflex) cameras introduced a lot of noise at ISO levels of 1,600 to 3,200. Some of the new mirrorless cameras can have much less noise apparent in photos taken at ISO levels of 6,000 to 8,500. To know more about the tolerance of noise in photos compared to ISO settings, take a lot of test shots and know your camera before attempting to composite images. View your images at 100% and look through areas where you see a lot of solid color. That's usually an area where you can find noise if it exists.

- **Film grain and noise:** The thing to look out for when you try to composite two or more images is where there's a lot of disparity in the noise level between the images. If you shoot one image at 100 ISO and another at 12,000 ISO, you'll see quite a bit of disparity between the noise levels. In some cases, you might be able to use a background with high noise levels and blur the background to create a little more depth of field. But when using two or more foreground subjects and one has a high noise level whereas the other photo is absent of noise, the difference can be easily detected.

- **Scale:** Scale images appropriately for the perspective. Unfortunately, the Elements Photo Editor does not provide an option to create a Smart Object. If you have the Elements+ plug-in, you can create Smart Objects. A Smart Object enables you to edit a layer nondestructively.

- Nondestructive editing is particularly important when you scale a layer. While compositing, you find yourself moving, scaling, and observing results frequently. You try to finesse adjustments to try to get the best possible results that appear realistic.

  For more information on simplifying layers, see Chapter 4, "Working with Layers."

- If you scale a layer in the Photo Editor many times, the image will show obvious deterioration. One way to get around the problem is to use File > Place and place a photo on a layer in the Photo Editor. When using the Place command, the content comes in as a Smart Object. You can then scale and move the object many times without data loss. You need to convert the Smart Object to a simple layer using the Simplify Layer command in the Layer panel menu before you can apply other edits to the layer. However, use the File > Place command and address scaling as one of your first edits when compositing images in Photoshop Elements. For more on placing files in the Photo Editor, see the section later in this chapter "Placing Images."

- **Placement:** Scaling and matching perspective are very important when compositing images. Equally important is where you place an image in the composite. You have to continually be aware of the perspective and scaling as you move an image around the canvas.

- **Masking:** When you create selections and add Layer Masks, the selections and ultimately the masks should be precise. If you have images with shadows, it's often a good idea to include a part or all of a shadow in the mask. When you drop the image into a composite, you can edit the shadow to make a good fit.

- **Lighting:** When you bring two or more images together in a composite, carefully observe the lighting and, in particular, the direction of the lighting. You want to avoid having two images with lighting coming from different directions. In Figure 8.2, you can see the obvious difference in lighting between the foreground subject and the background. The background photo was taken in harsh sunlight. The foreground subject was taken with much softer light.

- **Color balance:** One of the last edits you make when compositing images is to balance color. Try to get the luminosity, saturation, and color balance matching in all images in the composite.

  For more on clipping groups, see Chapter 5, "Masking Photos."

FIGURE 8.2 Shadow on the subject is much less than the background elements.

- **Blending:** Be careful when using blending modes. The Darken group darkens all layers below the Darken layer. Likewise, the Lighten group lightens all layers below the Lighten layer. Areas that are darker make the background darker. When you want to use a blending mode to change values on one layer, be certain to create a clipping group. The same holds true for all Adjustment Layers.

Understanding Perspective

Perhaps the most important consideration to make when compositing images is to have your photos in proper perspective. You might be able to get away with oversights in brightness, lighting, color, saturation, and so on. However, when you're off with perspective, people squirm a little. They look at your photo, and although they might not be able to say what's wrong with it, they just know things aren't right.

There are many different types of perspective. You can have one-point angular perspective, two-point oblique perspective, and perspectives with three, four, five, and even six vanishing points. Once you get to three-point perspectives, things become a little confusing. For all intents and purposes, knowing all about one- and two-point perspectives is a good start and will handle most of your compositing needs.

Identifying the Horizon Line

One of the first things you want to do when editing photos is to look at the horizon line to determine if a photo needs some straightening with the Straighten tool. When you look for images you want to combine in a composite, first identify the horizon line. If the horizon line is high, it means the camera was on a low plane when the shot was taken. Conversely, if the horizon line is low, it means the camera was on a higher plane when the shot was taken.

Position of the horizon line has great impact on your ability to composite photos. If you need to position a subject very high or very low to maintain perspective, you may not be able to use photos you want to use in a composite.

It's very easy to find the horizon line when you see the sky meeting the land (or water) in a photo. In other photos, you may need to search for the vanishing point to find the horizon line (see Figure 8.3).

FIGURE 8.3 When you identify the vanishing point, it's easy to find the horizon line.

Visualizing Vanishing Points

Objects are shaped along a line in a photo toward the vanishing point. Where the opposing lines converge, you find the vanishing point (see Figure 8.4). At the vanishing point, you also find the horizon line.

FIGURE 8.4 A one-point vanishing point.

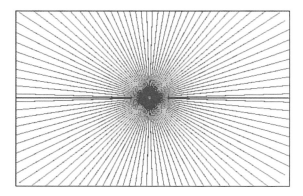

If you're standing in front of the horizon line and look ahead, a one-point vanishing point would be somewhere along the horizon line. If you look straight ahead at the vanishing point, you might see objects and buildings falling along lines similar to what you see in Figure 8.5.

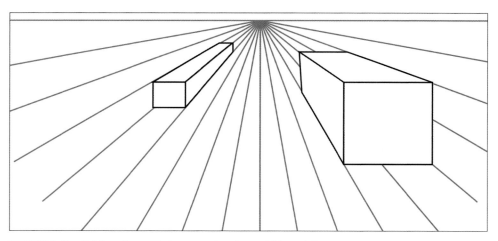

FIGURE 8.5 Parallel lines from objects converging at a vanishing point.

You can have more than one vanishing point in an image. A two-point vanishing point grid is shown in Figure 8.6. The parallel lines on two sides of an object converge at two different vanishing points.

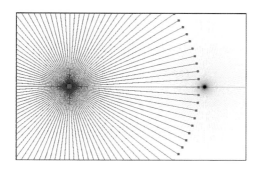

FIGURE 8.6 A two-point vanishing point grid.

Like one-point vanishing points, two-point vanishing points have parallel lines from two directions converging at the vanishing points. As shown in Figure 8.7, the objects have two sides with lines converging at two vanishing points.

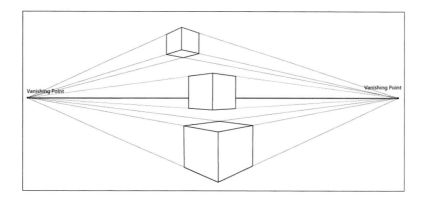

FIGURE 8.7 Objects with lines converging to form two vanishing points.

When compositing images, you want to know where the horizon line is in your images. When you have difficulty finding a horizon line, try to draw lines that converge to locate the horizon line.

Using Perspective When Compositing Images

When you have two images that you want to bring together on a single canvas, you start by creating a selection and Layer Mask on one or both images, depending on the content and what you want in your final photo. This example uses a Layer Mask on one image and brings it into the second image.

Finding the Horizon Lines

After you create a Layer Mask, find the horizon lines in both images. I'm starting with my photo with the mask. If you have a Layer Mask, press Shift and click on the mask to hide it. If the horizon line is easy to see, as shown in Figure 8.8, draw a line where you see the horizon line.

FIGURE 8.8 Locate the
horizon line in the first
image.

FIGURE 8.8 Locate the
horizon line in the first
image.

When you use the line tool, a new layer is automatically created. You can
later dismiss the layer when adding the photo to another photo. Save this
photo by choosing File > Save As and save the photo as a .psd file including
layers and a new name before moving on.

Open the second image. In my example, Figure 8.10 is the target image where
I'm creating the composite. Locate the horizon line in this image. In my example
photo, the horizon line is not as easy to detect. I draw two lines along the
base of the trees on either side of the photo. Where the lines converge is fairly
close to the horizon line, as you can see in Figure 8.9. Each line creates a new
layer. When you're sure the lines are as you want them, hide all other layers
and choose Merge Visible from the Layer panel menu. Only the line layers are
merged. Show all layers and save the file as a .psd including layers.

FIGURE 8.9 Locate the
horizon line by drawing
lines that converge at the
horizon.

Placing Images

Next, you want to create a Smart Object from the file you're importing into the final composite image.

Return to the first photo and hide all layers but the layer with the mask. Return to the composite target image and choose File > Place. When you place a photo in the Photo Editor, the file comes in as a Smart Object, which means you can scale the photo any number of times without destroying data.

As you can see in Figure 8.10, the placed photo comes in at the center of the image. Notice the horizon line for this photo is above the subject's head. Click the green check mark to commit the placement of the image. Notice that placing photos with Layer Masks retains the masked area. The placed image does not have a mask. The masked-out areas are deleted when you place the file.

FIGURE 8.10 A file placed in the target composite image.

Scaling Images

The next task is to scale and place the image in position. You can't use filters in the Filter menu or menu commands in the Enhance menu on a Smart Object. Therefore, you need to spend time deciding precisely what scaling you want for the photo. After scaling an image, you need to rasterize the layer by choosing Simplify Layer in the Layers panel menu.

In my example, I know the horizon line for the placed image is slightly above the subject's head. The horizon line is identified in the target image; therefore, I first need to move the placed image's horizon line so it matches with the target image's horizon line. When the placement looks good, press Ctrl/⌘

+ T to scale the image. Press Alt/Option + Shift and drag a corner handle to size the photo. When you use Alt/Option, the photo scales up or down while maintaining the placement on the horizon line. Pressing the Shift key constrains the sizing proportionately. In Figure 8.11, you can see the final scaling of the photo I placed in my target composite image. Compare Figure 8.10 with Figure 8.11. The subject looks more natural in respect to walking on the ground rather than floating above the ground.

> **TIP:** If you want to scale the placed photo, you can maintain the position on the horizon line as you scale up or down. First, press Alt/Option and click the tiny icon in the center of the image. This is an anchor point. Move the anchor point to where the horizon line intersects with the photo. Press the Alt/Option key and scale the image by dragging a corner handle. The image is scaled from the anchor point, thereby maintaining the same position on the horizon line.

FIGURE 8.11 Drag a handle to scale a photo while maintaining the placement.

At this point, you can hide the lines layer and begin to work on brightness/contrast and color matching. You also could look at creating a little shadow at the subject's feet and even a shadow for the figure, but I don't go into that detail here.

Using Photomerge Guided Edits

In the Guided Edits panel, there are six separate guided edits you can choose from for compositing images. That should give you an idea for how important photo compositing is.

The Guided Edits for Photomerge can provide for some quick photo compositing. In some cases, the final edits are very satisfactory. In other cases, you might want to also do some manual edits when merging photos. However, sometimes you may want to avoid a Guided Edit altogether and perform all steps manually. It all depends on the images you use and the results you want.

Using Photomerge Compose

The first Guided Edit is the Photomerge Compose item. This Guided Edit walks you through steps to bring objects from one photo into another photo. Open two files in the Photo Editor. In the Photo Bin, you should see only two photos.

Open the Guided Edit panel and click the Photomerge tab. Click the first item where you see Photomerge Compose. The first screen that opens asks you to drag and drop the file from which you intend to extract a subject or object.

Unfortunately, selections in the Guided Edit are very crude. You can muddle through the options for selecting and extracting a subject, but in the Photo Editor, you have so many more refined tools and methods for creating selections and extracting subjects. All in all, you're better off following manual methods than using this Guided Edit for compositing images.

Using Photomerge Exposure

You can use Photomerge Exposure in two ways. First, you can bring two totally different photos together in a composite and match exposures. The second option enables you to merge two or more identical photos. This feature is similar to merging HDR photos in Photoshop.

High Dynamic Range Photos

An HDR photo is a High Dynamic Range image. Many high-end cameras have an HDR setting that involves a rapid firing of three or more images shot at different f-stops. If your camera doesn't have an HDR option in the menu, you may have choices for bracketing photos.

HDR images are comprised of at least one photo for the highlights, one for the shadows, and one for the midtones. This essentially increases the dynamic range and enables you to capture highlight and shadow data that otherwise would not be captured in a single photo. If you have three photos taken at different f-stops, you need to merge the photos into a single image. Unfortunately, Photoshop Elements doesn't include a merge HDR option.

Merging Different Photos

Let's first take a look at merging two completely different photos. As a general rule, I wouldn't recommend using the Guided Edit for this kind of merge. You can match exposures much better manually than when using the Guided Edit.

You have an option for choosing Automatic or Manual. If you have two completely different photos, the Automatic setting lays one photo on top of the other and creates a double exposure look.

If you choose Manual, you can cut out one photo and merge it with the target document. In the Photomerge Exposure panel, click Manual at the top of the panel. Click the Pencil tool and draw around the object you want to add to another photo. You don't have to paint inside the object. Just draw an outline around it.

Painting the image for the cutout is very crude. You can do so much better with selection tools in the Photo Editor. For compositing images where you take a cutout from one image and add it to another, it's best to avoid this Guided Edit for compositing.

You may, however, find a different benefit for using this Guided Edit. Let's say you have two very different photos. You don't want to superimpose them; you just want to match the brightness in one image with another image. As a workaround, you could offset the photos so they don't overlap.

As an example, take a look at Figure 8.12. This photo has a reasonably good exposure, and the brightness values appear quite nice. Now look at Figure 8.13. This photo is a little dark, and the overall exposure isn't quite as good as the photo in Figure 8.12.

FIGURE 8.12 Photo with a reasonably good exposure.

FIGURE 8.13 Photo that's a bit underexposed.

If I take both these photos and bring them into the Photomerge Exposure edit, the final result is two photos superimposed. But I don't want to merge the photos; I simply want to match the exposure,

To set up the files, first size them to the same resolution and physical size by using the Image > Resize > Image menu command. After you size the photos to the same size, resize the canvas area. On one photo, you want to add more canvas (double the width of the photo) to the right. On the other photo, you want to add the same amount of canvas area to the left. After I've added more canvas area to the photos, they look like Figure 8.14.

As you might suspect, after using the Guided Edit, when the photos are merged, they won't superimpose one on top of the other. Each photo merges with the empty space added by resizing the canvas.

With the two photos open in the Photo Editor, click the Guided tab to open the Guided Edits. Click the Photomerge tab and click Photomerge Exposure. As you can see in Figure 8.15, the photos appear adjacent to each other. Use the tools in the Photomerge Exposure panel to refine the brightness. When you are finished editing, click Next and click Expert to open the merged photos in the Photo Editor. At this point, if you want the photos saved separately, duplicate the image and crop each one to retain the image you want to save.

As you can see in Figure 8.16, the photo on the right more closely matches the overall brightness of the photo on the left. At this point, you might add some refinement by adding a Levels Adjustment layer to refine the brightness.

FIGURE 8.14 More canvas area added to the two photos.

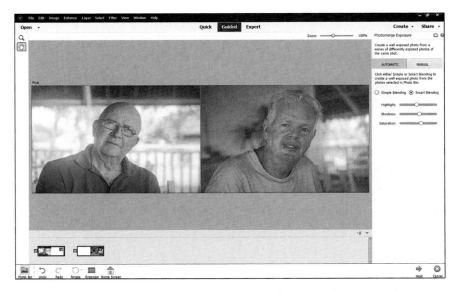

FIGURE 8.15 Photos appearing adjacent to each other in the Guided Edit Exposure panel.

If you need a quick fix for matching exposure between documents, this Guided Edit may be helpful.

Merging Photos for an HDR Effect

Remember, an HDR photo is one derived from three or more exposures of the same scene. You use your camera to shoot a scene underexposed, overexposed, and normal exposure. The photos can then be merged using the Photomerge Exposure Guided Edit. For this kind of edit, you don't have a manual method to achieve the same result. If you shoot three exposures of the same scene, you must use this Guided Edit to merge the photos when using the Photo Editor.

Figure 8.16 shows the three photos I use in this example. You can use five or seven photos. Whatever bracketing your camera accommodates is what you can use to merge the photos. Typically, three photos work quite well for most images.

In Figure 8.16, the photo on the left was shot with an average exposure. The middle photo was an overexposed photo capturing as much detail as possible in the highlights. The photo on the right was underexposed to capture as much detail as possible in the shadows.

FIGURE 8.16 Three photos shot for creating an HDR image.

With the three photos open in the Photo Editor, click the Guided Edit tab. Click Photomerge Exposure.

When you click Photomerge Exposure, the Guided Edit merges the three photos. The default option is Automatic, and this option is typically your best choice for merging photos for an HDR effect.

The Guided Edit panel, shown in Figure 8.17, provides some options for tweaking the composite image. When merging photos for an HDR effect, it's best to avoid using any settings in the Guided Edit panel. Click Next (see Figure 8.17). On the next screen, click Expert to return to the Expert editing mode.

You may want to tweak the overall exposure using a Levels Adjustment Layer and add some sharpening.

Figure 8.18 shows the photo shot with an average exposure. Figure 8.19 shows the same photo shot as an HDR and merged using the Photomerge Exposure Guided Edit. Notice the clouds have more detail in the HDR photo, and you also find much more detail in the shadows in the HDR photo.

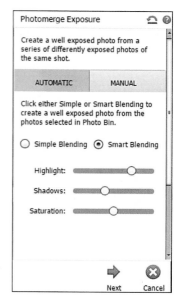

FIGURE 8.17 The Photomerge Exposure panel.

FIGURE 8.18 The merged HDR files.

FIGURE 8.19 The final HDR image after editing the merged files in the Camera Raw Editor.

Using Photomerge Faces

This Guided Edit is just a fun type of edit you use to distort faces and create some goofy photos as pranks. You can play with it if interested. For the purposes of this book, we'll look at some more serious kinds of edits that can help professionals and serious amateurs.

Photomerging a Group Shot

When taking group shots, you often find one person smiling in one photo and the same person frowning in another photo, one person looking away from the others, or one individual who has their eyes open in one photo and closed in another photo. An easy fix to these kinds of problems is to use the Photomerge Group Shot Guided Edit. It's not perfect and sometimes doesn't work well, but in some cases, you may find it useful.

Figure 8.20 shows a nice photo of a group of people. However, the man on the left is not looking at the individual who is talking.

FIGURE 8.20 Group photo with one individual who's not looking at the speaker.

If you have a second photo showing the individual looking in a different direction more consistent with the other subjects, you can merge the files. Use the second image as your final photo. Move the subject with the face forward from another photo to the final.

Open both images in the Photo Editor. Click the Guided Edit tab and click on the Photomerge Group Shot Guided Edit thumbnail. Drag the final image to the right placeholder. Select in the Photo Bin the image with the correct posture. Use the Pencil tool to draw around the subject in the left image in the Photo Bin. You can change the size of the pencil, and you can erase any unwanted selection. After you draw with the Pencil tool, you see a dynamic preview of the results, as shown in Figure 8.21.

Click Next and either save the photo or open it in Expert mode. In Figure 8.21, you can see the results of merging the photos. However, before I end this editing session, there's one more problem with the photo on the right. I need to do something about that sky. As you can see in the original image in Figure 8.20, the highlights in the sky are blown out.

FIGURE 8.21 Draw around the correct pose (left) to replace it in the final image (right).

Editing Skies

Quite often you can find photos that look good with foregrounds, but there are problems with the highlights, particularly with skies. You can see that the photo in Figure 8.20 has no detail in the sky. I need to add some color in the sky and perhaps add some clouds. Making these edits is quite simple.

You can edit a sky in a few different ways. You can copy a photo with a sky that will work well with your target image, or you can add a filter to create artificial skies.

Create a selection of the sky and press Ctrl/⌘ + J to create a new layer of just the selected area. Once you have a selection, you can copy a sky from another photo and choose Edit > Place into Selection.

TIP: If you use the Render > Clouds filter and you don't like the result, choose the filter again. Keep choosing the same filter to see different patterns. You can keep using the same filter, and each time the pattern changes. Choose the one that looks good to you.

If using a filter, click the foreground color swatch to open the Color Picker and choose a blue tone. Make sure you don't choose a highly saturated color. Click OK to return to the Document Window.

Choose Filter > Render > Clouds. Look over the results. Quite often, you may find the saturation of the sky color is too strong. If you create a layer, you can easily fix the problem of the oversaturated sky by moving the Opacity slider in the Layers panel to reduce the opacity in the layer.

The advantage you have with copying and pasting a sky photo is that you can easily see a preview of the sky. With a filter, you need to experiment and try different iterations of the clouds image.

In Figure 8.22, I copied a sky and pasted it into the target document.

FIGURE 8.22 The final image after edits to the sky.

Photomerging a Panorama

This Guided Edit is used to stitch photos together from multiple photos to create a panorama photo. Before using the Guided Edit, you should make adjustments to the photos you'll be using to make preliminary adjustments for brightness, contrast, and color. You can add additional edits on the merged photo after composing in the Photomerge Guided Edit.

Editing Panorama Images

If you shoot Raw images, open all photos to be merged in the Raw Editor and synchronize edits. Make adjustments for Exposure, Contrast, Highlights, Shadows, Vibrance, and Saturation. Open the photos in Expert mode in the Photo Editor and choose Image > Mode > 8 Bits/Channel to reduce bit depth for each photo. Save the files; then open the Guided Edits and use the Photomerge Panorama option.

Shooting Panorama Images

If you want to take panorama images, you should always use a tripod and set your camera in portrait mode. You want to capture as much height in the image as possible. The panorama image will ultimately be very wide, so height is very important.

When shooting the frames, leave about ½-inch overlap between frames. If you're shooting several panoramas, take a picture of your hand before the first image and take another photo of your hand after the last image. If you keep shooting, turn your hand around and take a picture of the back before and after. By the time you get to post processing, it will be easy to sort the photos and know what photos belong to what panorama.

Open all images in the Photo Editor and click the Photomerge Panorama thumbnail in the Guided Edit panel. When you arrive at the panel, your first choice is to decide what setting you want. You can choose Auto Panorama or click the down arrow to open a pop-up menu and make a choice from the available options. First, choose the Auto Panorama (see Figure 8.23). If you don't like the results, you can choose another option from the pop-up menu.

FIGURE 8.23 Photomerge Panorama panel with Auto Panorama selected.

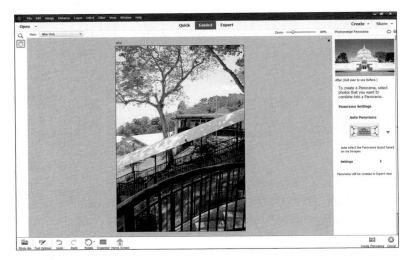

You can make some choices for Settings below the panorama layouts. Among your choices is the Content-Aware Fill Transparent Areas. You can try checking this box to see how well the content-aware fill handles the transparent areas. If you don't like the results, you can take care of the fills later when you open the image in the Photo Editor.

When you click Create Panorama at the bottom of the Photomerge Panorama panel, Elements goes about automatically creating layers and masks and merges the photos into a composite image. After merging the photos, a dialog box opens and prompts you to confirm whether you want to automatically fill edges with content-aware fill. If you click No, the merging process completes, and the Photomerge Panorama panel offers options for sharing or opening the file. Click Expert in the panel, and the file opens in Expert mode. You see something similar to Figure 8.24, where the Layers, Layer Masks, and composite image are shown. As you can see, I chose not to fill the transparent areas.

FIGURE 8.24 Composite image without edges filled.

Filling in Edges

You can choose to autofill the edges when you create a composite using the Photomerge Panorama Guided edit. Autofilling edges works quite well in many cases. However, if there are some slight adjustments you need to finesse, it's much easier to control the fills after creating the composite without autofilling the edges.

If you choose to manually fill edges, start by selecting one part of the photo to work on. This could be half or quarter of the photo. If the photo is very large, Elements will perform slowly, and you may need to wait some time before it finishes filling the edges. For this example, I chose to select half the photo edges to perform the fills in two steps.

Before selecting any area, open the Layers panel menu and choose Flatten Image. Save the flattened image. This reduces the memory, and you can perform steps much faster when editing a smaller photo.

Select the area you want to fill using the Magic Wand or Quick Selection tool. If you want to take the fills-in steps, select just a part of the photo. After making a selection, choose Select > Modify > Expand. Enter **5** in the Expand By text box to expand the selection 5 pixels. You need to grab some of the image edges so Content-Aware Fill will have a reference for the area to clone.

Press Shift + Backspace/Delete to open the Fill Layer dialog box. Choose Content-Aware from the Use drop-down list, as shown in Figure 8.25.

Notice in Figure 8.25 that only half the photo is selected. Click OK in the Fill Layer dialog box and the edge is filled with a clone sample of the edges.

FIGURE 8.25 Fill selections using content-aware fills.

Check the results. If the fill looks okay, move on to another part of the photo. Continue filling the edges. If you need to polish up an edge, you might try using the Clone Stamp tool. In Figure 8.26, you can see the final result of creating a panorama image.

FIGURE 8.26 Final panorama image after using the Photomerge Panorama Guided Edit.

Other than the Panorama Exposure for HDR photos and the Photomerge Panorama, it may be a trade-off as to whether you want to use some of the other Photomerge Guided Edits. The Scene Cleaner and Group Shots can be helpful for some quick edits. Just be certain that the perspective matches in all photos you merge. For more on matching perspectives, see the section "Understanding Perspective" earlier in this chapter.

Matching Color

Color matching is important when compositing images. If the color temperature is off or color casts appear in one or the other images, the composite will obviously be a fake image. Your task when compositing photos is to create the most realistic looks.

Quite often, you can use the same steps for adjusting brightness and contrast, and the color may balance between two images in a composite photo.

I took one photo and added a subject from another photo to create a composite, as shown in Figure 8.27.

FIGURE 8.27 Subject added to a background image.

I copied the subject to the background image and duplicated the subject. I added a Hue/Saturation Adjustment Layer and brought the Saturation slider to the left to –100 to create a black-and-white copy of the subject image.

I then added a Levels Adjustment Layer and sampled black, white, and midtones in the background image and clipped the layer. Before you sample tones, be certain to open the Tool Options panel for the Eyedropper tool and choose either 3x3 or 5x5 in the Point Sample area of the Tool Options.

Sampling Black, White, and Midtones

To sample black, white, and midtones, you first click the black Eyedropper tool in the Layers panel and then click in the darkest area of the image you're sampling. You then click the white Eyedropper tool and sample the lightest area in the photo. The last sample is handled by the midtone Eyedropper tool. Click in an area where you can find a neutral gray.

After I hid the black-and-white layer, the subject color match looked fairly close to the color in the background, as you can see in Figure 8.28.

If the brightness adjustment isn't quite right, you can use a very fast and easy adjustment for creating color balance by first duplicating the background. Move the background to the top of the layer stack.

Since you don't need the black-and-white layer anymore, you can delete it to make it easier to see before and after adjustments. Click the black-and-white layer, press Alt/Option, and click the Delete icon in the Layers panel to delete the layer. Likewise, you can delete the Hue/Saturation Adjustment layer.

FIGURE 8.28 A close color match between two photos in a composite image.

Select the top layer (the duplicate of the Background layer) and choose Filter > Blur > Gaussian Blur. In the Gaussian Blur dialog box, move the Radius slider far to the right. You want to blur enough to show some distinction in the colors but no detail.

Select the Blur layer and choose Color from the blending modes drop-down list.

You should always adjust brightness and contrast first when trying to color match photos.

As a last edit, flatten the layers or press Ctrl/⌘ + Alt/Option + Shift + E to create a composite layer and retain all layers in case you want to make any additional edits.

Adding Subjects in Grass

When you bring together photos where you show the feet of your subjects, you need to avoid creating composites where it appears the subject is floating above foreground elements. In particular, grass presents a problem. When you drag a subject to a photo with grass in the foreground, the subject looks like its feet are floating. A natural photo would show the feet sunken into the grass a little, with some grass surrounding the feet. Figure 8.29 shows the images I use for this example. Here are the steps to create this type of composite:

1. Bring a subject with a Layer Mask with the feet visible into a background with grass. Duplicate a selection of grass and bring it to the top of the layer stack. Cover the feet slightly with the grass copy.

2. Choose a brush you can use for grass. For this example, I used the 134 brush tip shown in Figure 8.30.

FIGURE 8.29 Two photos to composite.

3. In the Tool Options panel, click Brush Settings and move the scatter to around 10% and the Spacing to around 20%. You can make adjustments as necessary.

4. Create a new layer at the top of the layer stack. Set the blend mode to Multiply.

5. Select the Brush tool. Press Alt/Option to temporarily switch to the Eyedropper tool. Sample a color in the grass and apply brush strokes to the new empty layer at the top of the layer stack. If necessary, you can make opacity adjustments to the layer, and you can change the Opacity in the Brush tool options.

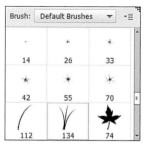

FIGURE 8.30 Brush settings to replicate grass.

In Figure 8.31, you can see the results of editing the photos shown in Figure 8.29.

FIGURE 8.31 Final result of adding grass around the feet to create a more realistic view.

PART V

WORKING WITH COLOR

You may find this part exciting because Chapter 9 examines color sampling and identifying color. Chapter 10 moves on to color toning and color grading. Once you master working with color, you will definitely see improvement in your photo editing.

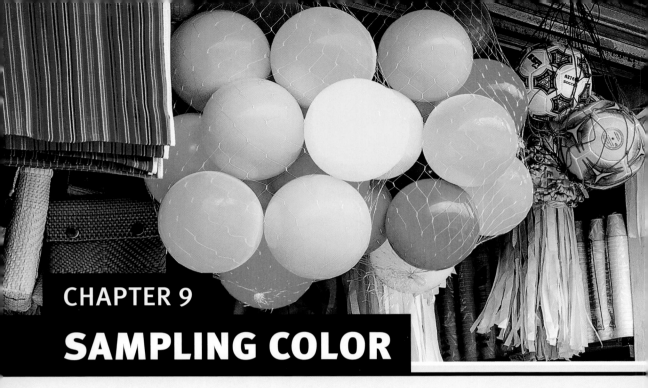

CHAPTER 9
SAMPLING COLOR

Chapter Goals

There's so much to color and working with color in photo editors that three separate books still would not explain all you should be aware of. Rather than engage in a lengthy explanation for color theory, this chapter covers a few practical applications for handling color, such as sampling color that you might want to apply to photos, applying color when color toning photos, and applying color variations using editing tools and commands. Topics in this chapter include the following:

- Sampling color in Adobe Color
- Color toning with gradient maps

Using and Applying Color

Sometimes you want to colorize a photo, add a background color, create a solid color adjustment layer, color a texture, or add color to a photo, but you're not sure whether the color works well with your photo. Sometimes it's helpful to know a little bit about color theory. It would be nice if you had a guide that tells you what color is complementary to the dominate color in your photo. Or how can you easily find a lighter or darker shade of the same color? Or maybe you want to see a range of earth tones or sky tones to experiment with.

Fortunately, you have a great assistant at your disposal. It's called Adobe Color, and you'll find a great number of ways to explore choosing colors for any project.

Using Adobe Color

Adobe Color is a web service provided by Adobe Systems. You find the website at https://color.adobe.com. Prior to 2015, the site was called Adobe Kuler. More recent access is made through this current URL at https://color.adobe. com/create/color-wheel.

> **NOTE:** Different browsers may show different options. For all these examples, I used Firefox.

When you arrive at the Adobe Color site, you land at the Create tab, as shown in Figure 9.1.

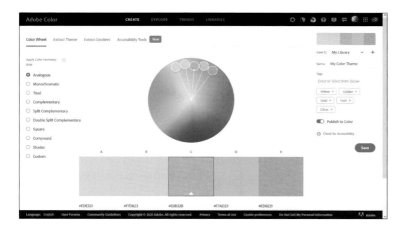

FIGURE 9.1 The default web page for Adobe Color.

As shown in Figure 9.1, you have tabs at the top of the window and a number of radio button choices on the left. In the center of the page, you see a color spectrum with five points plotted on the circle. Below the color spectrum, you see five color swatches representing the five points plotted on the color spectrum.

> **NOTE:** Figure 9.1 shows the Adobe Color website when you're logged in with your Adobe account. If you're not logged in, the items in the top-right corner are not available.

If you are logged in to Creative Cloud with your Adobe ID, you see four tabs at the top of the window. If you do not have an Adobe ID, you can easily acquire a free account. To sign up for a free Adobe ID, do an Internet search for "sign up for an Adobe ID."

If you don't log in with an Adobe ID, the Libraries tab is not available, which means when you find or create color swatches, you won't be able to save them. If you are signed in, you can load the saved swatches in the Photo Editor Swatches panel, as well as save them to libraries in Adobe Color.

Below the color spectrum you find the individual color swatches for each of the five plotted colors, and below the swatches are the hexadecimal values (see Figure 9.2). You can copy the hexadecimal values and paste them into the Color Picker in Elements.

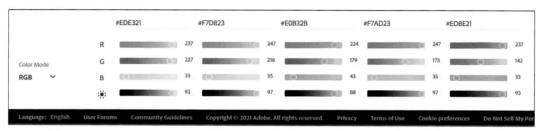

FIGURE 9.2 Color values shown in hexadecimal and RGB/Black values.

If you want all five values as shown in Figure 9.2, you can take a screen shot and open it in the Photo Editor. You can use the Eyedropper tool to sample colors.

To take a screen shot in Windows, press Shift or Alt and press the Prt Sc key. You can also use the snipping application. Press the Windows key + Shift + S when using the snipping application. When you press the keys, a pop-up toolbar opens at the top of your screen. The first tool on the left is used for drawing a rectangular box that captures the content with the rectangle. The second tool is the Freeform Snip you use for irregular shapes. The third tool is for capturing the foreground active window. The final tool on the right is the Fullscreen Snip tool used for capturing the entire screen.

On the Mac, press ⌘ + Shift + 3 to capture the full screen. Press ⌘ Shift + 4, and you see the cursor change to a crosshair. In MacOS Big Sur and later, you can use ⌘ + Shift + 5 to get a crop rectangle where you can move handles to trim the selection. Drag the crosshair around the area of the screen you want to capture and release the mouse button to complete the capture. If it's difficult to precisely capture what you want, capture a little extra area outside the area you want to capture and crop in the Photo Editor.

Both Windows and the Mac screen captures place a copy of the capture on the clipboard. To save the capture, you need to paste the clipboard contents in a new document. After capturing on either Windows or the Mac, open the Photo Editor. Choose File > New > Image from Clipboard. The exact size of your screen capture is the same size the Photo Editor creates when you choose File > New Image from Clipboard. The file is pasted in a new document automatically when you choose the menu command.

Choosing Colors in the Create Panel

The default color rule is Analogous. The five colors can be moved simultaneously while maintaining their proximity relationships by dragging the center circle around the color spectrum. If you drag in toward the center, you add more white, changing the tint.

Drag one of the outside colors, and they all move equidistant from each other, as shown in Figure 9.3. The color swatches below the spectrum always change accordingly when you move a point in the spectrum.

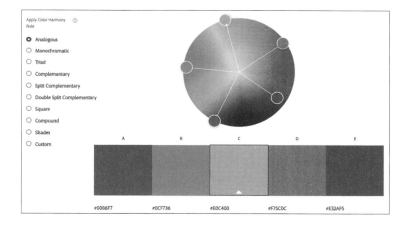

FIGURE 9.3 Analogous colors separated.

Along the left side of the window, you have a number of different color schemes:

- **Analogous:** As shown earlier in Figure 9.1, the Analogous colors are in close proximity. You find a lot of analogous color in nature photos, such as forests, autumn leaves, and various landscapes. There should be enough contrast when you add Analogous color to your photos.

- **Monochromatic:** Monochromatic is based on only one color or a single-color tint. It uses variations of shades of a single hue by changing saturation and brightness of the base color.

- **Triad:** The Triad color scheme is a variant of the Split Complementary color scheme with equal distance between the three colors. The three colors are equidistant on the color wheel.

- **Complementary:** Complementary colors are exact opposite each other on the color wheel. High contrast of complementary colors creates a vibrant look, especially when used at full saturation. Complementary colors are used well with subjects having a dominant color and the backgrounds having a complementary color. See Figure 9.4 for a view of the Complementary scheme.

FIGURE 9.4 The Complementary colors are opposite each other on the color wheel.

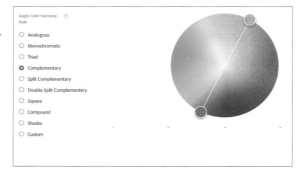

- **Split Complementary:** The Split Complementary color scheme uses one base color and two secondary colors. The two colors are placed symmetrically around the color spectrum. Using the Split Complementary scheme, you might think of using the base color as the main color in your image and the secondary colors should be used for highlights and accent colors.

- **Double Split Complementary:** Double Split Complementary schemes consist of four colors. Two colors are on either side of the color wheel. They form an X on the color wheel. An example is yellow, green, red, and violet.

- **Square:** The Square color scheme has four colors spaced evenly around the color spectrum. Using a Square color scheme works best if you have one color as a dominant color.

- **Compound:** When you select a color on the color wheel, the two colors adjacent to the base color are said to be a Compound color scheme. Compound colors create a pleasing color palette with less contrast.

- **Shades:** Shades is a single color with black or white added to a base color to produce light to dark variations of the base color.

- **Custom:** The Custom scheme in Adobe Color contains colors that you choose randomly. You can start with a color scheme, such as Analogous, and then click Custom. When you move the points on the color wheel, they move independently of the other colors. You use this scheme to choose five different random colors.

Below the color swatches, you find the colors represented in hexadecimal values, and below those values, you find sliders for Red, Green, Blue, and Black (refer to Figure 9.2). RGB values are only available when you choose RGB from the Color Mode drop-down list at the left of the color sliders. Select one of the five colors from among the swatches. You can move each of the sliders to change the RGB values for that particular swatch. If you move the black slider, you change the brightness values of the selected color.

Exploring themes

Click on the Explore tab at the top of the browser window, and you arrive at the Explore window, as shown in Figure 9.5. Here you find a number of Color Themes. When you see a thumbnail image, move the mouse cursor over a thumbnail. The thumbnail changes to a set of five swatches, a pop-up showing buttons for adding the swatches to one of your libraries, and a download button. (The latter two are only available when you're logged in with a Creative Cloud account.)

FIGURE 9.5 The Explore tab in Adobe Color.

On the right side of the window, you see a View drop-down menu that is by default set to All Sources. When you click on the arrow to open the list, you see commands for Color Themes, Creative Projects, and Stock Photos. Scroll to Color Themes, and you find a submenu with a variety of different themes you can choose to have displayed in the browser window. (See Figure 9.6.)

Perhaps one of the great advantages for using the Themes panel is searching for the kind of palette you want. You might want earth tones, for example. In the Search text field at the top of the window on the Explore tab, type *earth tones*. The browser displays palettes containing earth tones. Search for *sky tones*, and you see another set of palettes containing sky tones.

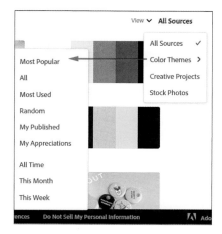

FIGURE 9.6 Menu options for choosing different themes.

My favorite aspect for searching in the Explore panel is performing searches for great artists. You can search for painters like Van Gogh, Da Vinci, Rafael, Picasso, or any other famous historical artists. I particularly like the earth tones used by Cezanne. When I search for Cezanne in the Search text box, I see a number of palettes used in some of Cezanne's paintings, as you can see in Figure 9.7.

FIGURE 9.7 Color palettes shown after searching for Cezanne.

As you can see in Figure 9.7, you find some nice palettes for various earth tones and you also see some thumbnails of some of Cezanne's paintings. As you mouse over a painting, you find a palette of colors used in that particular painting. When you mouse over a thumbnail, you see the color palette and you also have buttons for adding the palette to one of your libraries or downloading the swatch file.

NOTE: To add to a library or to download a set of swatches, you need to log on with a Creative Cloud account.

NOTE: Once again, the Firefox web browser is used in Windows and Safari is used on the Mac in these examples. If you use another browser, some options may be different.

Downloading Swatches

If you have an Adobe Creative Cloud account, you can click a swatch set, and you see options for adding to a library or a button for Download. Click Download, and in Windows, a dialog box opens, as shown in Figure 9.8.

FIGURE 9.8 Click to download a swatch palette, and a dialog box opens, prompting you to open or save the file.

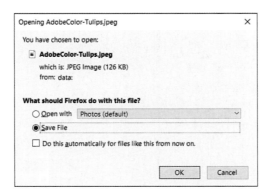

You have a choice for opening the swatch library or saving it. The file cannot be opened directly. It needs to be loaded in the Swatches panel. Therefore, choose Save File and click OK. The file is saved to your User Downloads folder.

On the Mac, when you click Download in Adobe Color, the file is automatically saved to your User Downloads folder.

The files saved on both platforms are saved as Adobe Swatch Exchange files with an .ase file extension.

Uploading Photos

If you want to see a set of swatches derived directly from one of your photos, you can upload a photo, and Adobe Color will draw from its library of photos to provide you with some selected matches between the color in your photo and the color of photos in the Adobe library with similar hues.

In both the Explore and Trends panels, you see a Camera icon at the end of the search text field. Click the Camera icon, and a File Upload dialog box opens. Browse your hard drive and locate a file. Select the file to upload and click the Open button. You should save files you upload as JPEGs and reduce the resolution to 72 ppi for faster uploads before attempting to upload photos to Adobe Color.

In Figure 9.9, you see a photo I uploaded to Adobe Color. This photo has a broad range of hues.

FIGURE 9.9 File uploaded to Adobe Color.

After the upload, Adobe Color offers you a number of photos with similar hues to the file you uploaded. In this example, there are a number of photos showing a similar range of hues as my original upload.

A number of different files are shown in the Adobe Color browser window. Scroll through the samples to find a color palette that appears similar to your sample image. Below each image is a swatch set available to you for download if you have a Creative Cloud account. If you don't have a Creative Cloud account, mouse over a photo to see a larger image for the swatch set and take a screen shot. In Figure 9.10, you can see the results of comparing my file to the matches provided by Adobe Color.

FIGURE 9.10 Samples returned by Adobe Color that closely match hues in an uploaded file.

Using Swatches

So far in this chapter, I've covered a lot of theoretical stuff that won't mean much to you until I show you how to apply the information. If you've read everything up to this point, bravo! Now it's time to look at some practical applications of the knowledge learned thus far.

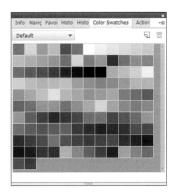

FIGURE 9.11 The Default Color Swatches panel.

When you open the Swatches panel in the Photo Editor, a library of swatches opens in the panel. By default, the library is called Default. Among other libraries, you have Windows and Mac OS swatches, Web Swatches, and Photo Filter Swatches. Click the Default drop-down list to choose another swatch set.

Loading Swatches

You load swatches in the Color Swatches panel. To open the Color Swatches panel, choose Window > Color Swatches. You can also click the More icon in the lower-right corner of the Panel Bin. When the Color Swatches panel opens, you find it nested together with a number of other panels, as shown in Figure 9.11. Click the Color Swatches tab and drag it away from the other panels so the Swatches panel is a single panel. Click the X in the top-right corner (Windows) or the top left-corner (Mac) on the other panels to close them.

You can choose a color in the Color Picker and load that color in a swatch library. First, select the library where you want to add a new color swatch. With the Foreground color set as you like, open the Color Swatches panel (Window > Color Swatches) and place the cursor after the last swatch in the Color Swatches panel. Click, and the Foreground color is added.

Suppose you want to add some colors derived from Adobe Color, and you don't have Adobe Creative Cloud. Take screen shots of one or more sets of color swatches and open them in the Photo Editor. You can merge the files as different layers and then crop and flatten the layers. In Figure 9.12, you can see three different sets of swatches I created from screen shots in Adobe Color and merged in the Photo Editor.

Unfortunately, Elements doesn't provide an easy method for adding individual color swatches to the Color Swatches panel from screen shots. You cannot add colors in groups. You have to add them one at a time.

Sometimes, you may have several different swatch sets you want to combine in a single library. If this is the case, you may want to separate the swatches with an identifier so you can easily see individual sets among a group of different swatch sets. I recommend you add a white color swatch as a separator. To do so, click the Eyedropper tool in the Color Swatches panel and click on a white swatch. If you don't have a white swatch, set the foreground color to white. With either a white swatch selected in the Color Swatches panel or white as your foreground color, click the Create New Color Swatch of Foreground Color icon panel to the left of the trash can icon at the top of the Color Swatches. The Color Swatch Name dialog box opens.

Type a name for the swatch. If you load different swatch sets, you may want to name individual swatches according to the swatch set names used by Adobe Color. Click OK, and a new white color swatch is added at the end of your swatches in the current library.

Using the different swatch sets shown in Figure 9.13, I added the individual swatches separately to the Color Swatches panel. Between each set, I added a white color swatch, as shown in Figure 9.13.

NOTE: There's really no reason to bother with screen shots. An Adobe ID is all you need, and it's free. If you don't have an Adobe ID, search the Internet for Adobe ID sign up. It takes a few minutes, and you can then access many features in Adobe Color.

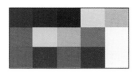

FIGURE 9.12 Swatches from screen shots taken on the Adobe Color website.

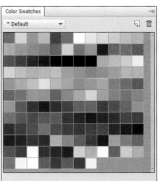

FIGURE 9.13 Swatches loaded in the Color Swatches panel.

TIP: If you have an Adobe ID, I can give you a much easier method for loading swatches from Adobe Color. You can use the Download button on a color swatch set and download multiple sets. For more on downloading a color swatch set, see the "Downloading Swatches" section earlier in this chapter.

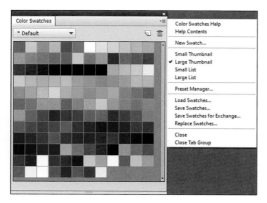

FIGURE 9.14 The Color Swatches panel.

Elements presents another minor problem in Windows when loading swatches files. As I mentioned earlier in the section "Downloading Swatches," the files are saved as Adobe Swatch Exchange files (.ase). The swatch libraries installed with elements are Adobe Color files (.aco). It's an annoyance, but it's not a major problem because .ase files can be loaded on Windows. On the Mac, there's no issue.

To load a swatch library in the Color Swatches panel, open the panel menu, as shown in Figure 9.14. As you can see, there are several options in this menu. You use the Load Swatches command to add swatches to the Color Swatches panel.

When you click Load Swatches, the Load dialog box opens. Navigate to the folder where you save swatch libraries. When you open the folder in Windows, you see nothing. That's because .ase files are probably not selected in the Load dialog box. In Windows, you need to open the pop-up menu adjacent to the Name text box on the far-right side of the Load dialog box and choose Swatch Exchange (.ASE). Any .ase files in the folder will be listed. Select one and click the Load button to load the swatches in the Color Swatches panel.

On the Mac, you don't have a menu in the Load dialog box. All files are recognized when you choose Load Swatches, and the Load dialog box opens.

Replacing Swatches

When you use the Load Swatches command in the Color Swatches panel and load a swatch library, the new swatches are, by default, appended to the current library. If you want to eliminate the current library and see only new swatches you load in the Color Swatches panel, choose Replace Swatches.

Saving Swatches

If you make a change by loading swatches or deleting swatches, you need to choose Save Swatches from the Color Swatches menu if you want to retrieve them again at a later time. If you don't save swatches and you change libraries, any changes you made to add or delete swatches won't be viewed when you load the library again.

Deleting Swatches

Managing swatches in the Color Swatches panel in Elements is a bit cumbersome at times. Adobe doesn't make it easy to rearrange your color swatch library and add new libraries from scratch.

If you want to delete swatches from the Color Swatches panel using the Panel options, you can only delete a single swatch at a time. To delete a swatch from the Swatches panel, press the Alt/Option key so the scissors icon becomes available. Click a swatch you want to delete. If you want to delete multiple swatches, you need to individually delete them in the panel.

Fortunately, there is an easier way to handle swatches. Rather than use the Color Swatches panel, you can use the Preset Manager and find some much easier ways to manage your color swatches.

Managing Swatches in the Preset Manager

Suppose you want to create an entirely new swatch library. There is no option in Elements to start a blank new library. You can get around this limitation by using the Preset Manager.

To create a new library, first select the Photo Filters presets swatches in the Color Swatches panel. This library has the fewest color swatches, so it will be easiest to delete them all. Open the Preset Manager by choosing Edit > Preset Manager. From the Preset Type drop-down menu, choose Swatches. The current active swatch library in your Color Swatches panel is opened in the Preset Manager.

Just to be safe, save this library as a new set. To save a set, you need to select all the swatches first. Press Ctrl/⌘ + A to select all the swatches; then click the Save Set button in the Preset Manager. The Save As dialog box opens. Navigate to the location where you keep your presets, type a name in the File Name field, and click Save.

Select all swatches again and click the Delete button to create a new blank library. Click the Add button to add new swatches to the library. If you have more than one swatch set, click Append on all subsequent additions you make to the library. When finished, press Ctrl/⌘ + A and click Save Set. Choose the location, type a new name for the set, and then click Save. Figure 9.15 shows a new color swatch library as it appears in the Preset Manager.

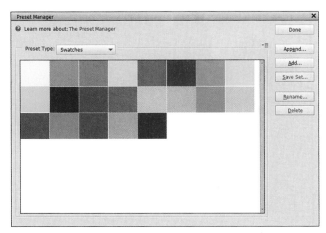

FIGURE 9.15 A new color swatch library as it appears in the Preset Manager Swatches group.

Applying Color

I've explained ways to create different color swatches. Now I'll give you a look at how you might use them. Obviously, you can paint with colors, but you can do so much more once you know the different color schemes and how to apply them to photos.

Colorizing Backgrounds

Take a look at Figure 9.16. It's a nice photo of a lovely model. The photo was taken outdoors. If we want to make this photo appear more like a studio shot with a solid color background, we can apply color to the background area.

FIGURE 9.16 Raw photo unedited.

As an experiment, let's see what we can do with creating a background using a complementary color. There are a few colors in this image, but we have some dominance in the blues and cyans. The model's shirt is bit of a teal color. You can use the Color Picker, select a color, and fill a selection for the blouse.

Select the Background layer and fill it white. When you use Adobe Color to extract the colors in the photo, you won't have a range of blues and cyans to complicate the process. Reduce the resolution if necessary by choosing Image > Resize > Image Size or press Ctrl/⌘ + Alt/Option + I. Save the duplicate file as a .jpeg.

Next, upload the file to Adobe Color. You're presented with a range of photos and color swatches. I pick a teal swatch that somewhat closely matches the teal color in the model's blouse. The new swatches appear when you click the Create tab if you're not already on this page.

Click Complementary to show a complementary color for a blue swatch. As shown in Figure 9.17, you see the complementary colors shown in the color swatches below the color wheel. For this example, I chose swatch B.

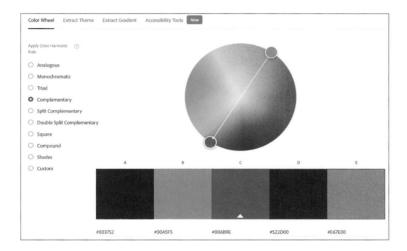

FIGURE 9.17 Finding complementary colors in an uploaded photo in Adobe Color

The hex code is reported below the swatches. Copy this code and return to the Photo Editor. Open the original file. Open the Color Picker and paste the color in the hashtag text box. This color now becomes the foreground color in the Tools panel. The Layers panel is shown in Figure 9.18.

FIGURE 9.18 The Layers panel after changing the background color.

Fill the background selection with the foreground color. The results of the edits are subjective. I wanted the model to stand out and appear as though this shot was taken in a studio with a solid color background. See the final result in Figure 9.19.

FIGURE 9.19 Final photo with a background color change.

Adding Graphics to Favorites

The Graphics panel, which you open by clicking the + at the bottom of the Panel Bin, offers a number of graphics. If you use a particular design frequently, you can add it to your Favorites panel. You get to the Favorites panel by clicking the More icon at the bottom of the Panel Bin or by choosing Favorites from the menu that opens when you click the down arrow adjacent to the More icon.

In Figure 9.20, I added a graphic to my Favorites panel by opening the Favorites panel and dragging the graphic from the Graphics panel to the Favorites panel. At this point, I'm not interested in the color of the graphic. Rather, I'm looking for a texture I might want to use frequently.

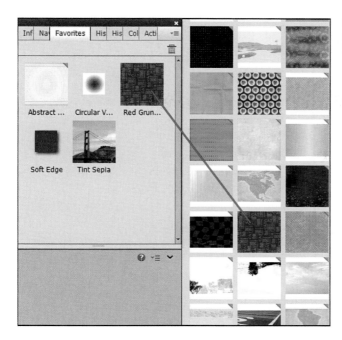

FIGURE 9.20 Graphic added to the Favorites panel.

In Figure 9.21, you see the original photo I use for this example. I want to change the background to a different color and use the texture from the graphic I copied to my Favorites panel. To begin, first duplicate the Background; then create a selection on the duplicate layer. In this example, I want to select the subject. After creating and refining the selection, create a Layer Mask.

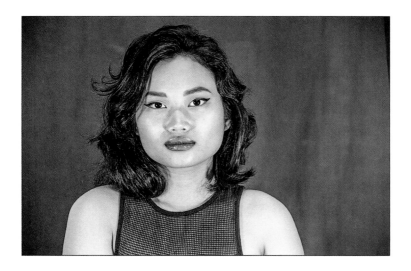

FIGURE 9.21 Original photo.

Drag a graphic to your photo. In this example, I dragged the graphic from my Favorites panel to my photo. Notice when you drag a graphic to a photo, the graphic always becomes a new background. If you have a layer selected and a selection, Elements ignores that layer and selection and still copies the graphic to the background.

At this point, activate your selection and inverse it by pressing Ctrl/⌘ + Shift + I to select the background. Click the graphic (the new background) and press Ctrl/⌘ + J to create a new layer.

To change the color of the graphic, add a Color Fill Adjustment Layer and choose a color from the Elements Color Picker that opens when you create the Color Fill Adjustment Layer. In this example, I choose a blue color.

To preserve the texture after coloring, set the Color Fill Layer to the Color blend mode in the Layers panel. Your Layers panel should now look like Figure 9.22.

FIGURE 9.22 The layers panel showing edits for Figure 9.21.

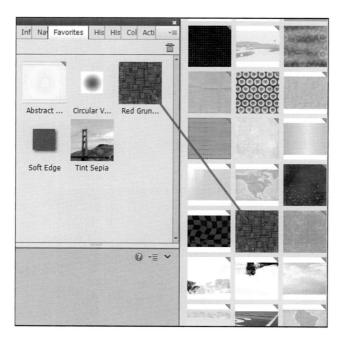

The Color blend mode only affects color in the layer and has no effect on the texture. As you can see in the final image in Figure 9.23, the texture and color are changed from the original photo in Figure 9.20.

FIGURE 9.23 Final photo after adding a graphic and changing the graphic color.

CHAPTER 10

COLOR TONING AND COLOR GRADING

Chapter Goals

Chapter 9, "Sampling Color," covers some basics for handling color. This chapter takes color handling a step further and looks at color grading photos, which is the process of improving the appearance of an image for presentation in different environments on different devices. You also get to apply some of the theoretical principles from Chapter 9 to photos. I discuss methods for the following:

- Color toning with gradient maps
- Color grading with Levels and Curves
- Creating duotones
- Removing color casts
- Color editing using Elements+
- Creating cinematic color toning

The exciting methods for color toning and color grading in this chapter can help you bring your images to the vision you have for your photo's final look!

Color Toning with Gradient Maps

Chapter 4, "Working with Layers," introduces and briefly mentions gradient maps. There's quite a bit to understand about gradients and gradient maps, so this chapter gives more detail.

In the Photo Editor, you have two options when using gradients. You can create a gradient fill, such as creating a new layer and applying a gradient to it using the Gradient tool, or you can create a Gradient Map Adjustment Layer.

You need to know that there's a different between a gradient and gradient map. If you apply a gradient to a new layer, once you commit to the gradient, there's no way to go back and refine the gradient, change colors, or change opacity stops. If you create a Gradient Map Adjustment Layer, you can reopen the gradient and change colors, shift the brightness, change the opacity stops, and edit the gradient as if it's a new custom gradient.

The other difference between a gradient and a gradient map is that a gradient layer applies a gradient to the layer with no regard for the colors and tones in the underlying layer. The gradient map maps out the color values from 0 to 255 and replaces them with colors in whatever gradient you have selected. Essentially, you can create two different looks to a photo using the gradient on a layer and a Gradient Map Adjustment Layer.

In Figure 10.1, you can see an example of an unedited photo with a gradient applied to a layer on the left and the same photo with a gradient map using the same gradient. On both photos, I applied the Soft Light blend mode with reduced opacity in the layers

FIGURE 10.1 Gradient on a layer (left) and a gradient map using the same gradient as an Adjustment Layer (right).

Creating a Gradient Map

Gradient maps are marvelous for color grading photos. You have an abundant number of choices for how you create gradients and map them to photos. To get familiar with creating and applying gradient maps, follow these steps:

1. Open an image in the Photo Editor.

2. Click the Create Fill or Adjustment Layer icon to open the drop-down list and choose Gradient Map. With an Adjustment Layer, you can always go back and double-click it to reopen the Gradient Map dialog box, where you can edit the gradient or choose a different gradient.

3. Almost invariably, you'll want to choose a blending mode from the Layers panel Blend Modes drop-down list. At 100% opacity, the only blend modes you can use are Overlay and Soft Light. The remaining blend modes require opacity settings around 20% or less.

NOTE: The blending mode in Figure 10.2 is Soft Light with a 20% opacity.

In Figure 10.2, you see a Gradient Map Adjustment Layer on a photo using a teal to orange gradient. When you double-click the Adjustment Layer, the Gradient Map dialog box opens. Click the down-pointing arrow to open a drop-down list where you can choose another gradient or gradient library.

FIGURE 10.2 Double-click the Gradient Map layer to open the Gradient Map dialog box.

Another way you can create a gradient is to choose the Layer > New Fill Layer menu command to open the New Layer dialog box. Name the layer and decide whether you want to clip it to the underlying layer; then click OK.

For more on editing gradients and creating new gradients, see Chapter 4.

The next dialog box that opens is the Gradient Fill dialog box. Here you can choose the style of the gradient. Most of the time, when you create a gradient fill, you'll probably use either Linear or Radial style for the gradient. You can also choose the Angle and Scale for the gradient. A Gradient Fill is just like using a new layer and drawing with the Gradient tool. It does not take into consideration mapping out colors and replacing them with colors in the gradient.

Loading Gradient Maps

Before I show you how to load gradients, I want to explain where you can find gradient libraries to load. Fortunately, there are a number of free gradients you can find on websites. Do an Internet search for *gradient library*, and you can easily locate many free downloadable gradients. When you find a gradient library you want to use, decompress the file and copy it to the folder where you save other presets.

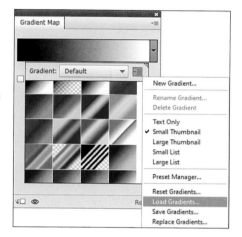

Both the Layer > New Fill Layer > Gradient command that opens the Gradient Fill dialog box and the Gradient Fill Adjustment Layer support loading gradients. In either the Gradient Fill dialog box or the Gradient Map dialog box, open the dialog box drop-down list and choose Load Gradients. When the Load dialog box opens, select the file you want to load and click Load. In Figure 10.3, you can see the menu command for Load Gradients in the Gradient Map dialog box.

FIGURE 10.3 Open the dialog box drop-down list and choose Load Gradients.

Creating Black-and-White Photos

When you shoot in RGB color, you have a number of ways you can convert an image to black and white. You can choose Image > Mode > Grayscale. You can open the Hue/Saturation dialog box and move the Saturation slider to the far left to –100. You can open a file in the Camera Raw Editor and move the Saturation slider in the Basic panel to the left to –100. You can also use the Enhance > Convert to Black and White menu command.

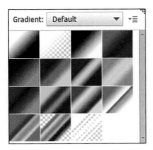

FIGURE 10.4 The Gradient Map dialog box.

Converting Color to Black and White Using Gradient Maps

There's one more way to convert RGB color to black and white. It's your best choice by far. Open a photo in the Photo Editor and add a Gradient Map Adjustment Layer by clicking the Adjustment Layer icon and choosing Gradient Map from the drop-down list. The Gradient Map dialog box opens, as shown in Figure 10.4.

Choose the Black, White gradient in the Default group (see Figure 10.4). That's it. Your RGB image is now a black-and-white photo. Figure 10.5 shows the image on the left where I applied the Enhance > Convert to Black and White menu command, and on the right is the same photo with a Gradient Map using the Black, White gradient.

FIGURE 10.5 RGB to grayscale using the Enhance > Convert to Black and White (left) and using a gradient map (right).

Colorizing Black-and-White Photos

After converting to black and white, you can colorize photos using gradient maps. You have a huge range of opportunities using gradient maps with several different blend modes and an infinite number of different gradients you can use. You can use one color and change blending modes, and you can apply different gradient maps using a variety of different color gradients.

In Figure 10.6, you can see a single color gradient (in this case, an orange value of ffa800 to white) applied as a gradient map to the same image using several different blending modes. All settings were the same for each photo except the blending mode and opacity settings. All photos were at 100% opacity unless so specified under each thumbnail.

FIGURE 10.6 The same color gradient map applied to the same photo at different blending modes.

Multiply

Screen – 25% Opacity

Soft Light

Hue

Luminosity – 25%

Color

Figure 10.7 shows the same photo converted to black and white using different gradient maps, and all images had the same Color blend mode.

FIGURE 10.7 Different colors used in gradient maps with the same Color blend mode applied to each photo.

Red, Green

Violet, Orange

Orange, Teal

Custom

Custom

Custom

Replacing Color with Gradient Maps

The previous section covers color toning on black-and-white photos. You also can use similar methods for color toning on color photos. You can use gradient maps to replace color, or you can mix and match and use both the Color Replacement tool and gradient maps.

One limitation you have with the Color Replacement tool is some difficulty with getting precise selections. Sometimes you might be best served by using selection tools and refining selections before replacing color. For example, if you want to replace color in hair, you will find it much better to use selection tools and Refine Edge to first make a selection and then replace the color. In other circumstances where you can easily make a selection with the Color Replacement tool, the tool works well, such as what you see in Figure 10.8.

FIGURE 10.8 Original photo (left) and after using the Color Replacement tool (right).

If you make a selection and then use the Color Replacement tool, you brush within the selection to change color. If making a selection is necessary, then it's just as easy to fill the selection using a gradient map as it is using the Color Replacement tool. If you need to have the replaced color on a separate layer, you need to make a selection and duplicate the selection on a new layer. When you create a gradient map, new layers are automatically created by Elements.

To see how you can use gradient maps to replace colors, I'll start by using the image of the lovely model shown in Figure 10.9. The photo looks a little flat, and I need to punch it up a little. I could use a little more color on the lipstick, brighten up the skin tones, maybe add a little color to the flower arrangement on her hair, and work on the eyes. Perfecting the eyes will help bring the viewer into the image.

FIGURE 10.9 Original photo that needs some edits.

There are several areas where we want to apply different adjustments and need to first make selections for each area we want to edit. In this example, I want to isolate the flower arrangement, the hair, the skin tones, the eyes, the lips, and the shirt (sweater).

To change colors in separate areas of a photo using gradient maps, follow these steps:

1. Open a photo in the Photo Editor. Try to find a photo where you can easily make selections in separate areas of the photo.

2. Create Layer Masks for each separate area. I want to isolate the mouths, face, blouse, flowers, and hat. Duplicate the background for each area you want to isolate and make selections and create layer masks for each area. Name each layer with a descriptive name. After I selected the different areas in the photo, my Layers panel looks like Figure 10.10. Notice the layer for the mouth is a very small selection of just the subject's lips. It may be difficult to see in the printed version of the Layers panel, but the selection is there.

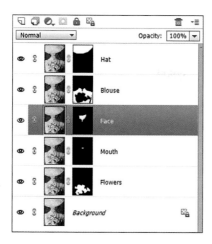

FIGURE 10.10 Layer masks created for separate selections for the distinct areas of the photo.

3. I'll start by replacing the color of the lips. Move the Mouth Layer to the top of the layer stack

4. Choose a lipstick color. For a guide showing various shades of lipstick, you can download images of lipsticks applied to models' lips from advertiser's websites. This method gives you a more authentic color.

    When you find an image showing various shades, download it, or take a screen shot and open the file in the Photo Editor.

    When you sample color, you want a setting other than the default Point Sample choice for the Eyedropper tool. A Point Sample samples the point where you click a photo. You could have dark and light tones mixed among the color value you want to sample. A better choice is to use a 3 × 3 or 5 × 5 average sample. Click the Eyedropper tool in the Tools panel and open the Tool Options panel. Where you see Color Picker, click on either 3 × 3 or 5 × 5. In my example, I used a 5 × 5 average. Figure 10.11 shows the various shades of lipstick in a photo along with the Eyedropper tool options.

    Click the Eyedropper tool on the shade of lipstick you prefer to set the color as the foreground color.

5. Press Ctrl/⌘ and click on the layer mask for the Lips layer to create a selection.

6. Be certain the Mouth layer is at the top of the layer stack. With the Mouth layer selected, click the Adjustment Layer icon at the top of the layers panel. From the drop-down list, choose Gradient Map. Choose the Black, White gradient and click on the gradient in the Gradient Map dialog box to open the Gradient Editor, as shown in Figure 10.12.

TIP: As a matter of default, you should almost always use either a 3 × 3 or 5 × 5 choice for the point sample when sampling with the Eyedropper tool. Select the Eyedropper and make the setting in the Tool Options panel.

FIGURE 10.11 Photo of lip-stick shades and the average point sample options for the Eyedropper tool.

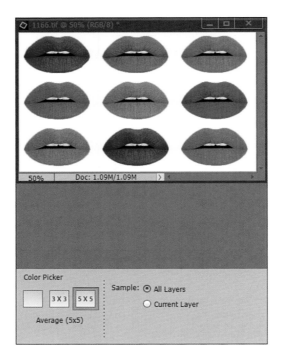

FIGURE 10.12 Click below the gradient to add a Stop in the Gradient Editor dialog box.

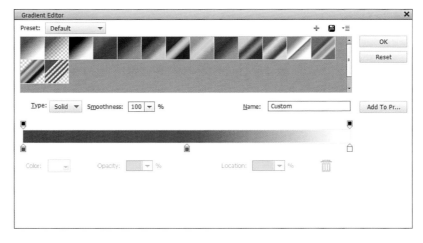

7. In the Gradient Editor, place a stop at the midpoint. Click anywhere below the gradient to add a stop, and type **50** in the Location text box. Click the midpoint stop, move the cursor to the Tools panel, and click the Foreground color. The stop now uses the foreground color. Click OK to return to the Photo Editor window.

8. As a matter of practice, you typically find that when coloring lips, the saturation is too much, and the color looks like it's pasted on the lips. In this example, such is the case. To bring the color to a more realistic view, reduce the opacity. In my example, I reduced opacity to 25%.

   In these series of edits, I replaced the original color of the lips to a darker red color, as you can see in Figure 10.13.

9. Proceed to each layer, creating selections from the layer masks and applying a gradient map to each layer. In my example, I added some blue to the hat, some red to the blouse, cooler skin tones, and a little more brightness in the flowers.

FIGURE 10.13 After replacing color on the lips.

FIGURE 10.14 Final edited photo.

Color Grading with Gradient Maps

Color grading, or the process of improving the appearance of an image for presentation in different environments on different devices, is most often used in film production, but you also use it with still images. Various attributes of an image, such as contrast, color, saturation, detail, black level, and white point, may be enhanced.

Color Toning with Gradient Maps

You can use the same techniques used on black-and-white photos for color toning on color photos. Again, you can download a number of different gradient maps, and you can create custom gradient maps. It's fun to experiment and observe results as you toggle through a variety of gradients.

To add some color toning with custom colors in a gradient map, follow these steps:

1. Open a photo that you want to add some color toning. In my example, I use the photo shown in Figure 10.15.

FIGURE 10.15 A photo that's flat with low saturation.

2. Click the Add Fill or Adjustment Layer drop-down list and choose Gradient Map.

3. Click the Gradient in the Gradient Map dialog box to open the Gradient Editor.

4. Click the mouse button with the cursor below the gradient to add a stop.

5. You can move the Color midpoints toward lighter and darker tones. Click a stop and drag left/right to move the stop. In this example, I added two stops on either side of the gradient. I adjusted the black on the left and added a white stop on the light side on the right. Figure 10.16 shows the Gradient Editor with the stops I used in this example.

NOTE: It doesn't matter what gradient you begin with if you change colors on the beginning and end stops. In the example cited here, I started with the Black, White gradient and left the black color on the first stop. I changed the end stop to a different color, as shown in Figure 10.16.

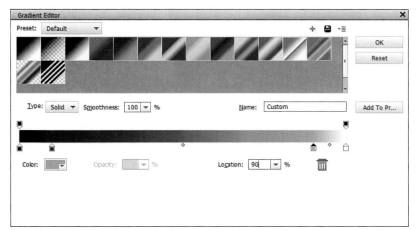

FIGURE 10.16 Additional stops added in the Gradient Editor.

6. In this example, I added a Levels Adjustment Layer by clicking the Add Fill or Adjustment Layer icon in the Layers panel and choosing Levels. The adjustment you make depends on your photo. Adjust the levels to add brightness/contrast.

7. Press Ctrl/⌘ + Alt/Option + Shift + E to create the composite layer. You can save the layered photo if you want to return to it for further edits.

8. As a final adjustment in the example photos, I adjusted shadows high-lights. Choose Enhance > Adjust Lighting > Shadows/Highlights.

The final edited image—which has much more saturation and a warmer image—is shown in Figure 10.17. This is only a single gradient map applied to this photo. Keep in mind you have thousands of options when you add Gradient Map Adjustment Layers to a photo.

FIGURE 10.17 Final color toning a photo using a gradient map.

Adding More Punch to Your Photos

You may have some photos that were underexposed. Some of your images may appear dingy without good contrast and some snap in appearance. In this exercise, I explain how to add more punch to your photos and make them more vivid in appearance:

1. Open a photo in Adobe Camera Raw. If your photo is not a raw image, in the Photo Editor, choose File > Open in Camera Raw. If you start with a Raw image, double-click to open in Adobe Camera Raw. In Figure 10.18, you can see a photo I have open in the Raw editor. Notice the photo appears very flat. It's underexposed and lacks contrast.

2. Work your way through the Basic panel and adjust Exposure, Contrast, Highlights, and Shadows and add some Vibrance. After completing the Camera Raw edits, click Open to open the photo in the Photo Editor.

3. In the Photo Editor, create a new blank layer and click the Spot Healing Brush. Make sure Sample All Layers is checked in the Tool Options panel and click on blemishes and artifacts in the photo while the new blank layer is selected.

4. Click the new blank layer and press Ctrl/⌘ + E to merge the layers.

5. Press Ctrl/⌘ + J to duplicate the layer.

FIGURE 10.18 Original file open in Adobe Camera Raw.

6. To sharpen the photo, while the duplicate layer is selected, choose Filter > Other > High Pass. Move the Radius slider to where you begin to see an outline of the subject. Don't move the slider too far.

7. Select the High Pass layer and press Ctrl/⌘ + E to merge the layers.

8. Open the Adjustment Layers list in the Layers panel and choose Gradient Map. The Gradient Map dialog box opens, as shown in Figure 10.19.

9. Open the Gradient Editor. Click the default Black to White gradient in the Gradient Map dialog box.

10. Click below the gradient in the Gradient Map editor. In the Location text box, type **50** to plot a stop at the 50% location, as shown in Figure 10.20.

11. Double-click the 50% stop to open the Color Picker.

12. Set the brightness (the B radio button) to the same value as the Location. In this case, I typed 50 in the B text box, as shown in Figure 10.21.

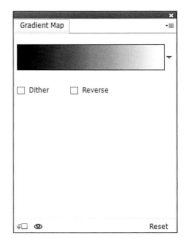

FIGURE 10.19 The Gradient Map dialog box.

FIGURE 10.20 The Gradient Map Editor with a stop plotted at the 50% location.

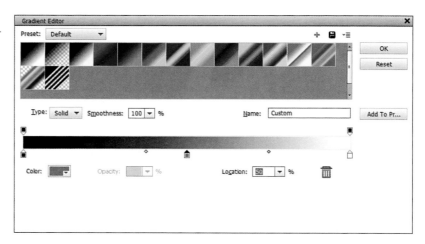

FIGURE 10.21 Color Picker with 50% set in the Brightness radio button text box.

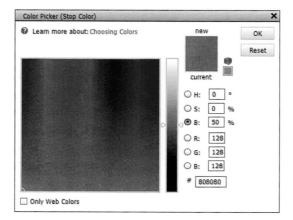

13. Click OK in the Gradient Editor. You return to the document window.

14. Set the Blend Mode drop-down list to Luminosity. Use this blend mode because you don't want to change the color in the photo—only the brightness values.

15. Divide the distance between the 50% stop and the 0% stop (the far-left side of the gradient) and plot a new stop. Type **25** in the Location bar. Double-click the stop and set the brightness to the same value as the Location value. Continue dividing two more times and set brightness values the same as the Location values. On the right side, if you need a little more lightness in the image, follow the same steps of dividing the distance by two and setting brightness to match Location values. Figure 10.22 shows the final stops I plotted for my example.

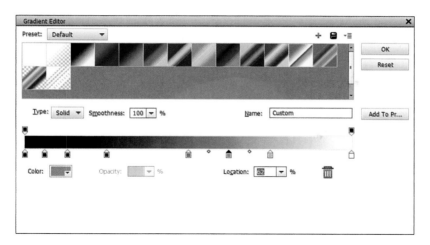

FIGURE 10.22 Final adjustments in the Gradient Map Editor.

16. If the photo requires some more brightness adjustments, open the Adjustment Layers list and choose Levels. At this point, your Layers panel should look like Figure 10.23.

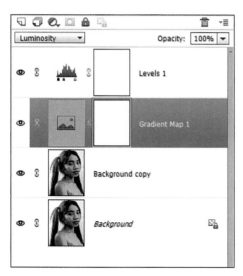

FIGURE 10.23 Layers panel up to this point.

17. Look over the photo and make any edits needed to polish up the photo, such as a little more sharpening and blemish removal. For portraits, you may want to edit eyes and lips and add some sculpture to the face, as I discuss in Chapter 14. For now, just focus on improving the overall brightness of the photo.

18. Save the file.

19. Open the edited file in Camera Raw.

20. If the photo needs a little more pop, move the Vibrance slider to the right. Figure 10.24 shows the results of my final edits. Compare this figure to the original image in Figure 10.18.

FIGURE 10.24 Final edited photo.

FIGURE 10.24 Final edited photo.

Adding Cinematic Color Effects

What exactly is color grading? You may have heard the term before, and we used a gradient map to color grade a photo in the previous section. Briefly, *color grading* is a term used most often by cinematographers and video editors. If you saw the raw film of a Hollywood movie, it would probably look pretty drab to you. The film editors are the real magicians when it comes to making commercial films.

Film editors shift colors in scenes, so they complement each other. Color grading helps develop the story of a movie and contributes to setting the mood. You might see a scene in a movie where the perpetrator is shown with split lighting (dark on one side of the face and light on the other), indicating perhaps there is good and evil in the character. To further contribute to the story, one side of the face may be warm tones emphasizing compassion for the hero seeking revenge, whereas in other scenes, you may see cooler tones contributing a sense of unease to evil personalities. All in all, color grading helps you tell a story within a photo and emphasize a mood or feeling.

The movie *Traffic*, for example, used a lot of film cross-processing and color grading. The scenes with yellowish tints are most often scenes of Mexico and the desert. Scenes with blue tints (showing actor Michael Douglas and his daughter) emphasize a dark drug-laden life. Other scenes were shot using natural light without much color toning.

One of the most commonly used color grading effects is a teal to orange color grading effect; it's known as the *blockbuster look* because of its popularity in Hollywood films. You see orange/teal color grading in many photos and extensively in cinema. Orange and teal are complementary colors that always work well together. Furthermore, using the colors creates contrast—not brightness contrast, but color contrast. To get an orange/teal effect, you push blues/teals into the shadows and oranges/yellows into the highlights, thus creating contrast and adding depth to a photo or movie clip.

There are several ways you can apply orange/teal color grading to a photo to give it a cinematic look. You can use the Hue/Saturation dialog box, create a gradient map, or, if you use Elements+, you can use the Channel Mixer panel, Selective Color panel, or the Elements+ Camera raw editor to create a split tone image.

Let's take a look at adding a teal/orange color grade to a photo using the Hue/Saturation Adjustment Layer. To add the effect, follow these steps:

1. Open a photo in the Photo Editor. Make any contrast/brightness adjustments using a Levels Adjustment Layer.

2. Open the Create New Fill or Adjustment Layer drop-down list and choose Hue/Saturation. In the Master channel, set the Hue slider to −20. Set the Reds Hue to +20. Set the Blue Hue to −20. Set the Yellows Hue to −20 and the Cyan Hue to +20. Set the Green Saturation to −100.

3. Color grading often looks matted. To create a matted look, choose Levels from the Create New Fill or Adjustment Layer drop-down list. Move the Output sliders in 20 levels on either side. You can click the number below the sliders and type new values. On the left for the shadows, type **20**. On the right for the highlights, type **235**.

The final teal/orange color grade photo appears in Figure 10.25.

FIGURE 10.25 Color grading teal and orange colors using Hue/Saturation adjustments.

Follow along as I work through another way to apply an orange/teal cinematic effect using the Gradient Map Adjustment Layer in the following steps:

1. Open an image in the Photo Editor.

2. Convert the photo to grayscale. You can use a gradient map with the Black, White gradient. Choose Gradient Map from the Adjustment Layers in the Layers panel.

3. Click the gradient displayed in the dialog box to open the Gradient Editor.

4. Click and drag the two color stops in about 4% each. Alternatively, you can type **4** and **96** in the Location text box.

5. Add two stops at the ends of the gradient by clicking below the gradient.

6. On the left side, double-click the second stop to open the Color Picker. Chose #00eaeb in the Color Picker and click OK. On the right side, double-click the second stop in from the right to open the Color Picker again. Add the color #ffa800 and click OK.

7. Add a stop in the center by clicking below the gradient.

8. Double-click the stop to open the Color Picker and chose the same orange color value #ffa800). This all depends on your photo. In some cases, you may want to add more teal color.

9. I moved the stop left to the 75% location (see Figure 10.26). By moving the teal center stop left, you can apply more of the teal colors to the shadows.

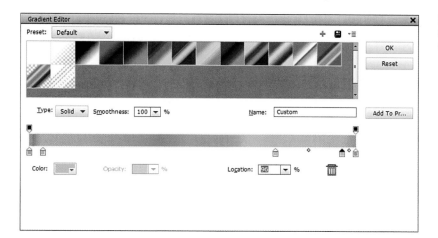

FIGURE 10.26 Stop positions shown for the orange/teal color gradient.

10. Click OK in the Gradient Editor.

11. Select the Gradient Map layer and choose Soft Light for the blend mode.

12. Look over the image. If you want less teal/orange color, move the Opacity slider left to reduce opacity. In my example, I reduced opacity to 75%.

13. Click the Background and select Levels from the Create Fill or Adjustment Layer drop-down list.

The final result is shown in Figure 10.27. As you can see, the teal/orange color grading using this method results in a flatter image with less vibrance and saturation. Because both methods use Adjustment Layers, it's easy to return to the settings and adjust the colors. Just double-click the Adjustment Layer in the Layers panel to open the Hue/Saturation panel or Gradient Map panel.

FIGURE 10.27 Color grading using teal and orange colors with a gradient map.

Color Grading Using Levels

We can also use the Levels adjustment to color tone images. Elements doesn't have a Curves dialog box like Photoshop. The Color Curves adjustment won't do for color grading. However, if you have Elements+, you have available a Curves adjustment similar to the Curves adjustment in Adobe Photoshop.

There are two ways to access the Levels adjustment in Elements. You can choose Enhance > Adjust Lighting > Levels, or you can create a Levels Adjustment Layer in the Layers panel. If you use an Adjustment Layer, be certain you have the Levels icon selected in the layer and not the mask. If you select the mask, all reassignment of colors appears in white only. To apply a color grading effect using Levels, follow these steps:

1. Open an image in the Photo Editor.

2. Press Ctrl/⌘ + J to duplicate the Background layer.

3. Choose Enhance > Adjust Lighting > Levels to open the Levels dialog box or create a Levels Adjustment Layer. If you create the Adjustment Layer, click the Levels icon in the layer and double-click to open the Levels dialog box. On the right side of the dialog box, just below the Auto button, you see three eyedroppers, as shown in Figure 10.28.

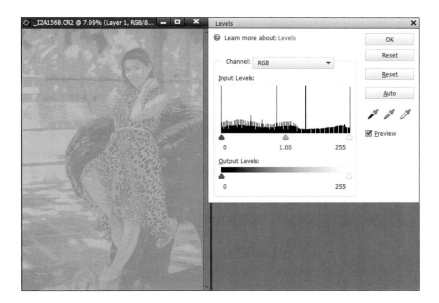

FIGURE 10.28 Set colors to the Shadow and Highlight eyedroppers.

4. Double-click the Black (shadows) Eyedropper tool and the Color Picker dialog box opens. Choose a color in the Color Picker. For my example, I want to create an orange/teal cinematic image. Therefore, for the shadows, I want the teal color. The value I used is #00aeab. Click OK.

5. Double-click the White (highlights) Eyedropper tool and choose another color. In this example, I chose orange with a setting of #ffa800.

6. After setting the colors for the shadows and highlights, you need to click the Black Eyedropper tool on the darkest area of your photo.

   If you want a more precise view of the darkest area, press the Alt/Option key and move the left-most black slider below the histogram in the Levels dialog box slowly to the right. Pressing the Alt/Option key turns the Document Window white. As you move the slider right, you begin to see black. When you first see black, note where in the photo you see the black and return the slider to the zero (0) position. Move the Black Eyedropper tool to the photo and click in the black area where you first discovered black appearing in the Levels dialog box.

TIP: You make color choices for hexadecimal values such as #ffa800 in the Color Picker by typing the numbers in the text box at the bottom of the dialog box.

7. Click the White Eyedropper tool in the lightest area of the photo.

   Follow the same procedure for the white highlight slider as with the Black Eyedropper. Press Alt/Option and drag the white slider below the histogram in the Levels dialog box to the left. The Document Window turns black. As you move the slider to the left, you begin to see white appear in the photo. Return the slider back to the 255 position and click the White Eyedropper tool in the area where white first appeared in the photo.

8. Click OK in the Levels dialog box. When you click OK, a dialog box opens prompting you to save the new target colors as defaults that you applied to the Eyedropper tools. Click No so the settings don't become the new defaults.

9. When you return to the Document Window, select the top layer and choose Soft Light for the blending mode.

10. Adjust the opacity in the Layers panel for the color grading effect you want. Figure 10.29 shows the final image for my example.

FIGURE 10.29 Final image after color grading in the Levels dialog box.

Creating Duotones

When Photoshop Elements 2021 was released, Adobe introduced a duotone Guided Edit, which you can use to perform similar color grading effects. If you have Elements 2021, open an image in the Photo Editor and follow these steps:

NOTE: To use a Guided Edit for creating duotones, you need Photoshop Elements 2021 or later.

1. Click the Guided tab and click on the Fun Edits tab when you arrive at the Guided Edits panel.

2. Determine the size of your output. If you want to leave the size at the default value of the open image in the Photo Editor, move on to the next step. If you want to change the size, click Original, and a drop-down list opens showing thumbnails of various choices. You can choose from a number of choices, and you have optimized choices for Instagram, Facebook, and Twitter.

For more on saving files for social media, see Chapter 16, "Sharing Images."

3. Choose between two Duotone effects. The Normal button creates a duotone that applies color to highlights and shadows. The Gradient effect applies the two colors in a gradient that follows the direction you determine below the Opacity adjustment. You can rotate the angle 360°, and you can choose a style like Linear, Radial, Angle, and so on. When you make your choices, the effect is applied as a gradient map; however, the colors are not applied to highlights and shadows. The photo is essentially divided in two. One half of the photo uses one color, and the other half uses the second color according to the Style and Angle you specify.

   In both options, you can choose the two colors by clicking on the swatches below the thumbnails in the panel on the right side of the window. Click a swatch to open the Color Picker and make a color choice. Click OK and click the second swatch to choose the second color.

   Choosing the Normal mode provides you with a more realistic Duotone. In Figure 10.30, you can see a photo where I applied a teal/orange effect using the Normal mode.

When you examine the Layers panel after creating a Duotone using either method, you find one layer for an RGB to grayscale conversion and another layer with a gradient map. The grayscale conversion may produce some banding. If this is the case, you might be best off performing an RGB-to-grayscale conversion using a gradient map, as I mentioned earlier in the section "Creating Black-and-White Photos."

Depending on the look you want, you may want to apply a Soft Light blend mode and adjust opacity on the gradient layer.

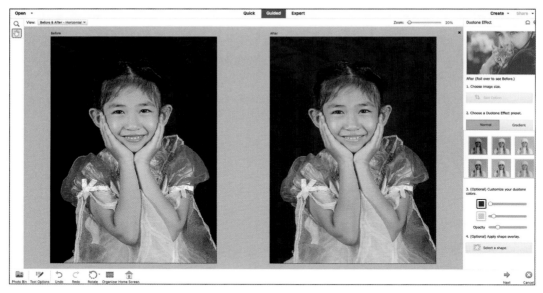

FIGURE 10.30 Duotone created using the Guided Edit Duotone effect.

Removing Color Casts

Photoshop Elements doesn't provide a number of color tools that are available with Adobe Photoshop. Many of the color adjustments in Elements are intended for users to apply auto adjustments. Some the auto adjustment features work quite nicely, but auto adjustments are not necessarily beneficial for all photos.

Figure 10.31 shows a photo that has a cyan color cast.

FIGURE 10.31 Photo with a cyan color cast.

We have a few ways to approach correcting this photo. In many cases, you might want to first try to use Enhance > Adjust Color > Remove Color Cast. This is a straightforward adjustment; when you choose the menu command, Elements just uses an algorithm to make a guess on how to color balance the photo. There are no dialog boxes and no choices to be made. You just select the menu command, and the result is immediately returned. In Figure 10.32, you can see the result for using Enhance > Adjust Color > Remove Color Cast on the photo shown in Figure 10.31. As you can see, in many cases you might see little difference between the original and the photo after using the menu command.

FIGURE 10.32 Photo with a color cast corrected using Enhance > Auto Color Correction.

Another way to color correct photos is to use the Levels dialog box. You can use the Enhance > Adjust Lighting > Levels command, or you can create a Levels Adjustment Layer. Before you open the Levels dialog box, click the Eyedropper tool and be sure to set the Color Picker to either 3 × 3 or 5 × 5 average in the Tools panel.

When you open the Levels dialog box, take the Black Eyedropper tool and click in the darkest area of the photo. Select the White Eyedropper tool and click in the lightest area of the photo. Click the midtone Eyedropper tool and click on a neutral gray tone. You may have to click a few times with the midtone adjustment. As you click on the photo, it dynamically updates so you can observe changes as you make them. In Figure 10.33, you can see the results using this method for color correction on the same photo shown in Figure 10.32.

FIGURE 10.33 Color correction using Levels adjustments.

Color correction is one area that you want to take as many precautions as possible before you start postproduction. Try to get the best results you can with your camera; then making corrections will be that much easier.

One thing to do when shooting, especially portraits and head shots either outdoors or in a studio, is to use a color checker or an 18% gray card. An

X-rite Passport Color Checker costs about $100 at Amazon.com, and 18% gray cards cost you around $10. When you use a color checker, have your subject hold it up while you shoot a photo. All subsequent photos under the same lighting conditions won't need a shot of the color checker on each photo. You only need to shoot it again if the light changes dramatically. Figure 10.34 shows a studio shot with a subject holding the X-rite Passport Color Checker.

FIGURE 10.34 Use a color checker in one shot during a photoshoot for correcting color when you edit your photos.

When it comes time to color correct photos, you can sample the black, white, and gray swatches in the color checker.

Creating Cinematic Color Toning

You can apply color grading and color toning effects on photos using a variety of methods from tools and menus in the Photo Editor. It's not necessary to use an additional plug-in to handle these editing tasks.

Color grading has been used by film editors even before films were shot in Technicolor. Master filmmakers have pushed the envelope when it comes to color grading films. There are many memorable films you can probably think of that use complementary colors, heavy saturation, triatic colors, pastels, and more to create moods and stimulate the audience's senses. Think of films like *A Clockwork Orange*, *The Aviator*, *Catch Me if You Can*, *Sin City*, *The Martian*, *Mad Max*, *Traffic*, *The Matrix*, *Wonder Woman*, and more, and you can probably recall scenes where color grading effects were applied in interesting ways to help set the mood.

If you like an effect used in a film, you can watch a trailer and take screen shots. Capture images containing colors you want to apply to a photo, and then you can duplicate the colors and color grade one of your photos.

I like the contrast between warm and cool tones in the movie *Traffic*. They represent different moods associated with the emotional highs and lows in the movie.

NOTE: Due to copyright issues, I cannot show the screen shot I used from the movie *Traffic*. The image had a predominately blue color throughout the photo.

To see how you can add a cinematic color grading effect to a still photo, follow these steps:

1. Open a file from which you want to capture the dominant colors.

2. Save the file as a GIF image by choosing File > Save for Web to open the Save for Web dialog box.

3. In the Save for Web dialog box, type **3** in the Colors text box. You can go as high as 5, but three colors will generally do nicely. The file type should be GIF, and below the GIF selection, choose Custom, as shown in Figure 10.35. Click Save.

NOTE: In Figure 10.35, you see the preview boxes void of an image. Due to copyright issues, the images are not shown. When you use Save for Web, you will see a preview of the original photo you choose to save and a preview of the export.

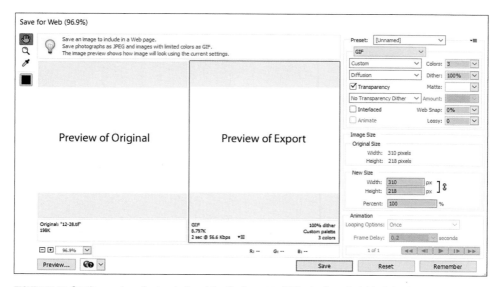

FIGURE 10.35 Set the number of colors to 3 and the file format to GIF in the Save for Web dialog box.

4. Choose Image > Mode > Color Table. The color Table dialog box opens, as shown in Figure 10.36. In this dialog box, you can see the three colors extracted from the image you saved in the Save for Web dialog box.

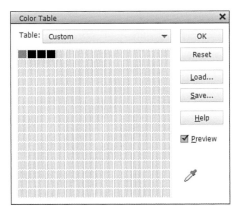

5. Click Save to save colors as a color swatch file (.aco).

6. Choose Window > Color Swatches. Click the Color Swatches tab and drag it away from the panel. Close the panel so you have only the Color Swatches panel visible.

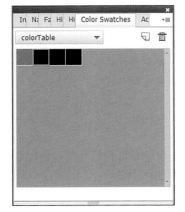

7. In the Color Swatches panel, click the icon to open the panel menu. Choose Replace Swatches in the menu. The Load dialog box opens. In the Load dialog box, locate the .aco file you saved from the Color Table. In Windows, you need to choose the file type from the drop-down list in the lower-right corner of the Load dialog box. Open the list and choose Swatches (*.ACO). Select the file and click Load.

On the Mac, when you open the Load dialog box and locate the saved swatch file, it automatically appears in the Load dialog box. Select the file and click Load.

FIGURE 10.37 Color Swatches panel showing the replaced color swatches.

The current swatches are replaced with the new swatches. In my example, my three colors plus black are shown in the Color Swatches panel in Figure 10.37.

8. Open the photo to which you want to apply the color grading in the Photo Editor. For this example, I used the photo shown in Figure 10.38.

FIGURE 10.38 Unedited photo.

9. Duplicate the Background layer by pressing Ctrl/⌘ + J.

10. Open the Create Fill or Adjustment Layer menu in the Layers panel and choose Gradient Map. You know the colors you want to use for the gradient and already have them loaded in the Color Swatches panel.

    Be certain the Color Swatches panel is open and place it aside the open photo in the Photo Editor. Also be certain the swatches saved from the color table appear in the Color Swatches panel. Click the Eyedropper tool. Open the Tool Options panel and select either 3 × 3 or 5 × 5 for the point sample.

11. When the Gradient Map panel box opens, click the Gradient to open the Gradient Editor. Double-click the Shadow Stop (or click the color swatch below the first stop) to open the Color Picker. Click the darkest color swatch in the Swatches panel with the Eyedropper tool. Before you exit the Color Picker, make note of the Brightness value.

12. Add the brightness value in the Gradient Editor. In my example, the Brightness value for the darkest color is 0% in the Color Picker. After clicking OK in the Color Picker, type **0** in the Location text box in the Gradient Editor. You'll notice the Shadow slider move to that location.

13. Repeat the same process for the bright side of the gradient and choose the lightest color swatch. Take note of the Brightness value and type that value in the Location text box when you return to the Gradient Editor.

14. Click below the gradient to add a new stop and double-click it (or click the Color swatch) and sample the midtone color swatch in the Color Swatches panel. Likewise, note the Brightness value in the Color Picker and supply

that value in the Location text box when you return to the Gradient Editor. Click OK in the Gradient Editor to return to the Document Window. The stops in my example appear as shown in the Gradient Editor in Figure 10.39.

FIGURE 10.39 Final position of the stops in the Gradient Editor.

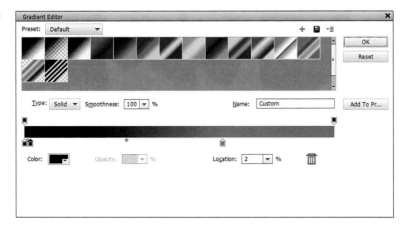

15. Select Soft Light or Color for the blend mode in the Layers panel for the Gradient Map layer. Try both Soft Light and Color to see which one works best for you. The Soft Light blend mode will be a little more subtle. In my example, I set the blend mode to Color to evenly distribute the cool tones.

The gradient may appear too dark. You might want to tweak the adjustments a little. You can simply reduce opacity on the Gradient Map layer. In this example, I reduced opacity to 82. The final image is shown in Figure 10.40.

FIGURE 10.40 Final image.

Color Editing with Elements+

So far, this chapter has explored color toning mostly by using tools and commands in the Photo Editor. The Elements+ plug-in includes some additional kinds of color toning and grading edits.

Elements+

There's plenty to do with the Photo Editor default tools and menu commands, so if you don't have the Elements+ plugin, you're not at a total loss. The plug-in just offers some extra methods and some different ways to approach similar color toning edits.

Color Grading Using the Channel Mixer

The Channel Mixer is one tool you don't have available in Photoshop Elements. You have some limited access to the three RGB channels in the Photo Editor. You can make some changes to the color in each channel by using the Levels dialog box either from the Enhance > Adjust Lighting > Levels menu or by using a Levels Adjustment Layer. You can see dynamic previews using the Levels adjustment, and the edits you make using the Channel Mixer are quite similar to using the Levels dialog box.

Elements+

Figure 10.41 shows a photo containing a lot of greens and blues. The photo has a somewhat cool feeling. Suppose you want to make this photo appear much warmer, like a hot scene. There are a number of ways you can handle this, and the Photo Editor provides you with many ways without using a plug-in. However, for this example, I'm showing you how to do it with the Elements+ plug-in.

FIGURE 10.41 Photo with some cool colors.

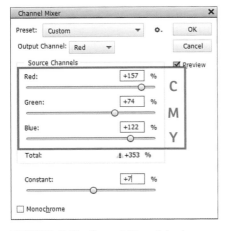

FIGURE 10.42 The Channel Mixer dialog box.

Open the Effects panel and choose Elements+ from the drop-down list at the top of the panel. Drag the 1. Color and Tone icon to the Document Window. At the bottom of the list, you see Channel Mixer.

Click Channel Mixer and click the check mark at the top of the panel or double-click Channel Mixer. The Elements+ Channel Mixer opens, as shown in Figure 10.42.

Like so many other dialogs and adjustment windows in Elements, whenever you see a slider with RGB on the left, the right side is always CMY. Therefore, if you move the Red slider right, you add more cyan to the photo. If you move the Green slider to the right, you add more magenta to the photo. And if you move the Blue slider to the right, you add more yellow to the photo.

Move the sliders left/right to create the color look you want. In Figure 10.36, you see a yellow exclamation point appearing next to the total value. If the value is more than 100, the colors are out of gamut, meaning they won't reproduce as shown on a monitor if you want to print the file. Some digital printers can come close to the colors, but if you send the file off for commercial printing and color separations, the colors will change radically. If you want to share photos on social media, the colors are fine, and you don't have to worry about being more or less than 100. If you want to print the files commercially, try to stay as close to 100 as you can.

For this example, I want to radically change the color by adding some cyan (by moving the Red slider to the right), some magenta (by moving the Green slider to the right), and a lot of yellow (moving the Blue slider right) to the photo to render a much warmer-looking photo. Unfortunately, the final result won't look like the print in this book, but you can open a similar image on your computer and work to get a similar look.

The print in this book looks a little diluted compared to the original photo shown in Figure 10.43.

FIGURE 10.43 Adding a warmer look to the photo using the Elements+ Channel Mixer.

Using Selective Color

The Selective Colors Adjustment Layer you can create with Elements+ enables you to intensify and add more saturation to colors in a photo or completely change a color. Colors become richer and more vibrant while making the tones appear more natural. Additionally, you can change hue values.

Figure 10.44 shows a photo where I want to change the red shirt on the subject to make it look a little lavender. If I want to change only the subject's shirt color, I first need to make a selection. Add a Layer Mask, then press Ctrl/⌘ and click to make the selection active, and your selective color adjustment is applied only to the selection.

FIGURE 10.44 Original image to be used for editing selective colors.

To access the Selective Color Adjustment Layer, you must use a plug-in like Elements+. There is no Selective Color panel in the Photo Editor.

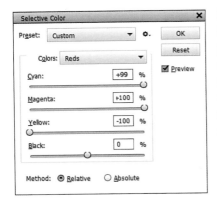

FIGURE 10.45 The Selective Layer panel from the Elements+ plug-in.

In the Effects panel, choose Elements+ from the drop-down list. Click on the 1. Color and Tone icon or drag the icon from the panel to the Document Window. The 1. Color and Tone panel opens. Scroll down the list and locate Selective Color. Click Selective Color and click the check mark or double-click Selective Color. The New Layer icon opens. Type a name for the layer if you like. If you want to clip the layer to the layer below the new layer, check the box where you see Use Previous Layer to Create Clipping Mask. Click OK, and the Selective Color panel opens, as shown in Figure 10.45.

When the Selective Color panel opens, make sure the Relative radio button is selected. Relative puts a cap on the adjustments you make and won't let you push the adjustments to extremes that move colors to more unrealistic views.

The first color option is Reds. This is the color I want to change in my example image. If you have multiple colors to adjust, as you make changes to one color, select another color from the Colors drop-down list.

You may need to toggle back and forth to get the color combinations you want for your photo. Click the Preview check box if it's not enabled so you can see a dynamic preview in the Document Window.

Click OK when finished and examine the results in the Document Window. As an Adjustment Layer, you can return to the Selective Color panel to make changes. However, you cannot double-click the Selective Color layer in the Layers panel to open the Selective Color panel. You must use Elements+ to return to the settings you made in the panel.

To do so, click 1. Color and Tone to open the 1. Color and Tone panel in Elements +. When you open the panel, at the top of the various tools and adjustments, you find Edit Adjustment Layer. This item only appears after you created an Adjustment Layer. Double-click, and the Selective Color panel opens with the last settings you applied in the panel.

If you have several Adjustment Layers and you want to edit one layer, select the respective layer in the Layers panel and open the 1. Color and Tone panel from Elements+. When you double-click Edit Adjustment Layer, the respective Adjustment Layer is opened in the panel.

In my example, I simply changed the color of the red stripes in the subject's shirt, as you can see in Figure 10.46.

FIGURE 10.46 The final image after editing with the Selective Color panel using the Elements+ plug-in.

Using 3D LUTs

LUT stands for LookUp Table. In a simplistic way, you can visualize applying LUTs to photos to create effects similar to using various choices for remapping colors when uploading Instagram photos or when you have an app on a cell phone that permits you several choices for how you want your final photo to appear.

Elements+

Understanding LUTs

LUTs can be defined as a set of instructions for remapping pixel values. There are 1D LUTs and 3D LUTs. A 1D LUT contains a single table for converting an input luminance value to an output luminance value. A 3D LUT contains three tables: one for each of the three RGB channels. To gain a more visual description of a 3D LUT, take a look at Figure 10.47. You see a 3D LUT where you can remap the luminance value of one pixel to another pixel within the RGB color space.

FIGURE 10.47 3D Color LUT cube.

I could talk about more technical aspects of LUTs by going into nodes, mathematical tables for remapping colors, and looking up input luminance values and finding corresponding output luminance values, but it's a little more practical to just explain that you use LUTs to remap colors and look at the results after applying a 3D LUT Adjustment Layer. You can apply cinematic looks to photos, add warm or cool tones, increase color intensity, and do a variety of other applications when using LUTs.

Unfortunately, Photoshop Elements doesn't include any LUT Adjustment Layers. You need a plug-in like Elements+ to remap colors using LUTs.

Downloading 3D LUTs

Like brushes, textures, and patterns, you can find websites that host downloads for LUTs, including some with free downloads. As with other downloadable files, many sites advertise free downloads only to offer a trial and require that you make purchases after downloading. Plan on spending a little time poking around websites to find free downloads if you're not interested in making purchases.

In a web browser perform, search for *free 3D Photoshop LUTs*. A number of returns are provided. Browse some of the sites and look for the kind of cinematic or color toning effect you want to use.

Installing 3D LUTs

After downloading LUTs, you can keep the new LUT files either in a folder outside Elements or create a folder inside the Elements Presets folder. To add LUTs to Elements Presets, make a folder and copy the folder to your Elements application folder. In Windows, you find the Elements Presets folder at the following path: Program Files\Adobe\Photoshop Elements [version number]\ Presets. On the Mac, look for Macintosh HD\Applications\Adobe Photoshop Elements [version number]\Support Files\Presets.

To use the LUTs with Elements+, you can use LUTs stored either inside the Elements Presets folder or an external folder where you keep other presets. Name a folder 3D LUTs so you know what is contained in the folder. Also, make a backup of the folder if you store the LUTs inside the Elements Presets folder in case you lose the folder when you upgrade Elements or delete the folder to reinstall the application.

Once you create a folder, decompress all downloads for any LUT files you downloaded. Select the decompressed files and copy them to your new 3D LUTs folder, as shown in Figure 10.48.

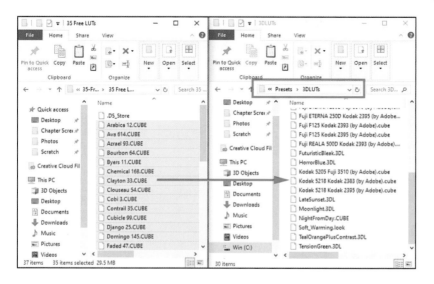

FIGURE 10.48 Copy downloaded LUTs to a folder inside your Elements Presets folder.

Using 3D LUTs

Elements+

If you installed new LUTs in your Elements Presets folder, the Elements+ plug-in recognizes all the LUTs contained in that folder. To apply a LUT to a photo, open a photo in the Photo Editor. Open the Elements+ Effects panel and choose 1. Color and Tone from the drop-down list at the top of the panel.

Mouse over the icons to see a pop-up description for each tool. Look for the Color Lookup tool, which is in the second row from the bottom. Click the tool to open the New Layer dialog box. Color LUTs created using Elements+ create new Adjustment Layers. Click OK, and the Color Lookup dialog box opens, as shown in Figure 10.49.

FIGURE 10.49 The Color Lookup dialog box from the Elements+ plug-in.

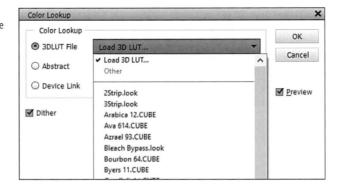

If you stored your LUTs inside the Elements Presets folder, click the Load 3D LUT drop-down list, and you find all the LUTs copied to your Elements Presets folder. If you store LUTs in another folder outside the Elements Presets folder, click the 3DLUT File radio button, and a Load dialog box opens. Browse your hard drive and locate the folder where you keep your LUT files. Select a LUT from the folder and click OK. As a matter of convenience, you'll find working with LUTs much easier when you copy them to the Elements Presets folder.

> **TIP:** Many LUTs you download will not have very descriptive names, so it will save you some time if you rename your LUTs more clearly. After loading LUTs, you may want to experiment to see what kinds of color remapping any given LUT does. Open the folder where you store your LUTs, check out what each one does, and rename it with a descriptive name.

In Figure 10.50, you can see the original image (left) and the edited image after I applied a Moonlight LUT I took from a Photoshop LUT preset.

FIGURE 10.50 Original image (left) and after remapping colors with a 3D Color LUT.

Creating 3D LUTs

If you want to create custom LUTs, you have to use Photoshop. Unfortunately, there's no way you can create a LUT from Elements. If you use Photoshop, or you have a friend who uses Photoshop, add a new layer to a photo in Elements. Make a new Adjustment Layer and apply color corrections to that layer.

Save the file as a .psd Photoshop file and open it in Photoshop or send it to a friend to open in Photoshop. In Photoshop, choose File > Export Color Lookup Tables. Choose settings and click Save.

Sizing Images for Cinematic Views

If you create cinematic color toning, you may upon occasion want to crop your photo to a realistic cinematic view. Cinema sizes have 21:9 ratios. LCD TVs typically have 16:9 ratios. You may want to crop your photos to one of these sizes for a more realistic look in a final image.

Preparing a Cinematic Look

Before you set the size for a cinematic view, you first need to prepare a photo with some color toning. In Figure 10.51, you can see the photo I started with.

FIGURE 10.51 Raw unedited image.

There are a number of different approaches you can use for color toning, some of which I covered in this chapter. It's completely up to you to decide what works best for you to create your vision of the final image you want. In Figures 10.53 and 10.54, I used 3D LUTs for the color grading.

Setting the Ratio for a Cinema Image Size

As I mentioned earlier, a cinema size is a 21:9 ratio. To crop the photo to a cinema view, select the Crop tool. Open the Tools Panel and type **21** in the W text box for the width and type **9** in the H text box for the height.

I created two versions of the image cropped to a cinema ratio from a warmer scheme and a cooler scheme using 3D LUTs. You can the results in Figures 10.52 and 10.53.

FIGURE 10.52 Color toned image with a warm sunset 3D LUT cropped to a cinema ratio.

FIGURE 10.53 Second color toned image using a blue 3D LUT also cropped to a cinema ratio.

PART VI

WORKING WITH TEXT AND PHOTO EFFECTS

It's important that you understand a few basic principles of typography before adding type to your photos, so in Chapter 11, I cover some basic principles of typography and explain how to create various text effects.

Chapter 12 deals with creating photo effects. This is a fun chapter where you can further your creativity and create some interesting results with your edits.

CHAPTER 11

WORKING WITH TYPE

Chapter Goals

This chapter is all about working with type and text fonts. The concepts contained herein include the following:

- Learning some typography basics
- Working with fonts
- Using type characters
- Creating type effects

When you want to add some type to a photo, or when you want to create a sign or poster, there are some basic rules you should follow regarding working with text. There's as much, or even more, to learn about typography as you can learn about Photoshop and Photoshop Elements.

However, this is not a book on typography, so I'm sticking to a few basic principles you should understand about working with type before moving on to applying different effects to type.

Working with Fonts

Adding type to a document requires more thought than just choosing a font from the Type Tool Options drop-down list and clicking a type font. If you use two fonts, you should be aware of making sure the fonts work together harmoniously. You should devote as much attention to creating a mood with a typeface as you do to color grading photos. Even if you add type to a texture, you should give some thought to the mood you're trying to create and choose a font that matches the mood.

Understanding Font Attributes

What is a font? Simply put, a *font* is a collection of characters that have a similar design. The characters can be upper- and lowercase, special symbols, numbers, and punctuation marks. A typeface, or a family, might be something like Helvetica, Garamond, Goudy Old Style, Eurostyle, Trajan, and so on. A font might be something like Helvetica 10-point Bold within the typeface family of Helvetica.

The important thing to know about fonts when constructing a document is that some fonts work well together, and some fonts don't work well when combined in the same document. If you're using more than one font, keep the total number of fonts in a single document to a maximum of two. To find out whether the fonts work well together, you can often perform a search in your web browser. For example, just type something like *what font goes well with Goudy Old Style* in a search engine. Quite often, your search results return a list of fonts that work well with the font you search. This little trick won't make you a typographer, but it will set you on a path to avoid some gross mistakes, like matching a font like Cochin with Eurostyle.

If you find yourself setting type frequently in documents, you might want to learn about font pairing to understand what fonts work well together and what font pairs you should avoid. There's a wealth of information on the Internet. Perform searches on font pairing and fonts to avoid.

Examining Font Types

When you choose a font from the Search For and Select Fonts drop-down list in the Type Tool Options panel, you see fonts installed by your operating system and any additional fonts you may have loaded in your Fonts folder. Within your Fonts folder, you may have any one of three different types of fonts. There are more types of fonts, but today most of the fonts you encounter are among these three different types:

■ **TrueType fonts:** Development of TrueType fonts was a collaborative effort by Apple and Microsoft to be a competitor to Adobe PostScript fonts. Back in the 1980s, Adobe was charging $60 to $80 for families containing as few as two to four fonts. Apple saw this as outrageous and decided to develop another technology. Ultimately, many TrueType fonts were distributed free of charge. TrueType fonts are fully scalable; you can fill, outline, and mask the fonts. Most of the TrueType fonts print well on commercial printing devices, but there are some exceptions. For screen use, TrueType fonts can be used without any problems. When you see a TrueType font in the Elements Photo Editor, a TT symbol appears, as shown in Figure 11.1.

■ **OpenType:** OpenType fonts are cross-platform fonts developed jointly by Adobe Systems and Microsoft. You can copy an OpenType font from a Windows machine to a Mac and vice versa. They are completely cross-platform. Adobe discontinued its entire PostScript font libraries and converted them to OpenType. OpenType fonts are now the de facto standard in the graphic design industry. OpenType fonts are represented by an O character when you view them in the Photo Editor fonts list (see Figure 11.1).

■ **TypeKit:** TypeKit is a free service by Adobe for Creative Cloud subscribers only. Adobe continually adds more fonts to the TypeKit library. To use the fonts, you need to be logged in to your Creative Cloud account. TypeKit fonts are identified in the Photo Editor font list with a Tk symbol (see Figure 11.1).

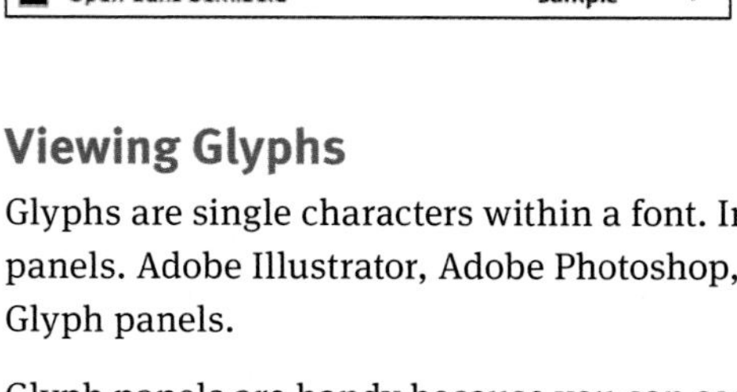

FIGURE 11.1 Three font types as shown in the Photo Editor font list.

Viewing Glyphs

Glyphs are single characters within a font. In many programs, you find Glyph panels. Adobe Illustrator, Adobe Photoshop, and Adobe InDesign all have Glyph panels.

Glyph panels are handy because you can see all the characters within a given font, including special characters. For example, if you want to type a trademark symbol (™), a Glyph panel shows you the trademark symbol to make it easy to find it on the keyboard. You can just double-click in a Glyph panel and the character is placed at the insertion point in an application document window that supports Glyphs panels.

Unfortunately, Photoshop Elements doesn't have a Glyphs panel. To access a panel where you can see all glyphs within a given font, you need to use tools provided by your operating system.

On Windows, open the Start menu, type **charmap**, and press Enter to search for the Character Map. The Windows Character Map dialog box (see Figure 11.2) enables you to choose a font from the Font drop-down list.

Below the font name, you see all the characters from the selected font in a scrollable list. If you want to add a character to a document in the Photo Editor, click a character, and the character appears zoomed in. Click the Select button, and the character is added to the Characters to Copy text box. Click Copy, return to your Photoshop Elements document, and choose Edit > Paste at a text insertion point. You must have a text insertion point active before you can paste the character.

FIGURE 11.2 The Windows Character Map dialog box.

Below the characters in the Character Map dialog box is a check box for an Advanced view. Click the check box to expand the dialog box so you can choose additional options. Among the Character set items shown in the drop-down list is Unicode. When you choose Unicode and mouse over a character, you are provided with a Unicode value. The codes can be used when you want special characters shown in web page designs.

On the Mac, you have something similar, but it's not as handy as Windows. On the Mac, you use a dialog box called the Character Viewer, and you can easily add a button in the top-level menu bar to open it. Apple put everything but the kitchen sink in this dialog box. You can view tons of different languages, see bullets and stars, see roman characters, see emoji icons, currency symbols, and a huge array of other special characters. If you want to see special characters, emojis, and character graphics on the Mac, press Ctrl + ⌘ + Spacebar to open Apple's Character Viewer.

However, the fundamental thing people want is to be able to change fonts and see character sets within a given font. Unfortunately, the programmers at Apple decided to not afford users this option.

The alternative you have on macOS computers is to use the Apple application Font Book, which is installed with your operating system in your Applications folder. Double-click Font Book, and the application opens as shown in Figure 11.3.

FIGURE 11.3 Apple's Font Book application.

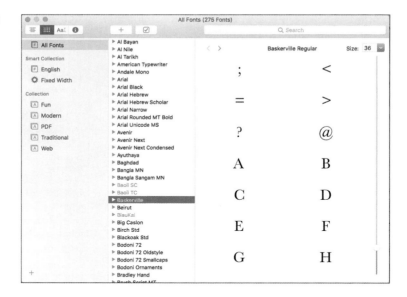

With Font Book, you can click installed fonts in the left panel and view characters associated with the font in the right panel. Select a character and choose Edit > Copy or press ⌘ + C and choose Edit > Paste (Ctrl/⌘ + V) at an insertion point in a document in the Photo Editor. If you choose a font in Font Book, you should have the same font chosen in the Photo Editor. If you have something like Wingdings selected in the Photo Editor and copy a character from Times New Roman, the pasted character will appear as a Wingding using the same keyboard key as the font copied from Font Book.

Looking at Font Types

You basically have two different font types within any given font. Fonts are categorized as either serif or sans serif.

Styles, widths, shapes, and designs can vary among serif fonts, but they all have what we call *serif extenders*. Figure 11.4 shows some examples of serif fonts.

FIGURE 11.4 Serif fonts.

Serif Fonts	
Adobe Caslon	Georgia
Baskerville	Goudy Old Style
Century	Minion
Cochin	Palatino
Courier	Perpetua
Garamond	Times New Roman

As a general rule, you don't want to use serif fonts at small sizes when exporting for screen displays. More modern fonts are more forgiving, but older fonts can present some problems for users being able to read the text. Sans serif fonts always work well on screen displays.

Among the serif fonts is a subgroup known as *slab serifs*. These fonts have sharp 90° corners, and the horizontal strokes are the same width as the vertical strokes. Slab serif fonts make for good headline type and applying special effects, and you can use them effectively with the right kind of complementary fonts. Some examples of slab serif fonts are shown in Figure 11.5.

The next category is sans serif fonts, samples of which are shown in Figure 11.6. There are more than 200,000 fonts available to you on computer systems today. More than 170,000 of those fonts are san serif fonts. San serifs are generally good for display type. Type is used in two manners: display and text. Display type is what you might think of as headline type. Text type is what you might think of as body copy. A headline might be a sans serif font on a printed document, and the type below it may be text type. On printed paper, serif fonts tend to read easier than sans serif fonts.

Slab Serif Fonts

Memphis
Rockwell
Serifa

FIGURE 11.5 Slab serif fonts.

Sans Serif Fonts

Arial	Kabel
Century Gothic	Myriad
Eurostyle	Optima
Franklin Gothic	Stone Sans
Gill Sans	Univers
Helvetica	Verdana

FIGURE 11.6 Sans serif fonts.

Changing Character and Line Spacing

Most programs offer you options for changing the tracking of words and the kerning of characters. Tracking is the overall spacing between characters, words, and large bodies of type like paragraphs. Kerning is the spacing between characters. When you set type in Elements, the Photo Editor uses some auto tracking and auto kerning.

If you want to change tracking, click the Type tool and open the Tool Options panel. You can open the pop-up menu and choose a fixed size or type a value in the Tracking text box. The higher the number, the farther the characters and words are spaced from each other.

In Figure 11.7, you can see the Tracking text box. There's also a label named Asian Text. By default, Asian Text is not active, and you may not see it in your Tool Options when you click a Type tool. You must first open Preferences (Ctrl/⌘ + K) and click Type in the left panel. Then check the box where you see Show Asian Text Characters. You also see two icons under the Anti-Aliasing check box: the Character orientation toggle and the Create Warped Text tool. You can choose to change text orientation between horizontal and vertical on the fly by clicking the first icon. The second icon, which is much more practical, is the Create Warped Text tool (which creates warped text). Make sure to click in a document with a Type tool to make the tools appear.

FIGURE 11.7 The Type Tool Options panel showing the Toggle Text Orientation and the Create Warped Text tool.

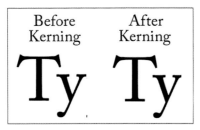

FIGURE 11.8 Type set in the Photo Editor using the Adobe Caslon font (left) and after kerning 100% in the Asian Text menu (right).

Photoshop Elements does not provide options for kerning characters. A workaround is to use settings in the Asian Text options. Select the characters where you want to decrease the intercharacter spacing and open the Asian Text pop-up list. You have fixed choices from 0 to 100% at 10% increments; choose the percentage by which you want to decrease the spacing. Below 100% is a minus (–) sign. If you want to increase the spacing, click the minus sign to add some spacing between characters.

Unfortunately, you only have limited control in Elements for kerning characters. A single application of 100% is as tight as you can kern characters together. As you can see in Figure 11.8, adding 100% kerning on the right side of the figure resulted in only a slight move of the y under the T.

Leading is the space between lines of type, and this is another type of spacing you can change. The default Auto Leading distance is close to 2 points greater than the text point size, although the measure is more precisely calculated when you set type in Adobe applications.

You can control leading by adjusting the Leading in the Type Tool Options panel. Open the drop-down list and choose a fixed value or type a value in the Leading text box. The higher the value, the greater the distance between the selected lines of type. If you have a paragraph of type and select only three of six lines, leading is applied to only the selected three lines.

Sizing Type

When you add type to a document, you see a green check mark and a Cancel symbol. Click the green check mark to confirm setting the type. As soon as you commit to the size and font attributes, you see a bounding box and handles on the corners and midpoints on all four sides.

Never drag the center handles. When you do, you distort the type by horizontal or vertical scaling. Fonts are works of art, and they're carefully calculated for each character's heights, ascenders, descenders, kerning pairs, and more. When you drag a horizontal or vertical midpoint, you destroy the artwork. Never scale any font horizontally or vertically.

The four corners can be moved to scale the type proportionately larger or smaller. When you move the cursor outside each corner, you see a semicircle with two arrowheads. Drag to rotate the text clockwise or counterclockwise. When you're finished transforming the type, click the green check mark to confirm the adjustment. In Figure 11.9, I created some type. I sized it up by dragging handles for proportional sizing and rotated it.

FIGURE 11.9 Type scaled and rotated.

One more thing to avoid when setting type is the Vertical Type tool. Software developers add tools like this for people to quickly apply vertical type. However, if you design a poster or announcement, never use vertical type. It looks amateurish and clumsy. If you need to have type run vertically, rotate the type 90°.

Viewing Type Samples

Elements includes a number of examples of type fonts used in designs that you can explore. You can poke around and see Adobe's examples of how some font pairs work together.

In Photoshop Elements 2021, a feature called *Quote Graphic* was introduced. You can access the Quote Graphic feature either in the Tool Options panel or from the Create menu. In the Tool Options panel, the Quote Graphic (labeled as Text Overlay Templates in the Tool Options panel) item appears on the right side of the Text Tool Options, as shown in Figure 11.10.

FIGURE 11.10 The Quote Graphic link appears in the Text Tool Options panel.

When you click the Text Overlay Templates icon or choose Quote Graphic from the Create panel, the Quote Graphic panel opens. In the panel are a number of samples and two options for creating your own Quote Graphic. Figure 11.11 shows some of the Quote Graphic templates.

FIGURE 11.11 The Quote Graphic templates.

For information on preparing images for social media, see Chapter 16, "Sharing Images."

Double-click one of the samples. Find one that has a type you like. You can also see a number of different layout sizes. Double-click a sample layout where you want to see the fonts, and look over the font pairing. A variety of different layouts appear for your selected design, as shown in Figure 11.12. Among the layouts are several social media sizes. When adding images for social media sites, you can use the template sizes as a guide for setting up your own designs.

When you've decided what type of template you need, double-click it to open the template. The template opens and displays the size you selected in the Quote Graphic panel.

Double-click in one of the lines of text. In the right panel, you see the type font displayed in a drop-down list at the top of the panel, as shown in Figure 11.13. You can choose one of the other fonts in the list to see how it works in the design. Most of the designs include two type fonts. You can use these templates as a guide for your own designs.

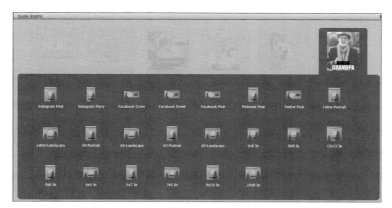

FIGURE 11.12 A template with a number of different size samples.

FIGURE 11.13 Click one of the lines of text to view the font information in the right panel.

Downloading Fonts

As I said earlier, there are more than 200,000 fonts. Almost all of those fonts are available for download either for commercial sale or as free downloads. If you're a Creative Cloud subscriber, you can access Adobe TypeKit and download TypeKit fonts free as a service with your Creative Cloud account. You can purchase and download other fonts from software vendors at a number of websites. The third option is downloading fonts that are free and don't require purchase.

Finding Fonts

There are a number of sites where you can download free fonts. Try one of these:

- www.1001freefonts.com

- www.fontsquirrel.com

- www.dafont.com

Alternatively, do an Internet search for *free fonts* to find some more sites that provide you with free downloads.

When you visit a site and you want to download a font, be certain to look on the website for any licensing requirements. If you download a font that's accompanied with a PDF or README file, be certain to look it over. Some sites will provide free downloads for personal use but want exorbitant fees if you use the fonts commercially, post on social media, or even print on paper.

Figure 11.14 shows some fonts I downloaded from www.1001freefonts.com. Each of the fonts on that website is free, but some can be used only for personal use. Some request that you make a donation, and others require that you buy a commercial license. Be sure to look over each font before you download so you know the restrictions, if any, for using the font.

FIGURE 11.14 Free fonts downloaded from the www.1001freefonts.com website.

Installing Fonts

If you have a huge library of fonts, it will serve you well to use a font management tool. My personal favorite is Font Agent Pro from Insider Software, which is available for both Windows and the Mac. Visit www.insidersoftware.com for more information about their font management tool.

If it's not a problem for you to install/deinstall fonts, then you can manually move them around on your computer. On Windows, after downloading a font, first decompress the file (if it's compressed) by right-clicking and choosing Extract. Move the extracted files to the Windows > Fonts folder. Unfortunately, you can't keep the fonts in separate folders, so they all have to be lumped together in a single folder.

On the Mac, go to a Finder view. From the Go menu, choose Go to Folder. The Go to Folder dialog box opens. In the text box, type **~/Library/Fonts** and press Enter. The Fonts folder opens. Copy all decompressed fonts here.

Deinstalling Fonts

One thing you want to be certain of is that you keep your computer lean, especially if you don't have a lot of RAM. Installing a lot of fonts slows Elements down to a snail's pace on computers with 8G or less of RAM.

Create a folder where you want to keep disabled fonts. Copy fonts that you want to delete temporarily from your Fonts folder to the new folder. On Windows, copy fonts from the Windows > Fonts folder; on the Mac, open the Go menu in the Finder and type **~/Library/Fonts** to open the fonts folder. Copy fonts you don't need for an editing session to the folder where you store disabled fonts. After you've copied the fonts to the folder, delete them from the source folder.

If you have Elements open, either in the Organizer or the Photo Editor, quit all Elements applications and restart the Photo Editor after disabling some fonts. You need to relaunch the program in order to see new fonts added.

Creating Type Effects

Now that you're familiar with some font basics, it's time to apply some editing tasks to type. There are hundreds of different effects you can apply to type in the Photo Editor. It's well beyond the scope of this book to cover every possible effect, but I can take you on a tour of some of the more popular effects you can use with type.

Adding Styles to Type

When you add text to a document, the text is a vector shape. You can scale the type up or down an infinite number of times without losing any quality, but you cannot apply any options available in the Effects or Filters panels. To use Effects or Filters, you must convert the vector layer to a raster layer. To convert text from a vector shape to pixels, use the Layer panel menu and choose Simplify Layer or choose Layer > Simplify Layer.

For more information on vector and raster data, see Chapter 3, "Making Selections."

When you click Styles in the Panel Bin, you have a number of choices from which to choose for various style effects that you can apply while the text remains as a vector layer. You can also apply the same effects if you simplify the layer. However, you may experience unexpected results if you want to edit and refine a style applied to a simplified layer. It's best to complete all edits and then simplify the layer if you need to perform an edit that cannot be applied on a vector layer.

Click Styles and open the drop-down list at the top of the panel. As shown in Figure 11.15, there are many different style categories from which to choose. All the styles from all the different categories can be applied to the vector type. You don't need to simplify type layers when applying Styles.

FIGURE 11.15 Styles drop-down list.

Within each category are many different options. Some categories have fewer choices, whereas other categories have several choices. There are 26 different choices in the Patterns category, for example.

NOTE: You can change the type after applying any style. The text changes, but the style remains unaffected.

You have an array of effects that you can apply using the Styles panel. You can create bevel and embosses, glows, neon effects, plastic, chrome, and many more. At the top-right side of the Styles panel, you see a symbol commonly used to represent settings. By default, this item is grayed out. You need to first apply a style to an item before you can access the Style settings.

Apply a simple style such as a Bevel. You can use any one of the different styles. The Show Style Settings icon appears on all panels within the Styles categories. Just select a Bevel and drag it to a type layer or select the type and click a bevel in the Bevels panel. Click the Show Style Settings icon at the top-right side of the Bevels panel. The Style Settings dialog box opens, as shown in Figure 11.16.

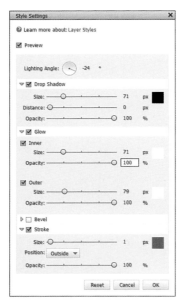

FIGURE 11.16 The Style Settings dialog box.

All the Styles have different options applied. The Style Settings dialog box by default shows you all the settings for a given style. You can change settings by moving sliders to edit the amount of a given effect. You can change colors by clicking swatches to open the Color Picker. You can add or delete drop shadows, glows, bevels, and strokes or change their attributes.

For example, if I apply a Wow-Neon Yellow effect (in the Wow-Neon styles group) to type as shown in Figure 11.17, I can open the Style Settings and see what settings were made to create the effect. Figure 11.16 shows the settings used for the Wow-Neon Yellow.

If I want to make some changes for the size of the Inner/Outer Glows, the Stroke attributes, the Drop Shadow size and distance, and so on, I can make those edits, click OK, and customize the style. You can also eliminate all settings and create a new style from scratch. If you click the Reset button, it has no effect on the other styles.

FIGURE 11.17 A Wow-Neon Yellow style applied to type.

In Figure 11.18, you can see some adjustments I made in the Style Settings for the Wow-Neon Yellow effect I applied in Figure 11.17.

You're not limited to type when using styles. Any photo can be a target for applying a style. You can use raster images, or if you want to create a Smart Object, choose File > Place and place a photo in an open document, and it comes in as a Smart Object.

FIGURE 11.18 The Wow-Neon Yellow effect edited in the Style Settings dialog box.

There are far too many styles you can apply to discuss each one in this book. Most of the styles are self-explanatory. To see the results after applying styles, play around with type and the options available to you.

All the styles are intended for easy application to type or photos where you want to change appearances of a given style. You can also start from scratch and manually apply similar effects to type and photos.

Creating Gold Type

The Style Settings in Elements are very limiting. There's only so much you can do with creating effects you might like to have. In Photoshop, the Layer Styles panel offers much more than what's available in Elements. But you can make a try at creating some effects using the Photo Editor. One of those effects is creating gold type. It doesn't turn out as well as it would with Photoshop, but here are the steps to creating gold type in Elements:

1. Create a new document and use the Default Photoshop Elements Size from the Document Type drop-down list. Fill the background with black.

2. Open the Text Tool Options and choose a serif font with a narrow body width, such as Garamond, Trajan, or Times New Roman. Type body widths vary. An extra bold font has a large body width. An ultralight font has a very narrow body width. Type a word with a font size of around 140px. In my example, I typed the word Gold. Select the text.

3. Select the type and open the Color Picker by clicking the foreground color swatch. Choose an orange or orange/yellow color. I used the same color I used in Chapter 10 when I created Orange/Teal gradients, so I typed ffa800 in the # text box and clicked OK.

4. Open the Bevels panel by clicking Styles. By default, the Bevels should appear. If Bevels is not showing in the Styles panel, choose Bevels from the drop-down list at the top of the panel. Select the text on the top layer.

5. Select Wacky Metallic (the last item in the Bevels list), and the bevel effect is applied to the type, as shown in Figure 11.19.

FIGURE 11.19 The Wacky Metallic bevel applied to the text.

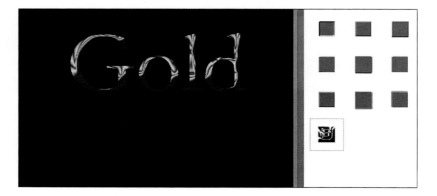

FIGURE 11.20 Adjustments made in the Style Settings dialog box.

6. The text doesn't look right. I need the gold color applied more evenly through the text. Double-click the *fx* symbol at the far right of the layer or click the Style Settings icon at the top of the Bevels panel to open the Style Settings.

7. Change the lighting angle to **−50** and move the Bevel slider to the left to 21, as shown in Figure 11.20. Leave the default Up check box alone and click OK. The gold color now appears more evenly throughout the text, as shown in Figure 11.21.

FIGURE 11.21 Final gold type image.

Splitting Text

Breaking or splitting type is often used in different designs. To split type, follow these steps:

1. Create a new document and type a character or word. Select the text, create a Layer Mask, and duplicate the layer. You now have two layers with two layer masks.

2. Use the Lasso tool and draw a diagonal line through the center of the text. Press the Alt key or select the Polygon Lasso tool, click, move the cursor, and click again to create a straight-line selection.

3. Move the selection around the top of the text. Click the mask so it's selected and fill the selection with black. Half of the character or word should be hidden in the mask, as shown in Figure 11.22.

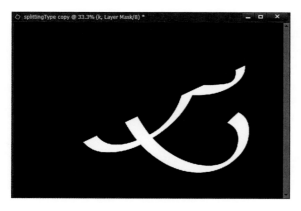

FIGURE 11.22 Fill half of the text with black to hide the top part of the text.

4. Keep the selection active and press Ctrl/⌘ + Shift + I to inverse the selection.

5. Click the original Layer Mask to select it and press Alt/Option + Backspace/Delete to fill the foreground with black. At this point, you have two layers with the top and bottom half of the type masked in the layers.

6. Apply a bevel or glow to each layer.

7. Click the Move tool and press the arrow keys to move a layer. The final split text is shown in Figure 11.23.

FIGURE 11.23 Type split in final image.

Warping Type

For a long time, users have wanted a tool to warp objects, and finally in Elements version 2022, we have a means of warping both type and objects.

The difference between warping type and warping objects is that to warp type using the Type Tool Options panel adjustments, you need to apply the warp to vector objects. As I mention earlier, adding a type layer creates a vector object. If you use the Warp transformation tool, you need to work on a raster layer.

Warping Vector Type Using Tool Options

Let's take a look first at warping type using the Type Tool Options panel. Follow these steps to warp type:

1. Create a new document and add some type to the new file.

2. Open the Type Tool Options panel and click the Create Warped Text tool (refer to Figure 11.7) to open the Warp Text dialog box. You'll warp the text and then add a gradient.

3. Click the Style drop-down list to see a list of preset warp options, as shown in Figure 11.24.

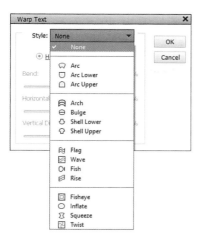

FIGURE 11.24 The Warp Text fixed presets in the Style list.

The warp effect you apply to type using this method limits you to the presets. The only way you can modify the style you choose is in the Warp Text dialog box.

4. Select a preset, and you return to the Warp Text dialog box adjustments for a given preset, as shown in Figure 11.25.

5. From the Style drop-down list, you have many options for creating warped text. For this example, I used the Bulge option to raise the center of the text. Adjust sliders in the Warp Text dialog box to your liking. As you move sliders, you see a dynamic preview of the results.

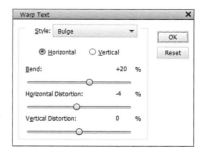

FIGURE 11.25 The Warp Text dialog box adjustments.

6. If you want to change the color of the warped text, apply a fill, or apply a gradient, you can do so while the text is still a vector object. In this example, I added a gradient to the text.

For more information on creating clipping groups, see Chapter 5, "Masking Photos."

7. Create a new blank layer at the top of the layer stack. If you use Layer > New Layer, the New Layer dialog box opens. Check the box for Use Previous Layer to Create Clipping Mask. If you use the Create a New Layer icon in the Layers panel, place your cursor between the new layer and the type layer below it. Press Alt/Option and click to create a clipping group. This action fills the text with the gradient and clips the gradient to the text.

8. Select the top layer and click the gradient tool. Choose a gradient by clicking the gradient in the Tool Options panel. Draw a gradient from one side of the top layer to the other. The resultant layer is clipped to the text below it.

9. Click the Type layer to select it. Open the Styles panel and choose Strokes from the drop-down list at the top of the panel. Choose a stroke you want to apply to the type. In my example, I used the Black Stroke 0.5px option, as shown in Figure 11.26.

FIGURE 11.26 Warped type filled with a gradient and black stroke.

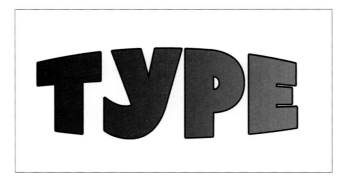

Warping Raster Type Using the Warp Transformation Tool

With the Warp transformation tool, you can warp text or anything else on a layer, including images and objects. Use the following steps to see how to do warp transformations using this tool:

NOTE: You must have Elements version 2022 or greater to use the Warp Transformation tool.

1. Create a new blank document. Set the file attributes as you like. For my example, I created a document with a transparent background.

2. Select the Horizontal Type tool and click in the document. In the Tool Options panel, set the type attributes you want. In my example, I used the Impact Regular font, a size of 300 points, and a blue fill for the type. To change the color from the current foreground color in the Tools panel, click the swatch where you see Color in the Tool Options panel. Type the text you want to use. My example is shown in Figure 11.27.

FIGURE 11.27 "Type" with a blue fill added to a new blank document.

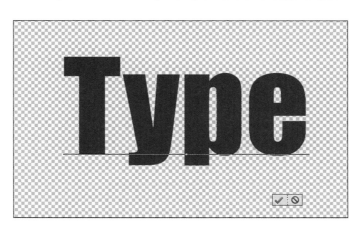

3. To add a stroke while the type is still a vector object, you can right-click the type and choose Edit Layer Style from a context menu. The Style Settings dialog box opens. Click the Stroke check box and open the menu by clicking the right-pointing arrow. The options you have for a stroke setting include setting the stroke point size, choosing the position of the stroke (Outside, Center, Inside), and an adjustment for Opacity. In my example, I chose an 8-point stroke positioned at the Center, as shown in Figure 11.28.

    After you've adjusted the settings, click OK to return to the document window.

4. You cannot warp the text while it remains as a vector object. You need to convert the text to a raster image first. To do so, open the Layers panel menu and choose Simplify Layer, and the vector object is converted to a raster image. At this point, you can use the Warp tool.

5. Select the text. In my example, I created the text on a transparent layer, and if the text is created on a transparent layer, you can easily select the text by pressing Ctrl/⌘ and clicking the layer in the Layers panel. All nontransparent data are selected. With the text selected, choose Image > Transform > Warp.

    After selecting the Warp command, you find handles at the corners of the object and points plotted along each side of the bounding box rectangle. You can move any one of the points along all four sides to shape the object and warp it. When you select a point, you also get anchor points and direction lines that you can use to create Bezier curves. Take a look at Figure 11.29. You can see the object warped, handles along the edges, and Bezier curves with points at the ends of the curves.

FIGURE 11.28 The Style Settings dialog offer options for adding a stroke and setting stroke attributes.

NOTE: The Warp tool is a menu command, and it's part of the Transformation tools. Remember to access warp features by first selecting a raster object and then choosing Image > Transform > Warp.

NOTE: When you make a selection, the peripheral selection is called the **bounding box** of an object.

FIGURE 11.29 Text warped using the warp transformation.

For an example where a photo is warped using the Warp tool, see Chapter 14, "Creating Photo Effects."

You can use the warp tool with any raster data on a layer. Just remember to first make a selection and then choose Image > Transform > Warp.

Creating Type on a Curve

You can create effects to show type carved in material such as stone or wood. My first example is for carving type into stone. Later, I'll show you carving type into wood.

Creating Type on Stone

This exercise calls for a marble or granite texture. You can scan a piece of marble or tile and use it for the background of the image. If you don't have any marble or tile handy, search for marble and granite images on the Internet.

I wanted my final image to have an old Roman look, so I used a font that has characteristics of an old Roman typeface. The font Trajan is common to most Elements users (pronounced TRAY-jen and named after Caesar Nerva Trajanus Augustus who ruled from 98 to 177 AD). Add type using the Trajan 3 font. If you don't have the Trajan font, choose a similar serif font.

Open the Bevels panel and choose the Simple Sharp Inner bevel. Click the Style Settings icon to open the Style Settings. Set the Lighting Angle to −50 and move the bevel Size slider to a position where it splits the type evenly between the dark and light shades, as shown in Figure 11.30.

FIGURE 11.30 Adjust Style Settings to balance the light and dark areas of the text.

Apply any color you like to the text. If you're using a medium to medium-dark granite texture, leave the text color black. If you're using marble and you want to color the text, click the Eyedropper tool on the marble in an area where you want to lift the color or use the Color Picker to choose a color.

In my example, I chose the text Marcus Aurelius after the Roman emperor from 161 to 180 AD. I also added a photo of a statue of Marcus Aurelius to the image, as shown in the final result in Figure 11.31.

FIGURE 11.31 Type on marble.

Carving Type on Wood

You can scan pieces of wood on a flatbed scanner or take a photo of a wall, table, or other wooden object to use if you want to follow along with these steps:

1. Open the file in the Photo Editor.

2. Choose a typeface in the Type Tool Options panel and type a word on your wood background. If you want to sample a color in the wood, set the Point Sample for the Eyedropper tool to 3 × 3 or 5 × 5. Click on one of the darkest areas of the photo.

3. Select the type with the Type tool by dragging across the type to select it. Click the foreground color swatch with the new color appearing as the foreground color. The Color Picker opens. Click OK and the foreground color is applied to the type.

4. Open the Styles panel and choose Bevels from the drop-down list. For the bevel in my example, I wanted a softer bevel shape applied to the text, so I chose the Simple Inner Bevel.

5. If you want to edit the Style Settings, click the Style Settings icon in the Bevels panel and make adjustments for Angle and Size.

6. Click the Layers panel icon in the Panel Bin and apply the Soft Light blend mode to the layer. As you can see in Figure 11.32, the Soft Light blend mode brings out the wood grain through the type.

NOTE: When you use the Eyedropper tool to sample a color, always set the Average Point Sample in the Tool Options dialog box to 3 × 3 or 5 × 5. If you leave it at the default Point Sample, it samples only a single pixel, and you might sample a pixel much lighter or darker than the color you want. The 3 × 3 and 5 × 5 choices use an average for a range of 3 × 3 and 5 × 5 pixels. The sample results in a more representative match for the color you sample.

FIGURE 11.32 Final image with type on wood.

Creating Grunge Type

To create a grunge background, use these steps:

1. Create a portrait document—maybe 4 × 6 at 300 ppi.

2. Click the Brush tool and open the Tools Panel. If you have some grunge tip brushes, it helps, but you can usually find a grungy brush in the default brushes. Set the brush size to a large size, like 1500 or greater.

3. Click and apply dabs on the canvas. In my example, I used a default brush tip and clicked some dabs on a blank canvas. I then rotated the canvas for a landscape view, as shown in Figure 11.33.

FIGURE 11.33 Brush dabs using a grunge brush tip.

4. Add type to create a new type layer. For my typeface, I wanted a Slab Serif font, so I choose Rockwell Bold for the font.

5. Place the type layer below the grunge brush strokes. Create a selection for the type and press the Alt/Option key. With the cursor between the layers, click the line separating the layers to create a clipping group. Essentially, you are clipping the grunge layer to the selection from the type.

6. Create a Layer Mask from the selection on the type layer. Click the mask to select it. Make sure the foreground color is white and set the brush size

to a smaller size. Click some dabs in the mask to add a little more grunge appearance on the type.

7. If you want to add a color layer below the type, click the Create a New Layer icon in the Layers panel and move it below the type.

8. Fill the bottom layer with a color as you like. The final result of my example is shown in Figure 11.34.

FIGURE 11.34 The final image with grunge type.

Creating Type Shadows and Reflections

You might want to add a shadow or reflection to type you add to a photo. In the following steps, I demonstrate how a shadow is applied to type:

1. Create type on a photo and duplicate the type layer. In my example, I duplicated the layer twice. One type layer is used as a drop shadow. If you don't want a drop shadow, then create only one duplicate.

2. On the first layer above the Background layer, select the type, open the Layers panel menu, and choose Simplify Layer. Press Ctrl/⌘ and click the layer to select the type. Fill the text with black. Deselect and apply a Gaussian blur. The amount depends on your image and how much you want the shadow to feather out.

3. Hide the top two layers and adjust opacity on the shadow layer. Set the opacity to your liking.

4. Place the layer above the shadow in view. Click the Move tool and tap the arrow keys to nudge the shadow so it offsets from the layer above.

5. Click the layer above the shadow and press Ctrl/⌘ + E to merge the two layers.

6. Select the top layers and choose Image > Rotate > Flip Layer Vertical. Move the layers below the vertical type layer.

7. Open the Layers panel menu and choose Simplify Layer. You need to use the Perspective transformation on one layer, and Elements permits you to alter perspective on raster layers only. Therefore, you cannot use a vector type layer.

8. Select the layer after simplifying it and press Ctrl/⌘ + T to transform the type.

9. Open a context menu on the selection and choose Perspective. Drag the corner handles out to create a perspective view for the shadow.

10. Press Ctrl/⌘ and click the distorted type to create a selection. When the selection is active, add a Layer Mask. Be certain the inside of the selection is white when you click on the mask.

11. Select the Gradient tool and open the Gradient Tool options. Click the gradient shown in the Tool Options panel. When the Gradient Editor opens, set the Foreground to Transparent gradient and click OK.

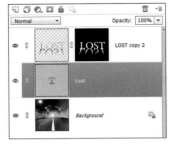

12. Press D on your keyboard to select default black foreground and white background colors.

13. In the Tool Options panel, be certain the gradient type is Linear.

14. Create a selection by pressing Ctrl/⌘ and clicking on the mask and selecting the mask. Draw a gradient in the mask. The type should gradually fade out. If the gradient doesn't look right, try again. Keep reworking the gradient until it looks right. In my example, I used the Soft Light blending mode. At this point, the Layers panel looks like Figure 11.35.

FIGURE 11.35 Layers panel showing two type layers.

15. Try experimenting with blending modes. Try Soft Light, Linear Burn, and Normal to see what effect looks best for you. My final image for this example is shown in Figure 11.36.

FIGURE 11.36 Final image with a type shadow.

Masking Type

Masking type is very straightforward. You create a type layer and add a Layer Mask. You can use the Horizontal Type Mask tool. Type the characters you want and click the Add Layer Mask icon in the Layers panel. Place a photo on top of the type layer. Select the photo layer and load the selection from the mask by pressing Ctrl/⌘ and clicking on the mask. Press the Alt/Option key and click between layers to create a clipping group.

Once you mask the type, you can move the photo inside the type mask. Select the Move tool and click on the photo layer. Move the cursor inside the type while you're still on the photo layer. Click and drag to move the photo around to a desired position. In Figure 11.37, you can see a type mask I created for this example.

FIGURE 11.37 Final image with a type mask.

Creating Type on a Path

When you click on the Type tool and open the Tool Options panel, you see seven Type tools. The Vertical Type tool and the Vertical Type Mask tools are somewhat worthless. As I mention earlier in this chapter, using vertical type is not good graphic design.

The other tools after the Horizontal Type tool and the Horizontal Type Mask tools include the Text on Shape tool and the Text on Custom Path tool. Earlier versions prior to Elements 10 didn't have this tool.

If you want to add type to geometric shapes like circles, rectangles, polygons, and some custom shapes, you use the Text on Shape tool. When you want to draw freeform paths, you use the Text on Custom Path tool.

You may have the line tool, rectangle tool, or another tool currently selected, but before you create a path, you need to select the Custom Shape tool. The Custom Shape tool is to the right of the Eyedropper tool in the Tools panel. Click the Custom Shape tool to open the Tool Options panel. Click a shape. In my example, I use the Ellipse tool to draw a circle. Click on the Type tool and select the Text on Shape Tool (the tool below the Horizontal Type Mask tool).

This tool is needed if you need to modify paths when you draw paths with the Text on Shape Tool.

Suppose you want to add text on a circle. Take a look at the following steps to see how you can do that:

1. Choose File > New > Blank File. In the New dialog box, set the background color to white. Use any resolution you like for your file and set the Color Mode to RGB. Click OK to create the new blank file.

2. Select the Text on Shape tool and open the Tools panel. To the right of the Text on Shape tool, you see icons for various shapes, as shown in Figure 11.38. Select the Draw Ellipse tool. Note that the only time you see shapes in the Type Tool Options panel is when you select the Text on Shape tool.

Shape Selection Tool

FIGURE 11.38 Tool Options for the Text on Shape tool.

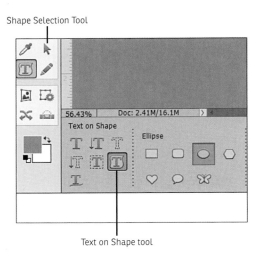

Text on Shape tool

3. Press Alt/Option + Shift and draw an ellipse.

TIP: Alt/Option + Shift enables you to draw a circle from center.

4. Move the cursor to the circle. When the cursor is placed over the circle, you see the cursor icon change to a text insertion over a diagonal wavy line, as shown in Figure 11.39.

5. Move to the left side of the circle and click. Type what you want for the text to add it to the circle.

6. In the Tool Options panel, choose a font and set the point size.

7. Press Ctrl/⌘ + J to duplicate the layer.

8. Press Ctrl/⌘ + T to transform the circle. Press Alt/Option + Shift and click on a corner handle. Be certain in the Tool Options panel that the center circle is selected for the Transform settings. Keep the keys depressed and move a corner handle to size up the circle and text. Size the circle up about twice the point size of the type.

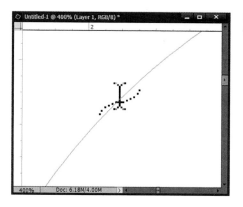

FIGURE 11.39 Move the cursor over the circle to see the text insertion cursor.

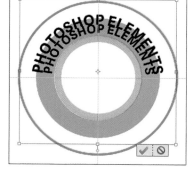

FIGURE 11.40 Size up the duplicate so the baseline of the duplicate layer is on top of the first text layer.

9. Try to size the duplicate circle so the baseline of the text is right on the top of the text in the first layer. It should look something like what you see in Figure 11.40.

10. When the size appears right, click the green check mark to confirm the adjustment.

11. Click the text on the duplicate circle. You should see a cursor with an insertion symbol and a left-pointing arrow off the middle, similar to Figure 11.41.

12. Type text for the bottom half of the circle. Rotate the text so it appears centered at the bottom of the circle.

13. Move the cursor to the bottom of the circle. You should see a cursor icon with two opposite arrows, as shown in Figure 11.42. Click and drag up to move the text to the inside of the circle.

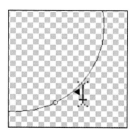

FIGURE 11.41 The cursor icon changes when you click the text and move the cursor over the circle.

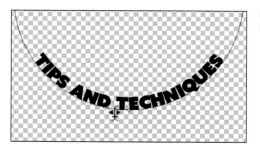

FIGURE 11.42 Drag up so the text moves to the inside of the circle.

14. Sizing the circle with the type changes the font's point size. In the Tool Options panel, set the point size for the type to match the same size as the original type.

If you want to add some color, you can create additional shapes below the text layers and fill them with colors. In Figure 11.43, you can see the final image I have for this exercise.

FIGURE 11.43 Final image with two type layers.

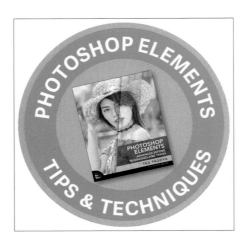

Adding Watermarks

Unfortunately, as of this writing, it's not possible to process multiple files with graphic symbols in Photoshop Elements 2022. If you want a graphic for a watermark, you need to place the graphic individually on photos. You can open a photo with a watermark image and keep it in the Photo Bin. As you want to apply the graphic to a photo, you open it from the Photo Bin and drag the layer from the graphic photo to your final image.

If you want to use text for a watermark, you can apply text using a batch processing technique where you can target a folder of files and have Elements automatically watermark each photo without having to open and save the photos individually. Use this method:

1. Choose File > Process Multiple Files. You don't need any file open in the Photo Editor to use the menu command. After choosing the menu command, the Process Multiple Files dialog box opens, as shown in Figure 11.44.

2. Choose the folder that contains your photos to be watermarked by clicking the Browse button in the Source area of the dialog box. Click Browse in the Destination area to identify where you want to save the watermarked files. If you want to overwrite the source files, select the same folder for the Destination.

NOTE: You can also use brushes for watermarks. You need to apply brush strokes manually on each document. To learn how to create brush strokes for watermarks, see online Chapter 17, "Working with Brushes."

3. In the Labels section, be certain Watermark is selected from the dropdown list. Type the text you want for the watermark in the Custom Text field.

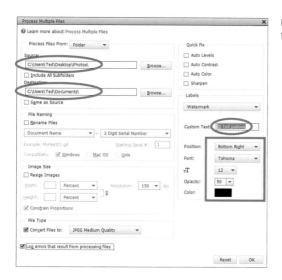

FIGURE 11.44 The Process Multiple Files dialog box.

4. Choose a position in the Position drop-down list. Also choose a font, font size, opacity, and color for the watermark from the respective drop-down lists. Click OK when finished. Figure 11.45 shows a photo I watermarked for this exercise.

FIGURE 11.45 Watermarked photo.

CHAPTER 12

CREATING PHOTO EFFECTS

Chapter Goals

In Chapter 7, "Using Effects," I explained how to use effects from a variety of methods that you can apply using the Effects panel. In this chapter, I take you through some photo effects to create some interesting artistic photos and some other effects to help you improve your photos. The various effects I discuss in this chapter include the following:

- Low key and high key images
- Infrared photos
- Effects with photo filters
- Pixel stretch images
- Low poly artwork
- Custom portrait effects
- Tattoo removal
- Multiple masks

- Portrait brush effects
- Paint drip effect
- Cartoon effects
- Caricature effect
- Pencil Drawing effect
- Dispersion effect
- Creating low and high key photos

A low key photo is one that is predominately black with little brightness. Low key photos are usually dramatic and somewhat mysterious, and they convey atmosphere and mood. High key photos, on the other hand, are predominately white with a lot of brightness and very little black. These photos generally feel airy and light.

Creating a Low Key Photo

You can create low key photos from color, black and white, color converted to black and white, photos that begin with predominately dark tones, or photos with normal exposure values. When converting a photo to low key, the Low Key Guided Edit is a good place to start.

To begin converting a photo to low key, click Guided at the top of the Photo Editor. Click on the Black and White tab. Even though the High and Low key options are contained in the Black and White Guided Edit tab, you can use color photos and keep them in color after you complete the conversions.

Click Black and White in the Guided Edit panel. Scroll down to Low Key and click the Low Key thumbnail to open the Low Key panel. In the Low Key panel, your first option is to use Color or Black and White for the final low key image. In this example, I clicked on Color to leave the photo in RGB Color mode. As shown in Figure 12.1, you also have an option to use a Background Brush to fade out some areas of the photo.

FIGURE 12.1 The Low Key Guided Edit panel.

If you want to darken some of the background, use the Background Brush. You can adjust size and opacity in sliders below the Background Brush button. If you add too much darkness to the background, you can erase some of the darker areas of the photo by selecting Reduce Effect below the Background Brush options.

When you finish editing in the Low Key panel, click Next, and you have a choice for saving the file, uploading to social media, or opening the file in Expert mode in the Photo Editor. For this example, I used the latter option.

When you arrive back at the Photo Editor, open the Layers panel, and you can see several layers that were added to the file. Before proceeding, create a selection of the subject containing only the brighter tones in the photo. After creating the selection, add a layer mask on a duplicate layer of the background. At this point, your Layers panel should look like Figure 12.2.

FIGURE 12.2 The Layers panel after completing the Guided Edit.

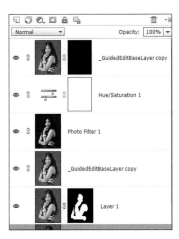

The Guided Edit is a good start in producing a low key image, but most photos will require some more editing. You may want to create a Levels layer and adjust brightness for the subject. Press Ctrl/⌘ and click on the mask you created. Add a Levels Adjustment Layer. Edit the brightness of the subject by adjusting the sliders.

For my example, I wanted to create a black-and-white photo. I could have chosen black and white in the Guided Edit panel, but I prefer using my own method for converting color to black and white. For this conversion, I use a Gradient Map Adjustment Layer. Choose Gradient Map from the Add fill or Adjustment Layer drop-down list in the Layers panel and then choose Black, White.

After some additional adjustments in the Levels dialog box, the final image looks as shown on the right in Figure 12.3.

FIGURE 12.3 Low key image (right) created from unedited photo (left).

Creating a High Key Photo

Sometimes you take a shot with your camera and find some things you like about the image but decide it has too many distracting elements. The subject may look good, but the overall photo is terrible.

This was the case once when I attended a friend's wedding. The bride and groom hired a photographer, so I was always conscious of staying away from the photographer's work. I couldn't pose the subjects or move them to more appealing areas around the wedding site. I just had to take candid shots as best I could.

One photo I liked was a candid shot I took of the bride. She was a lovely bride and the shot captured her in a pleasing and flattering way. However, the background was horrible, and the photo was cluttered, as you can see in Figure 12.4. I thought about this photo and decided I'd try to convert it to a high key image to see what I could do to make the photo look much better.

The first step in this conversion was to convert the color to black and white. There was no way to make this photo look better with the original color, so I decided to eliminate it.

To convert to black and white, use Enhance > Convert to Black and White. The Convert to Black and White dialog box opens, as shown in Figure 12.5.

FIGURE 12.4 Original unedited photo used for conversion to high key.

FIGURE 12.5 The Convert to Black and White dialog box.

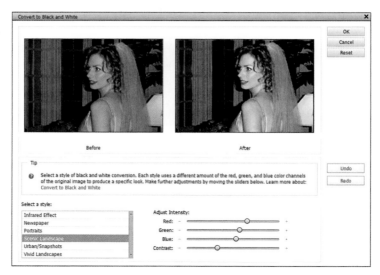

In the Convert to Black and White dialog box, the best choice for the style for this photo is the Portrait option. If necessary, adjust the RGB and Contrast sliders. In this example, I just accepted the defaults and clicked OK.

For more on selecting sub-jects, see Chapter 3, "Making Selections."

The next step is to create a selection of the subject. You need to isolate the subject to do something with a horrible background. I created a selection around the subject and the bouquet of flowers, as shown in Figure 12.6.

FIGURE 12.6 Create a selection of the subject.

Add a Layer Mask by clicking the Add Layer Mask icon in the Layers panel. Click the mask and inverse the selection by pressing Ctrl/⌘ + I or choosing Select > Inverse.

Add a Levels Adjustment Layer by clicking the Create Fill or Adjustment Layer icon in the Layers panel and choosing Levels. The Levels dialog box opens, as shown in Figure 12.7.

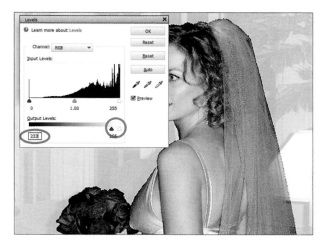

FIGURE 12.7 The Levels dialog box.

When the Levels dialog box opens, move the Output slider to the right. In my example, I move the slider to 233. This fades the background considerably, resulting in a high key image because most of the black has been eliminated from the photo.

Make a Color Curves adjustment to the selection of the background. Choose Enhance > Adjust Color > Adjust Color Curves to open the Adjust Color Curves dialog box, as shown in Figure 12.8.

FIGURE 12.8 Adjustments in the Color Curves dialog box.

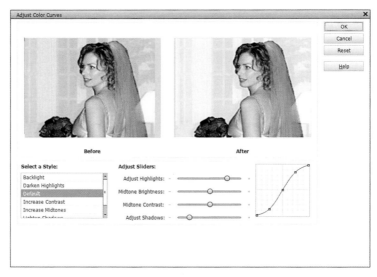

In this example, I darkened the shadows just a bit and brightened the highlights by moving the Adjust Highlights and Adjust Shadows sliders, as shown in Figure 12.8.

FIGURE 12.9 Final high key image.

The image is now complete. If you want to add a tint or sepia tone to the photo, you can bring in some tones that enrich the look of the photo. In this example, I use a Levels Adjustment Layer. When the Levels dialog box opens, I select the Red channel and set the midtone slider to 1.41. I select the Green channel and set the midtone slider to 1.12. In the Blue channel, I set the midtone slider to .89. Changing the midtone values of the RGB channels adds a sepia effect to the photo.

The final photo is shown in Figure 12.9. As you can see, the final high key image is something we might see in *Bride* magazine. Compared to the original image, it's a huge improvement.

Creating Infrared Photos

The human eye can see wavelengths between 400nm (nanometers) and 700nm. This is a range from purple to red. Infrared is the light beyond 700nm ranging from around 700nm to 1200nm. The result of infrared photos is that they appear with some very distinct effects that typically make the images very pleasing. With infrared color photos, you see some shifts in the colors. The yellows and greens often found in grass turn to an orange color. This type of color shift is very common among infrared photos. You also find blue skies turning to cyan. Foliage on trees bounces light, and you get a sort of snowy white effect.

Some photographers who regularly shoot infrared have their cameras modi-fied by a technician to shoot photos with an infrared look. In Photoshop Elements, you have an option to convert a photo to an infrared image, and it provides you with a nice starting point for tweaking a photo you want to convert to infrared.

For this example, I used the photo you see in Figure 12.10.

FIGURE 12.10 Unedited photo.

To apply an infrared effect to a photo, follow these steps:

1. If the photo you use needs some adjustments for brightness and color, open the photo in Camera Raw. We'll use the Raw Editor to prepare the photo for conversion to infrared by making adjustments for brightness and contrast. If your file doesn't need any adjustments, skip this step and step 2.

2. Make brightness and color adjustments in Camera Raw. In the Basic panel, adjust the Exposure, Contrast, Highlights, and shadows. In this example, I also made some adjustments for Temperature and Tint to warm up the photo, as shown in Figure 12.11. After making the edits, click Open Image to open the photo in the Photo Editor.

For more on opening files in Camera Raw and using the Camera Raw Editor, see Chapter 2, "Using Camera Raw Hacks."

FIGURE 12.11 Edits made in the Camera Raw Editor.

3. If your photo is currently in 16-bit mode, choose Image > Mode > 8 Bits/Channel.

4. Duplicate the Background by selecting it in the Layers panel and pressing Ctrl/⌘ + J.

5. Select the new layer and choose Enhance > Convert to Black and White. The Convert to Black and White dialog box opens, as shown in Figure 12.12.

6. Select Infrared Effect from the Select a Style list. Make adjustments to the Adjust Intensity sliders, as shown in Figure 12.12. In this example, I added some green and took down the blues. I lowered the contrast. Each photo is different, though, so you need to choose the adjustments you think will work for your photo. When you're finished with your changes, click OK.

7. Duplicate the Background again by pressing Ctrl/⌘ + J.

8. Select the new Background copy and choose Enhance > Convert to Black and White. This time, choose Scenic Landscape as the Style and click OK to accept the rest of the defaults.

9. Click the top layer and click the Add Layer Mask icon in the Layers panel to add a Layer Mask to the top layer.

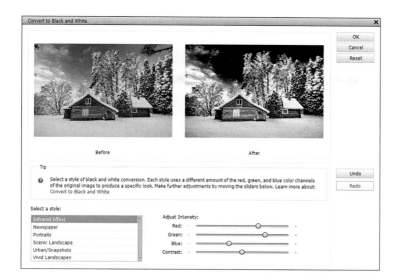

FIGURE 12.12 Select the Infrared effect in the Select a Style list and make adjustments for the color channels and contrast.

10. Select the Brush tool and choose a large soft brush around 300 pixels. Set the Opacity to 10%.

11. Press D on your keyboard to return to default colors.

12. Click in the mask to select it and make sure the foreground color is black. Move the brush over the highlights in the layer where you converted to black and white using the Scenic Landscape style. In my example, I brought down some of the highlights by painting with a low opacity brush, as shown in the Layers panel in Figure 12.13.

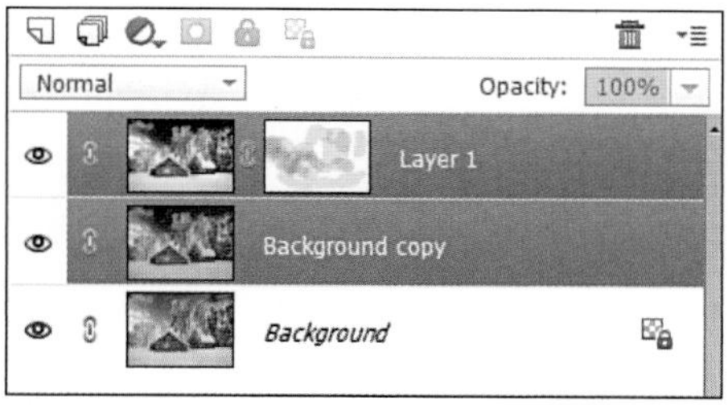

FIGURE 12.13 Layers panel shown with painting in the top layer with a Layer Mask.

13. When you're finished adding brush strokes, select the top and middle layers and press Ctrl/⌘ + E to merge the layers.

14. Add a new Layer Mask to the merged layers by selecting the top layer and clicking the Add Layer Mask icon in the Layers panel.

15. Select the mask and open the Gradient Editor. Open the Tool Options panel and click the Gradient. The Gradient Editor opens.

16. Choose the Black, White gradient in the Gradient Editor. If you do not see the Black, White gradient, open the Preset drop-down list and choose Default. Select the Black, White gradient and click OK.

17. In the Tool Options panel for the Gradient tool, select Radial from the icons shown in the panel.

18. Draw a gradient from the center to the edge of the mask. The outside of the gradient should be white. If the gradient is reversed, check Reverse in

the Tool Options panel and draw the gradient again. The gradient should appear in the mask in the Layers panel, as shown in Figure 12.14.

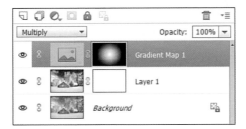

19. Choose Multiply from the Blend Mode drop-down menu. If the image appears too dark, reduce Opacity.

20. Merge the blend mode layer and the middle layer; select the top layer and press Ctrl/⌘ + E to merge the layers.

The final image is shown in Figure 12.15.

FIGURE 12.15 Final image after applying an infrared look to the original photo shown in Figure 12.10.

Using Photo Filters

In previous chapters, I explained using the Solid Color Adjustment Layer. You have another Adjustment Layer that works similar to the Solid Color Adjustment Layer: the Photo Filter Adjustment Layer. Both apply color to the underlying layer(s).

For this example, I used the unedited photo shown in Figure 12.16.

The big difference between the two Adjustment Layers is with Solid Color; you apply a completely opaque color. You can change the transparency of the color by adjusting the layer opacity, and you can use blending options in the Layers panel.

With the Photo Filter Adjustment Layer, you work with something very similar to using a filter on a camera lens. Other than ND (Neutral Density) filters, the other filters on camera lenses are not opaque and just filter lighting many different ways depending on the filter. You still have Opacity adjustments available in the Layers panel, but you also have a Density slider in the Photo Filter dialog box. Whereas Solid Color can completely block out a layer at 100% opacity, the Photo Filter can't be used for a 100% opaque effect.

FIGURE 12.16 Raw unedited image.

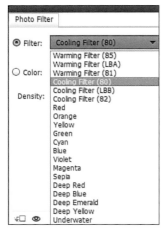

FIGURE 12.17 Photo Filter dialog box.

To apply a photo filter, choose Photo Filter from the Adjustment Layer drop-down list. The Photo Filter dialog box opens, as shown in Figure 12.17.

When you select Warming Filter (85), the drop-down list shows you several warming filters and several cooling filters as well as an assortment of different colors. Applying a Photo Filter to your photo does not require you to use opacity or a blending mode to see the effect on the photo. Of course, you can reduce opacity and use blending modes, but it's not necessary because the filters provide you a degree of transparency.

The warming and cooling filters add some dramatic effects to photos. In Figure 12.18, I applied the Warming Filter (85) to the photo shown earlier in Figure 12.16. This filter added a warmer tone to the image with a rich tonal range. To get a feel for what these filters do, apply different filters to different images to understand more about the effects that you can create using the Photo Filter Adjustment Layers.

FIGURE 12.18 The Warming Filter (85) applied to the photo.

Creating Pixel Stretch Images

Many Photoshop users create some interesting images with a technique called Pixel Stretch. You can stretch pixels horizontally, vertically, and in a circular shape. I'll first show pixels stretched horizontally; later, I'll show you how to create a circular pixel stretch.

Horizontal Pixel Stretch

Pixel stretch is most commonly used to show motion when creating horizontal patterns. The standard way to create a pixel stretch image is to have a subject on one layer and a single pixel (or few pixels) copied from the subject on another layer. It's not complicated, but the most important edit you need to make is the selection of the subject. The better your selection, the better the results you can expect. So, be prepared to take some time and get the best selection you can when you start creating a pixel stretch image.

To create a horizontal pixel stretch design, follow these steps:

1. Open an image in the Photo Editor. Choose a photo where you can easily select the subject. Try to find photos with some saturated colors and a subject showing some motion. This can be a variety of different photos, like runners, ballet dancers, motorcycle riders, horseback riders, and a huge range of people in motion. For this exercise, I used a man running, as shown in Figure 12.19.

2. Use the selection tools that work best for you to select the subject in the photo. You might try using Select > Select Subject first and then refine the selection.

3. Keep the selection active and press Ctrl/⌘ + J. The selection is added to a new blank layer, as shown in the Layers panel in Figure 12.19.

FIGURE 12.19 Subject selected and isolated on a new layer.

4. Duplicate the new layer by pressing Ctrl/⌘ + J.

5. Select the Background layer and press Alt/Option and click the Delete icon in the layers panel to delete the layer.

6. Use the Marquee Rectangle tool and draw a marquee vertically beginning at the top of the image about ¼ inch wide and down as far as you can go while staying on the subject. You need to make several selections, especially if you have a subject who's running. Press Alt/Option + Shift + V and drag the selections to the right of the image to duplicate the selections. Continue copying parts of the subject until you get a horizontal patch similar to what you see in Figure 12.20.

7. Select one or a few pixels in the vertical bar. Try to get as close to a one-pixel selection as you can. If you select more than one pixel, in most cases, it's OK.

8. Press Ctrl/⌘ + T while the selection is active to transform it. You should see handles on three corners and sides of the selection.

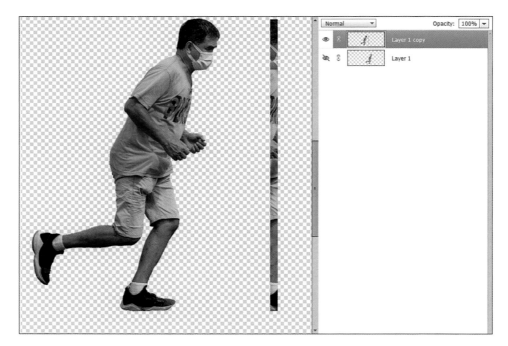

FIGURE 12.20 A vertical bar created from copies of the subject.

9. Drag the middle horizontal handles outward from either direction. You should see a pattern similar to Figure 12.21.

10. Select the subject by pressing Ctrl/⌘ and clicking on the bottom layer.

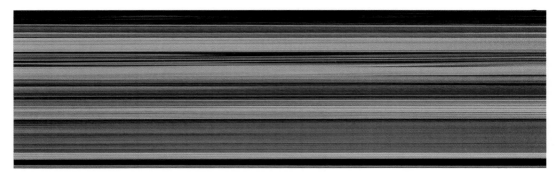

FIGURE 12.21 A one-pixel selection stretched across the canvas.

11. Select the layer with the pixel stretch. The selection should be still active when you select the layer. Essentially you are selecting the subject, but you're going to work on the layer above the subject.

12. Press Ctrl/⌘ + Shift + I to inverse the selection.

13. Click the Eraser tool and drag around the right side of the selection to erase the pixel stretch pattern in front of the subject. In Figure 12.22, you can see the subject selected and the pixel stretch pattern removed from in front of him.

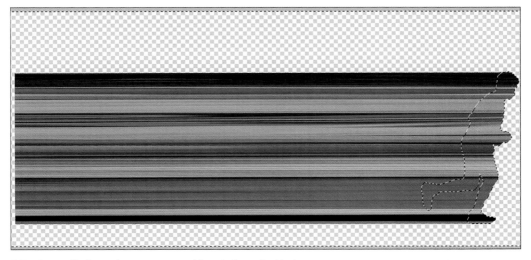

FIGURE 12.22 Pixel stretch pattern removed from in front of subject.

14. Click the layer with the subject in the Layers panel and drag it up if the subject is below the pattern.

15. In the Layers panel, choose Merge Layers or press Ctrl/⌘ + E.

16. If you'd like, warp the beginning of the pattern. Remember, you need Photoshop Elements 2022 to create a warp effect. To warp the pattern, choose Image > Transform > Warp. You don't need a selection to warp the layer content. Drag the end handles to shape the design. The final image I created is shown in Figure 12.23.

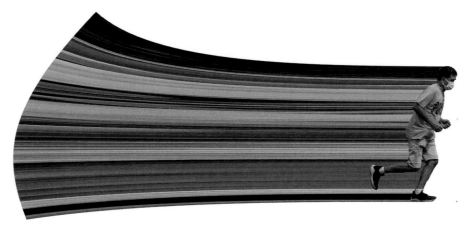

FIGURE 12.23 Pixel stretch pattern removed from in front of subject.

Circular Pixel Stretch

Another type of pixel stretch is a circular pattern. This pattern can be used in many interesting ways and with many different types of photos that show movement or motion. To create a circular type of pixel sketch, follow these steps:

1. Open a file in the Photo Editor. A photo of a ballerina, gymnast, or athlete in movement makes for good source material. For this example, I used the photo shown in Figure 12 24.

2. Select the subject. Make the selection similar to how you made a selection for the horizontal pixel stretch.

3. With the selection active, press Ctrl/⌘ + J. This action duplicates the selected subject on a new layer. Press Ctrl/⌘ + J again to duplicate the subject layer.

4. Press Alt/Option and click the Delete icon in the Layers panel to delete the Background layer.

5. On the first layer above the Background, perform a similar task as when you created the horizontal pixel stretch. Use the Marquee Rectangle tool and make selections. Press Alt/Option + Shift and drag aside the subject. Continue making selections and duplicates to create a vertical line.

FIGURE 12.24 Original unedited image.

6. Use the Marquee Rectangle and select a one-pixel vertical line. Press Ctrl/⌘ + T to create a transformation rectangle. Grab a center handle and move to the right. Grab the left center handle and drag to the left. The pattern should appear horizontally across the canvas, as shown in Figure 12.25.

FIGURE 12.25 Drag the center handles outward to the edges of the canvas.

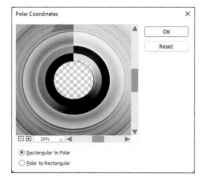

FIGURE 12.26 Make certain Rectangular to Polar is selected in the Polar Coordinates dialog box.

7. With the second layer active and the pattern deselected, choose Filter > Distort > Polar Coordinates. The Polar Coordinates dialog box opens. Select the Rectangular to Polar radio button, as shown in Figure 12.26, and click OK.

8. The result of the Polar Coordinates filter is an elliptical shape. You want this shape to appear more like a circle. Press Ctrl/⌘ + T. Drag the center handles on each side inward to make the shape more circular. When the shape appears as you like, click the green check mark (see Figure 12.27) to accept the edit.

9. If you have a square pattern as shown in Figure 12.27, you need to delete any data outside the circle. Use the Elliptical Marquee tool. If you need to make the center more visible, open the Rulers (View > Show Rulers or Ctrl/⌘ + Shift + R). Move the cursor to the center point and press the Alt/Option key as you drag outward. Try to create an elliptical selection that matches the outside circle in the pattern.

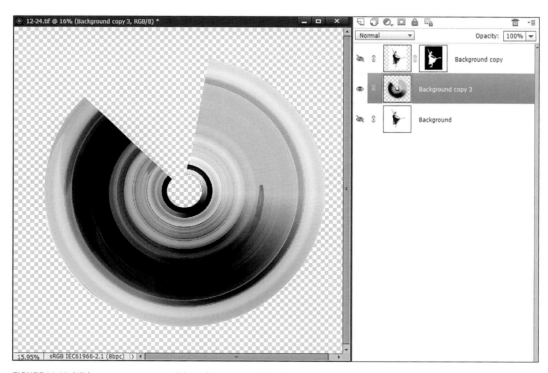

FIGURE 12.27 With a square pattern, delete the area outside the circle.

10. Press Ctrl/⌘ + Shift + I to inverse the selection.

11. Press Delete with the selection inversed to delete the excess outside the circle.

12. Use artistic freedom to create the appearance you want in your final image. If you want to delete part of the pattern, use the Eraser or Lasso tool to remove some of the pattern.

13. Create a new empty layer. Use the Elliptical Marquee tool and draw a small ellipse below the subject. In my example, I put the ellipse below the ballerina's right foot. Fill the selection with a 50% black fill. Deselect and apply a Gaussian Blur. Adjust the opacity in the Levels dialog box.

14. Duplicate the subject layer. Select the subject and fill the selection black. Deselect, and apply a Gaussian blur. Move the shadow slightly offset from the subject above it. Use the Eraser tool to remove shadow in areas where you don't want the shadow to appear. The results of the edits along with the layers panel up to this point is shown in Figure 12.28.

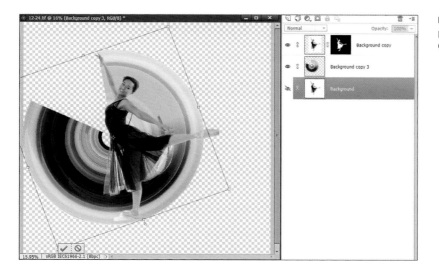

FIGURE 12.28 Part of the pattern is removed, and a drop shadow is added.

15. If you want a color for the background, you can add a layer at the bottom of the layer stack and create a gradient, pattern, or solid fill. In my example, I added a solid color fill for the final image, as shown in Figure 12.29.

Creating Low Poly Illustrations

Low poly illustrations are comprised of multiple small polygon shapes that render a chiseled look to what was once a photo. Ideally, the best way to create a low poly illustration is to use Adobe Illustrator and Photoshop. However, you can create a low poly illustration using only Photoshop Elements.

Creating low poly illustrations is simple enough. It just takes a lot of time and patience. Most people who create low poly illustrations use solid colors to fill the polygons. I prefer to use gradients, which adds considerable time to creating the final illustration.

To create a low poly illustration, follow these steps:

1. Open an image in Photoshop Elements.

2. Create a new blank layer.

3. Select the Lasso tool. You can use either the Lasso tool or the Polygon lasso tool.

4. Press Ctrl/⌘ + plus (+) to zoom in or use the Zoom tool in the Tools panel.

5. Draw a triangle in an area of the image. The triangle should be small (less than .5 inches), and it should be in an area with a lot of common color. To draw a triangle with the Lasso tool, press Alt/Option and click. Keep the key depressed and move the mouse to the next location and click. The final stop should be a return to the point of origin to create the triangle. Release the keys and you have a selection.

6. Click the Eyedropper tool in the Tools panel and click 3 × 3 Average in the Tool Options panel.

7. The smaller the polygons you create, the more detail you ultimately end up with in the final illustration. Zoom in close to the photo. Click the darkest color within the selection. Press Alt/Option an click the Lightest area in the selection. You should have the dark pixels color as the Foreground color swatch and the lighter color as the background color swatch.

8. Fill the selection with a gradient. You should still have the selection active while sampling the colors. Click the Gradient tool in the Tools panel and draw a foreground-to-background linear gradient.

   As an alternative, you can fill the selection with a color you sample from within the selection. The result won't be as refined as when using gradients, but it will work.

   You can keep the same gradient for multiple selections as long as the colors remain similar. When you see changes in hues or brightness of one or the other color, create a new gradient in the Gradient Editor.

   If you don't zoom to a zoomed-in view where you can clearly see the area you're working on, it's very easy to misalign the selections. As you can see in Figure 12.30, there are some gaps between the polygon shapes that I filled with gradients.

9. If you find gaps between polygon shapes, create some selections covering the gaps and draw new gradients.

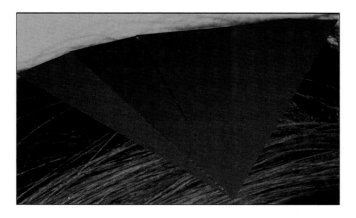

FIGURE 12.30 Zoom in tightly to clearly see the shapes you draw and ensure they overlap slightly.

You can draw a variety of polygon shapes. In my example, I chose to use triangle shapes for all polygons. You can use different shapes, and you can combine different shapes in the same illustration. It's up to you to use the shapes you want for creating the illustration that satisfies your taste.

In Figure 12.31, you can see one illustration I made using polygons and gradients.

FIGURE 12.31 A low poly illustration.

Creating Custom Portrait Effects

You can apply tons of different portrait effects in portraits and head shots. Let's take a look at a few effects that work well on portraits.

Creating Longer Necks

In Chapter 14, "Editing Portraits," I talk about stretching out subjects for longer necks and bodies. When we look at making necks longer, we apply the effect on a subject's neck when the neck is in clear view and separate from surrounding objects like shoulders or clothing.

If you take photos where the camera is higher than the subject or you use wide-angle lenses, the subject often appears distorted in the final photo. Many of these shots may show subjects in awkward poses just because of the camera angle when the shot was taken. On frequent distortions you find in many photos is when the subject's neck appears too close to their shoulders, resulting in an awkward appearance.

To bring the neck up to make it a little more pronounced and separate from the shoulders, use the Liquify filter. To open the Liquify dialog box (see Figure 12.32), choose Filter > Distort > Liquify. The Liquify dialog box opens.

The secret to using the Liquify filter is to work slowly and in very small adjustments. In the right panel, you have sliders to adjust Size and Pressure. You can use the same sizing alternatives you have available with brushes. Press Alt/Option and right-click the mouse button; move left to size down or right to size up the brush tip.

The Pressure slider controls the amount of moving areas as you drag the brush. Moving the slider left applies less movement. Moving the slider to the right increases the amount of what you move. You can also use the mouse and keyboard to control pressure. If you press Alt/Option, right-click, and then move up, you lower the pressure. If you press Alt/Option and right-click and drag down, you increase the pressure.

When you apply Liquify edits to a photo, keep the pressure low and drag the brush with very short strokes, moving edges of the subject in small amounts at a time. When finished, click OK.

In Figure 12.33, you can see the Liquify filter applied to the right image and the original unedited image on the left.

FIGURE 12.33 Unedited image (left) and after applying Liquify filter adjustments (right).

Notice in Figure 12.33 that the edited photo shows just a little change made with the Liquify filter, but the end result shows quite an impact on the image. The model looks thinner and the neck looks more natural. The original image has a bit of distortion, so the final edit looks a little more authentic.

Making Hair Appear Fuller

Sometimes you shoot a portrait, and everything looks good in the shot but maybe the hair doesn't look quite right. Perhaps the hair was pushed back and not enough of it shows in the photo, the portrait would look better if the hair were fuller, or the shot would look better if the hair followed the shape of an object such as a hat.

For these kinds of edits, you again turn to the Liquify filter. Open a photo in the Photo Editor and choose Filter > Distort > Liquify. The Liquify filter dialog box opens, as shown in Figure 12.34.

FIGURE 12.34 Liquify filter dialog box.

With most edits you make with the Liquify filter, and particularly when you edit hair, it's best to zoom in on the image. You want to see how the strands of hair are affected when you move areas of the photo with the Liquify brush.

Move about the hair and once again use very small adjustments with a relatively low pressure. When finished, click OK.

The photo I used for this technique didn't have much wrong with the subject's hair. It was just a personal choice for making the hair appear fuller. Figure 12.35 shows the edited image (right) compared to the original image (left). The change is very slight, but the hair appears a bit fuller in the final image. I also edited the file by changing the background and editing some blemishes. But, as you can see, the edit for the hair was very slight. The final image shows the hair a bit fuller on the right side of the photo.

FIGURE 12.35 Liquify edits applied to the subject's hair (right) on the original unedited image (left).

Applying Multiple Textures

You can use multiple textures to create artistic effects from photos. The possibilities are endless, and you have an abundance of textures from which to choose in the Graphics panel. Additionally, you can scan objects or download textures from many websites that offer free downloads.

To see how we use multiple textures on an image, follow these steps:

1. Open a photo in the Photo Editor.

2. Double-click the Background to convert it to a layer. The layer name should then be Layer 0.

3. Click the Create a New Layer icon in the layers panel and move it below the Background layer.

4. Select the Background layer (Layer 0) and press Ctrl/⌘ + J to duplicate the layer.

5. Click the Add Layer Mask icon in the Layers panel.

6. On Layer 0, choose Filter > Distort > Liquify. In the Liquify dialog box, set the Size to a large size and the Pressure to a high pressure. Move the edges of the canvas outward, as shown in Figure 12.36.

FIGURE 12.36 Distort the image by moving all the photo to the edges of the canvas.

7. Select the Layer Mask on the second layer. Use a grunge brush and paint black in the white layer mask. Change brush tips a few times to other grunge brushes.

8. Open a file with a sky or a texture.

9. Drag the sky image onto the current document. The file comes in as a new layer.

10. Transform the object to fit the canvas of the current document by pressing Ctrl/⌘ + A to select the sky layer and then dragging the handles to fit the layer to the new document.

11. Choose Filter > Filter Gallery. In the Filter Gallery dialog box, click Brush Strokes to open the Brush Strokes folder. Select Accented Strokes. Set the Width to 1, the Edge Brightness to 38, and the Smoothness to 3, as shown in Figure 12.37. Click OK.

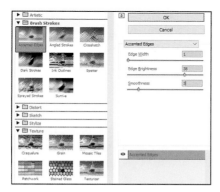

FIGURE 12.37 Choose Brush Strokes in the Accented Edges dialog box.

12. Press Alt/Option and click the Add Layer Mask icon in the Layers panel to add a negative mask.

13. Paint some white strokes with a grunge brush on the Layer Mask.

14. Select all the layers and create a composite by pressing Ctrl/⌘ + Alt/ Option + Shift + E.

15. Add one Adjustment layer for the Photo Filter, one for Levels, and one for Hue/Saturation. Choose a photo filter. In this example, I used a warming filter. Adjust brightness and contrast in a Levels Adjustment Layer and reduce the saturation in the Hue/Saturation Adjustment Layer. Settings vary according to different documents. Choose the settings you like for these adjustments.

In Figure 12.38, you can see the final edited image (right) aside the original unedited image (left).

FIGURE 12.38 Original photo (left) and after edits (right).

Creating Brush Effects

The possibilities for creating special effects using brushes are endless. You can have fun creating layer masks and painting in masks using different brush tips. The best way to know what kind of results you get is to play and experiment.

Painting in Layer Masks with Grunge Brushes

Many Photoshop users create negative Layer Masks and paint white in the Layer Mask to produce different edge shapes to photos, such as grunge edges.

To do this, you open a photo and convert the background to a layer. Add an inverted layer mask by pressing Alt/Option and clicking the Add Layer Mask icon in the Layers panel (the mask appears black). Then choose a grunge brush and paint a border for an effect, as shown in Figure 12.39.

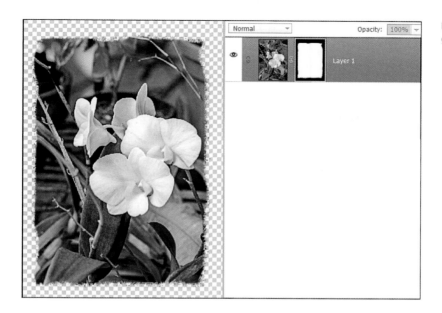

FIGURE 12.39 Photo with grunge edges.

Reusing Masks

Suppose you want to reuse the same mask for different photos. In Figure 12.40, I have a portrait orientation image. Suppose you want to use the same mask with a landscape photo. Here's how you do it:

1. Open a photo. In this case, I started with a portrait image.

2. Press Alt/Option and click the Add Layer Mask icon in the Layers panel to create a negative mask.

3. Select a grunge brush. You can download grunge brushes from the Internet. Search for Photoshop Brushes free downloads. Download some brushes and use the Edit > Define Brush menu command to add new brushes to your brush library.

4. Paint white in the Layer Mask. For this example, I created a border. To create a grunge border, use a grunge brush and paint white around the mask, as shown in Figure 12.40.

5. Open a second image in the Photo Editor. For this exercise, I used a landscape image.

6. Press Ctrl/⌘ + Alt/Option + I to open the Image Size dialog box. Look at the width text box. Make note of this number to use in the next step. Click Cancel to dismiss the dialog box.

7. Return to the portrait photo and choose Image > Resize > Canvas. Leave the anchor at the default position and type the same width value in the

Width text box as you noticed in the Image Size dialog box. Click OK. The canvas is sized horizontally to add more canvas area on each side of the image.

8. Drag the landscape photo to the portrait document.

9. Select the mask and press Ctrl/⌘ + T to set up a transformation. Right-click the mouse button and choose Rotate Right 90° from the context menu. At this point, your image and Layers panel should look like Figure 12.40.

FIGURE 12.40 Photos with the mask rotated.

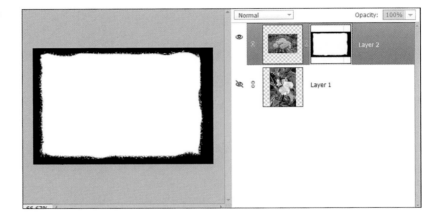

10. Delete the bottom layer.

11. Size the photo if it's not sized properly. To size the photo without the mask, duplicate the layer. Delete the mask on the new layer. Select the image and press Ctrl/⌘ + T. Drag the corner handles to resize the photo. Press Alt/Option and drag the mask to the layer where you resized the photo. Delete the bottom layer, and your final landscape image should look something like Figure 12.41.

You can save a copy of both the portrait and another copy of the landscape images with the masks. When you want to apply the same border to other photos, drag and drop them on the template files. Delete the old photos and drag the mask to the new photo. Be sure to save at least one copy of both the portrait and landscape images as Photoshop (.PSD) files with the layers intact, so you can continue using with the mask layer.

FIGURE 12.41 Copied mask added to another photo.

Creating Custom Grunge Brush Effects

You can download a variety of brushes from a number of websites, but at times, you might need a brush that's not quite like any you find with the default brushes in Elements or those you can download.

To create a new custom brush, begin by creating a new document with Background Contents set to Transparent and make the size square, such as 2 × 2, 3 × 3, 5 × 5, and so on. Select a brush to create the design you like. Use either a hard tip or soft brush and draw a shape. You can also use the pencil tool to draw a shape. In Figure 12.42, you can see a shape I created for a custom brush.

Before you create a new brush, be certain you add it to the library you want. When you open the Brush Tool Options panel and click on Brush, you see the current library selected. It may be Default Brushes or another library. From the Brush drop-down list, shown in Figure 12.43, select the brush library where you want to add the brush. When you create new brushes, they are added to the current selected library.

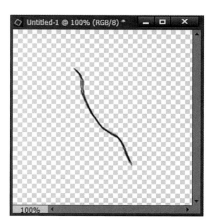

FIGURE 12.42 A shape drawn for creating a custom brush.

FIGURE 12.43 Select the library where you want to add the brush before defining a brush.

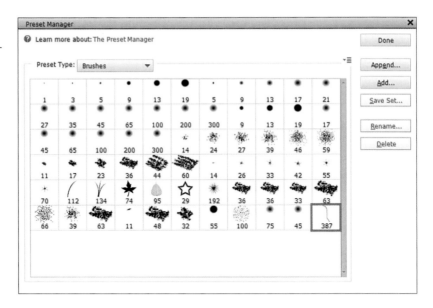

NOTE: If a document is transparent or white, you don't need to select an object or mark you want to convert to a brush. If the document has any background color above white, you need to select the object/mark if you don't want the background color as part of the brush.

When you select the library where you want to add the brush, choose Edit > Define Brush. When the Define Brush dialog box opens, type a name for the brush and click OK.

The brush is added to the current open library. But the brush is only temporarily added to the library. It has not yet been saved to the library. If you choose another library, the brush is lost if you don't save it first.

Before moving on, if you want to save a newly added brush, choose Edit > Preset Manager. The Preset Manager opens with Brushes as the default Preset Type. The current library is shown also by default. You should see your new brush added to the current library. In Figure 12.43, my newly added brush is 387.

To save the new brush, select all the brushes in the Preset Manager window and click Save Set. The Save As dialog box opens. Navigate your hard drive to where you save presets and type a name for the new set. Click Save, and the new brush is saved along with your other brushes in the respective library. If you want to save just the new custom brush to a new library, select just the custom brush you created and click Save Set. Type a name and click Save. A new library is created. You can add additional brushes to this library as you create them.

After creating the new brush, it's time to apply brush strokes to a photo. To see how you add a brush and use it on a document, follow these steps:

1. Open a photo in the Photo Editor.

2. Press Ctrl/⌘ + J to duplicate the Background layer.

3. Press Alt/Option and click the Add Layer Mask icon in the Layers panel to create a negative mask.

4. By default, the foreground color should be white. If it is not white, press X on your keyboard to set the foreground to white. You paint with white to apply brush strokes in a negative mask.

5. Use a basic soft brush to bring back areas in the photo where you don't intend to apply the new brush strokes.

6. Select the new custom brush. Apply strokes to the mask as shown in Figure 12.44.

FIGURE 12.44 The photo after new brush strokes were added to a negative mask.

Frequently change the size and opacity as you add more brush strokes. You can create multiple layers and copy the mask from previous layers. If you make a mistake, you can delete the layer and return to the previous layer with the original mask. If you see problems with transitions of brush strokes to the original photo, use the Clone Stamp tool and choose a low opacity setting. Brush across the areas where the transition of tones occurs.

If you mask a subject in the image, you can add a background by either using a texture or applying a color background. In this example, I created a gradient for the background, as shown in the final image in Figure 12.45. Notice in Figure 12.44, the custom brush strokes are more evident than you see in Figure 12.45.

FIGURE 12.45 Photo with a gradient background.

Creating a Red Carpet Photo Booth

You can create brushes from text, add vector shapes, and/or raster shapes and convert text and images to create a new brush.

Suppose you want to create a red carpet–style Hollywood photo booth. It's easy enough when you create brushes to help form the design. Just follow these steps:

FIGURE 12.46 Add text and graphics to a new document.

1. Start by choosing a subject in a photo. Create a selection and add a Layer Mask to isolate the subject from the background. Create a new blank square document, such as 2 × 2, 3 × 3, 5 × 5, or another square size. Set the resolution to 150 and choose RGB for color.

2. Add type and graphics if you want graphics along with the type. In Figure 12.46, you can see the type and graphic I created for a brush tip design.

3. Create a new brush from the text and graphics. If you have text only, you can create a new brush as well. Choose Edit > Define Brush. The brush is added to the current open library. If you want to save the brush, open the Preset Manager. Select all brushes in the current set (including your new brush) and click Save Set. Save the brushes where you save presets with the same name and overwrite the last saved version of the current set.

4. Create a new document. Set the size and resolution to your liking.

5. Open the Brush Settings in the Brush Tool Options panel. Set all the sliders to zero (0) except the roundness slider. Move this slider right to 100%.

6. Click around the new document window. Change brush size and add some smaller text to the document.

7. Click the Create New Fill or Adjustment Layer icon in the Layers panel and choose Levels. Darken the text in the document. Click OK and reduce opacity if necessary. Text at smaller sizes when used as brush tips tends to lose some brightness. You can bring back the brightness on the text in the Levels dialog box.

8. Open the file with the subject. Click the layer containing the subject and mask in the Layers panel. Drag the layer to the new document with the text. Size the subject and move it to the desired location.

Figure 12.47 shows the results of my example image.

FIGURE 12.47 Final image after applying text brush strokes to the background.

Creating Paint Drip Effects

An interesting effect is one we call a paint drip effect, which uses—unsurprisingly—an image of paint dripping. You can find images on various websites that appear like paint running down a wall. Perform an Internet search and look for some images in the public domain that you can download or copy.

To start from scratch and create your own paint drip design, follow these steps:

1. Open a photo in the Photo Editor. This effect works well for photos containing subjects, although you could use the effect on landscape and other photos. In this example, I used a group shot.

2. Click the Create a New Layer icon in the Layers panel.

3. Click the Gradient tool. Open the Tool Options panel and click the gradient to open the Gradient Editor.

4. Double-click the first stop below the gradient to open the Color Picker. Select a color for the gradient and click OK. Select the last stop below the gradient and double-click to open the Color Picker. Choose a second color and click OK. In my example, I chose white for the second color to blend from the first color to white.

5. Open the Tool Options panel and click the Radial Gradient icon. Determine where you want the center of the gradient, press Alt/Option, and drag out to create a radial gradient. The new layer with a radial gradient is shown in Figure 12.48.

FIGURE 12.48 The gradient appears as the background fill.

6. Press Ctrl/⌘ + J to create a duplicate layer. Move the Background copy to the top of the layer stack.

7. Add a graphic containing a paint drip effect. For my example, I have a piano with a paint drip effect, as shown in Figure 12.49. I used this graphic to create a selection.

8. Look for the midpoint of the subject and a place where you want the paint drip effect to begin. Select the rectangle Marquee tool and draw a selection from the midpoint of the subject to the bottom of the photo.

9. Press Ctrl/⌘ + T and then drag handles to resize the effect. You want the width to match exactly the same horizontal width as your subject. You can size either proportionately by holding the Shift key down as you drag a handle, or disproportionately by dragging handles without using the Shift key.

Notice in Figure 12.50 that the object is wider that the subjects. In this example, I sized the object to match the width of the subjects.

FIGURE 12.49 Drag the paint drip image to position.

10. Create the mask on the image you use for the paint drip effect— in my example, the piano image. Select Add Layer Mask from the Layers Panel. Fill the selection black to hide that portion of the photo.

11. Press Ctrl/⌘ and click the layer containing the paint drip image to create a selection. Click the Layer Mask and fill the selection in the mask white. In Figure 12.50, you can see Layers panel as it should look at this point.

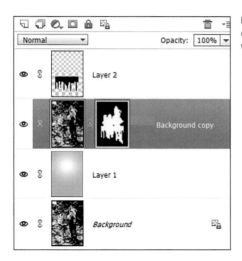

FIGURE 12.50 Layers showing the paint drip image and the Layer Mask filled white from the paint drip selection.

12. Delete the paint drip (top) layer. At this point, you can delete the paint drip layer. Select the layer in the Layers panel and press Alt/Option. Click the Delete icon in the Layers panel to delete the layer.

13. Click the Styles icon in the Layers panel to open the Styles panel. From the drop-down list at the top of the panel, choose Drop Shadows. Click on the Noisy drop shadow.

14. Open the Style Settings by clicking on the Style Settings in the top-right corner of the Styles panel. Adjust the size and opacity of the shadow. Check the box for Bevel and click OK.

The final image from the example file is shown in Figure 12.51.

FIGURE 12.51 Final image with paint drip effect.

Creating Cartoon Illustrations

In this section, I explain a variation for creating something close to an illustration or cartoon effect. To properly create more illustrated art and effects similar to cartoon illustrations, you need the Pen tool as you find in Adobe Photoshop. Elements doesn't have a Pen tool, and we're not likely to see one added to the program. Therefore, you have to be content with the tools available in the Photo Editor.

You can make selections using the Lasso tools and stroke the selections by choosing Edit > Stroke (Outline) Selection to create illustrated lines. It can be difficult, but it is possible.

After you open a photo, create a selection around the subject and add a Layer Mask. Create a selection from the mask and choose Filter > Artistic > Poster Edges. The Artistic filters open with the Poster Edges filter selected, as shown in Figure 12.52. In the Poster Edges dialog box, set the Edge Thickness to 2, the Edge Intensity to 1, and the Posterization to 1.5. If you want a few more shadows showing in the image, set the Posterization slider to 2. Then click OK.

FIGURE 12.52 Make adjustments in the Poster Edges dialog box.

If you want to try adding strokes to the photo, create selections around the eyebrows, eyes, lips, nostrils, and chin. These areas should have more pronounced detail. In some cases, you may need to use the Lasso tool. Create a thin line lasso selection. Don't include any area outside a line. As you create selections, create separate layers for each selection.

After the selections are added as separate layers in the Layers panel, load a selection and choose Edit > Stroke (Outline) Selection. Continue selecting from the layers by pressing Ctrl/⌘ and clicking on a layer to load the selection. Use Edit > Stroke (Outline) Selection to stroke the selections.

If you want to add a background, create a new layer and move it just above the Background layer and below the Background copy layer. With the Layer Mask, use a texture or add a solid color background.

In my example, I added a gradient for the background, as shown in the right image in Figure 12.53.

FIGURE 12.53 Final edits made to raw unedited image (left) and to create a cartoon illustration effect (right).

Creating a Caricature Cartoon Effect

To create a caricature effect in Adobe Photoshop, you use the Oil Paint filter in a few of the steps. Unfortunately, Elements doesn't have an Oil Paint filter, so you need to use a workaround. To create a caricature cartoon effect in the Photo Editor, use the steps in the following sections.

Preparing the Photo

First, you need to prepare the photo:

1. Open an image in the Photo Editor. Make sure the horizontal or vertical dimension is 1,500 pixels or more. In my example, I used the image shown in Figure 12.54.

2. Adjust brightness and contrast.

3. Duplicate the layer.

4. Create a selection around the subject and add a layer mask. See Figure 12.55.

FIGURE 12.54 Image used for caricature.

FIGURE 12.55 Layer mask created from selection.

5. Add a Levels Adjustment layer to increase contrast. See Figure 12.57 for the Layers panel adjustment made for the example image.

6. Merge the Levels and Copy layers by selecting the Levels Layer and pressing Ctrl/⌘ + E.

7. If your photo requires editing for blemishes and skin tones, make those edits now.

8. Press Ctrl/@@cmd + J to duplicate the layer.

9. Add some sharpening with the High Pass filter. Set Radius to 2.0. Click OK and choose Overlay for the Blend mode.

10. Select the High Pass layer and the Background copy layer and choose Merge Layers from the Layers panel menu.

11. Choose Enhance > Unsharp Mask. Keep the amount to less than 150%—for example, set it to 135%. Set the Radius to 2.0 and leave the Threshold at 0, as shown in Figure 12.56.

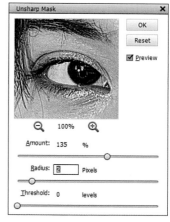

FIGURE 12.56 Unsharp Mask dialog box.

Shaping the Caricature

Now that the photo is prepared, you can move on to some steps to create the caricature shape:

1. Choose Filter > Stylize > Diffuse. In the Diffuse dialog box, shown in Figure 12.57, choose Anisotropic. Click OK. You need to apply the Diffuse filter three to five times. But to avoid adding unwanted artifacts, you need to rotate the image 90° each time you apply the Diffuse filter.

2. Choose Image > Rotate > 90° Right to rotate in a clockwise direction.

3. Apply a second Diffuse Filter by choosing Filter > Stylize > Diffuse, as shown in Figure 12.57. Continue rotating and applying the Diffuse Filter.

4. Choose Filter > Noise > Reduce Noise. Set the Strength to 10 and the remaining sliders to 0. Click OK.

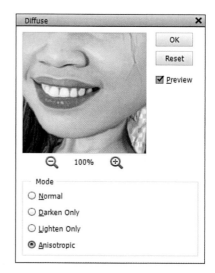

FIGURE 12.57 The Diffuse dialog box.

5. Choose Enhance > Unsharp Mask. Set the amount to less than 100. I set this example to 98. Set the Radius to 2.0 and the Threshold to 0. Click OK.

6. Press Ctrl/⌘ + J. Name the layer. Change the name from Background copy to another name. In my example, I named the layer Painting. Press Ctrl/⌘ + J to duplicate the layer.

7. Choose Filter > Other > High Pass. Type 2.0 for the Radius and click OK.

8. Choose Overlay in the Blend Mode drop-down list.

9. Merge the High Pass layer with the layer below by selecting the top layer and press Ctrl/⌘ + E to merge the layers.

10. Use the Lasso tool and make a selection of the subject's head.

11. Press Ctrl/⌘ + J to create the layer of the selection.

12. Select the subject's head layer and inverse the selection by pressing Ctrl/⌘ + Shift + I. Click the composite layer. Press Ctrl/⌘ + J to duplicate the layer. At this point, you should have one layer at the top of the subject's head and below it a layer of the subject's body minus the head.

13. Select the head layer and press Ctrl/⌘ + T. Drag one of the corner handles and move outward to size the image up. In Figure 12.58, you can see the transformation for the head and the Layers panel.

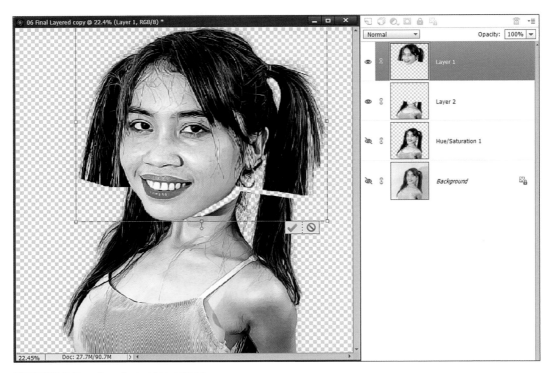

FIGURE 12.58 Transform the head layer head.

14. Select the body layer and press Ctrl/⌘ + T. Drag a handle inward to size down the body.

15. Click the Move tool and drag the head or body to position the two elements.

16. Select the head layer (at the top of the layer stack) and press Ctrl/⌘ + E. The body layer should be just below the head layer. This creates a composite of the body and head layers.

Finishing Up the Caricature

At this point, the subject's head and body will distorted because the head is much larger than the body. You need to shape the figure so the head and body fit together. This will be the most difficult part of your edits. You need to use the Liquify filter and bring the head and body together in a seamless flow with these steps:

1. Select the composite layer and choose Filter > Distort > Liquify. The Liquify dialog box opens, as shown in Figure 12.59. Move the hair and face to fit with the body layer. (For this particular image, I couldn't get a perfect match.) Move the elements as close as possible and click OK.

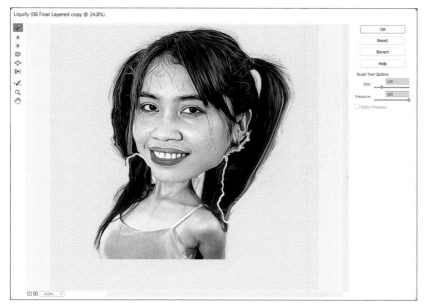

FIGURE 12.59 The Liquify dialog box.

2. Move the hair and face to match the position in the head to the body. Use the Clone Stamp tool to fill in the gaps.

3. Distort the eyes, nose, lips, and forehead with Enhance > Adjust Facial Features. In the dialog box shown in Figure 12.60, you can make these adjustments. If you make an adjustment and it isn't enough—for example, you size up the eyes and you decide you want them to be larger—click OK after the first adjustment and then reopen the Facial Features adjustment to make another adjustment. You may need to return to the adjustment several times.

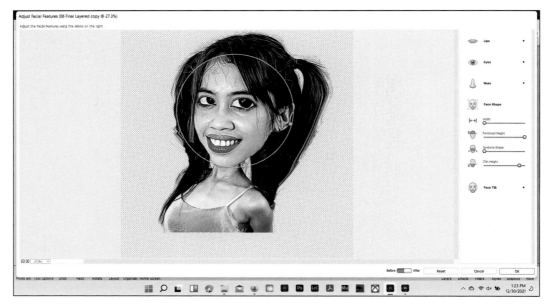

FIGURE 12.60 The Adjust Facial Features dialog box.

4. Click the top layer and press Ctrl/⌘ + Alt/Option + Shift + E.

5. Choose Filter > Filter Gallery > Posterize. In the Filter Gallery, click Poster Edges. Set the Thickness, Intensity, and Posterization to your liking. In my example, I set Edge Thickness to 10, Edge Intensity to 4, and Posterization to 1, as shown in Figure 12.61.

6. If you need to smooth out some edges or remove artifacts, use the Clone Stamp and Healing Brush tools.

7. Select the top layer, press Ctrl/⌘, and click the Create a New Layer icon in the Layers panel. This adds a layer below the top layer.

8. You can add a texture, a fill color, or a gradient for the background. In my example, I added a radial gradient.

9. Open the Layers panel menu and choose Flatten Image. I also added a border to the image in my example, as shown in Figure 12.62.

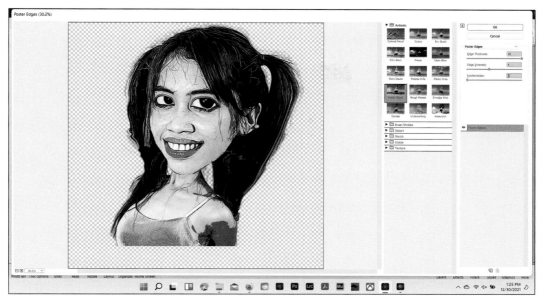

FIGURE 12.61 Choose Poster Edges in the Filter Gallery.

FIGURE 12.62 Final caricature image.

Creating a Pencil Drawing

There is a Line Drawing Guided Edit in Photoshop Elements that produces a pencil sketch from a photo. You find the Guided Edit by clicking Guided at the top of the Photo Editor window and then clicking the Black & White tab.

The Guided Edit does a fair job in creating a pencil drawing effect. However, my opinion is that the Guided Edit doesn't produce as nice of a drawing as you can achieve using manual methods. You can use some different methods for creating a pencil sketch. Following are two ways you can manually create a pencil sketch.

Pencil Sketch 1

Use these steps to manually create a pencil sketch:

1. Open a photo and press Ctrl/⌘ + J to make a copy of the Background. In my example, I used the image shown in Figure 12.63.

FIGURE 12.63 Original image.

2. Open the Adjustment Layers list in the Layers panel and choose Hue/Saturation. Drag the Saturation slider to the far left. This creates a black-and-white photo.

3. Select Layer 1 (above the Background layer) and choose Color Dodge from the Blend Modes drop-down list.

4. With the same layer still selected, press Ctrl/⌘ + I to Invert the layer. The image should appear white.

5. Choose Filter > Blur > Gaussian Blur. Add a blur amount you like for the amount of detail you want in the photo. In my example, I used 27.7 for the Radius, as shown in Figure 12.64.

FIGURE 12.64 Gaussian Blur applied to image.

Notice how light the sketch appears. This will be the result of using this method on just about any photo you attempt to turn into a pencil sketch. Don't worry. You'll fix this later in step 7.

6. Select the layer and press Ctrl/⌘ + J to make a duplicate. Name the layer **Multiply**.

7. As you can see in Figure 12.64, the sketch is very light. You can only do so much with a Levels adjustment. To add more data to the photo, select the Multiply layer and choose Multiply from the Blend Modes list.

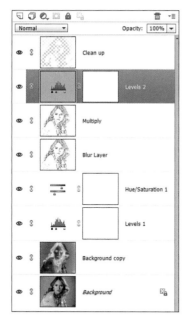

FIGURE 12.65 Layers panel up to this point.

FIGURE 12.66 Final pencil sketch image.

8. Choose Levels from the Adjustment Layer list in the Layers panel. Move the Black input slider to the right to the amount you want for the contrast.

9. If you find some areas too dense, select the Brush tool. Set the brush tip size in the Tool Options panel to 400px. Set hardness to 0 and set the Opacity to 40%. Brush over the dense areas. The foreground color should be black.

10. Invert the Foreground/Background colors by pressing X on your keyboard to reverse the colors.

11. Set the brush tip to 100 and Opacity to 100%. Brush over areas that need to be cleaned up. At this point, your Layers panel should look like Figure 12.65.

12. Choose Filter Gallery from the Filter menu. Click Poster Edges. Set the Edge Thickness to 10, the Edge Density to 4, and the Posterization to 0.

13. Paint again with a white brush set to 40 percent and brush over high-density areas. The final image is shown in Figure 12.66.

Pencil Sketch 2

A Guided Edit can help you create a pencil sketch. This edit makes the photo look a little too perfect without quite enough of a rustic appearance you might see in a hand-drawn pencil sketch. In Figure 12.67, you can see the Line Drawing Guided Edit, which is used to create a pencil sketch on the left and some manual steps to produce a pencil sketch on the right.

FIGURE 12.67 Guided Edit pencil sketch left, manual pencil sketch right.

In the following steps, we look an another manual methd for creatinga pencil sketch:

1. Open a photo in the Photo Editor. Make corrections for brightness and contrast and be certain the image appears with good contrast.

2. Duplicate the Background layer by pressing Ctrl/⌘ + J.

3. If you want to isolate the subject, create a selection and add a Layer Mask.

4. Desaturate the duplicate layer by choosing Enhance > Adjust Color > Adjust Hue/Saturation. When the Hue/Saturation dialog box opens, move the Saturation slider to the far left to −100. This setting renders the image black and white and eliminates all color. You could use a Hue/Saturation Adjustment Layer, but there's really no need to return to the Hue/Saturation dialog box. You're simply converting the image to black and white.

5. Duplicate the Background Copy layer by pressing Ctrl/⌘ + J. At this point, you have the original Background layer and two copies.

6. Invert the top layer by pressing Ctrl/⌘ + I.

7. Still working on the top layer, choose Color Dodge for the blend mode. If the image turns all white, don't worry. You'll bring it back momentarily.

8. On the top layer, select the Invert layer and choose Filter > Blur > Gaussian Blur. In the Gaussian Blur dialog box, move the slider to the position that displays the kind of sketch appearance you like. In my example, I moved the Radius slider to 30, as shown in Figure 12.68.

FIGURE 12.68 Add a Gaussian Blur to the Invert layer.

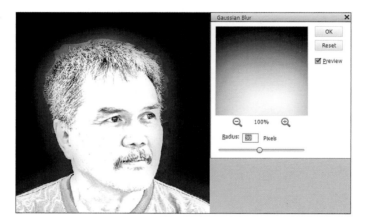

9. Add a Levels Adjustment layer. At this point, you can make a levels adjustment to add more contrast and darken the pencil strokes in the Layers dialog box.

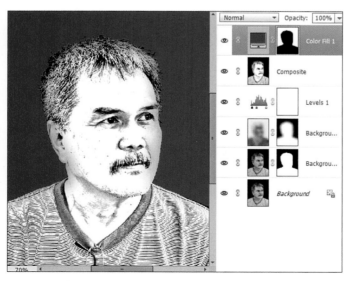

10. Select the layers in the Layers panel and press Alt/Option + Ctrl/⌘ + Shift + E to create a composite layer. Name the layer Composite.

11. If you want to add a background, texture, or color fill outside the mask, you can add a new layer with a mask and set it up for using the Texturizer or use a graphic from the Graphics panel. In Figure 12.69, you can see the layers I used to create the pencil sketch and a color fill I applied to the background.

FIGURE 12.69 Layers used to create the pencil sketch.

Creating a Dispersion Effect

If you want to add a dispersion effect to an image, you can find a huge number of free downloadable brushes on the Internet. Just search for *free Photoshop brushes*. Any brush designed for use in Photoshop can also be used in Photoshop Elements. You can also visit www.brusheezy.com, which has a large number of free downloads available. If you visit the site, search for *dispersion* to find brushes specifically for this exercise.

After you've found appropriate brushes, follow these steps:

1. After downloading a brush set, you typically need to decompress an archive. Most often, the download is saved in your Downloads folder. Locate the download file and double-click it to extract the file(s). In Photoshop Elements, you can load brushes in one of two areas: either the Brushes pop-up list in the Brush Tool Options or in the Elements Preset Manager. Choose Edit > Preset Manager. You can add the brushes, in which case the current brush set is dismissed, or you can append brushes, in which case the current set is preserved, and the new set is appended at the end of the list. In my example, I appended some Dispersion brushes I downloaded from www.brusheezy.com. In Figure 12.70, you can see the brushes I appended to my default set in the Preset Manager.

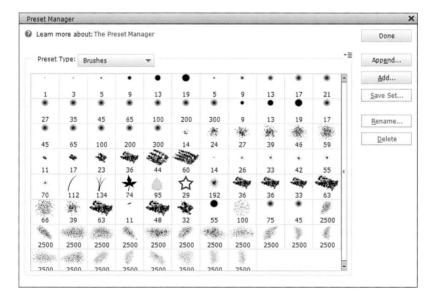

FIGURE 12.70 Dispersion brushes appended to the default brushes.

2. Choose File > Open and select a file to open. You can also use the Organizer, right-click a photo, and choose Edit with Photoshop Elements Editor. In Figure 12.71, you can see the photo I start with.

FIGURE 12.71 Original photo.

For more on creating selections and refining edges, see Chapter 3.

3. If you have a subject where you want to apply the dispersion effect, you need to isolate the subject with a selection. The same holds true for an object. You'll find using either a subject or object will work best with this effect. Choose Select > Subject to begin with the selection. You may need to refine the edge. If so, choose Select > Refine Edge. If you need to use additional selection tools, use them to create a good selection of the subject.

4. Keep the selection active and press Ctrl/⌘ + J to create a layer from the selection.

5. Select the Background layer and click the Delete icon in the Layers panel to delete the background layer.

6. Click the Layer name to select it and name the layer **Liquify**.

7. You need about the same amount or more space to the right or left of your image as the image itself. For example, if your image is 3 inches wide, you need to add 3 to 4 inches on one side of the subject. The side where you add the space is dependent on where you want the dispersion effect to appear. One side of your subject should be clear and unaffected by the effect, whereas the opposite side should appear with the effect. In my example, I needed more space to the right side of my photo.

    To add more canvas area, you can choose Image > Resize > Canvas Size (Alt/Option + Ctrl/⌘ + C), or you can use the Crop tool. If you're using the Crop tool, choose No Restriction in the pop-up menu in the Tool Options panel after selecting the Crop tool. Drag the Crop tool outside the image to the distance you want to add to the canvas. Note that you can make the canvas larger by dragging the Crop tool outside the existing canvas. In Figure 12.72, you can see the canvas I enlarged for my example image. Notice the Crop tool selection is extended beyond the existing canvas.

FIGURE 12.72 Crop tool is used to create a larger canvas

8. Click the New Layer icon in the Layers panel and name the layer **Background**.

9. Open the Add a Fill or Adjustment Layer drop-down list in the Layers panel and choose Gradient. Be certain to choose Gradient and not Gradient Map because Gradient Map will add a new layer, and you don't want that. Choose the Black, White gradient. In the Gradient Fill dialog box that opens when you choose Gradient, adjust the angle to your liking by moving the radius in the dialog box. Choose Radial from the Style drop-down list and check Reverse. Set the scale to lighten the edges. See Figure 12.73 for the adjustments I made in my photo.

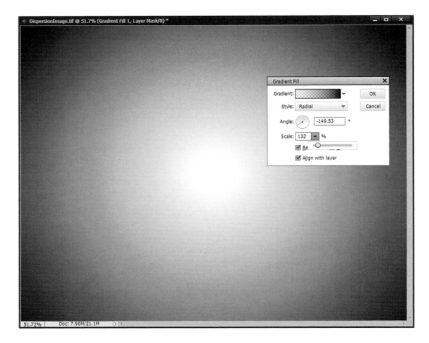

10. Move the Gradient Fill 1 layer below the Liquify layer. At this point, you should have only two layers. The Liquify layer should have your subject with the area around the subject transparent, and the Background layer should have the gradient.

11. Click the New layer icon to create a new layer. Press D on your keyboard to make sure you have default foreground/background colors. Press Ctrl/⌘ + Backspace/Delete to fill the layer white. Name the layer **Background**. Drag the layer to the bottom of the layer stack. This action will let you see the other layers without transparency.

12. Select the Liquify layer and press Ctrl/⌘ + J to duplicate the layer. Name this layer **Subject**.

13. Select the Liquify layer and choose Filter > Distort > Liquify. The Liquify dialog box opens. Size the brush very large and stroke from one side of the photo to the edge of the canvas. In Figure 12.74, note the brush size in my example is 700%. Click OK when finished with the Liquify filter.

14. Select the Liquify layer. Press Alt/Option and click the Add a Mask icon in the Layers panel. Holding the Alt/Option key when you create the mask creates a mask filled with black.

FIGURE 12.74 Move the image data in the Liquify dialog box to the edge of the canvas.

15. Press the Shift key and click on the black mask to hide it.

16. Select the Subject layer. Click the Add a Mask icon in the Layers panel. The mask should appear with a white fill. At this point, your Layers panel should look like Figure 12.75.

17. Select the Brush tool in the Tools panel and open the Tool Options. Click the Brush setting. To see more brushes, you can drag the top-right corner to the right to open up the panel (see the callout in Figure 12.76). You should see the Dispersion brushes you added in step 2. The brushes I loaded are shown in Figure 12.77. All the Dispersion brushes in my example are named 2500. Select a brush by clicking on the brush icon in the pop-up panel.

18. Click the eye icon on the Liquify layer to hide the layer.

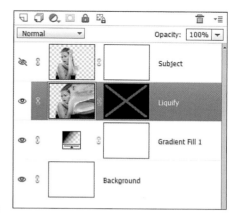

FIGURE 12.75 Layers panel showing the three layers added up to this point.

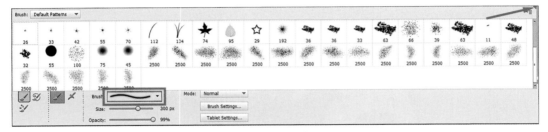

FIGURE 12.76 Brushes panel expanded and showing the Dispersion brushes.

19. Paint the edge of the subject toward the Dispersion effect. In my example, I painted on the right side of the subject toward the right. For this edit, you want to slightly brush the edge of where you want the Dispersion effect to begin, but don't move it too far off the subject. After every few strokes, change the brush tip size by pressing Alt and right-click as you drag right or left to size the tip up and down (Windows). On the Macintosh, press Ctrl + Option as you left-click and drag right or left to size the brush tip. Be sure not to overdo it. In Figure 12.77, you can see the results of my edit.

FIGURE 12.77 Set the foreground color to black and paint with a Dispersion brush in the mask on the Subject layer.

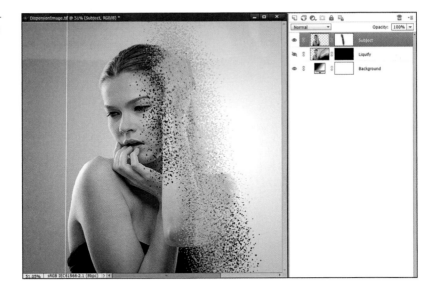

20. Unhide the Layer Mask if it's hidden by pressing the Shift key and clicking on the mask. Set the foreground color to white and click on the mask. Paint with several different dispersion brushes on the outside of the subject. Be certain to change brush sizes, and be sure you paint on the mask. At this point, your photo might look similar to Figure 12.78.

For more information about creating custom colors for gradient maps, see Chapter 10, "Color Toning and Color Grading."

21. The background currently has a dull black-to-white gradient. To add some color to the photo, open the Add Fill or Adjustment layer drop-down list and choose Gradient Map.

FIGURE 12.78 Paint white in the mask on the Liquify layer.

22. Chose a color gradient in the list or add your own colors.

23. Choose Soft Light from the Blend mode drop-down list in the Layers panel. Drag the Opacity to the level you like for the color effect. In Figure 12.79, you can see my final result.

FIGURE 12.79 The final image with background gradient edited.

PART VII

EDITING PHOTOS OF PEOPLE

At some point, you may want to restore a vintage photo or give a newer photo a vintage look. In Chapter 13, I cover techniques for these tasks.

Regardless of the type of photography you favor, you will undoubtedly take many photos of people such as portraits, senior photos, athletes engaged in sports, children, families, infants, and many others. Chapters 14 and 15 delve into portrait editing, where I show you ways to remove skin blemishes, edit skin tones, and edit facial contours and body shapes.

CHAPTER 13

EDITING VINTAGE PHOTOS

Chapter Goals

This chapter covers some editing tasks you might use when restoring old or damaged photos. In this chapter, I cover the following topics:

- Restoring photos
- Color grading vintage photos
- Adding vignettes and frames
- Creating a "vintage" photo

You may have relatives who have—or you yourself may have—old photos taken in the film days. You may have 35mm slides, prints, or Polaroids taken years ago. Perhaps they were thrown in a box and have been crumpled up with a Howdy Doody marionette or an old Post Toasties box.

The old photos may have been shot with poor exposures or maybe they faded over the years. Regardless of the condition, you can try the techniques in this chapter to resurrect old photos for printing or sharing with family on social media.

Restoring Photos

Photo restoration involves several different kinds of edits. You typically need to address brightness and contrast first. Next, you need to look at major repairs to a photo, like reconstructing missing pieces, fixing crumpled-up areas, and repairing cracks and torn edges. Finally, you need to remove dust and scratches. If you want to colorize a photo or add a tint, you'll do those edits at the end of your editing session.

Restoring Faded Photos

In Chapter 4, "Working with Layers," I talked about adding more data to photos. If you take a photo that's horribly underexposed—where the image appears washed out—your first step is to see if you can bring back detail in highlights by using brightness controls. If the photo is devoid of too much data, making a brightness adjustment may not be enough.

In Figure 13.1, I have a vintage photo my father brought back from his tour of Italy during WWII. This photo is faded and needs, among other things, a contrast boost.

FIGURE 13.1 This vintage photo appears as though it's underexposed.

The first step to restore a photo like this is to create some more data you can work with. Follow these steps:

1. Create a duplicate layer in the Layers panel by pressing Ctrl/⌘ + J.

2. Select the top layer, and from the Blending Modes drop-down list in the Layers panel, choose Multiply. The Multiply blend mode adds more black to any value above 50% gray. You can take care of values lower than 50% when you adjust brightness/contrast. If the image still looks weak, you

can duplicate the top layer, add Multiply for the blend mode, and adjust opacity if necessary.

3. Open the Layers panel menu and choose Flatten Image. Save the file and close it.

4. Choose File > Open in Camera Raw in the Photo Editor and select the file you just saved to open it in the Raw Editor.

5. If the photo isn't in 16-bit mode, set the Depth to 16 Bits/Channel at the bottom of the Raw Editor. From the Profile drop-down list, select Monochrome.

6. Make adjustments in the Basic panel for exposure, contrast, highlights, shadows, and clarity. Adjust the Black and White sliders as necessary. Figure 13.2 shows the adjustments I made to my example.

FIGURE 13.2 Adjustments made in the Camera Raw Editor.

7. Click the icon for the Detail panel and add a slight bit of sharpening, but don't overdo it. If the file is low resolution, you may want to avoid sharpening in Camera Raw for now.

8. Click Open when you're finished editing in the Raw Editor.

Using the Dust & Scratches Filter

You can apply some edits while in 16-Bit mode, including using the Dust & Scratches filter. Choose Filter > Noise > Dust & Scratches. When the Dust & Scratches dialog box opens, move the Radius slider to a low value—1 to 3. For my example, which you can see in Figure 13.3, I set the Radius slider to 3.

You need to drop from 16-Bit mode to 8-Bit mode to move on, so choose Image > Mode > 8 Bits/Channel and then follow these steps:

FIGURE 13.3 Choose a low Radius value in the Dust & Scratches dialog box.

1. Open the original image you opened in the Camera Raw Editor. You could also Duplicate the original image before opening it in the Raw Editor. The point is you want two copies of the image: one with the Dust & Scratches filter applied and one without a Dust & Scratches adjustment.

2. Open both copies in the Photo Editor. Make sure they are both 8-bit images. Press the Shift key and drag the photo without the Dust & Scratches filter to the other image. The end result is you want the Dust & Scratches adjustment on the bottom layer. Pressing the Shift key when you drag a layer to a second image ensures the layers are aligned.

3. Create a selection of the subjects in the photo and inverse the selection by pressing Ctrl/⌘ + Shift + I.

4. Create a Layer Mask from the selection. At this point, you are showing through the background area to the dust and scratches layer. You want to maintain sharpness in the subjects' faces and bodies. However, you can let the dust and scratches show through to the clothing.

5. Select a brush and paint black in the mask in the clothing and areas where you don't need detail. You now have the dust and scratches layer at the bottom of the layer stack, and you're blocking out areas that need sharpness, like the subjects' faces.

The areas needing more sharpness are exposed, whereas the areas that don't need sharpening, such as the background and large areas of common tonal values, remain blurred. The result is that you've eliminated some dust and scratches, tears in photos, crimpled edges, and other imperfections.

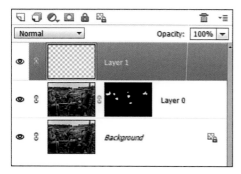

FIGURE 13.4 Create a new layer at the top of the layer stack.

TIP: Remember to press the Alt key and right-click (on Windows) or press Ctrl _ Option and left-click (on Macintosh) and then drag left or right to size brush tips.

For more on creating sepia tones, see the "Creating Vintage Photo Looks" section later in this chapter.

Removing Imperfections

Using the Dust & Scratches filter won't take care of all the imperfections in a photo. You may have long and wide scratches, tears, and missing pieces. The Dust & Scratches filter works best for some of the minor dust specs that would take considerable time to edit out of a photo.

To remove other imperfections, you need to use the Healing brushes and the Clone Stamp tools. Here's what you need to do:

1. Create a new layer. When you work on restoring photos, create layers for each distinct editing task. The Layers panel should look like Figure 13.4 at this point.

2. Select the Healing Brush tool (not the Spot Healing Brush). Check the box for Sample All Layers. Choose a medium brush tip. You can change brush tip sizes using the left and right bracket keys to make the tips smaller and larger, respectively. You can also make the brush tip smaller and larger with Windows by right-clicking the mouse button while pressing the Alt key and dragging left to make the size smaller and right to make the brush larger. On a Mac, press Ctrl + Option and left-click the mouse button while dragging left/right, or press Alt and right-click and move up to make the brush tip softer and down to make it harder. On the Mac, press Ctrl + Option and left-click the mouse button while dragging up or down to change hardness. If you want to change brush tips, right-click the Brush tool to open the Brush choices.

3. Make sure Sample All Layers is checked in the Tool Options panel. Press Alt/Option to sample an area and click; then click the new layer and paint to cover additional dust and scratches in the photo. Continue working through the document to remove all imperfections. Work slowly, and remember to change layers when sampling and then applying brush strokes. You need to continuously work back and forth.

Vintage photos are often best viewed with a sepia tone or a tint. Unless you have a good-quality black-and-white photo, you'll likely want to add some color tones to the photos. In this example, I added a sepia-tone effect. I set the Layer blend mode to Overlay and reduced opacity on the layer to 25%. The final image is shown in Figure 13.5.

FIGURE 13.5 Final edited photo.

Using the Clone Stamp for Fixes

When you have photos with severe problems, the Healing brushes may not do the job. You may need to use Clone Stamp or Content-Aware Fill, or you might need to copy sections of a photo and paste into other areas, like you're patching the image.

For cloning adjacent areas in a photo, click the Clone Stamp tool. Like all restoration edits, you first create a new layer where you add our Clone Stamp tool effects. For full-strength cloning, use 100% opacity. If some areas present a greater challenge, you may want to lower opacity and build it up gradually.

Sample areas next to the areas you want to clone and add your clone edits to the new blank layer, as shown in Figure 13.6. Remember to use shortcuts to change the brush size and hardness by pressing Alt as you right-click and drag to change size and brush hardness on Windows, and press Ctrl + Option while you left-click the mouse button and drag on the Mac.

Continue moving around and cloning areas. When a Healing brush will do the job, change tools, sample, and then apply with the Healing brush. If you need to edit a stroke, press Alt/Option and click the Eye icon on the edit layer. Only that layer will be visible, and you can see your brush strokes. Use the Eraser tool or make selections and delete brush strokes. If some strokes are too intense, select them and press Ctrl/⌘ + J to create a new layer of the selected items. Change the opacity to edit the strokes.

FIGURE 13.6 Cloning with the Clone Stamp tool.

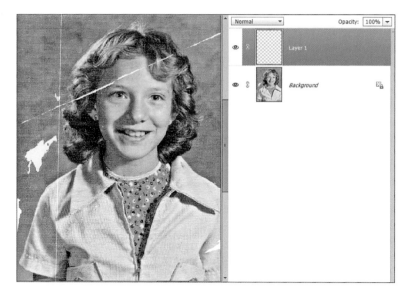

I added a duplicated layer and used the High Pass filter; then I used the Overlay blend mode to sharpen the photo. In many cases, you might need to add some sharpening. The final image using the Clone Stamp tool is shown in Figure 13.7.

FIGURE 13.7 Final edited photo.

Color Grading Vintage Photos

Quite often, you find old photos have color casts. Even photo prints taken as black and white will carry a color cast over time. When you scan the photos, the color casts may appear in the Photo Editor when you open the images. Before colorizing vintage photos, you want to remove color casts.

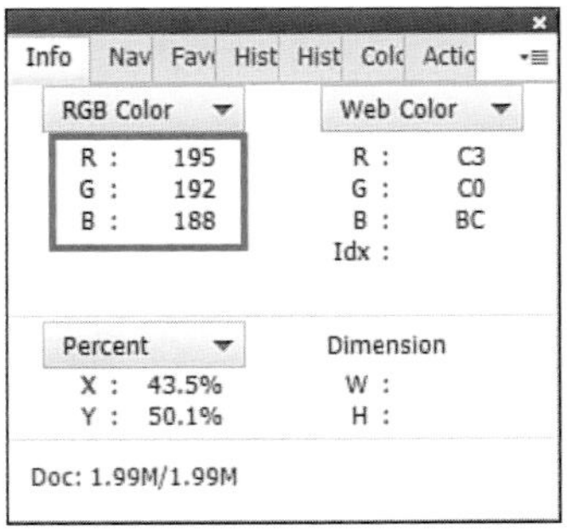

If you're not sure whether a photo has a color cast, you can easily check to see if there's color in the photo. Open the Info panel. Click the More button in the Photo Editor Panel Bin, and the miscellaneous panels open. Select the Eyedropper tool and click in an area of the photo. Move the Eyedropper tool around the photo to see if you find any values in the RBG readouts in the Info panel. As you can see in Figure 13.8, there's a color cast in the photo shown in this figure. If the photo has no color, the RGB values are equal.

FIGURE 13.8 Open the Info panel and drag the Eyedropper around a photo to check for a color cast.

To remove color from a photo, choose Enhance > Adjust Color > Remove Color, or you can use Enhance > Convert to Black and White. If you open the Info panel and move the Eyedropper tool around the photo, all the RGB values are equal wherever you move tool, showing no color in the photo.

Assuming you don't have to perform any restoration edits, you may want to move on to color grading the photo. The first thing to do is adjust the brightness and contrast. Click the Create Fill or Adjustment Layer icon in the Layers panel to open the drop-down list; then choose Levels. Add a Levels Adjustment Layer and make brightness and contrast changes.

Add a new layer and create a gradient. In my example, I used an orange/teal gradient and set the stops as shown in Figure 13.9.

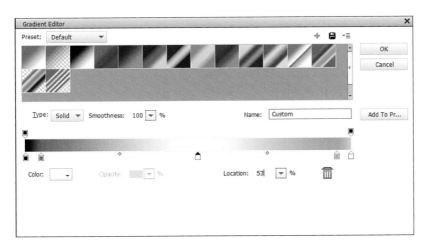

FIGURE 13.9 Custom color gradient edited in the Gradient Editor.

I added a new layer and applied the gradient to the new layer. I then set the blending mode to Soft Light and reduced opacity to 25%. The final image is shown in Figure 13.10.

FIGURE 13.10 Final vintage photo with a color grading effect.

Adding Vignettes and Frames

Vignettes darken the edges of a photo. Vignettes are used to help bring the viewer's eye to the center of a photo.

As far as vignettes go, just about any kind of photo—whether portrait, landscape, street, travel, head shot, fashion, or glamour—can benefit from having a vignette. Traditional vintage photos are often viewed in frames. You can add many different kinds of frames to photos that perhaps you wanted to share on social media. For printed photos, you may want to include or exclude borders. Quite often, printed photos are best viewed in actual frames rather than as printed photos with applied frames. There are exceptions, though, and you may want to include a photo frame with prints you frame.

Creating Vignettes

There are many different ways you can add vignettes to a photo. You can create a selection with a feather, fill the selection black, and then apply different blend modes. You can add feathering after the fact. You can copy the outside of a photo, add it to another layer, and then apply blend modes.

You can also use a Guided Edit to create vignettes, and the Vignette Guided Edit does a pretty good job at creating a nice vignette. Using the Guided Edit, you can choose to have a black or white vignette, and you have control over the opacity, feathering, and roundness of the vignette shape. The Vignette Effect Guided Edit is in the Basics Guided Edits panel. Scroll to the bottom of the panel to find Vignette Effects. In Figure 13.11, you can see a vignette effect nicely created in the Guided Edits panel. Notice the effect is slight and not overpowering. This little bit of a vignette helps focus attention on the subjects.

FIGURE 13.11 Vignette created from the Vignette Effect Guided Edit.

The only thing you don't have available using the Guided Edit Vignette Effect is the ability to create a custom shape. The Guided Edit Vignette Effect does create a layer with a mask that you can manipulate in Expert mode in the Photo Editor if you want to add more edits, so it is somewhat flexible.

Another way to create a vignette is to make the edits manually using the Hue/Saturation Adjustment Layer. To create a vignette using a Hue/Saturation Adjustment Layer, first open a photo and add a new layer. Create an elliptical selection with the Elliptical Marquee tool on the blank layer. Press Alt/Option and click the Add Layer Mask icon in the Layers panel. The mask has a black fill for the elliptical selection. Only the outside of the ellipse is the selected area.

Next, create a Hue/Saturation Adjustment Layer from the drop-down list in the Layers panel. Press Alt/Option as you click and drag the mask from the empty layer to the Hue/Saturation layer. If prompted to replace the mask, click Yes.

Double-click the Hue/Saturation icon in the Hue/Saturation Adjustment Layer to open the Hue/Saturation dialog box. When you open the Hue/Saturation Adjustment Layer, the elliptical shape doesn't look very good. It has a hard edge, as shown in Figure 13.12. Don't worry about that. You'll fix it later.

FIGURE 13.12 Create a Hue/Saturation Adjustment Layer.

FIGURE 13.13 Apply a high value for the Radius in the Gaussian Blur dialog box.

At this point, you want to move the Lightness slider to the left in the Hue Saturation dialog box to darken the outside of the shape.

Select the Hue/Saturation layer and choose Filter > Blur > Gaussian Blur. Move the Radius slider right to add a significant blur. In my example, I moved the slider to 30 pixels, as shown in Figure 13.13.

Choose Multiply from the Layers panel for the Blend mode. Reduce the opacity to what looks best to you. In Figure 13.14, you can see the final image and the layers used for this edit.

FIGURE 13.14 Final image with a vignette effect.

Creating Borders and Frames

You have a huge number of choices and ways to approach adding a border around a photo or adding a picture frame.

Adding Borders

You can add a simple border to a photo quite easily. To add a border, choose the color you want for the border color. If you want a simple white border, press D on your keyboard for default colors. Default colors are black foreground and white background. If you choose another color, make sure it's the background color.

Choose Image > Resize > Canvas Size. You can also press Ctrl/⌘ + Alt/Option + C to open the Canvas Size dialog box. The Canvas Size dialog box opens, as shown in Figure 13.15.

By default, the center anchor is selected. Make certain you leave it alone because you'll size the canvas up from the center so it's equidistant on all sides. Add .25 or whatever size you want for your border to both the Width and Height text boxes.

If the size of the canvas is an odd size—something like 4.32 × 6.17, cancel out of the Canvas Size dialog box and click the Crop tool. Round off the width and height values. In this case, type **5.5** in the W (width) text box and **3.5** in the H (height) text box. Crop the image to cut off the little bit on the edges

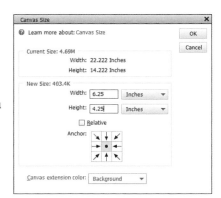

FIGURE 13.15 The Canvas Size dialog box.

and press the Enter key to accept the crop dimensions. This makes the size consistent with standard sizes and much easier to add .25 or another size to the Width and Height text boxes. The final image with a .25 border will be 6 × 4 inches, which is a standard print size.

Again, Choose Image > Resize > Canvas Size to open the Canvas Size dialog box. In my example, I added .25 inches, and my background color was white. The final result is shown in Figure 13.16.

FIGURE 13.16 A simple white border added to the photo.

Adding Frames

Elements provides a lot of frames when you install the program. This may be of particular interest if you use Elements for scrapbooking.

Adding one of the preinstalled frames is easy, but you can experience a few quirks if you don't set up your file properly before adding a frame. The most important thing to do is flatten your image if you have multiple layers. You can get some unexpected results if you try to add a frame on a photo having two or more layers. If you want to keep your original photo with layers, press Alt/Option and choose File > Duplicate. Holding the Alt/Option key bypasses the Duplicate Image dialog box. You can also press Ctrl/⌘ + Alt/Option + Shift to create a composite layer in the event you want to keep layers if you need to start with a new frame or add several frames and compare results. Save a copy of the file; then flatten the layers and save as a new name.

To flatten a layered file, open the Layers panel and choose Flatten Image in the Layer panel menu. Open the Graphics panel by clicking Graphics at the bottom of the Layers panel. At the top of the Graphics panel, you have three drop-down lists. The top-left list offers several choices for categories for the type of graphics you can add to your photo. Choose By Type to access the Frames panel.

TIP: If you have odd sizes and you don't want to crop, use a percentage increase for upsizing the canvas, such as .25 or .5 percent. Be sure to change the Width/Height to Percent before typing in the Width/Height text boxes.

The drop-down list to the right of the By Type drop-down list offers a few choices, one of which is Frames. Choose Frames from this list. Figure 13.17 shows the various frames available in the Graphics panel.

If you use an Elements version that's earlier than 2022, adding frames is a little more complicated. You drag a frame from the Graphics panel and the frame comes in on top of your image. You have to finesse the layers and placement of the photo. In Elements 2022, adding frames became so much easier. You just drag a frame on top of a flattened image, and the frame is added to the photo. You can resize the photo to fit the frame, but the process is much easier than earlier versions of Elements. In Figure 13.17, you can see the result of dragging and dropping a frame on a photo.

FIGURE 13.17 A frame dragged from the Graphics panel to a photo.

When you examine the Layers panel, you see the layers that Elements creates for you, as shown in Figure 13.18. Before sharing or printing the file, be certain to flatten the layers.

When you flatten layers, you may find excess canvas outside the frame. Crop the photo to the frame for the final image.

In Figure 13.19, I have dragged a frame to a flattened photo, and you can see the result properly shows the

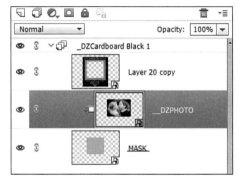

FIGURE 13.18 Layers created automatically by Elements after adding a frame from the Graphics panel.

FIGURE 13.19 Result after flattening layers and cropping to the frame.

FIGURE 13.20 Final image and the layers panel displaying the Color Fill layer.

photo through the mask and the excess canvas deleted after cropping the photo.

Painting Layer Mask Frames

A very simple but creative way you can add a frame to a photo is by using a Layer Mask and painting the edges of the mask. You can apply a frame to backgrounds and layered files.

Open a photo and click the Create New Fill or Adjustment Layer icon. Select Solid Color for the type of Adjustment Layer. The Color Picker opens. You can choose any color you want for your frame. If you want white, select the white color (ffffff) in the Color Picker and click OK.

The mask is filled white. Click the mask and press Ctrl/⌘ + I to invert the mask so the mask becomes black.

Click the Brush tool. Open the Tool Options panel and choose a grunge brush or a decorative brush for the effect you want on the edges of the frame. Set the brush tip size between 300 and 400 pixels. If you want the frame size smaller or larger, press Alt/Option as you right-click and drag to make the tip smaller or larger.

Click the mask to select it. Be certain the mask is selected, and the foreground color is white. Click one corner. Move the mouse to the opposite corner and press Shift and click. Pressing Shift and clicking creates a straight line for the brush stroke. If you want the line to be more freeform, drag the brush across one side. Continue brushing all four sides.

I started out with a terrible image. It was a Polaroid photo taken more than 50 years ago. The frame in Figure 13.20 shows the result of creating a frame in this manner.

Using Shapes as Frames

All of the shapes contained in your Custom Shapes library can be used as frames. Here's what you need to do:

1. Open an image and click on the Custom Shape tool. Open the Tool Options panel and scroll through the shapes. You can choose any shape; however, if you open the drop-down list for Shapes and choose Frames, you're offered some shapes that were designed specifically for frames.

2. Click and drag a shape on the photo. The shape is added as a new layer.

3. Press Ctrl/⌘ and click to create a selection.

4. Press Ctrl/⌘ + Shift + I to inverse the selection or choose Select > Inverse.

5. Click the Add Layer Mask icon in the Layers panel to create a Layer Mask.

6. When you add a frame or a shape, the objects are vector objects. You cannot change the pixel value of the objects because they are not yet pixels. Therefore, you cannot change colors of the shapes once they're created. If you want a color applied to a shape or frame, you have to first select the color and then create the shape or frame.

   You can, however, convert the shape to pixels. Then you can use painting tools and apply fills with different colors to shapes. To convert a vector shape to pixels, open the Layer panel menu and choose Simplify Layer. Apply this menu command to your shape layer.

7. If the frame is smaller than the photo and you need to delete some excess photo area in the image, double-click the Background to convert it to a layer. Load the frame selection and click the Background layer. Select the Eraser tool and use a medium-size brush. Paint over the edges. The area inside the selection is protected, so the only areas you erase are the edges outside the innermost selection.

8. To use a color in the photo, click the Eyedropper tool and sample a color in the photo. Press the Ctrl/⌘ and click on the shape layer to select it. Make sure the shape is selected and choose Edit > Fill Selection. The foreground color is the fill color.

   If you change your mind and want another color, move the cursor to the photo. When the cursor is on the photo, it turns into the Eyedropper tool. Click on the color you want to sample and click OK. Make sure the shape is selected and choose Edit > Fill Selection. In the Use drop-down list, choose Foreground Color and click OK. The color you sampled is now the fill for the shape.

The final result of these edits is shown in Figure 13.21.

FIGURE 13.21 Shape frame with a drop shadow.

Creating Frame Templates

You can create some templates for your favorite frames. Open several images in the Photo Editor. Open Preferences and check Allow Floating Documents in Expert Mode in the General Preferences.

Minimize the photos by clicking the top-left features button (represented by a minus symbol) on Windows. On the Mac, click the middle circle icon at the top-left corner of the photo window.

Choose a frame you like to use frequently and add it to a new document window. Pick another frame if you want more than one on a page and add it to the same document.

At this point, you have two empty frames. Open the Photo Bin at the bottom of the Photo Editor window to show the open files. Drag photos to the frames. In Figure 13.22, you can see photos added to two different frames.

FIGURE 13.22 Photos added to different frames.

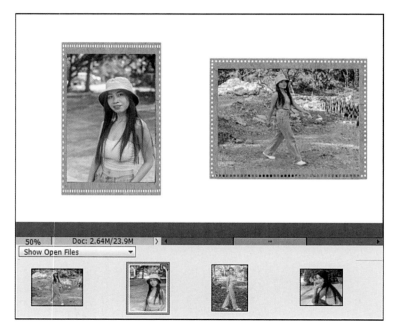

Save the file as a .psd file. Name it something like FramesTemplate. When you want to add the same frame for different photos, open this file and open additional photos. Drag photos from the Photo Bin to the frames to replace the photos within the frames.

Creating Frame Favorites

The My Frames panel is more of a favorites location than a place where you can create custom frames. Files need to be saved as .psd files to be added to the My Frames panel. Unfortunately, you cannot create a .psd file, save it, and add the design to your My Frames panel. The only way to add frames to this panel is by adding a .psd file that contains a frame.

You need to create a new document and add a frame from the Other Frames panel. Then open the My Frames panel. To do so, choose By Type in the first drop-down menu and choose Frames in the second menu adjacent to the By Type menu. Open the menu below the By Type menu and choose My Frames. From the panel menu drop-down list, choose Add Frame.

The Load dialog box opens. Navigate your hard drive and locate a file you saved as a frame, select it, and click Load. When you save files containing a frame as a .psd file, you can only have a single frame in the document.

The frame is saved to your My Frames panel. You can continue locating some frames you might use frequently, add them to new blank documents, and save as .psd files. Load the frame files in the My Frames panel to keep your favorite frames in one panel.

Figure 13.23 shows the My Frames panel I have set up and a frame applied to a document by dragging from my Frames to a blank document and dropping a photo on the frame.

FIGURE 13.23 Frames added to the My Frames panel and one of the favorites applied to a photo.

Creating Vintage Photo Looks

Sometimes you may want to work the other way around. Instead of editing a vintage photo, perhaps you may have a photo to which you want to apply a vintage look. Perhaps you want to create an entire scrapbook of photos combining vintage photos with newer photos altered to have a vintage look. The photo I used for this example is in Figure 13.24.

Before you begin, you need a couple of grunge type textures. You can create your own or find some free downloads for grunge documents. One of the grunge files should contain black and white with little gray values, as shown in Figure 13.25.

FIGURE 13.24 Original
unedited photo.

FIGURE 13.24 Original
unedited photo.

FIGURE 13.25 Grunge file
with black and white and
few grays.

The second file contains gray values, blacks, and whites in a grunge pattern, as shown later in Figure 13.26 in the Layers panel labeled as the Grays layer. You can try downloading different textures and convert them to grayscale. Test them out to see if you get the look you want.

When you're set with your grunge files, use these steps:

1. Place the two grunge files in a single document as different layers. Add a photo to the file. When the photo comes in, press Ctrl/⌘ + T to transform the photo. Be certain you use a photo that's equal to the same size and resolution as the file size or one you can size down in the grunge layers file. Press Alt/Option and drag a handle to size from center. Bring the photo to the same size as the other two layers. Name the layers Grunge 1 and Grunge 2.

2. Double-click the Photo layer to make it a layer.

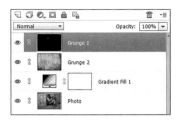

3. Select the Photo layer and open the Adjustment Layers drop-down list. Choose Gradient Map from the menu choices. Open the Tool Options panel and click the Gradient. Select the Black to White gradient and click OK in the Gradient Editor. The bottom layer is now a black-and-white image. Your layers panel should look like Figure 13.26.

FIGURE 13.26 Layers panel containing the two grunge layers and the photo converted to black and white.

4. Add a Levels Adjustment layer and darken up the image a little but not too much.

5. Combine the Background copy, Gradient Map, and Levels layers into a single layer by selecting the three layers and pressing Ctrl/⌘ + Alt/Option + Shift + E to merge the selected layers.

6. Select the Grunge 2 layer and choose Soft Light.

7. Copy the layer by pressing Ctrl/⌘ + J and setting the blend mode to Multiply. If the image appears too dark, reduce the Opacity.

8. Add a new layer and choose Edit > Fill Layer. Choose 50% Gray from the Use drop-down list. Click OK and choose Overlay for the blend mode. Duplicate the layer. When you duplicate the layer, the same blend mode is applied to the layer.

9. Label one layer **Dodge** and the other layer **Burn**. Use the Dodge and Burn tools to lighten and darken areas in the image. When you brush with the Dodge tool on the Dodge layer, set the foreground color as white. Set the Burn tool foreground color as black.

10. Select the other grunge layer. Set the blending mode to Screen. At this point, your layers panel should look like Figure 13.27. Remember, you merged the Gradient Map and Levels layers with the Duplicate Background layer, so those layers are not visible in the Layers panel.

11. Open the Adjustment Layers drop-down list and choose Levels. Select Red from the Channel drop-down list and move the midtone slider to the left to 1.41. You can type values in the midtone slider text box.

FIGURE 13.27 Grunge file showing layers.

12. Select Green from the Channels drop-down list. Set this value to 1.18. Select the Blue channel from the drop-down list. You need to add yellow to the image. (Remember, the opposite of blue is yellow.) Move the Blue slider right toward yellow and set it to .70. Click OK to apply a sepia effect to the photo.

The final image is shown in Figure 13.28.

FIGURE 13.28 Final edited photo.

You can use other methods for applying sepia toning to photos. You have Actions that have sepia effects. You can also use a Color Fill layer. And there are a number of other ways to apply sepia tone to images. In this example, I showed you how to adjust channels in the Levels dialog box. Set the opacity of the layer to what appears pleasing to you.

CHAPTER 14
EDITING PORTRAITS

Chapter Goals

This chapter and the next cover techniques you need to edit portrait photos. In this chapter, I cover selective editing for eyes, lips, facial contours, body shapes, and removing blemishes and artifacts. Chapter 15, "Editing Skin Tones," looks at editing skin tones. This chapter covers the following aspects of editing portraits:

- Using Camera Raw adjustments
- Editing blemishes
- Sculpting facial contours
- Editing eyes
- Editing lips
- Sharpening portraits
- Editing bodies

Many of the techniques we looked at in previous chapters can apply to portraits and glamour photos, but some options require some finesse and a gentle approach when they're applied for editing faces in portraits, head shots, and glamour photos.

There are two things to keep in mind when editing portraits and glamour photos:

- Always work on as many layers as needed. Each time you change a tool or use a blending mode, apply the edits to new layers.

- Work slowly and build up your edits. You can make some edits to backgrounds and create a lot of mistakes when editing. The final result may look fine to anyone viewing your photo. But with a portrait, the slightest overedit will be obvious to viewers. You want to try to create the most natural-looking subjects possible.

Using Camera Raw Adjustments

The first thing you want to look at with portraits and glamour photos is the brightness, contrast, and color temperature. Don't start performing other edits before you get the brightness/contrast of the photo right. This doesn't mean you won't later go back to Camera Raw or the Levels or Shadow Highlight adjustments. You may need to tweak the brightness and contrast as a last edit in some photos, but you should still start off with the proper adjustments for brightness/contrast and color temperature.

FIGURE 14.1 Choose Adobe Portrait from the Profile drop-down list.

When opening an unedited file for the first time, use the Camera Raw Editor as your first stop. Files saved as raw files from your camera open directly in the Raw Editor when you choose File > Open and select the file. If files are not saved in the raw format from your camera, then choose Open in Camera Raw in the Photo Editor.

The first panel that opens is the Basic panel. Your first choice is what profile to choose. For Portrait images, try the Adobe Portrait profile you select from the Adobe Profile drop-down list, as shown in Figure 14.1.

After choosing the profile, your next stop is the Temperature and Tint sliders. In many cases, using the default As Shot setting works well. However, you may want to warm up a photo or cool it down by adjusting the Temperature slider. The nice thing about using Camera Raw is that if you don't like the results when you start editing in the Photo Editor, you can close the file and start over. If you close a file and then choose File > Open Recently Edited File, the file opens in Camera Raw (if it's a raw file), showing the last adjustments you made in the Raw Editor.

As I covered in Chapter 2, "Using Camera Raw," you work down the Basic panel sliders to make adjustments and move back and forth to refine adjustments. For most of the slider adjustments, press the Alt/Option key as you drag a slider. The image window in the Raw Editor turns black. Move the slider slowly until you begin to see some data in the image window. In Figure

14.2, I pressed Alt/Option and dragged the Shadow slider. When you see data in the window, back it off a little to a point where the data just begins to show in the image window.

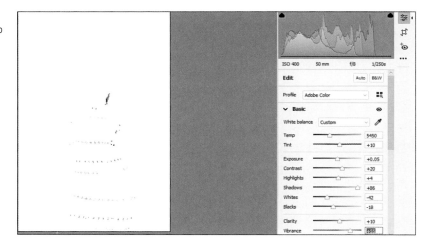

*For more on using the
Basic panel adjustments,
see Chapter 2.*

Move through the Basic panel sliders and make adjustments. As you continue refining the adjustments, look at the Histogram and the image window to double-check your adjustments.

After finishing with the Basic panel, click the icon for the Detail panel just to the right of the Basic panel icon. In the Detail panel, you can add some sharpening and noise reduction.

In this panel, you can also see a preview for how the data falls in the image when making the adjustments. Press the Alt/Option key while you drag a slider. For the Masking option, you see where sharpening is applied as you move the Masking slider as you press the Alt/Option key. All the white area is affected by the adjustment, whereas the black area receives no sharpening. (See Figure 14.3.)

When working with portraits, you want to apply minimal sharpening. Sharpening is applied to the entire image that remains within the mask. There may be some areas you want to sharpen more, and other areas where you want less sharpening. For example, a subject's eyes in portraits are the most important focal point. You'll want to add more sharpening to the eyes than other areas in the image. Hence, you want to apply a slight bit of sharpening in Camera Raw and handle the rest of the sharpening using sharpening techniques in the Photo Editor.

At the bottom of the panel, you see the Bit Depth setting. The Depth adjustment should be 16 Bits/Channel. When you click Open Image or Open Copy, the file containing the Raw Editor adjustments opens in the Photo Editor. When the file is opened, choose File > Save As and save a copy to work on.

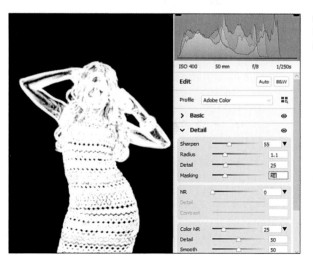

FIGURE 14.3 Press Alt/Option and drag the Masking slider to see where sharpening is applied in the photo.

If you need further adjustments to brightness/contrast, save your updates in the copy of the file and reopen the original image in the Raw Editor. Make further adjustments in the Raw Editor, and open the photo in Expert mode. Save another copy as another name. You need to reduce the file to 8 bit by choosing Image > Mode > 8 Bits/Channel. Open the original copy and also reduce it to 8 bit. If you added any Adjustment Layers to the original copy, you can drag them to the second copy. This way you can rescue some of the edits made on the original copy.

In Figure 14.4, you can see a file I used for this example. Adjustments to brightness and contrast and the shadow/highlight adjustments brought out detail in the hair. I applied a little bit of sharpening to the photo. This photo still needs some sharpening in the eyes and lips.

FIGURE 14.4 Photo edited in Camera Raw and then opened in the Photo Editor.

Editing Blemishes

Most novice Photoshop and Photoshop Elements users will grab the Spot Healing brush right away and start brushing over blemishes. Both the Healing brush tools are wonderful, but you shouldn't view them as a panacea for curing blemishes and artifacts on subjects. When it comes to editing portraits, there really isn't a quick fix you can apply to all your photos. You can make some overall improvements, but to create really nice-looking photos of family, friends, models, glamour shots, and even candid photos, it pays to work slowly and look at some effective alternatives.

Skin is critically important when editing portrait photos. You want to remove all temporary artifacts and blemishes from your subject's faces, but you don't want to make your subject unrealistic and have the individual appear completely different than their character or persona. When it comes to extreme editing and making subjects look unrealistic, you can leave that to those who create movie posters.

For certain characteristics such as moles, freckles, under-eye shadows, and so on, for the most part, you want to leave those alone. In some cases, you may want to smooth skin texture and make some corrections for how lighting affects the subject's appearance. For temporary skin blemishes, dust particles, exaggerated pores, lack of makeup, and so on, you want to make some edits to show the subject at his or her best. Just remember, if it's a temporary imperfection, take it out. If it's something permanent, like Harrison Ford's little chin scar, leave it in.

One thing that's a certainty when it comes to editing portraits is that it's very easy to overdo it. Too much of anything makes your subject look unrealistic and fake. Try to create a balance for perfecting skin while keeping the subject in a very realistic view. Whenever you can, use layers for skin editing. You can always reduce opacity to bring the adjustments down so that they appear more realistic.

With some of these thoughts in mind, let's take a look at how you can make edits to remove artifacts and blemishes in portraits.

Creating Selections

The first thing you want to do when editing portraits is create a selection for the skin tones in the face. You can use many different methods for creating a selection. In a lot of cases, just using the Quick Selection tool is a good start. Click the Quick Selection tool in the Tools panel. Open the Tool Options panel and select a soft-edged brush.

Adjust the brush size by pressing the Alt/Option key and right-clicking the mouse button (Windows) or pressing Control + Option and left-clicking (Macintosh) as you drag. To size down a brush size, drag left. To size up the brush tip, drag to the right. You can also use the left and right bracket keys to size the brush tip down or up, respectively. In Figure 14.5, you can see the selection I made using the Quick Selection tool on a photo used in this example.

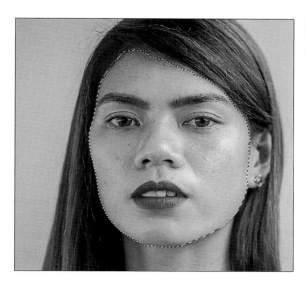

FIGURE 14.5 Selection made with the Quick Selection tool.

Refining Selections

After creating a selection, choose Select > Refine Edge. You can also click the Refine Edge button in the Tool Options panel when the Quick Selection tool is active. Either action opens the Refine Edge dialog box.

Click the View Mini Thumbnail icon to open the View drop-down list. Choose Overlay or press the V key on your keyboard. This choice shows the Quick Mask mode where all the nonselected area is displayed with a red overlay. Check the Smart Radius option and move the Radius slider to the right. How much you move the slider depends on your image. In my example, I moved the slider to 7.7, as shown in Figure 14.6.

Open the Output To drop-down list and choose New Layer with Layer Mask. Click

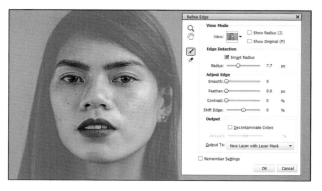

FIGURE 14.6 View the selection using the Quick Mask overlay and add some radius to the Smart Radius setting.

OK, and a new layer is created with a Layer Mask created from the refine edge selection.

If your first edit doesn't include an edit that duplicates the background, you should start by duplicating the background by pressing Ctrl/⌘ + J so you can work on a duplicate copy of the Background layer in case you want to toss the edits and start over. It's too easy to forget and press Ctrl/⌘ + S to save a photo. If you inadvertently press the keyboard shortcuts, you won't have an unedited image to return to if you want to start over.

In this example, I didn't need to duplicate the background because my first edit produced a duplicate of the Background layer. You want to add layers for all edits where you change tools, but you want to try to keep the number of layers to only those that are necessary. As you add more layers, you increase file size. If you're working on a Camera Raw photo, the file size is usually quite large. The more layers you add, the slower your computer's performance.

Blurring Skin Tones

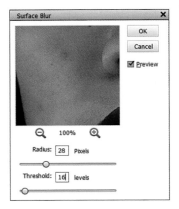

FIGURE 14.7 Make adjustments in the Surface Blur dialog box.

You can take care of some of the open pores and small blemishes by using a blur filter. Select the top layer (Background Copy) and choose Filter > Blur > Surface Blur.

You want to set the Radius and the Threshold levels to a combination where you hide some of the small blemishes and imperfections. Be careful to not push the Threshold slider too far to the right. The settings you apply in the Smart Blur dialog box depend on your image and the resolution of the file. In this example, I set the Radius to 28 pixels and the Threshold Levels to 16, as shown in Figure 14.7.

As you can see in Figure 14.7, the skin on the subject's face is smoothed out some. You may notice that some of the texture is lost with the Smart Blur filter. Don't worry about it now; you'll take care of that later.

Editing Layer Masks

One thing you want to do is keep some areas of the face as sharp as you can. When you apply a Blur filter, you lose detail in all areas where the blur was applied. In my example, I want to keep the eyebrows, eyes, eyelids, and lips sharp. Therefore, I edited the Layer Mask to remove these areas from the Surface Blur adjustment.

Click the mask on the top layer. Be certain the mask is selected. Click the Brush tool, and choose a hard-edge brush in the Tools Options panel. Open the Brush Settings by clicking the Brush Settings button in the Tools Options panel. Double-check the Hardness slider in the Brush Settings dialog box. The slider should be pushed to the far right to 100%, as shown in Figure 14.8.

Again, click the mask to be sure you apply brush strokes to the mask. The mask should be selected, but you should be seeing the photo in the Document Window. Check your foreground color. It should be black. If it is not, press D on your keyboard to return to default colors of a black foreground and white background. You want black as the foreground color. As you paint black in the mask, the respective areas in the photo are not affected by the edits you make on the photo. In this case, the Surface Blur edit won't be applied to the black areas in the mask.

With the mask selected and the foreground color set to black, paint over the eyebrows, eyes, eyelids, and lips on the photo. Because the mask is selected, the brush strokes are applied to the mask. You might also include some fine hair if your photo shows hair strands over the forehead and edges of the face.

After painting the target areas in the mask, press Alt/Option and click the mask. Look over the mask and paint over any areas missed when the photo was in view. The mask I used for the example image after painting over the eyebrows, eyes, eyelids, lips, and some hair is shown in Figure 14.9.

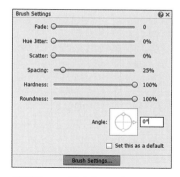

FIGURE 14.8 Click Brush Settings in the Tool Options panel to open the Brush Settings dialog box.

FIGURE 14.9 The Layer Mask shown after painting black over the eyebrows, eyes, eyelids, and lips.

Using the Blur Tool

The Surface Blur may not have caught all blemishes and skin imperfections, and you may need a little more blurring in some areas of the face. For this edit, you use the Blur tool.

Select the Blur tool and open the Tool Options panel. Select a soft-edge brush and check the Sample All Layers box. Set the Strength to 100%. If you find the blur to be too much when you first apply the brush, you can reduce the Strength amount by dragging the slider left.

Create a new layer and select it. All the blur you add to the image is applied to a blank new layer. If you don't like the results of using the Blur tool, you can delete the layer and start over. All the previous edits remain unaffected.

Press Alt/Option as you right-click and drag left or right (Windows) or press Control + Option as you left-click and drag (Macintosh) to size the Blur tool brush tip. Paint over areas where you see blemishes and imperfections. The larger areas you can take care of later if the blur tool doesn't have any effect on larger blemishes.

Using the Spot Healing Brush Tool

The larger blemishes you couldn't remove with the Surface Blur or Brush tool need some edits with a different tool. The Spot Healing Brush tool is the one you'll use to remove larger blemishes.

Create a new layer where you'll apply all the Spot Healing Brush strokes. If you make some mistakes, you can edit the layer to correct them, or you can delete the layer and start again without affecting your previous edits.

Select the Spot Healing Brush in the Tools Panel. Select a soft-edge brush and check the box for Sample All Layers. The Spot Healing Brush requires no sampling. Select the new top layer in the Layers panel and brush over blemishes.

If you apply some brush strokes and the edits are not right, you can Undo the edits or use the History panel. If you want to keep edits after the one you want to change, you can select a brush stroke and press the Backspace/Delete key to delete it from the layer.

Press Alt/Option as you right-click and drag left or right (Windows) or press Control + Option and left-click as you drag (Macintosh) to change brush sizes. You want to use brush tip sizes a little larger than the blemish you want to remove. Continue moving around the document, changing brush tip sizes, and applying brush strokes to the blemishes and skin imperfections.

Adding Film Grain

As a last edit, you can add some film grain or noise to the areas you edited. Film grain or noise brings back a little texture. Select the Duplicate layer with the mask and all layers above it and press Ctrl/⌘ + Alt/Option + Shift + E to create a composite layer.

FIGURE 14.10 Create a composite layer at the top of the layer stack.

At this point, all your layers should look like Figure 14.10.

Select the new composite layer and press Ctrl/⌘ and click the Layer Mask (on the Background copy layer). This creates a selection of the face on the composite layer.

Select Filter > Texture > Grain. You can also apply Noise. If you choose the Noise filter by selecting Filter > Noise > Add Noise, add a low amount of noise. Add something between 1 and 2.5. If it looks like too much after you apply it, press Ctrl/⌘ + Z to undo the last edit and add a lower amount.

If you use the Film Grain filter, choose Soft from the Grain drop-down list. Adjust the intensity and contrast sliders so a little grain appears in the preview image, as shown in Figure 14.11.

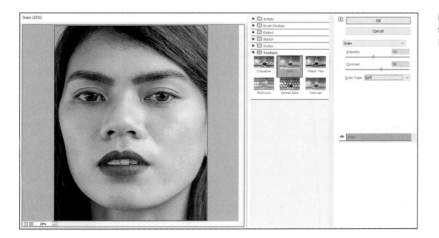

FIGURE 14.11 Add a little film grain by using the Film Grain filter.

Set the zoom level to 100% and scroll around the photo. Use the Spot Healing Brush to remove any slight imperfections that you may have missed. These should be minimal if you performed all the edits up to this point.

The final image I used in this example is shown on the right in Figure 14.12. On the left is the original photo after brightness adjustments in Camera Raw. As you can see in the image at right, the adjustments are subtle, but they do show a remarkable improvement.

FIGURE 14.12 Before (left) and after (right) applying the edits for removing blemishes.

Sculpting Facial Contours

Human faces have natural contours, but in photographs, some features are not emphasized enough and need sculpting help so faces have a little more dimension.

FIGURE 14.13 Areas of the face where highlights naturally fall.

You add more dimension by editing highlights and shadows to accentuate curves and features in faces; you do this by dodging and burning different regions of the face. The general zones for adding more highlights and shadows are shown in Figure 14.13. Those areas outlined with red are the zones for highlights. The shadows would appear on the left and right sides of the forehead highlight zone, at the edges of the face along the cheeks and to the left and right of the nose shadow zone, and slightly darkened on either side of the chin highlight zone.

Previous chapters included some simple dodge and burn techniques using a 50% gray layer set to the Overlay mode. Using this technique is but one way to create a dodge and burn effect. There are some other ways you can dodge and burn photos. Before we move on to editing a photo, let's look at some of the alternatives.

Using the Dodge and Burn Tools

One way to dodge and burn is to use the Dodge and Burn tools directly on a photo in the areas that need the effect. When you select the Dodge or Burn tool and open the Tool Options panel, you can choose an option from the range drop-down list for Highlights, Shadows, and Midtones. You also have a slider to set the exposure value. When dodging and burning, it's always best to start with low exposure values.

Several problems are associated with using the Dodge and Burn tools directly on a photo. First of all, you can't add the brush strokes on a layer. All your dodging and burning are applied to, at best, a duplicate copy of the photo. If you add too much dodging or burning, you need to travel back in the History panel to undo the edits. Furthermore, because you aren't working on a layer, you can't adjust opacity, which would offer you another level of editing.

Using 50% Gray Layers

You've seen this technique before in several earlier chapters. You create a new layer and fill the layer 50% gray and change the blend mode to Overlay.

You can then use either the Dodge or Burn tools or the Brush tool and paint over the areas that need dodging and burning. If you use the Brush tool, you need to paint white for dodging and black for burning.

Using Levels Adjustment Layers

You can create two levels Adjustment Layers. What you look for is how bright you want the maximum highlights to be and how dark you want the shadows to be. You set the levels correspondingly to the highlights and shadows. You add Layer Masks and fill both masks black to hide the levels adjustments. The two layers will be used for dodging and burning—one for dodge and the other for burn. You keep them separate in case you want to adjust opacity for one or the other.

You then use either the Dodge and Burn tools or the Brush tool. If you use the Brush tool, you paint with white on both Layer Masks. Be certain to set the brush hardness to the softest setting and reduce the opacity to around 5 to 7 %. You gradually build up the brush strokes to create the amount of dodging and burning you want.

If you use the Brush tool, it's best to have a tablet. It's a little more difficult to use a mouse for painting either on Layer Masks or when using the 50% gray Overlay layer.

In Figure 14.14, you can see the Layers panel where I applied each of the three methods to a 50% gray sphere.

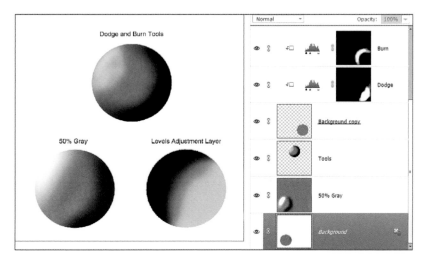

FIGURE 14.14 Three methods of dodging and burning.

Dodging and Burning a Portrait

To sculpt a portrait with some dodging and burning edits, you can use the method described earlier in the section "Using Levels Adjustment Layers."

Open a photo and create two Levels Adjustment Layers. In one Levels Adjustment Layer, move the midtone slider to the left for the highlights. Move the slider to the maximum amount of brightness you want for the highlights. The Adjustment Layer automatically creates a Layer Mask. Name the layer **Dodge**. Move the midtone slider left to the level of brightness you want, as shown in Figure 14.15. Fill the layer mask black to hide the adjustment.

FIGURE 14.15 Set the Levels adjustment to the lightest value you want for the highlights.

For the other Adjustment Layer, set the Levels to the brightest area you want for the shadows. Name the layer **Burn**. Fill the mask with black to hide the levels adjustment.

Select the Brush tool and choose a soft brush. Open the Tools panel and click Brush settings. Set the Hardness value to 0% for the softest brush. (Refer to the Brush Settings dialog box in Figure 14.8.)

Set the Opacity in the Tool Options panel to a low setting (somewhere between 5 and 7 %). The foreground color should be white for painting on both masks. Paint on the masks with the Brush tool.

In this example, I dodged and burned the photo, the result of which can be seen in Figure 14.16.

FIGURE 14.16 Final image (right) after dodging and burning using Levels Adjustment Layers.

On the left, you can see the original photo, and on the right is the photo after dodging and burning. Notice how the photo on the right adds some more dimension to the image.

Editing Eyes

When it comes to portraits, the eyes are the most important part of the photo. The viewers of your photos will immediately notice the eyes of a subject before they notice anything else. It's a magnetic attraction for all who view your photos. Editing eyes involves not only editing the irises but also the lashes and brows to bring all areas around the eyes within a correct exposure and amplified detail.

The following sections break this down and address the eyes, the lashes, and the brows separately to culminate in creating an improved photo.

Analyzing a Subject's Eyes

First of all, you need to analyze the construction of the subject's eyes. The eye itself includes the iris, the pupil, and the sclera (commonly known as the whites of the eyes). Typically, when you take portrait photos, the one area that suffers most from lack of brightness and contrast is the iris. Almost every portrait photo you edit needs some attention devoted to the iris.

You often find the appearance of tiny veins in the sclera (or whites of the eyes). Therefore, you need to pay some attention to the whites of the eyes.

The pupils are black, and sometimes you may find a color cast on the subject's pupils. Many photos show a catchlight in some area of the eye. Catchlights assume a shape from the light source. For example, if the portrait were taken in a studio with a beauty dish, the shape of the catchlight would be circular. In other cases, the shape may be rectangular or appear as a trapezoid. When a catchlight appears in the eye, the light hits the eye, and a reflection bounces out. Many times, however, the camera doesn't capture the catchlight, and you may need to create one artificially. The reflection from the catchlight is typically 180° on the opposite side of the eye. In Figure 14.17, you can see the different parts of the eye and how the reflection falls off the catchlight.

Whites
Pupil

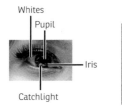

Iris

Catchlight

Catchlight

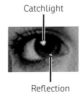

Reflection

FIGURE 14.17 Parts of the eye that need some attention when editing portraits.

Editing the Irises

The subject's iris is a good place to start. The first step is to create a Levels Adjustment Layer. In the Levels dialog box, you want to brighten up the image enough to see the detail in the subject's irises.

In the example in Figure 14.18, I moved the midtone slider far to the left to 1.85. When you look at the photo, it's obvious the adjustment is too much for a global Levels adjustment, but you don't need to be concerned with the entire photo. You'll mask out the area outside the subject's eyes.

FIGURE 14.18 Add a Levels Adjustment Layer and brighten the image enough to see details in the subject's eyes.

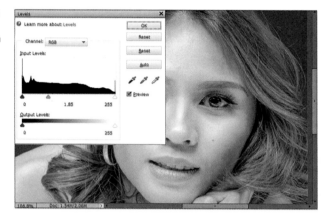

Don't be concerned if the Levels adjustment is too much. You don't want to overdo it, but the brightness adjustment doesn't have to be perfect. You're simply looking for some detail in the subject's irises. Continue with these steps:

1. Click on the mask for the Levels layer; the foreground color should be white, and the background color should be black. Press Ctrl/⌘ + Backspace/Delete to fill with the background black color. The Levels adjustment is now hidden from the image. You now want to bring back some of the brightness of the Levels adjustment in one iris at a time.

2. Select the Brush tool and choose a thin brush size of 1 pixel and set the Hardness to 0 (zero) to make a soft brush tip. The Hardness adjustment is in the Brush Settings dialog box shown in Figure 14.8.

3. Make sure the foreground color is white. Click in the mask and create straight lines in the iris. The lines should go from the outside edge of the iris toward the pupil at the center as if you're drawing radius lines in a circle. The lines I drew on my mask appear in Figure 14.19.

FIGURE 14.19 Lines drawn in the Levels mask.

In a zoomed-in view, when you look at the photo, you see the results of painting the mask with a 1 pixel brush. The zoomed-in view may not look right, as shown in Figure 14.20. However, when you zoom out, you see a far better representation of what the eye should look like.

FIGURE 14.20 Zoomed-in view of the edits made in the layer mask.

4. If the iris looks too bright all around the eye, you need to look at the catchlight and keep the area opposite the catchlight bright. The areas between the catchlight and the reflection need to be a little darker. To darken the area between the catchlight and the reflection, first put the Levels layer inside of a group. Select the Levels Adjustment Layer and choose New Group from the Layers panel menu. Click the Add Layer Mask icon to add a Layer Mask. Paint black in the new mask for the areas you want to hide.

5. To handle the whites of the eyes, create a new layer. Select the Healing Brush tool. Set the brush size to a small size (2 or 3 pixels) and the softness to 0 (zero) percent. Choose Lighten from the Mode drop-down list in the Brush Tool Options. Press Alt/Option and sample a light area in the photo. Paint over the veins and darker areas of the whites.

6. Duplicate the procedure in this section for the other eye.

Editing the Sclera

The sclera is the white part of the eye. Subjects' eyes may often appear quite bloodshot. To brighten up the sclera in a subject's eye, select the Healing Brush tool. In the Tool Options panel, open the Mode menu and choose Lighten. Sample the color tone lighter than the area you want to brighten and apply strokes. The darker areas will lighten up and remove veins and darker areas in the sclera.

Editing Eyebrows, Lashes, and Liners

Choose a small 1-pixel brush and sample color in the eyebrows. Create a new layer and paint strokes in the same direction as the hairs along the eyebrows.

This task is easier to do with a tablet. If you only have a mouse, move very slowly. Adjust opacity to lighten up the edits.

Next, work on the eyelashes. Choose a 1-pixel brush and sample the color of the lashes. If you need to construct new lashes, draw them very carefully on a new layer. For eyeliner, create a new layer and paint with a 1-pixel brush to match the same color as the lashes.

Create a new layer. Select the Sharpen tool and scrub across the lashes to sharpen them a little. If you apply too much sharpening, reduce the opacity.

Final edits on the eyes for the subject in my example are shown in Figure 14.21. The original image is on the left, and the final edited photo is on the right. Notice the edits didn't create fake or unnatural eyes. I just amplified the natural brightness and color of the subject's eyes.

FIGURE 14.21 Final image (right) after editing eyes, brows, lashes, and liner.

Editing Lips

Lips can be difficult to edit, primarily because Elements doesn't include tools to create the kind of perfect selection needed to select the lips. The ideal tools would be Paths and the Pen tool that are available in Photoshop.

Removing Artifacts Around the Lips

Create two new layers and make two selections—one for the upper lip and one for the lower lip. Create a Layer Mask on one layer and name it **Lower Lip**. Create another mask from the upper lip selection and name it **Upper Lip**.

Load the selection for the lower lip and use the Healing Brush tool to remove any artifacts. Lipstick can produce some bits of hardened masses, and chapped lips can be a problem. Load the selection for the lower lip and move around using the Healing Brush by sampling and brushing with a small brush tip. Inverse the selection by pressing Ctrl/⌘ + Shift + I and use the Healing Brush to polish up the areas outside the lip. Load the selection for the upper lip and perform similar edits.

Applying a Color for the Lipstick

After finishing with the Healing Brush tool, create a selection from one of the Lip layers, press the Shift key and press Ctrl/⌘, and click on the other lip layer so you have both lips selected. Choose Solid Color from the Adjustment Layers drop-down list in the Layers panel. Choose a color for the lipstick you want to apply to the lips.

In Chapter 10, "Color Toning and Color Grading," I suggested ways to choose lipstick colors. Look for a palette of lipstick colors or simply choose a color from the color picker. Choose OK in the Color Picker. Load a selection from the lips and fill the selection with the foreground color. The result is obviously horrible and looks like you painted a solid color over the lips. All texture is lost. To create a more realistic view, you need to reduce opacity. In my example, I reduced opacity to 30%.

Dodging and Burning the Lips

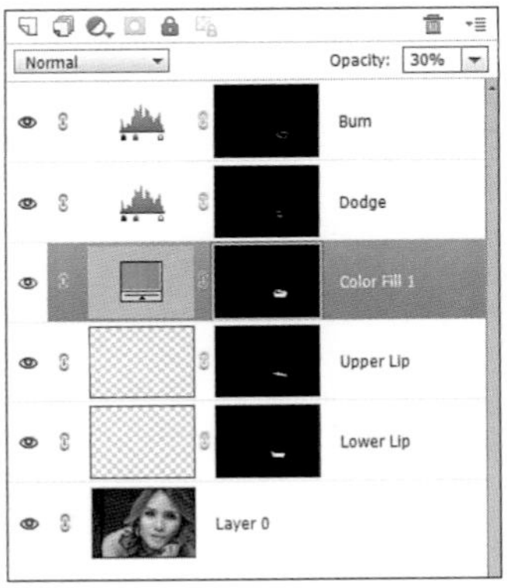

Open the Adjustment Layer drop-down list and choose Levels. In the Levels dialog box, move the midtone slider to lighten the photo to the lightest amount you want for the lightest part of the lips. With an Adjustment Layer, you can always reopen the Levels dialog box and refine the adjustment. Fill the mask with black to hide the Levels adjustment. Name the layer **Dodge**.

FIGURE 14.22 Layers panel showing Dodge, Burn, and Color Fill layers.

Create a second Levels Adjustment Layer and move the midtone slider to the right to darken the photo. Move the slider to the darkest amount you want to darken the lips. Fill the mask black and name the layer **Burn**. At this point, your Layers panel should look like Figure 14.22.

Select the Brush tool and choose a smooth brush tip. You can open the Brush Settings and move the Hardness slider to 0 (zero) for a soft brush. Set the Opacity to 12 to 15%. You want to slowly build up the brush strokes.

Press Alt and right-click (Windows) or press Control + Option and left-click (Macintosh). Drag horizontally to change brush tip size. If you prefer to change hardness using the mouse and keyboard, you can press Alt, right-click, and then drag up to soften the brush. You can start by using the same brush size and opacity for both the Dodge and Burn layers.

Apply strokes to the Dodge and Burn layers to paint white in the masks. With regard to the lips, the areas you will typically burn are the bottom of the top lip, both sides in the corners of the lips, the top and bottom of the lower lip, and any shadow that comes in one side or the other on the bottom lip. The areas you dodge are often the top of the upper lip and the middle of the bottom lip.

These areas targeted for burning and dodging can change according to the light projected on the lips. You can usually get an idea for how light falls on the lips before you start editing, so if light direction is different, you can make adjustments accordingly.

Brightening Teeth

Teeth always look fake when you paint the teeth or fill them with white. Most people don't have Whitney Houston white teeth. Most teeth are off color, and you want to brighten up the teeth because they may be in shadow or have a color cast. But do not brighten so much that it results in an artificial look.

Create a selection for the teeth and add a new Levels Adjustment Layer. Brighten up the teeth by moving the Levels midtone slider to the left. Name the layer **Teeth** and move the opacity slider on the layer to bring the brightness into a realistic view.

At this point, you're finished editing a portrait for the facial tone, eyes, brows, lashes, lips, and teeth. In Figure 14.23, you can see the original image on the left and the final image on the right. In the final image, I added a warming photo filter to warm up the image a bit. As you look at the final edited photo, notice the eyes. The edited version shows a much more dynamic view of the subject's eyes and brings the viewer into the photo.

FIGURE 14.23 Original image unedited (left) and final image (right).

Sharpening Portraits

When you sharpen portraits, you might want to address different sections of the photo with different levels of sharpening. For example, the skin tones should have a low level of sharpening applied. The subject's clothing and background might have a higher level of sharpening. Perhaps the subject's clothing would have one level of sharpening and the background another level. The subject's eyes and lips might have a level of sharpening between the skin and the background.

To apply different levels of sharpening to different areas in a photo, you need to create selections and Layer Masks. You should select the background and press Ctrl/⌘ + J to duplicate it. Duplicate the background for as many different selections as you intend to make.

On the first duplicate layer, choose File > Other > High Pass. Move the radius slider to a low level of sharpening. This adjustment applies sharpening to the entire photo, including all the skin tones. For skin tones, you need a low level of sharpening, so keep the radius in the High Pass filter dialog box low, but what you choose depends on your photo. In some photos, you may need more or less. What you're looking for is where you begin to see an outline of areas in the photo—not too much and not too little. Click OK in the High Pass filter dialog box. Choose Overlay for the blending mode.

On the next layer, create a selection of the background and the subject's clothing. If you want two different levels of sharpening applied to the background and the clothing, create a second duplicate layer and make the selection as needed. In my example, I'll apply sharpening to both background and clothing. After creating the selection, click the Add Layer Mask icon in the Layers panel.

Select the photo on the layer—not the mask. Before you apply a filter, change the blending mode to Overlay. When the mode is selected, you can see a dynamic preview in the Document Window as you make adjustments. Once you apply a filter in Elements, you cannot edit the settings. Unfortunately, you would need to create a Smart Object to readjust the filter's settings, but in Elements, Smart Objects aren't available without using a plug-in.

Choose Filter > Other > High Pass. Move the Radius slider to the right. Add an ample amount of sharpening. As you move the Radius slider, you can see the effect in the Document Window. Make sure you choose the right amount before leaving the High Pass filter dialog box. You can zoom in and out of the photo while the High Pass filter dialog box is open. Press Ctrl/⌘ + − (minus) to zoom out and Ctrl/⌘ + + (plus) to zoom in. After you're sure you have the right amount of sharpening, click OK in the High Pass filter dialog box.

Select the third duplicate layer. In this layer, create a selection for the eyes and lips. If you want separate adjustments for the eyes and lips, you can create a second layer and make the adjustments separately. Once again, choose Overlay for the blend mode. Choose Filter > Other > High Pass and adjust the Radius slider as you observe the results in the Document Window. Click OK when finished with the adjustment.

In Figure 14.24, you can see my Layers panel for applying sharpening to different areas of the example photo.

The sharpening you apply to photos is generally minimal. If you begin with a soft or out-of-focus file, there's little you can do to make the photo sharp.

You also have to be very careful to not overdo the sharpening. Sharpening adds contrast between adjacent pixels of different contrast

FIGURE 14.24 Layers panel for sharpening different areas of an image.

values and tones. If you sharpen too much, you'll see some sharp distinctions between tones; if too much sharpening is applied, you'll see outlines throughout your photo.

In Figure 14.25, you can see the results of my edits in this example. I started with a soft image, so the sharpening effect looks rather subtle, and the photo still isn't completely sharp. However, this is the best result you can get from this kind of photo.

FIGURE 14.25 Before sharpening (left) and after sharpening (right).

Editing Body Shapes

Richard Avedon was a famous photographer from the 1940s to 2000. Perhaps one of his most famous photographs of all time was titled "Nastassja Kinski and the Serpent," in which he posed actress Nastassja Kinski lying down with a boa constrictor covering her naked body. Avedon was one of the most creative photographers for over a half century. But his work among photographers is best known for the many *Vogue* and *Harper's Bazaar* cover photos of fashion models. His signature photographs were often photos of models with long necks. When photographers saw models that fit that form, they called them *Avedon women*. His famous photos of actress Audrey Hepburn captured her beauty and highlighted her neck.

There was something about Avedon's fashion photos that were both interesting and intriguing. Most professional female models are tall with long legs and thin bodies. If you have subjects that don't quite fit the look you want, you can do a little alteration in the Elements Photo Editor to achieve the results you are looking for. You should think of these edits as being minor and perhaps only a slight improvement on the photo. Don't take it to extremes and create unrealistic photos that don't capture the character of your subject.

Creating a Gradient Mask

Figure 14.26 shows the photo I used for this example. When you look at the photo, it appears darker at the top of the photo than the middle and bottom of the photo. Before you go about editing shapes, you always want to address the brightness and contrast as your first step.

This photo presents an interesting problem. I can't apply a Levels edit because the brightness and contrast will be applied to the entire image. I can't paint a mask because the transition of the tones needs to be more of a gradient. Therefore, the best bet is to create a Levels Adjustment Layer and apply a gradient in the mask. For this image, I created a black to white gradient and left the top 25% white, and the remaining part of the mask would be black at the bottom and graduate to white at the top.

In Figure 14.27, you can see the Layers panel with the gradient in a Levels Adjustment Layer mask.

Once the gradient is added, double-click the Levels (not the mask) to open the Levels Adjustment. Move the midtone slider left to lighten the top part of the gradient.

FIGURE 14.26 Unedited photo.

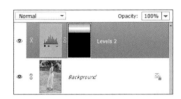

FIGURE 14.27 Levels Adjustment Layer with a gradient in the mask.

Making a Model Appear Taller

After adjusting brightness and contrast and performing all corrections to a photo, if you want to add a little more height to the model, your first step is to increase the canvas size of the document. Choose Image > Resize > Canvas Size or press Ctrl/⌘ + Alt/Option + C to open the Canvas Size dialog box.

In the Canvas Size dialog box, click the top-middle anchor, so when you size the canvas, the excess size will be added to the bottom of the image. Enter a value a few inches more than the Height in the Height text box. Click OK when finished, and you should see some excess canvas added at the bottom of your photo. If it doesn't look right, choose Edit > Undo and open the Canvas Size dialog box again.

FIGURE 14.28 Draw a rectangle below the knees and press Ctrl/⌘ + T.

FIGURE 14.29 Photo on the left is the original. Photo on the right is after adding two transformations.

Select the Marquee Rectangle tool and draw a rectangle from around midway at the model's thighs down to the beginning of the excess area created in the Canvas Size dialog box. Press Ctrl/⌘ + T to create a Transformation rectangle. Grab the middle handle at the bottom of the Transformation rectangle and drag down a little. Be careful to not overdo it. You want to move the transformation between ⅛ and ¼ inch, depending on the resolution of your photo. Click the green check mark to confirm the edit.

Draw another rectangle below the knees, as shown in Figure 14.28. Press Ctrl/⌘ + T to transform the selection.

Click on the bottom-middle handle, as shown in Figure 14.28, and drag down slightly, again around ⅛ to ¼ inch. The amount you drag the transformation is important. You want to make these adjustments ever so slight. If you need to make a model taller, then make slight transformations from other parts of the legs.

As you can see in Figure 14.29, just a few slight transformations make quite a bit of difference.

Creating Longer Necks

In Chapter 12, "Creating Photo Effects," I covered making models, necks longer. In many photos, you can immediately see where you want to make such edits. In other photos, you might see a little disparity between one subject and another in terms of body shape. In Figure 14.30, you see the original photo on the left and the result after I made a slight edit on the right. In this photo, the subject on the left looks like she's hunched down a little. The subject on the right looks like she has a longer neck. The objective here would be to assess the photo and determine that the subject on the left needs a longer neck to fit the photo more equally between the shapes of the subjects.

To make a subject's neck longer, you need to make a selection. In this example, I made a selection from the top of the head to below the chin. I moved the selection up about 18 pixels. To fill in the gap, I used the Clone Stamp tool.

The edit is very slight, but when you compare the before and after images, you can see that the figure on the right shows the subject with a much less hunched down look.

FIGURE 14.30 The original photo (left) and the edited image (right).

CHAPTER 15

EDITING SKIN TONES

Chapter Goals

This chapter takes off where Chapter 14, "Editing Portraits," ends. This chapter looks at adjusting skin tones and smoothing skin.

When retouching photos of people, it's common to find color problems with skin. Tan lines, tattoos, skin tonal changes, and skin discoloration are different kinds of retouching tasks much different than what is covered in Chapter 14. In this chapter, I offer some techniques for retouching skin after you have completed basic retouching for brightness/contrast, removal of blemishes, and improving facial features.

In this chapter, you find editing for the following:

- Adjusting skin tones
- Smoothing skin
- Using frequency separations
- Creating luminosity masks

Correcting Skin Tones

When retouching photos of people, it's common to find some issue with skin that could be improved with editing—tan lines, tattoos, and skin discoloration, for example. In this section, I offer some techniques for retouching skin after you have completed basic retouching for brightness/contrast, removal of blemishes, and improving facial features.

The first thing you want to do when retouching skin is to open the photo in the Raw Editor and adjust brightness, contrast, hue/saturation, and temperature. Temperature is very important. If you want to leave a photo at the default As Shot or choose Adobe Portrait for portrait shots in the Camera Raw Editor, that's fine. If you want to warm up a photo or make it appear cooler, you should change temperature after you retouch skin, which means you return to the Camera Raw Editor after working in the Photo Editor. Take care of all the edits you can in the Camera Raw Editor first and then open the photo in the Photo Editor.

You should also perform edits you make in the Photo Editor after opening from Camera Raw, such as dodging and burning, before you work on correcting skin tone and other issues. No matter what method of dodging and burning you use, some colors have a tendency to change and not match the rest of the skin, even if the adjustments have the same tone/brightness adjustments. The same thing happens when a makeup artist applies too much concealer or corrector on a subject's skin.

Using a Gradient Map for Skin Tone

There are some gradient maps to handle skin tones that you can download from various websites. You can do an Internet search for *gradient maps downloads for skin tones*. However, each photo is different, and it's impossible to use a set of gradients that can be used for all your retouching needs.

The best way to apply a gradient map to a photo is to create different gradient maps for each set of photos. If your subject is the same person under similar lighting situations, you can create a gradient and apply it to several photos. However, if you have different subjects and/or different lighting conditions, you need to create custom gradients for all noticeable changes in skin tones.

The following steps explain how to use gradient maps for skin tone:

1. Before you begin working on a gradient, select the Eyedropper tool in the Tools panel. Open the Tool Options panel and click either 3 × 3 or 5 × 5 for the point sample. If you leave the default at Point Sample, when you sample a color, you're only sampling 1 pixel. When you choose 3 × 3 or 5 × 5, you sample an average of a group of pixels where you click the cursor. This sample method provides a better sample, so the color is not

skewed if you click on a dark or light pixel that may be a single pixel darker or lighter among other values surrounding the sample.

2. Open a photo with a subject in which you can clearly see skin tones.

3. Select the Gradient tool and open the Tools panel.

4. Click the gradient in the Tool Options panel to open the Gradient Editor. Click any gradient from any of the Preset drop-down lists. Elements doesn't provide an option for creating a new blank gradient. Therefore, you need to select a gradient and modify it.

5. Drag all extra stops below and away from the gradient to delete them.

For more on editing gradient maps, see Chapter 10, "Color Toning and Color Grading."

6. There are three stops above the gradient. If you don't see three stops, click anywhere above the gradient to add a stop. On the far left and far right stops, enter 0% for the Opacity. Setting both stops at each end of the gradient to 0% creates a gradient that begins with transparency and ends with transparency.

7. Below the gradient, select the far-left stop and set the Location value to 3. Double-click this stop to open the Color Picker. Move the cursor into the document, and the cursor changes to an Eyedropper tool. Look over the image and click the Eyedropper tool on the darkest skin tone in the subject.

8. On the far right, move the stop below the gradient to 97% in the Location text box. Double-click the Stop to open the Color Picker and sample the lightest area of the skin tones in the photo.

9. Click below the gradient to add a stop. Set the Location to 50%.

10. Double-click the center stop and sample a midtone skin tone in the photo.

Figure 15.1 shows the Gradient Editor and my adjustments in the Gradient Editor thus far.

FIGURE 15.1 Add stops and apply colors to the stops in the Gradient Editor.

11. Click the Add to Presets button to add the gradient as a new preset. Click OK to dismiss the Gradient Editor.

12. In the open photo, apply any last-minute edits to the image. If you need some dodging and burning, do those edits first.

13. Choose Gradient Map from the Adjustment Layer drop-down list. Select the new custom gradient map preset (the last preset in the group). Creating the Gradient Map Adjustment Layer automatically adds a Layer Mask.

14. Select the Layer Mask and fill it black to hide the gradient map.

15. Select the mask on the Gradient Map layer.

16. Create a selection in the photo of the subject's skin tones. In my example, I selected the face, shoulder, and left arm.

17. After creating the selection, inverse the selection by pressing Ctrl/⌘ + Shift + I or choosing Select > Inverse.

18. Select the mask and press Backspace/Delete to fill the selection in the mask black. The selection was inversed, so all area except the skin is currently selected. Black should be the current background color. The white area remains the subject's skin and now reveals the gradient map.

19. On the Gradient Map layer, choose Color for the blend mode. If necessary, you can reduce opacity on the layer.

20. Press Ctrl/⌘ + Alt/Options + Shift + E to create a composite layer. In Figure 15.2, I added a composite layer so I could easily create a before and after look.

21. I also added a slight bit of dodging and burning before I added the Gradient Map Adjustment Layer. The Layers panel should look something like Figure 15.2.

The changes in the skin tones are subtle, but in Figure 15.3, you can see the color is more even in the after photo on the right and has an overall richer appearance for the skin tones.

FIGURE 15.2 Layers panel showing the Gradient Map Adjustment Layer.

In the image in Figure 15.4, I used a photo that had good color correction to start with and no color casts, so the retouching is very minimal. I decided to use a color complementing the subject's skin tones and apply it as a background color, which is a matter of personal choice. The original has a very pleasing background color, but another pleasing color would be a complement to the subject's skin tone.

FIGURE 15.3 Original photo (left) and final edited photo (right).

To learn how to find com-plementary colors using Adobe Color, see Chapter 9, "Sampling Color."

To create the background radial gradient on the right in Figure 15.4, I used Adobe Color to find the complement for the subject's skin tones. When you want a sample of a subject's skin tones, create a rough selection of the subject's skin. Then choose Filter > Blur > Average. Use the Eyedropper tool and sample the averaged color. Open Adobe Color and find a complement. Copy the hex code and use it as your foreground color.

On the right in Figure 15.4, I created a selection of the subject and added a Layer Mask. I added a blank empty layer below the layer with the mask and filled the layer with the color derived from Adobe Color. I then applied a radial gradient.

FIGURE 15.4 Original photo (left) and final edited photo (right).

Using Levels Adjustments for Correcting Skin Color

One very simple and fast way to correct skin color is to use a Levels Adjustment Layer. You first need to use an accompanying file that has an array of color swatches made of skin tones. There is no one single chart that works best. You can find a number of color charts for skin tones on various websites. Just do an Internet search for *skin tone charts*, and a number of returns for charts should be listed. In this example, I used the chart shown in Figure 15.5.

To use Levels for adjusting skin tones, follow these steps:

1. Open a photo in the Photo Editor.

2. Press Ctrl/⌘ + J to create a duplicate of the Background layer.

3. Select skin tones by using the selection tools that work best on your photo to create the selection.

4. Add a Layer Mask. The skin tone selection is white in the mask.

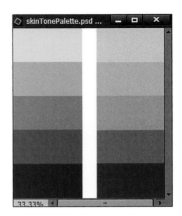

FIGURE 15.5 A skin tone chart.

5. Open your skin tone color chart and place it aside the photo you're editing, as shown in Figure 15.6. Set your Eyedropper tool to a 3 × 3 or 5 × 5 Average.

FIGURE 15.6 Place the chart aside the photo.

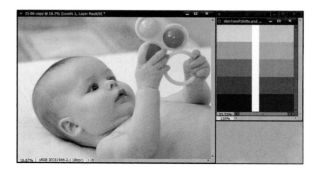

6. Press Ctrl/⌘ and click the mask to select the subject.

7. Add a Levels Adjustment layer.

8. With the Levels dialog box open, sample a color in the Skin Tone Color Chart.

9. Click the Midtone Eyedropper tool in the Levels dialog box, as shown in Figure 15.7.

FIGURE 15.7 Select the Midtone Eyedropper sampler in the Levels dialog box.

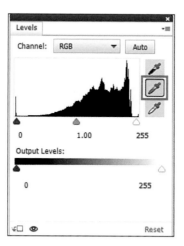

10. Move the eyedropper to the photo and sample a midtone.

The final result is shown on the right in Figure 15.8.

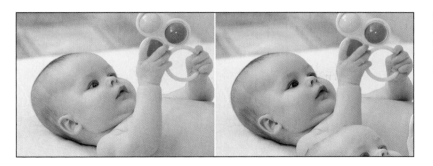

FIGURE 15.8 Click the Saturation radio button and move the slider in the gradient to change saturation.

Smoothing Skin

If you need to smooth the texture of a subject's skin, make sure you've removed blemishes and skin imperfections first. See the "Editing Blemishes" section in Chapter 14 for details on those editing techniques.

The major problem you face when attempting to smooth skin is that you can easily lose texture in the photo. You need to use the right tools and methods to smooth skin while protecting texture.

Creating Smooth Skin

In this section, I explain a quick and easy technique used by many Photoshop users:

1. Open a photo and duplicate the layer.

2. Select the duplicate layer and press Ctrl/⌘ + I to invert the photo or choose Filter > Adjustments > Invert. Set the blend mode to Vivid Light. At this point, it doesn't look like much, but don't worry. You'll bring it around momentarily.

3. Choose File > Other > High Pass. Set the radius amount to 24. Click OK in the High Pass filter dialog box and choose Filter > Blur > Gaussian Blur.

4. Set the Radius value between 3 and 4 in the Gaussian Blur dialog box. View the preview and make sure you don't apply too much blur that can result in eliminating all detail. Click OK when finished in the Gaussian Blur dialog box.

5. Press the Alt/Option key and click the Add Layer Mask icon in the Layers panel. A negative mask is created and filled black, hiding all the edits to the layer. Select the Brush tool and choose a soft brush. Set the Opacity to below 80%.

6. Click the mask to select it. Make sure the foreground color is white and paint on the mask in areas of the face, arms, and other skin tone areas. Avoid brushing in the highlights. Where you see transitions between highlights and shadows, lower the opacity of the brush and paint in the darker edges of the transitions.

Figure 15.9 shows my original photo (left) and the result after I performed all the skin softening edits.

FIGURE 15.9 Original photo (left) and final edited photo (right).

Using the Smooth Skin Dialog Box

Another quick skin-smoothing fix is to use the feature in the Photo Editor for smoothing skin. Choose Enhance > Smooth Skin and the Smooth Skin dialog box opens (see Figure 15.10). At the bottom of the Smooth Skin dialog box is a slider to adjust the amount of smoothness you want to apply.

FIGURE 15.10 The Smooth Skin dialog box.

The Smooth Skin dialog box uses facial recognition algorithms, and you automatically see a circle around your subject's face. If you have a group shot, each face is marked with a circle that indicates the areas where the smoothing effect will be applied. If you have a profile shot with only a partial face in view, Elements reports back to you that the face is too small, and the Smooth Skin task cannot be applied.

The final result of using this menu command is that it's very good but doesn't quite match up with creating a frequency separation, as you can see in the next section where I talk about cloning out texture and smoothing colors. Figure 15.11 shows the original photo (left) and the edited photo (right) after using the Smooth Skin command.

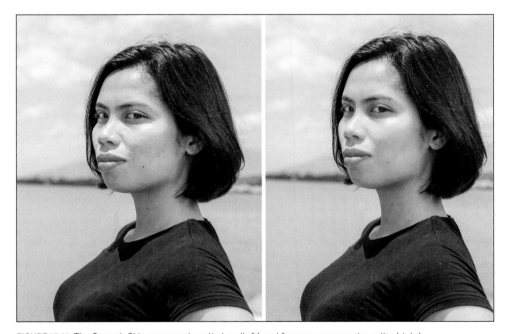

FIGURE 15.11 The Smooth Skin command applied on (left) and frequency separation edits (right).

Creating Frequency Separations

Don't let the term *frequency separations* frighten you. It's not that complicated once you understand where you're going.

Frequencies are all around us, and even if you don't already know what a frequency is, you've experienced it many times: different frequencies of light, frequencies in microwave ovens, with sound and audio signals, with moving objects, and more. All of these examples involve high and low frequencies.

In Photoshop terms, you have frequencies with color and texture. When you look at editing a photo, the high and low frequencies of the image require you to simultaneously edit both color and detail.

If you can separate the frequencies, you can edit the color independent of the texture and vice versa. To do this, you need to perform a frequency separation. In Figure 15.12, you see two frequencies coupled together in the middle of the diagram. By default, this is the way your photos appear when you open them up in Photoshop Elements. If I paint over the two frequencies, I affect both color and texture. At the bottom of the diagram, you see the low-frequency data representing color. At the top of the diagram, you see the high-frequency data representing the texture (or detail). If I paint over the top or bottom frequency, I affect only color or detail, depending on which frequency I paint over.

FIGURE 15.12 Frequencies coupled together at the top and separated at the bottom.

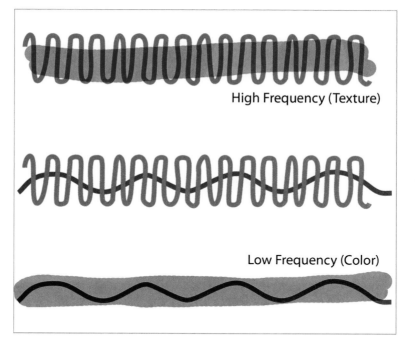

High Frequency (Texture)

Low Frequency (Color)

When editing photos, you use frequency separation primarily to work on the color in an image without affecting the texture and vice versa. To edit a photo's color and texture separately using a frequency separation, follow these steps:

1. Open a photo in the Photo Editor.

2. Duplicate the Background layer three times by pressing Ctrl/⌘ + J.

3. Name the layers. Name the second layer **Color**. Name the third layer **Details**. Name the top layer **Details Copy**.

4. Select the Color layer. Choose Filter > Blur > Gaussian Blur. Set the blur amount to a value between 3 and 4 depending on your photo. Look to blur pores and artifacts in the skin but not lose too much detail. When you move the Radius slider just to where the texture disappears, you're eliminating the detail frequency, leaving the layer with only the color frequency.

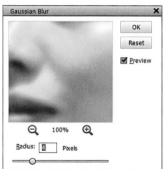

   In my example, I set the blur amount to 3.8, as shown in Figure 15.13. Click OK after setting the blur amount to your liking.

FIGURE 15.13 Set the blur amount to just where the texture disappears.

5. Select the top layer (Details copy). Blur this layer with the same amount as you applied in the Color layer. At the top of the Filter menu, you see Gaussian Blur. When you select this item, it applies the same amount as your last setting for that filter.

6. Press Ctrl/⌘ +I to invert the layer. Alternatively, you can choose Filter > Adjustments> Invert.

7. Reduce the opacity to 50%.

8. Select both the Details Copy and Details layers and press Ctrl/⌘ + E or open the Layers panel drop-down menu and choose Merge Layers. Name the layer **Details**.

9. Open the blend modes drop-down list and choose Linear Light.

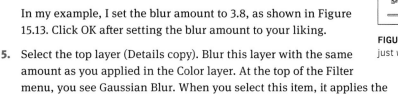

   At this point, when you inverted the top layer and merged it with the Details layer and then chose Linear Light, you created the second frequency for details only.

10. Before you apply any adjustments to the layers, create two new empty layers above the Color and Details layers. Name these layers **Color Layer** and **Detail Layer**, as shown in Figure 15.14.

11. Select the Clone Stamp tool. Set the opacity down to 70%. This adjustment may vary according to the textures in your photo. Be careful to not overdo the edits. Select Sample All Layers in the Clone Stamp tool Options panel.

FIGURE 15.14 The layers panel after adding two more layers.

12. Select the Details layer.

13. To edit the photo, begin with the texture area. Sample a clean area on the face in the photo by pressing Alt/Option and clicking with the Clone Stamp tool. Brush across adjacent areas that need the skin smoothed. Move around the photo to clean up all the texture in the photo.

14. Select the Color Layer. Using the Clone Stamp tool, sample areas in the Color layer. Brush across areas that need some smoothing for the color transitions. Check both layers. If you need to reduce opacity, move the opacity slider in the layers panel for the Color and Details layers. If you need to erase some edits on either layer, select the Eraser tool and brush across the strokes you want to eliminate in the Color Layer and Detail Layer layers.

In Figure 15.15, you can see the final image I edited for this example. The photo at left is the original photo. The photo at right is the edited final image.

FIGURE 15.15 The final edited photo.

Creating Luminosity Masks

You know what a mask is after using Layer Masks so many times in this chapter and several previous chapters. You know that when you create a mask, the black in the mask conceals, and the white in the mask reveals.

By virtue of its name, the term Luminosity Mask should give you a clue as to what kind of mask it is. Luminosity is brightness. Therefore, a Luminosity Mask is a brightness mask. What this translates to is all gray values brighter than 50% are revealed, and all gray values less than 50% are concealed. Another layer might represent the opposite, where brighter values are concealed, and darker values are revealed. In another layer, you might have all the midtones revealed, while the brighter and darker areas are concealed.

You can use Luminosity Masks on photos with a subject where we want to separate the highlights and shadows and make different adjustments to the different brightness levels. You can adjust the brightness contrast individually for highlights, shadows, and midtones. The reason you might want to do so is that perhaps the photo is dark, and you want to add more brightness adjustment in the shadows. But the highlights are bright and may need only a slight adjustment. Perhaps the midtones need an adjustment not as strong as the shadows but more than the highlights. A single Levels Adjustment would bring the shadows brightness level in fine but there would be too much brightening in the highlights and midtones. With a frequency separation, you could make a much better brightness adjustment by independently adjusting shadows, highlights, and midtones. Luminosity Masks provide you with a means for separating the brightness values between shadows, highlights, and midtones.

There are several ways you can create a Luminosity Mask. To make adjustments in Luminosity Masks, follow these steps:

1. Open a photo in the Photo Editor. For this example, I used a photo that was taken at night. In Figure 15.16, you can see the original photo I used to begin this exercise.

2. Press Ctrl/⌘ + J to create a copy of the Background layer.

3. Select the top layer and press Ctrl/⌘ + A to select all the layer data.

4. Create a Layer Mask by clicking the Add Layer Mask icon in the Layers panel. Select the mask and press Ctrl/⌘ to paste the data. Essentially, you have a copy of the photo in the mask. Name this layer **Highlights**.

5. Select the Highlights layer and press Ctrl/⌘ + J to duplicate the layer.

FIGURE 15.17 Original unedited photo straight out of the camera.

6. When you duplicate the layer, the Layer Mask is also duplicated. Click the mask and press Ctrl/⌘ + I to invert the mask. Name this layer **Shadows**.

7. Select the Background and press Ctrl/⌘ + J to duplicate the layer. Drag the duplicate Background copy to the top of the layer stack.

8. Create an Intersection selection. Select the Background copy layer at the top of the layer stack, and with the layer selected, press Ctrl/⌘ and click on the Highlights Layer Mask. Press the Ctrl/⌘ + Alt/Option + Shift and click the Shadows Layer Mask. By pressing Ctrl/⌘ + Alt/Option + Shift and clicking, you create an intersection of the selections. If you see a warning dialog box appear, just ignore it and click OK.

9. Create a Layer Mask by clicking the Add Layer Mask icon in the Layers panel. Name this layer **Midtones**.

10. Select the Background and press Ctrl/⌘+ J to duplicate it. Drag the layer to the top of the layer stack. At this point, your Layers panel should look like Figure 15.17.

11. Select the Background Copy layer. With the Layer selected, press Ctrl/⌘ and click on the mask in the Highlights layer. With the selection active, open the Add Fill or Adjustment Layer menu in the Layers panel and choose Levels. Images will vary, and the amount of the adjustment will likewise vary between images. Adjust the Midtone slider to a brightness level suitable for the photo. If needed, you can also move the highlight sliders inward to refine the adjustment. When the adjustment looks good, click OK. Name this layer **Levels Highlights**.

12. Follow the same steps using the Background Copy layer as the source and create selections in the Shadows and Highlights layers. Add a Layer Mask to each layer and name the layers **Levels Shadows** and **Levels Midtones**.

13. Add a Levels Adjustment Layer if necessary to adjust brightness.

14. Add a color fill to the shadows. This is optional. If you want to add a little color to the shadows, first create a composite layer by selecting the top layer and pressing Ctrl/⌘ + Alt/Option + Shift + E. Name the layer **Composite**. Open the Create New Fill or Adjustment Layer menu and choose Solid Color. When the Color Picker opens, select a color. In my example, I wanted to cool the photo down a bit, so I chose a blue hue.

15. I also added some sharpening by creating a duplicate of the composite layer, applying the High Pass filter, and then changing the blend mode to Overlay. At this point, your Layers panel should look like Figure 15.18. The High Pass Sharpen and Color Fill layers are optional.

The final figure in my example is shown in Figure 15.19.

FIGURE 15.17 Layers panel up to this step.

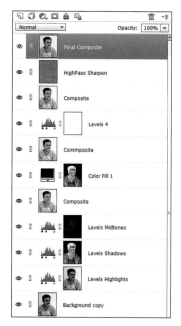

FIGURE 15.18 Layers panel showing layers from the Background copy shown earlier in Figure 15.17 with all the new layers added after the Background copy.

FIGURE 15.19 Final edited photo after making adjustments using luminosity masks.

PART VI

SHARING YOUR CREATIONS

One way for amateur and novice photographers to showcase their photos—whether they're of people or beautiful landscapes—is to share them on social media. This section looks at readying photos to be shared online.

Chapter Goals

Editing photos and keeping them on your computer is enjoyable, but most of us derive more joy when we can share our photos with family, friends, colleagues, or clients. Sharing photos on social media is very popular, and you've probably uploaded a photo or two to some social media sites. You have several choices for where you can share photos, and there are some distinctions for how providers want your files prepared. This chapter covers some basics for preparing photos you want to share, including these topics:

- Preparing images for Instagram
- Preparing images for Facebook
- Sharing photos on Twitter
- Printing photos

Preparing Photos for Instagram

Instagram is a popular social media site for sharing photos. If you've uploaded photos to Instagram, you may be confused as to why your photos are cropped differently than the cropping you'd used and perhaps have wondered why the photos don't look exactly like they do on your computer in other respects.

One reason Instagram—and almost all social media sites—show your photos differently on their sites than you see on your monitor is that they all have different algorithms for sizing and compressing your files. For example, if you save files with one color space and the provider uses a different color space, it uses an algorithm to change your color space to one acceptable for its use. This conversion can render unexpected results if the conversion produces color shifts and changes in brightness values.

The way to avoid problems is to use a provider's recommended settings for optimum results for displaying photos on their social media sites. All of the top providers offer help guides on the Web that inform you what settings are best suited for the sites.

Setting the Color Profile

Almost all social media sites use sRGB color as the color profile they use for all the photos you see online. If you use Adobe RGB or you receive a file from a Photoshop user who embedded a profile other than sRGB, the provider service converts the color profile. In some cases, you may see undesirable results.

When preparing photos for Instagram, use the Always Optimize Colors for Computer Screens choice in the Color Settings dialog box. To check your color settings, choose Edit > Color Settings to open the Color Settings dialog box shown in Figure 16.1.

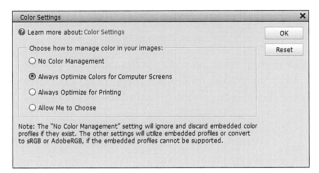

FIGURE 16.1 Color Settings dialog box.

When you save your file, embed the profile in the image. For saving files with embedded profiles, see "Saving a Photo for Instagram," later in this chapter.

Adjusting Brightness

As is the case with just about any set of editing steps, your first adjustments are for brightness and contrast. Before you make any brightness, contrast, or color adjustments, it's best to change your background color in the Photo Editor to match the background used by Instagram.

Unfortunately, Photoshop Elements 2022 no longer enables you to change the background color in the Editor window. You can create a new blank document and size it to be the size of the Document Window. To do so, first open Preferences by pressing Ctrl/⌘ + K. In the General Preferences, check the box for Allow Floating Documents in Expert Mode. Uncheck Enable Floating Document Window Docking, as shown in Figure 16.2. This allows you to size a new file to the full size of the Document Window.

FIGURE 16.2 Choose File > New > Blank Fill with a white background and click OK. Size the document up so it fills the entire screen except the menu bar.

Because the background color in the Instagram application is white, you need to change your user interface background to white, too. White is not available from the menu choices in the context menu, so choose Select Custom Color from the context menu to open the Color Picker. Select white in the Color Picker dialog box or type **ffffff** in the # text box. Click OK, and the user interface background changes to white. In Figure 16.3, I changed the Elements window from the default gray background color to white, and opened a photo. You can see the white background surrounding the photo.

Select the Adjustment Layer drop-down list in the Layers panel and choose Levels to add a Levels Adjustment layer. Press the Alt/Option key and move the Highlight and Shadow sliders. The preview area shows white when you press Alt/Option on the Shadow slider and black when you press Alt/Option and click the Highlight slider. Move the sliders until you first begin to see data in the preview area.

FIGURE 16.3 When preparing images for Instagram, change the Document Window background color to white.

Data are remapped when you move the sliders from 0 to 255 within the range of the sliders. If you want to change how the data are mapped—let's say from 20 instead of 0—you can move the Shadow Output slider, as shown in Figure 16.4. This changes the luminance level to 20 instead of the default value of 0. In this scenario, everything will be mapped from 20 to 255.

Choose the settings that work well for your image. Of course, the end result is you want a brighter image with sufficient contrast. In Figure 16.4, you can see a Levels Adjustment I made for the example image. As you can see, I moved the Output sliders in slightly and remapped the photo from 5 to 250.

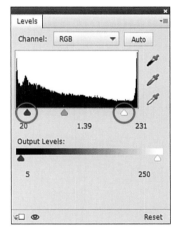

FIGURE 16.4 Correct brightness and contrast in the Levels dialog box.

Adding Punch to a Photo

I've offered many ways to add punch to a photo in earlier chapters. You can create gradient maps, apply color on layers, use blend modes, and use photo filters. In this example, I want to warm up the photo a bit. Therefore, I choose a Photo Filter Adjustment layer and choose a warm color.

To apply a warm photo filter, open the Create Fill or Adjustment Layer drop-down list in the Layers panel and choose Photo Filter. In this example, I use the Warming Filter (85). After applying a photo filter, look over the photo. If the warming of the photo is too much, reduce opacity.

In my example image, I made an overall Levels Adjustment. I made a selection of the subject's eyes and applied another Levels Adjustment to brighten

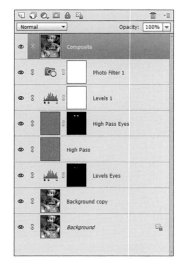

FIGURE 16.5 Layers panel showing edits for brightness and contrast and adding a warm tone to the photo.

the eyes. I added a High Pass filter to sharpen the photo, and another High Pass filter for sharpening the eyes. I set the blend mode to Overlay for both High Pass filter layers. I added a Photo filter at the top of the layer stack and created a composite layer.

With your photo, you may need other editing steps to prepare it properly for social media. The point is that you need to address brightness/contrast, color, and sharpening to preset the best-looking photo you can.

The Layers panel for the edits I made to my example image are shown in Figure 16.5.

Sizing a Photo for Instagram

Instagram photos default to a square format. If you use sizes such as 4×5 or 5×7, Instagram crops your photos to fit within a square format. Therefore, set your Crop tool to a square value like 2×2, 4×4, and so on. When you crop the photo, the crop tool initially goes to the photo bounding box. Release the mouse button and drag the handles if you need some extra canvas area to accommodate a square format.

In Figure 16.6, you can see the crop rectangle in the shape of a square.

FIGURE 16.6 Crop rectangle set to a square.

After cropping the photo, choose Image > Resize > Image Size. In the Image Size dialog box, shown in Figure 16.7, check the Resample Image box. At the top of the Image Size dialog box, type **1080** in the Width text box. Note that you can't access the Width text box unless you check the Resample Image check box.

FIGURE 16.7 Set the Width to 1080 pixels in the Image Size dialog box.

Comparing Photos with a Phone Display

You have a few choices for previewing the photo as it might appear on a mobile phone. Of course, mobile phones vary in sizes, so a precise preview for all phones is not possible. Just use your phone and hold it up to your computer monitor while you have the photo open that you want to upload to Instagram. You can also use a photo of your phone at an actual size. You can find a number of images on websites with actual-size photos of a huge range of phones.

Figure 16.8 shows my photo placed adjacent to a phone to give a preview of what I might expect after uploading the photo to Instagram.

FIGURE 16.8 Preview your photo against a mobile phone.

Saving a Photo for Instagram

Choose File > Save for Web. The Save for Web dialog box opens, as shown in Figure 16.9. In the right panel, choose JPEG for the file format in the drop-down list below Preset. Most social media providers use JPEG as the file format for photos you upload to their sites.

Set the Quality to **73**. This value is consistent with what most Photoshop users set when working with images shared on social media platforms. Check Embed Color Profile and the sRGB profile is embedded if you set your color settings to Always Optimize for Computer Screens.

If you adjusted size in the Image Size dialog box, you should see 1080 pixels for the Width and Height sizes. Click Save, and the file is saved in JPEG format.

FIGURE 16.9 Save for Web dialog box.

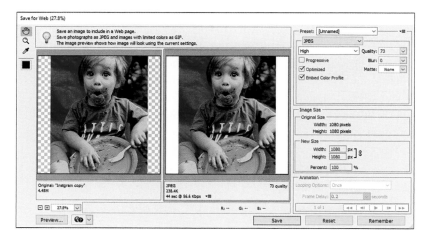

Uploading Photos to Instagram from Desktop Computers

You can upload photos to Instagram directly from your computer. To do so, you need to use the Google Chrome web browser. If you don't have Google Chrome, search the Internet for a download site. Google Chrome is free, and you can download and install it on your computer.

Launch Chrome after downloading, and go to instagram.com. When you arrive at the site, you are provided a log-in page, as shown in Figure 16.10.

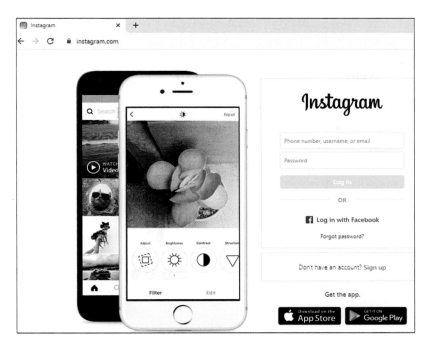

FIGURE 16.10 Instagram log-in page in the Chrome Web Browser.

Don't log in yet. First, click on the yellow exclamation (!) mark in the top-right corner of the browser. A drop-down list opens. Choose More tools > Developer tools in the list, as shown in Figure 16.11. At the top of the left panel, you see an icon for toggling the device toolbar, as shown in Figure 16.11. Click the icon, and the left pane assumes a cell phone view.

> **NOTE:** You can also access Developer tools in Safari on the Mac and Firefox on Windows and the Mac. In Safari, you find a menu titled Developer where you find all the Safari Developer Tools. In Firefox, select Tools > Web Developer > Web Developer Tools or use the keyboard shortcut Ctrl/⌘ + Shift + I.

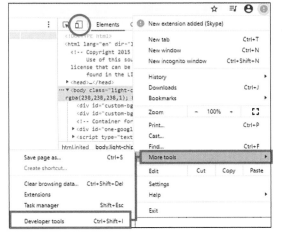

FIGURE 16.11 Choose Developer tools and click the Toggle Device Toolbar icon.

Type your username and password. The display is similar to your mobile phone. At the bottom of the left panel, you see the same tools as you find in the Instagram mobile phone app. Click the plus (+) icon to upload a file. In the Open dialog box, navigate your hard drive and locate the file you want to upload. Select it and click Open.

In Figure 16.12, you can see the example file I uploaded to my Instagram account.

FIGURE 16.12 Click the plus
(+) icon and select a file to
upload.

Photo: Courtesy Courtany
Jensen

Preparing Photos for Facebook

Facebook uses three different types of photos. You have a cover photo that spans the width of your Facebook page like a masthead. You have a profile picture inset in the cover photo, and then there are photos of varying sizes for your timeline and photo albums.

For the cover photo, you don't have much of a problem deviating from Facebook recommendations for cover photos until you add text on a cover photo. Ideally, it's best to follow Facebook's guidelines for cover photos regardless of whether you have text on the image.

The most important size you need to keep in mind is the width. As of this writing, the perfect Facebook cover size is 820 pixels wide by 312 pixels high. When you view a Facebook page on a mobile device, the display will show your cover photo at 640 pixels wide by 360 pixels tall.

Another important factor is image resolution, especially when you add text to the cover photo. The file size should not exceed 100K. As is with most screen displays, you should use the sRGB color profile.

TIP: At times, you can find social media sites change their standards, so you should routinely double-check to see if any updates use another standard. Perform a Google search and search for Facebook cover photo sizes. If the current Facebook recommendations are different than what you've been using, change your photos to match the current recommendations. This goes for all social media web sites. Any updates to the applications might change how a site handles photos.

When you know the dimensions and the file size, use the tools to render the appropriate size. First, crop your photo using the Crop tool. In the Crop Tool Options panel, set the width and height for the crop, as shown in Figure 16.13.

FIGURE 16.13 Set the width and height in the Crop Tools panel.

When you type 820 in the Width text box, be sure to type 820 px. By default, Elements supplies inches unless you use another unit of measure. Therefore, type **820 px** in the Width text box and **312 px** in the Height text box.

After cropping the photo, you need to change the Image Size Resolution setting if your cover photo contains any text. If there is no text in the photo, you don't need to make any changes in the Image Size dialog box. If your image includes text, choose Image > Resize > Image Size. In the Image Size dialog box, be certain the Resample check box is unchecked and type **100** in the Resolution text box, as shown in Figure 16.14. Be certain the top Width remains at 820 and the Height remains at 312.

After cropping and setting resolution, if necessary, it's time to save the photo and upload to Facebook. Choose File Save for Web. The Save for Web dialog box opens.

A PNG file is a better choice than JPEG when you have text in the file, so if your cover photo has text, you might consider saving the file as PNG-24. If the cover image is just a photo, choose JPEG for the file type. Set the Quality to **95** to minimize compression, make sure the sRGB file was used in your photo, and check Embed Color Profile. After making all the choices for the settings, click Save (see Figure 16.15).

FIGURE 16.14 Set resolution to 100 Pixels/Inch if your cover photo contains any text.

FIGURE 16.15 Choose PNG-24 if the cover image contains text; otherwise, choose JPEG for the file type.

NOTE: In earlier versions of Elements, you could upload files directly to Facebook from within the Organizer or Photo Editor. However, in the past several releases, the link to Facebook has been eliminated. Facebook began to prohibit other apps from uploading photos within external apps.

To upload your cover photo to Facebook, log on to your Facebook account on your computer. The Edit Cover Photo button appears on the page. Click the button, and a drop-down list opens. Choose Upload Photo to open a dialog box where you can navigate your hard drive and select a photo to upload. Select the photo you want to upload and click the Choose button.

With Profile pictures, there's no button. Just click the existing Profile picture and click Update Profile Picture. In terms of size, crop Profile pictures to 360 px by 360 px and save the same way you save photos that don't contain text for the cover photo.

Uploading Photos to Twitter

Twitter aficionados don't want to spend much time doing any kind of preparation for images. They just want to quickly type a tweet and click a button to upload a photo or video. Elements makes it easy for you to send off a tweet with a photo.

You open a photo in the Photo Editor and don't have to do anything to it. Elements automatically prepares the photo for uploading to Twitter. Open the Share panel at the top of the Photo Editor window and click Twitter in the panel. To open the Twitter dialog box, you must have only one file open in the Photo Editor.

When you click Twitter in the Share panel, Elements prompts you to authorize your Twitter account. A dialog box opens that takes you to the Twitter site in your default web browser and prompts you for your username and password. You log on, and a confirmation web page opens, confirming your logon.

Return to Elements and click Twitter with the photo you want to upload open in the Document Window. The Twitter dialog box opens, as shown in Figure 16.16. Type a message and click Tweet. The photo and your tweet are uploaded to your Twitter page.

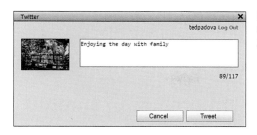

FIGURE 16.16 Type a Twitter message and click Tweet to upload to your Twitter account.

Printing Photos

There are many different options you can use for printing files. If you make your own scrapbooks and family albums, you might use a desktop color printer. If you want to print quantities of a photo for something like a wedding invitation, you might use a commercial printer. If you want to print banners and signs, you might use a commercial printer or a business specializing in tarpaulin printing. If you want art prints, you want to use a company that specializes in fine art printing.

Printing to Desktop Color Printers

Perhaps the most important thing for you to control when printing to desktop color printers is your monitor brightness. Ideally, it's best to use a monitor calibration device. In Chapter 9, "Sampling Color," I talked about calibrating your monitor and using a calibration tool like SpyderX.

If you don't have a calibration tool and you haven't calibrated your monitor, print a photo on your desktop printer. Choose a photo with a wide range of colors and one that has brightness adjustments appropriate to the image. Hold the photo next to your monitor. Adjust your monitor brightness in Settings > Display on Windows or Displays in the System Preferences on the Mac. Run some more tests and return to monitor brightness settings. Try to bring the monitor brightness to as close to the prints from your desktop color printer as you can.

There are a number of other issues to deal with when printing files. You should use color profiles supplied by your printer developer and use profiles appropriate for every kind of paper you use. If you print scrapbook and family photos on photo paper, in most cases, it's fine to let your printer determine the profile. Your photos for most desktop color printers would be in the sRGB color space.

For a more thorough explanation of color printing on desktop color printers, see the latest edition of *Photoshop Elements For Dummies* (Obermeier/Padova, Wiley Publishing).

Printing at Commercial Print Shops

There's not much you can do on your end without advice from your provider. Commercial printing on high-end devices is something you can't determine on your own. If you have a file you want printed on offset press, you need to save the file as sRGB and don't embed a color profile. If you have duotone photos and you want to have a two-color print job, you most definitely need to talk to your provider. You cannot set angles and determine color names in Elements—something that's critical for color separating duotones.

You cannot change color modes to CMYK, so you need to ask your printer if you can send sRGB files to them. For size and resolution, you should also listen to advice supplied by your provider.

As a general rule, when you want to have your photos printed at commercial printshops, your first step is to talk to your provider. Discuss the job thoroughly before submitting files for printing on offset presses.

Printing Oversized and Tarpaulin Prints

Large format print machines typically use a variety of different color profiles for each substrate they support. You cannot embed the provider's profiles in your photos, which is generally not a problem since the provider is likely to choose a given profile when printing your job.

TIP: Although upsizing images is not recommended, if you must upsize a photo, you can achieve some good results by upsizing in increments of 10 percent. If you start with a sharp image that has good resolution, you can upsize 10 percent quite a few times. But you must upsize 10 percent each time. In other words, you can't choose 150 percent. Specify 10 percent and upsize 15 times.

Large format printing devices can usually tolerate low-resolution images— some as low as 35 ppi—without loss of detail. The biggest mistake people tend to make when sending files for oversized prints is upsampling a photo. If your photo needs some upsampling, you need to discuss it with your provider. The provider has seen every kind of image sized at a huge number of different resolutions. With their experience, they can tell you what kind of tolerance limitations you have with upsizing a photo. Generally, it's best to avoid any kind of upsizing. If you need to size up a tiny bit, talk to your provider first.

Using Online Print Services

If you want art prints, then you may choose an online printing service. There are many different providers offering many different kinds of printing services. If art prints are what you're looking for, you might want to order *giclee* (pronounced "zhee-clay").

Giclee is a French term meaning *to spray*, referring to how inkjets lay down inks. The machines used for giclee printing use tiny spray heads, and the device holding the spray head matches both color and application of ink precisely. The prints are made on a variety of substrates, from canvas, glass, and fabrics to fine art archival papers.

Regardless of whether you want giclee prints or just some 8×10s of family and friends, sending out files for printing can be more advantageous than printing on your desktop printer for several reasons. First, ink and photo papers are costly for desktop printers. You may need to make three, four, or more prints before you get the image you ultimately want. Therefore, in many cases, online services are generally less expensive. Online services offer printing on archival papers. If you frame an 8×10 photo of a print made on your desktop printer, after a year it may look faded and discolored. Online archival prints will last longer than the years you have left to live. Turn-around is generally fast, and prints are delivered to your doorstep. So, using online services might be a viable option for you.

Forget about using one-hour photo services. Printing at Costco, Walmart, and rapid print centers typically produce terrible prints. If you want to have a service print your photos, use an online professional printing service.

In my opinion (and this can change any day as new providers open doors) the top five providers and prices as of this writing in the United States include the following:

- **Mpix:** Prints render great skin tones and deep blacks. The website is easy to use. The provider offers print sizes from 2.25×3.5 wallets to 16×20-inch prints. Wallets for a set of four are priced at $1.69. 16×20-inch prints are priced at $23.99. Standard 8×10 photos are offered at $2.99. Mpix is found at www.mpix.com.

- **WHCC:** Very close in quality to Mpix. The photos have great skin tones and good contrast, and the website is equally easy to use. WHCC provides a free sample photo from one you upload, showing a range of papers offered by the service. They offer a large range of printing on a variety of substrates such as vinyl, wood, bamboo, and metal, in addition to a variety of different papers. WHCC also offers fine art prints on canvas and archival papers, such as smooth matte, velvet, and torchon (a pure cellulose watercolor paper). Eight-up wallets are priced at $2.30. 16×20-inch prints are priced at $16.20, and standard 8×10 prints are priced at $2.30. WHCC also offers prints as large as 30×45+ priced at $6.45 per square foot. WHCC can be found at www.whcc.com.

- **Pro DPI:** Skin tones from this service are a little more pink than either Mpix or WHCC. They provide samples of different substrates from a photo you submit. The samples are watermarked, and they're provided free. They also provide samples of cards for the photos you submit that you want printed as cards. Pricing is set at four wallets for $1.35, 16×20 inches at \$16.20, and standard 8×10 at \$2.30. They offer prints as large as 30x50 priced at \$63.30. Pro DPI can be found at www.prodpi.com.

- **Bay Photo:** Colors are not as good as the previous three services. On the provider's website, you find fine art prints from 8×8 inches to 40×80. Eight wallets are priced at \$3.50, 16×20-inch prints are priced at \$22.99, and standard 8×10 prints are priced at \$3.50. Bay Photo provides the largest print size of 50×90 at \$223.59. Bay Photo can be found at www.bayphoto. com.

- **Nations Photo Lab:** Standard printing paper is thinner than the other providers. Prints are sharp and colors are good, although not as good as the top three. Nations offers printing on luster paper, metallic prints, glossy prints, and linen prints. Pricing for prints include four wallets at \$1.35, 16×20 at \$17.99, and standard 8x10 at \$2.49. Print sizes go up to 30×45 priced at \$65.47. Visit the site at nationsphotolab.com/.

All of the online printing services listed here are very good. Slight color shifts may be experienced with a few of the providers, but generally, you would be pleased with any of the services I've mentioned. All of the providers offer printing on several different papers and printing gifts, cards, and photo albums in addition to photo prints. A few offer fine art printing.

If giclee printing is what you want, there are some services that specialize in giclee and fine art printing. You can try one the services here that offers fine art prints or search online for other providers offering giclee prints.

INDEX